RIGHTEOUS REPUBLIC

Thomas J. Wilson Prize

The Board of Syndics of Harvard University Press
has awarded this book the forty-first annual
Thomas J. Wilson Prize, honoring the late director of the Press.
The prize is awarded to the book chosen by the
Syndics as the best first book accepted
by the Press during the calendar year.

RIGHTEOUS REPUBLIC

The Political Foundations of Modern India

ANANYA VAJPEYI

HARVARD UNIVERSITY PRESS
Cambridge, Massachusetts, and London, England

Printed in India

First Harvard University Press paperback edition, 2014

Library of Congress Cataloging-in-Publication Data
Vajpeyi, Ananya.
Righteous republic : the political foundations of modern India /
Ananya Vajpeyi.
p. cm.
Includes bibliographical references and index.
ISBN 978-0-674-04895-9 (cloth : alk. paper)
ISBN 978-0-674-41732-8 (pbk.)
1. Political science—India—Philosophy—History.
2. India—Politics and government—Philosophy.
3. Self-determination, National—India.
4. Nationalism—India. I. Title.
JA84.I4V23 2012
320.0954—dc23 2012005074

For

Roopa Vajpeyi
mātā gurutarā bhūmeḥ
"The mother is weightier than the earth"

and

Kailash Vajpeyi
khātpitoccataraḥ
"The father is taller than the sky"

Contents

Preface

The Search for the Self in Modern India

Reflect on the crisis of the self as a crisis in the tradition which has formed the self.

Alasdair MacIntyre, *The Tasks of Philosophy*

From the last two decades of the nineteenth century until the middle of the twentieth century, Indians saw themselves as engaged in a struggle for *swaraj*. What is *swaraj*? This word, understood widely across many modern Indian languages, meant "political independence" (i.e., freedom from colonial rule, an end to the British Empire). The Sanskrit form whence *swaraj* is derived has two elements: *rājya*, meaning "rule," "dominion," or "mastery," and *swa*, a reflexive particle meaning "of the self," "to do with the self," or "having reference to the self." A common translation of *swaraj* in English, then, is "self-rule." The ambiguity in the exact nature of the ligature between *swa* and *raj*, evident in the Sanskrit and preserved both in Indian languages and in English, results in two meanings: "rule by the self" and "rule over the self"—the "self" thus is either the subject of rule, or the object of rule, or both the subject and the object at the same time. In the context of India's anticolonial movements between 1885 and 1947, the word "swaraj" thus signified India being able to recapture from the British the power to rule over itself. It was to be a relationship of the self with the self—India was to be the ruler; India was to be the ruled. In the simple story of Indian nationalism, after much effort and strife, this goal was achieved: on August 15, 1947, British dominion over India ended; India became a free country. A historic transition was made, from British Raj that lasted from 1857 to 1947, to swaraj that began in 1947 and continues even today.

But who or what is the "self," the rule of which was the prize that India's nationalists were after, for a good three or four generations? To say that the "self" is "India" and "India" is the "self" is only to defer the question, for next we would have to ask: What is India, the rule of which was the ultimate goal of Indian nationalism? Colonial India's political and cultural leaders, who were in many cases also the principal intellectuals of their time, grappled with this question in very serious ways. The history of India's decolonization, so far, has focused for the most part on how the Indian nationalist elite understood raj, or political sovereignty, and how they came to wrest it back from their British rulers through both violent conflict and nonviolent resistance, spread out over about seven decades, culminating in the foundation of the new nation-states of India and Pakistan. Many men and women were involved in this long struggle, which unfolded over large parts of South Asia, but it is unquestionable that a few names stand out when we really want to identify those who led both the battle for sovereignty and the search for the self. In this list, undoubtedly, among India's founders we may count as first among equals Mohandas Karamchand Gandhi (1869–1948), Rabindranath Tagore (1861–1941), Jawaharlal Nehru (1889–1964), and Bhimrao Ramji Ambedkar (1891–1956).

This book is about five men. Four of them fought to regain India's sovereignty, and the fifth, Abanindranath Tagore (1871–1951), a prominent artist and close associate of many leading nationalists, posed a question neglected by most historians: What constitutes India's "self"? What is the substance of the "swa" in "swaraj"? When we say "India," what do we mean? In my view, these five founders expended an equal amount of energy thinking about self and sovereignty, though it is only the latter quest that we hear about in most historical accounts, while the former has so far not been examined very much. A classic formulation of the problem can be found in Jawaharlal Nehru's celebrated book *The Discovery of India*—part memoir, part history, and part political treatise—at the very beginning of the third chapter, tellingly titled "The Quest":

> As I grew up and became engaged in activities which promised to lead to India's freedom, I became obsessed with the thought

> of India. What was this India that possessed me and beckoned to me continually, urging me to action so that we might realize some vague but deeply felt desire of our hearts? The initial urge came to me, I suppose, through pride, both individual and national, and the desire, common to all men, to resist another's domination and have freedom to live the life of our choice. It seemed monstrous to me that a great country like India, with a rich and immemorial past, should be bound hand and foot to a faraway island which imposed its will upon her. It was still more monstrous that this forcible union had resulted in poverty and degradation beyond measure. That was reason enough for me and others to act.
>
> But it was not enough to satisfy the questioning that arose within me. What is this India, apart from her physical and geographical aspects? What did she represent in the past; what gave strength to her then? How did she lose that old strength, and has she lost it completely? Does she represent anything vital now, apart from being the home of a vast number of human beings? How does she fit in to the modern world?
>
> This wider international aspect of the problem grew upon me as I realized . . . how isolation was both undesirable and impossible. The future that took shape in my mind was one of intimate co-operation . . . between India and the other countries. . . . But before the future came, there was the present, and behind the present lay the long and tangled past, out of which the present had grown. So to the past I looked for understanding.[1]

In these three short paragraphs, Nehru adumbrates every theme necessary to chart my main argument. The nationalist intellectual—here Nehru himself—having had his early education and a variety of personal experiences (described in this instance in chapters 1 and 2 of *The Discovery of India*), comes into political maturity by becoming "engaged in activities which promised to lead to India's freedom." The quest for India's freedom is the firmament against which we can see the very horizon of the political. But even as he is engaged in his political activities, the freedom fighter becomes "obsessed with the thought of India." He struggles to define his telos, the object that urges him to action, that possesses him, that beckons to him continually—"What was this India . . . ?" he asks. He recognizes that initially his urge to seek India's freedom came from a common desire, shared by all human beings, regardless of India's particular circumstances, to be our own masters and to bow to no one in living "the life of our choice." Liberty, in Nehru's understanding, is a universal human aspiration.

More specifically, he knows that he first felt prompted into political action by the fact of British imperialism, by the shameful and intolerable circumstance of India being "bound hand and foot to a faraway island which imposed its will upon her" and, moreover, by the "poverty and degradation" that this "forcible union" of master and slave, colonizer and colonized, had produced in India, once a "great country . . . with a rich and immemorial past." Nehru acts out of injured "pride, both individual and national"; he becomes involved in nationalist politics because his own personal sense of self-respect, as an educated and cognizant Indian who belongs to the ruling classes, is threatened, and because the dignity of the political community to which he belongs—that of Indians as an incipient nation—has been violated through the wrongful imposition of the domineering will of the small, distant island of Britannia upon the entire subcontinent of India. In other words, Nehru and others like him (whom he does not name) have plenty of reason to engage in anticolonial activity. The chain of cause and effect is straightforward—colonial rule prompts nationalist resistance that is both universally human and specifically Indian, realized in the actions of Jawaharlal Nehru the individual as well as of millions of other patriotic, freedom-loving Indians who chafe against foreign domination.

Nationalism, though perfectly justified, is, however, "not enough to satisfy the questioning that arose" within Nehru. He has found a rationale and an explanation for the widespread politics of anticolonial resistance that is consuming him and all of India, but still the question has not been answered: "What is this India . . . ?" Yes, India has a spatial definition: a finite area it covers, specific features of that land, and fixed territorial boundaries, but surely "physical and geographical aspects" are inadequate as answers, as is the huge population inhabiting this expanse, or the fact of India being "the home of a vast number of human beings." Although there is a sense in which they empirically exist and are verifiable, in truth neither cartographic territory nor sheer population can, in and of itself, be the "what" of what India is. Perhaps the answer has to come from the past, then, suggests Nehru, before colonialism, when India was a "great country," strong, free, and self-ruling. Maybe India can only be defined with a reference to a time when it was still "vital," not half-dead from "poverty and degradation beyond measure," listlessly lying there "bound hand and foot" to another nation and its will to power.

For what troubles Nehru is that he cannot see an evident relationship between India and her own prior self, on the one hand—"that old strength," now lost, perhaps completely—nor, on the other hand, can he see the relationship between India and any other country in the world—"the wider international aspect of the problem," as he calls it. At the present moment, the only thing he can discern about India is India's relationship with Britain, which is one of servitude and oppression; a relationship that denies India her right to self-determination and robs Indians of their self-respect. For India not to be isolated in the future, she has to have both a sense of self—a self-image that is clear and a self-knowledge that is confident—and the motivation for "intimate cooperation" with other countries of the world. For the moment—"before the future came, there was the present"—Nehru faces a wall. He confronts what he encounters. He does not know the answer to the question that keeps on bothering him, that he has raised twice already without making any headway: "What is this India?" He has some inkling, though, that the answer lies in history, in the earlier time when India still had her vitality and her greatness, her capacity for self-rule—"the long and tangled past, out of which the present had grown." The answer to Nehru's persistent question does not appear to be coming from the given reality, the colonial rule that constitutes India's miserable present, nor from India's status in the modern world, which is currently nil. All signs seem to point in just one direction. Nehru makes a call: "So to the past I looked for understanding."

Nehru was not alone. All five of the founders discussed in my study—Gandhi, the Tagores, Nehru, and Ambedkar—looked to the past for understanding. Understanding what? Understanding the self whose sovereignty they sought; understanding the India that was in their time ruled by the British but that once had been free in the past and once again would be free in the future. If the quest for swaraj were only the quest for raj, then it would be half a quest. If the story of the quest for swaraj were only the story of the quest for raj, then it would be only half the story. I try to tell the story of the search for the self in modern India, the swa in swaraj, seeking which the founders delved deep into the texts, monuments, traditions, and histories of India, "rich and immemorial" in Nehru's resonant words. They understood, each one in his own way and by his own unique formula comprised in equal parts of intellectual engagement and political judgment, that raj would have to be found in the future, that swa would be discovered in the past, and that the effort made in the present was itself the necessary but forever ambiguous ligature between past and future, between swa and raj, between self and sovereignty. "What is this India?" they all asked; or, put another way, "What is Indian self-rule the rule of?" In other words, to come full circle, we are back to the question, but this time the complete and not the partial question: What is swaraj?

The philosopher Alasdair MacIntyre—whose work, particularly on the theory of "tradition," on the crises that traditions face, and on the processes by which traditions confront those crises, informs this study of India's search for the self—has written that "a crisis in the self is a crisis in the tradition which has formed the self." Treating this as an axiomatic statement (what in Sanskrit philosophical systems is called a *sūtra-vākya*), let us look at the predicament of Indian intellectuals, especially those who were also nationalist thinkers and political leaders, in the late nineteenth and early twentieth centuries. They experienced a crisis in the self. The swa of swaraj was unclear; the subject (rule by X) and object (rule over X) of anticolonial politics, or the "India" whose freedom was sought, remained undefined or underdetermined. This was true not just for the five figures I have chosen, but for the entire spectrum of intellectuals during that period, running into hundreds if not thousands of men and women who comprised the founding generations. Nehru's first-person account was considered so truthful and so moving when it came out, on the cusp of Independence, precisely because it gave voice to the unspoken sentiments of literally every major or minor, famous or unrecognized Indian nationalist who had struggled for swaraj any time in the preceding three-quarters of a century. The feeling that there was a crisis of selfhood was ubiquitous.

This widespread crisis of the self, to follow MacIntyre's lead, was the result of the fact that the traditions that had formed the selfhood of Indians in the centuries leading up to colonial rule were themselves in a severe state of crisis. Partly they had atrophied from internal decay or entropic logics about which very little, still, is understood by historians of knowledge or theorists of history. An excellent example of an extremely long-running and fecund knowledge tradition in India, one of the greatest the world had ever seen, going into an irreversible decline and coming to a more or less complete end by the middle of the nineteenth century, has been laid out at length by Sheldon Pollock and his colleagues. At first Pollock called it "The Death of Sanskrit," though the historical description has been slowly deepening and growing to encompass the state of Sanskrit knowledge (as a totality) on the eve of colonialism, which showed remarkable elements of flashing newness and flaring renewal as well, in an overall and inexorable trend toward extinction. Colonialism and its forms of knowledge were only partially to blame for what happened to Sanskrit—Pollock's essay was never titled "The Rape of Sanskrit." At least some of the degeneration and exhaustion of the tradition was the result of its own peculiar historical trajectory, its uniquely encumbered entrance into and swift, painful exit from what we may call, as a convenient shorthand form (and with a nod to the single most important text of the Sanskrit language, the *Mahābhārata*), the dice game of modernity.

The atrophy of Sanskrit was but one symptom of the crisis. Indian science and mathematics, which had in two millennia, the one preceding and the one following Christ, given to the world many of its fundamental starting points for advanced theories across a wide array of disciplines, also ceased to be productive in the modern age, ceding the leadership role to Europe, and thereby hastening the conquest of Asia and Africa by the three *C*s—colonialism, capitalism, and Christianity. Indian political traditions, broadly speaking of a mixed Hindu and Islamic character, as theorized and practiced in the precolonial kingdoms of the Mughals, the Deccani Sultans, the Nayakas, the Marathas, the Rajputs, and the Sikhs, among others, were severely delegitimized and weakened, not to say destroyed, through the gradual colonization of much of India by the East India Company between 1757 and 1857, followed by the dramatic defeat of the Indian rebels by British forces in the mutiny of 1857 and the decisive establishment of the Crown Raj from 1858 onward. By the time men like Gandhi came of age, the rout of Indian traditions of either thinking about the political or practicing politics was so complete that we find at one stage India's nationalist elite consisting of men (for it was almost entirely men, and practically no women, until much later) who were schooled purely in Western political thought. Except for the color of their skin, they could in no way be distinguished from the liberals, conservatives, socialists, Marxists, and eventually Fascists and Communists of Europe and Anglo-America.

Indian traditions of theorizing the self—a great deal of Sanskrit philosophy could be described as having this function—and Indian traditions of theorizing sovereignty—Sanskritic, Islamic, or other—were therefore effectively unavailable to India's nationalist intellectuals when they started to try and figure out the meaning of swaraj, its subject, its object, and its purpose as the marker of the principal political project of their age. Many of them were not just formed, but also persuaded by the tenets of liberal politics—they became enthusiastic students and later passionate proponents of egalitarianism, democracy, and liberty. They did not think to turn to Indian traditions, in whatever state of survival, flourishing or disrepair, as legitimate sources of authority on almost any matter concerning modern life, whether that of the individual or of the community as a whole. ("Religion" and "custom" were supposedly the last bastions of native identity and indigenous pride to hold out against the West, but even these began to undergo, inevitably, some kind of modernization or other through the mechanisms of "secularization" induced from the outside and internal reform driven by self-criticism.)

Educated at Harrow and Eton, Oxford and Cambridge, London and Edinburgh, Indian youth from elite families were taught to think like Englishmen, and indeed they did, creating a class that they would eventually come to disparage, at moments of self-hatred, as "brown sahibs." They were estranged from Indian traditions by both force of habit and free choice; by the persistent condescension of their white masters and by their own growing skepticism about the value of whatever was Indian; by the empirical vanishing of entire cultures of Indian knowledge and by their own migration, in spirit if not in body, to more "cosmopolitan" parts of the world. Some other history of Indian nationalism will one day look at the young Rabindranath's home schooling and abandoned English education; the young Aurobindo's return to India to teach himself Sanskrit and Bengali, overwriting the Greek and Latin he had studied in England; the middle-aged Gandhi's complete change of dress and personal appearance as he silently traveled the length and breadth of India upon his return from South Africa; and countless other such episodes of a "turn" and a "return" that punctuated and in some cases punctured these lives. Each of these men and many others, too, had to come to

India to find himself, and to find India to come into himself: the two processes were the same.

A good indication of the extent to which nationalist intellectuals became unmoored from all established protocols for the authorization of knowledge—whether knowledge about the self, or knowledge about sovereignty, or indeed knowledge about any other matter of let us say a moral or political description—is, for example, the sudden proliferation of modern commentaries and critiques on a traditional text like the *Bhagavad Gītā,* by men like Bankimchandra, Tilak, Aurobindo, and Gandhi himself, not to mention Vivekananda, Savarkar, and Ambedkar. One way to understand this remarkable phenomenon is that their exposure to Western modernity gave to these men the requisite insouciant confidence to pick up and read an ancient and difficult text according to their own lights. Another way to understand it is to see that they had no choice but to take on a text like this on their own, barehanded, as it were, for there no longer existed the entire edifice of traditional learning with its scholastic, religious, and popular authority to provide any kind of structured and systematic access to the recondite meaning of this text. There was literally nowhere else to turn, except the book itself—sometimes mediated, ironically (and if at all), by translations into English, such as Edwin Arnold's *Song Celestial*—as European Indology stepped in to replace the fugitive Sanskrit traditions.

Elsewhere Indian mutineers had already made the bitterly disappointing discovery that Bahadur Shah Zafar, the last Mughal, was emperor only of the realm of poetry: he had neither the political vision nor the material resources of his fabulously wealthy ancestors, who had in the sixteenth century been the richest and most powerful monarchs on the planet, to offer to those who looked to him to stand up to the coming colossus of the British Empire. A "faraway island," having swallowed India whole, became the whale inside which sat the entire leadership of the future nation-state, unable to recall, recapture, or reconstruct the vast ocean—the past "rich and immemorial" that had once been India's reality—unable to swim out into the wide deep waters of the traditions that had once been their own. The crisis of the self, we noted, is a crisis in the tradition that has formed the self.

The nationalist elite experienced the crisis in Indian traditions as a crisis for two reasons, the first being that many of these traditions had gone into decline and were in the process of lapsing into incoherence. The second reason for this profound sense of crisis was that Indian intellectuals at the end of the nineteenth century had become in many ways insiders relative to Western political traditions, especially liberalism. The problem was a very difficult one. They could not turn to Indian traditions in any simple sense, because these had foundered. Nor could they turn away from Western traditions, because these had become familiar and acceptable, even desirable. And yet many Indian thinkers could see that it would not be possible to continue in limbo for very much longer. European ideas, while backed by the political power of the colonial state and reinforced by the globally dominant paradigm of capitalist modernity, were not socially embedded in the Indian milieu. Gandhi recognized this with the greatest clarity and was consequently able to introduce into mass politics a number of new concepts and tactics that drew intelligently on extant and remembered Indian political cultures.

On the other hand, Indian traditions, weakened though they were, were still seen as the repositories of a number of political norms, moral values, and aesthetic resources that, with some effort at revitalization and recalibration, would make sense to, and work for, ordinary Indians because they belonged within India's precolonial history and emerged from it into the colonial moment. All five of the founders were acutely aware of the limits of European liberalism in an Indian political context, as well as the residual normative appeal of Indian traditions to the people of India. The five men had different strengths—Gandhi focused on everyday lived experience and techniques of self-discipline, the Tagores on poetry and the arts, Nehru on politics proper, and Ambedkar on legal and juridical scholarship. But each one, I argue, entered into a prolonged engagement with Indian traditions in search of sources of the self, a move without which none of them would have been able to restore the delicate balance within swa and raj, the two terms that together (and inseparably) defined the project of nationalism.

All five of the founders under discussion here had to some degree attempted to plumb the depths of India's past, but it is notable that they did not go in any obvious or direct way to the religious traditions that were, according to Orientalist wisdom, supposed to be India's mainstay, the heart of what India was about. In this sense the relationship of these five to tradition was completely distinct from that of say, Ramakrishna, Vivekananda, and Aurobindo on the one hand; Bankim, Bhartendu, Tilak, and Savarkar on the other hand; and Iqbal and Azad in yet another direction. When Gandhi turned to Hindu *(Vaiṣṇava)* texts, say the *Rāmāyaṇa,* the *Rāmcaritmānas,* the *Bhagavad Gītā,* or the devotional songs of the medieval *bhakti* poets of northern and western India, what he sought from them was a moral—possibly even a didactic—vision that could help an individual to cultivate self-mastery and acquire self-knowledge, and at the same time regulate the affective life of communities. Ritualism, the rigidly hierarchical relations of caste society, the authority of orthodox Brahmins, and dry scholasticism—the very aspects of Indian religions that had come in for severe criticism from the modern West—were discarded by Gandhi as well, though he did cling stubbornly, for a variety of reasons, to social conservatism in some respects (including patriarchal caste strictures), much to the irritation of his critics.

The Tagores looked to religion—mainly the religious traditions found in their native Bengal, such as Sakta cults, Gaudiya Vaisnavism, Sahajiya Buddhism, Sufi Islam, certain kinds of tantric and yogic beliefs shared across low-caste Hindu and Muslim groups, tribal systems, and Christianity—to construct what Rabindranath called "the religion of man": a synthesis of universalism, humanism, and nature worship from which all traces of organized religion had been removed. Tagore's grandfather and father, close to Ram Mohan Roy, had been the founders and proponents of a new reformist Bengali sect called the Brahmo Samaj, loosely based on the tenets of Advaita Vedānta and Unitarianism. But Rabindranath Tagore never quite stayed within this fold, being too inventive and too individualistic to be able to fit into a given system, even one that originated in his own family. By instinct he was suspicious of the esoteric dimensions of most of the religions prevalent in Bengal and distanced himself especially from orgiastic practices involving animal sacrifice; the consumption of meat, alcohol, and hallucinogens; rituals that incorporated sexual activity; and other extreme forms of either corporeal indulgence or self-mortification. Even his vaunted love for Baul poetry and music came after he had made a highly selective, sanitized, and stylized interpretation of Baul praxis. Abanindranath Tagore was relatively more willing to explore the emotional states *(bhāva),* imaginative play *(līlā),* and aesthetic essences *(rasa)* associated with the characters, narratives, and rituals of different religious traditions. Besides, he was interested in the history of religions in India because it provided him with a parallel history of Indian art and architecture over the course of more than two millennia. Unlike his uncle, Abanindranath came from the Hindu rather than the

Brahmo branch of the Tagore family, which meant that Sakta worship was very much a part of his upbringing. Some of this early exposure may be seen in the ease with which he incorporated Tantric and Puranic imagery into his later painting.

Nehru and Ambedkar had a far more complicated relationship to religious traditions—not that Gandhi and the Tagores did not, but at least they were not as adversarial in their attitude to religion as the two modernists. Born a Brahmin (a Kashmiri Pandit), Nehru was a self-confessed atheist and moreover the architect of postcolonial Indian secularism; born an Untouchable (a Maharashtrian Mahar), Ambedkar converted to Buddhism in the last months of his life, but to what extent that gesture was either "religious" or a "conversion" is in fact the main topic of discussion in my chapter on Ambedkar. Nehru was completely opposed to the Partition of India along lines of religious difference and did not permit the new Indian nation to become a "Hindu Pakistan." Ambedkar, however, even though he was not given to "communal" sentiment any more than Nehru was, thought in terms of majorities and minorities, federalism and democracy, rights and reservations, because of which intellectually (though not politically) he understood and felt compelled to support Partition. After Independence, the two men together, as prime minister and law minister respectively, and as the prime movers of the Indian Constitution, made a serious attempt to reform and modernize Hinduism through the Hindu Code Bill, but they failed, fell out, and parted ways. After this unhappy experiment—at both collaborating with one another and enlightening their countrymen—Nehru took the route of compromise, and did what he could to curb the evils of caste and temper the tendencies inherent in religion to further fragment and vitiate the polity. Ambedkar, however, undertook an aggressive foray into religion, thoroughly studying and testing Islam, Christianity, Sikhism, and finally Buddhism to figure out the best option outside of Hinduism that might be available to Untouchables.

Nehru understood that although he personally did not care for religion, the majority of his compatriots did, and that therefore religion, blanched and attenuated but recognizable, had to be incorporated into the story of India that he was trying to tell. For him, tradition may have been the past, but it was necessary to acknowledge and validate it because in the tradition, counterintuitive as that seemed, lay coiled the teleology of a future democracy. Ambedkar, whose critique of the Hindu caste system and of upper-caste socioreligious practices *tout court* was the most scathing that the modern age has seen, regarded tradition as the axis of subordination, the reason for the relentless oppression and exclusion of lower castes and Untouchables over centuries of Indian history. Yet in the end he too had to recognize that in India, as far as religion went, there was no way beyond it except through: traditions could be criticized and attacked, but not simply jettisoned. Traditions of various kinds were the bones and sinews of the Indian body politic, not extraneous tumors to be cauterized and removed, howsoever aged or afflicted their present condition might be.

The search for the self—the self whose political sovereignty had to be reinstated—took the form of an attempt to recover a line of moral inquiry from a welter of Indian traditions. It should be clarified that the founders were not nostalgic revivalists: they did not waste time extolling the glories and virtues of the religion, culture, or philosophy of premodern India, because their concern was with the present and the future, not with the past as such. While they embraced the ideas of liberty, equality, and fraternity that they learned from their European colonizers, they were concerned not to replicate the exact structure of Western sovereignty with what they regarded as its many obvious flaws—it had its foundations in violence, it gave the monopoly of force to the state, it thrust individual interests into combative and competitive relations with one another, it exploited nature and dehumanized society through an excessive reliance on technology, and in the worst case it could always become uncontrollable, even demonic, in its exercise of power. Indian sovereignty, especially in Gandhi's theorization, had to construct itself as self-limiting, as reined in by culturally grounded conceptions of a polity and how power is to be wielded. Gandhian nonviolence *(ahimsa)* took an alternative Indian theory of rule (raj) and self-rule (swaraj) to another extreme, ultimately unrealizable within the horizon of the modern nation-state, but it came out of his engagement with multiple Indian political and moral traditions that had refined to the utmost degree a number of strategies to liberate the self from the primordial, irrational, and almost insuperable impulse to violence that comes with the human condition.

In defining what constitutes a tradition, I follow MacIntyre, in that I treat texts as the building blocks of tradition. A tradition proceeds through the reading and rereading, through the continuous critical reinterpretation, of a corpus of texts over time. This corpus suffers some deletions and admits some additions, but it is largely stable, so that a tradition retains its identity even in the *longue durée:* there is a core set of texts, with a finite set of issues; there are methods of reading; there are protocols of evidence; and there are authorities that must be followed. Those who enter into the tradition, even as critics, rebels, dissenters, agnostics. or skeptics, must grasp this architecture and these principles, must know where the conversation is at, even if that conversation has gone on over hundreds of years in multiple languages before arriving at the present (or at whatever is the latest juncture). In the Sanskrit traditions, the structure of the textually defined tradition *(paramparā)* is even tighter, with a strongly defined root text *(sūtra),* and subtended from that a series of commentaries *(bhāṣya),* further differentiated as major *(mahābhāṣya)* and minor *(ṭīkā),* onto even finer classifications of subcommentaries. Rather than trying to figure out where the five founders stood with regard to the idea of "Tradition" as such (which is after all rather vague), I examine particular intellectual engagements with traditional texts that each one undertook, and bring out the categories of selfhood that emerged from these acts of interpretation.

I follow Gandhi's reading of the *Bhagavad Gītā,* a text that he treated as perhaps his single most consistent source of moral reflection and ethical guidance, to show how this engagement yielded the category *ahimsa,* the self's orientation toward others, an orientation devoid of the intent to harm. For Rabindranath, the text in question is the *Meghadūta,* a long poem in Sanskrit by the fifth-century classical poet Kalidasa, a text whose principal category turns out to be *viraha,* the self's longing, a yearning for reunion with a beloved who has become estranged, perhaps permanently and irreparably so. For Abanindranath, we have to treat the term "text" somewhat expansively, to admit the greatest of the Mughal monuments in India, Shah Jahan's Taj Mahal, built in the mid-seventeenth century, which yielded for the modern painter *samvega*—the self's shock—a specific type of aesthetic experience that produces both the momentary pleasure of art and the abiding knowledge of truth. I will look at Nehru's fascination with the texts and artifacts of the Mauryan Empire (320–185 BCE), notably the moral edicts of Emperor Aśoka carved on rocks and pillars, and the *Arthaśāstra* of Kauṭilya, a treatise on statecraft, arguably India's oldest text of political theory, more or less contemporaneous with Aristotle's *Politics.* For Nehru, what emerged from his engagement with these materials was *dharma,* the self's aspiration, its tendency toward its own perfection, and *artha,* the self's purpose or purposive character, its ability to act in goal-oriented ways. Finally, for Ambedkar, who was a scholar and a self-taught philologist, there were many texts to choose from, but I focus on his reading of the Buddhist canonical literature in the last stage of his life, because it was here that he discovered *duḥkha,* the self's burden, which is nothing other than the suffering, individual and collective, produced in any society that is weighed down and immiserated by caste.

The founders drew these understandings of selfhood from Hindu and Buddhist texts, from Buddhist and Mughal artifacts, from traditions that were classical and vernacular, living and dying, ancient and recent, relatively pure in their instantiations in India and relatively mediated by colonial knowledge practices. The sources are a hodgepodge of genres, languages, regions, periods, and even modalities (textual/artifactual). Yet once the past has been thoroughly engaged with and interrogated and partially absorbed and partially rejected by the founding fathers, what we get at the end is a new corpus of texts that we may call a modern Indian tradition of thinking about self and sovereignty. The Tradition, of moral and political reflection broadly construed, has, in effect, been reconstituted. It is a remarkable new tradition that India produces because while India is in the process of becoming a modern democracy, her founders reject the violence of the nation-state form (Gandhi), reject nationalism as an ideology (Rabindranath), transform a nonmodern and sectarian history into an enabling precursor for secular democratic modernity (Nehru), and shift the bases of human happiness from the pursuit of individual interest to the alleviation of social suffering (Ambedkar).

Every tradition that lives a long and robust life, according to MacIntyre, must at some point face an epistemological crisis. There can be three responses in such an event. First, a tradition can fail to resolve its crisis, and more or less come to an end. In my view this is what happened to Sanskrit knowledge in India. Second, a tradition can recognize its own crisis, but not be able to change itself enough to save itself, and so it can accept the superiority of another tradition, take that other tradition into itself, and carry on. This is more or less what happened to Indian science: it now continues as Western science. Third, a tradition can resolve its own crisis by itself, using its internal resources, reconsidering its own neglected aspects, overcoming its own contradictions, eliminating its own weaknesses, refreshing itself by critically recombining elements from within and without. This is what happened to India's political tradition. Under the sign of swaraj, the founders revised and remade Indian intellectual traditions, traditions that had meditated on self, sovereignty, and their ligature for as long as anyone could remember.

Righteous Republic

Introduction

Swaraj, the Self's Sovereignty

This book is an account of the search for the self in modern India, the very self that is the ground of the Indian polity, or indeed of any polity that seeks to be independent, liberal, democratic, egalitarian, and just.[1] If there was one word that dominated Indian politics from the 1880s, when the Indian National Congress was first founded, until Independence in 1947, this word was swaraj. Swaraj literally means "self-rule": the rule of the self, or the rule over the self. Both the subject and the object of "rule" (raj) is the "self" (swa). A subjugated country is ruled by others; a free country rules itself. After the failure of the rebellion of 1857, Britain became India's ruler. Intellectuals all across colonial India, from Bengal in the east to Maharashtra in the west, via Banaras in the Gangetic north, began to use this word to describe their ultimate political aim in response to and reaction against foreign rule, which had formally passed from the East India Company to the British Crown in 1858. The ligature between "self" and "sovereignty" is swaraj. One way to understand this word is of course to focus on the sovereignty sought by the early ideologues and advocates of swaraj, men like Bankim Chandra Chattopadhayay (1838–1894), Bhartendu Harishchandra (1850–1885), and Bal Gangadhar Tilak (1856–1920). Most of the history of

India between the creation of the Congress in 1885 and the birth of India and Pakistan in 1947 is written precisely as a history of India's search for its "freedom"—its political sovereignty, its power to rule itself. Other prominent synonyms of swaraj, like *swadhinata* (literally, "the state of being under one's own control") and *swatantrata* (literally, "the state of being in charge of oneself"), and its close relative *swadeshi* (literally, "indigenous," "belonging to one's own country"), tellingly share the reflexive particle "swa" that points back to the speaker, positing a self to whom this sovereignty belongs and over whom this sovereignty is exercised.

The entire weight of the historical exercise could just as legitimately be put upon the self as it could be—and has been—upon its sovereignty. All major schools of modern Indian history—Nationalist, Marxist, Subalternist, Hindu, and Liberal—since the 1940s have produced accounts of how India made the journey from subjugation to sovereignty, from colonialism to independence, from British rule to self-rule. Where did the dominant notions of sovereignty come from—Western thought or Indian thought? What methods were used to win sovereignty? Whence did Indians derive the form of the modern sovereign nation-state? Once sovereignty was achieved, how has it been preserved in the postcolonial era? Is this sovereignty equitably distributed among different sections of Indian society? What institutions are used to uphold and strengthen it? These and other similar questions have preoccupied all the major historians of modern India throughout the twentieth century and up to the present moment, from Bipin Chandra and Sumit Sarkar, to Ranajit Guha and Partha Chatterjee, to Sunil Khilnani and Ramachandra Guha. The "raj" part of "swaraj" has dictated the historical narrative for the past two generations of scholars trying to understand the creation of the Indian nation. The self to whom this sovereignty belongs, and over whom this sovereignty is exercised, so far seems not to have a history at all. The history of modern India has, for some reason, bracketed its own subject, as though that subject were either implicit, given, or understood, or as though that subject did not matter. I attempt to write a history of the search for the self that has all along run parallel to the search for sovereignty in and for India.

The domain of the self extends over politics, religion, art, and culture. While it seems obvious that one would look for the lineaments of political thought either in political actions or in texts about politics, the self is not so narrowly constrained—if anything, it is, rather, a bit too diffuse. Surely every kind of action or event in history, and every kind of text or discourse, has or can have reference to a self. This book follows five of India's founders through their engagements with a range of classical texts whose primary description may or may not conform to our prior expectations regarding the genre of political thought. My sources, in other words, range across poetry, painting, scripture, epigraphy, architecture, and sculpture; across texts that are as likely to be expressive and aesthetic as they are to be didactic and ethical; and spread out in their production and reception over a period that begins as early as the life of the Buddha (ca. fifth century BCE) and comes right up to the twentieth century. I try to illuminate aspects of selfhood that seem to be the most salient in the thought of my protagonists. Who these figures are, why I chose them and not others, and what the emergent aspects of selfhood were for them, are subjects that I address in detail.

But first a small detour by way of setting the stage of the intellectual and cultural context in which the five founders—Mohandas Gandhi, Rabindranath Tagore, Abanindranath Tagore, Jawaharlal Nehru, and Bhimrao Ambedkar—were embedded. The British philosopher Alasdair MacIntyre uses the term "epistemological crisis" to describe a state affecting the consciousness of either an individual or culture, wherein existing epistemologies, or ways of knowing, no longer seem adequate to accurately comprehend or describe the world.[2] From long habit, people understand things a certain way, until one day they encounter some unexpected piece of information that calls into question their entire epistemological framework up until that moment. In MacIntyre's celebrated examples, European science on the verge of the Copernican-Galilean revolution was in the throes of an epistemological crisis, as was Shakespeare's character Prince Hamlet when he found out about the betrayals of his family and friends. The crisis in Europe's scientific tradition in the late sixteenth century is to my mind an excellent analogy for the epistemological crisis engulfing India's knowledge traditions in the late nineteenth century.

Old ways of knowing the world that were extant in India—and that had been evolving in certain directions for centuries—were giving way before the onslaught of colonialism and its more up-to-date forms of knowledge.[3] Indian intellectuals struggled with the competing pulls of tutelage from their colonial masters and rebellion against them. Many examples of a sclerosis in intellectual cultures across South Asia at the advent of colonialism may be adduced, but suffice it for now to cite the phenomenon that Sheldon Pollock has famously called the "Death of Sanskrit" by the early to mid-nineteenth century.[4] Sanskrit literature, criticism, philosophy, and science effectively ceased to be produced in India by about the 1830s—or rather, while texts continued to be written and taught, nothing that was new, or that made much sense in the face of rapid and irrevocable change, ever again came out of the Sanskrit ecumene after that point in time. Sanskrit as a living locus of epistemology, of a mode of knowing and acting upon reality, ceased to exist. In the 150 years since then, all that has occurred by way of intellection in Sanskrit is the repetition and transmission of old knowledge, knowledge that in its own day had the power to reimagine and reconfigure the world but is now the mere shell of a "dead" language. Apart from this, the historian Sudhir Chandra has documented in some detail the widespread sense of epistemological crisis voiced by nineteenth-century intellectuals in colonial Bengal, Maharashtra, Gujarat, and Hindi-speaking north India; Urdu literary culture in the cities of Lucknow and Delhi experienced an even more concentrated and dramatic moment of deluge and ending after the cataclysmic violence of 1857.[5] Both cities picked themselves up by the bootstraps over the course of the following eighty or so years, only to be comprehensively brought down again as centers of poetic excellence in Urdu during the Partition of 1947—a blow from which Delhi subsequently recovered not at all, and Lucknow only very little, and only very briefly.

MacIntyre's account of the fate of traditions does not stop at the epistemological crisis, however. In order to survive such a crisis, a tradition must undergo what MacIntyre calls an "epistemological break": a reconfiguration of epistemology such that new ways of knowing and new pieces of knowledge come into proper alignment with one another. The break for European science came in the form of Galileo's revolutionary text of 1632, *Dialogue Concerning the Two Chief World Systems (Ptolemaic and Copernican)*. This text allowed a knowledge tradition in crisis to become reoriented and to proceed onward into its future; perhaps without the Galilean turn, science in Europe might have foundered forever, like many other premodern knowledge systems in different parts of the world. Without such a critical recalibration between what is known and ways of knowing, a tradition may lapse into incoherence; an individual—like the unfortunate Hamlet—may stumble into madness or suicide. The option, MacIntyre says, is between a timely epistemological breakthrough, and tragedy.[6]

India's political traditions, which were experiencing a profound crisis around the turn of the century, were rebooted and rejuvenated by Gandhi's short tract of 1909, *Hind Swaraj, or Indian Home-Rule.* What Galileo was to the European scientific tradition, Gandhi was to the Indian political tradition: not so much an inventor or a discoverer as the first one to see that new historical circumstances necessitated new ways of being in the world, new ways of processing what was known, and new strategies for coping with what was still unknown. If Gandhi became the leader of India's apex nationalist movement from 1919 until his death in 1948, if Gandhi was seen during his lifetime and is still seen today as the very father of the Indian nation, it is because at some level, in implicit or explicit ways, we understand that he effected the breakthrough that first arrested and then reversed a crisis of historic and potentially tragic proportions in India's traditions of political thought and in Indian politics as such.

Gandhi's was the crucial breakthrough, and the reason for this is that his manifesto took as its subject the meaning of the one category that was already very important at the time and would only become even more so, in fact, would become central in the coming decades (viz., swaraj). *Hind Swaraj* is Gandhi's meditation on India's self and India's sovereignty, without which it is not possible to imagine how he would have gone on to lead India to freedom from colonial rule. It is the taking of a deep breath in the moment before the Mahatma, and together with him all of India, plunged right into the turbulent waters of history, to emerge on the other shore nearly four decades later as a sovereign nation. Everything that Gandhi knew, intuited, believed, or hoped, the entire scaffolding of the vast and complicated architecture of his thought, is contained in this short book, written in ten days, printed at his own expense, translated from homely Gujarati into unpretentious English under his own supervision, widely distributed despite an instant ban by the British government, and read in millions of copies by the subjects of the British Empire in India, South Africa, and England. In twenty cryptic chapters, Gandhi races through his preoccupations, which would soon be shared by all of India—Self and Other, East and West, true civilization and consumer capitalism, violence and non-violence, cowardice and courage, colonial reliance and swadeshi self-reliance, nature and culture,

Britain and India, craft and technology, truth and lies, freedom and subjugation. The text is brief but the magnitude of its epistemological departure from nationalist politics as it had been lurching along in the preceding two or three decades is so patent and so enormous that it pushed a foundering political tradition over a nearly insurmountable hump, and launched it into futurity.

Gandhi's was the pivotal epistemological break, the Galilean moment, the hinge between past and future—but it was not the only one. Needless to say, no one man, not even Mahatma Gandhi, can win or lose the game for an entity the size, the age, and the complexity of India. In the first two decades of the twentieth century—up to the beginning of the first Gandhian non-cooperation movements and civil disobedience campaigns circa 1919/1920—signs of a breakthrough are everywhere to be found in India. These signs are of necessity diverse and diffuse, but once we begin to look for them, we see them rampant. The epistemological break—which is now, to modify MacIntyre's metaphor a little, more like a breaking wave than a thunderclap—comes on as the Swadeshi movement of 1905–1908 in Bengal, the formation of the Muslim League in 1906, the split in the Congress between moderate and extremist factions in 1907, the publication, in the single momentous year of 1909, of Gandhi's *Hind Swaraj,* of Kauṭilya's *Arthaśāstra,* and of Vinayak Damodar Savarkar's *The Indian War of Independence—1857.* It keeps on coming, in the form of Rabindranath Tagore's repudiation of Swadeshi politics and the articulation of his critique of nationalism via his novel *The Home and the World* (1916) and his speeches titled *Nationalism* (1917);[7] it comes as Sri Aurobindo's renunciation of terrorist nationalism in 1910 and his resurfacing as a yogi in Pondicherry four or five years later, never to return to active politics.

New institutions of higher learning proliferate—Tagore's Santiniketan is founded as a school in 1901 and deemed a full university by 1921; the Bhandarkar Oriental Research Institute (BORI) (1915–1917), the Banaras Hindu University (BHU) (1916), and Jamia Millia Islamia (JMI) (1920) are all created within five years of one another. These become the loci of entirely new fields and disciplines, like the tribal and popular arts of Bengal (Santiniketan), nationalist philology and Indian Indology (BORI), the history of Hindi language and literature (BHU), and progressive, anticolonial, and Pan-Islamic Muslim politics (JMI). To this apparently chaotic and confusing list of events, texts, and institutions, which I am arguing in fact belong within a single analytic envelope—that of the epistemological break that delivers the Indian political tradition from its debilitating crisis—we must also add the departure for Columbia University in 1913 of Bhimrao Ambedkar, a poor Untouchable graduate student from western India who was to eventually preside over the drafting of the Constitution of the Indian Republic between 1946 and 1949. It may be that Gandhi alone knew this with the *claritas* and the *veritas* that qualify an epiphany, but there came a point when India broke through a historical sound barrier, never to turn back.[8] Within a few years, between the 1920s and 1950s, India developed an intricate ecology of political thought, running the entire gamut from socialism, Marxism, and Communism, to democratic liberalism and republicanism, to Fascism and National Socialism, to a variety of homegrown political and quasi-political creeds, including Gandhian activism, Hindutva, and the radical humanism of the later M. N. Roy (at first the founder of India's Communist Party, in 1920).

Other indices also point to the epistemological climate—with its successive and sometimes overlapping phases of crisis, breakthrough, and resolution—in which I want to locate India's search for the self. Again, the data are seemingly disparate, but in my view, their pattern can be discerned. In the far south, the ancient Tamil Sangam literature—an enormous poetic canon that establishes the antiquity and sophistication of the Tamil language and its literary culture—was discovered and published between 1887 and 1915: a development that might seem potentially limited in its impact but in fact causes the equivalent of an earthquake in the politics of Tamil cultural nationalism.[9] In Pune, at the Bhandarkar Institute, Marathi scholar-nationalists led by V. S. Sukthankar prepared a critical edition of the *Mahābhārata,* the epic that they called "the Book of Books" and India's "national poem," from about 1916, a philological exercise of absolutely stunning proportions that was completed half a century later in 1966.[10] Eastward, a literary and artistic efflorescence of unparalleled beauty and productivity unfolded over the course of the aesthetic career of Rabindranath Tagore and his extraordinary extended family of relatives, disciples, and friends: the Bengal Renaissance, which began around 1890 and ended in the early 1940s—another half century that would form, shape, and change India's cultural identity. These phenomena have to be seen together, as premonitions, iterations, and aftershocks of a gigantic epistemological transformation that we usually subsume under omnibus labels like "tradition and modernity," implying a conflict between these terms, or the passage from the former to the latter, or the loss of the former and the achievement of the latter.

* * *

This book follows five founders of modern India, Mohandas Gandhi (1869–1948), Rabindranath Tagore (1861–1941), Abanindranath Tagore (1871–1951), Jawaharlal Nehru (1889–1964), and Bhimrao Ambedkar (1891–1956), on a particular journey of ideas that each of them made in the course of the struggle for Indian freedom from British rule. At the height of the British Raj during the late nineteenth and early twentieth centuries, they shared the intuition that there was a crisis in India's traditions of both political thought and political practice. Each one in his distinctive way tried to address this crisis by thinking about a problem that I believe has three parts: First, What is the self? Second, What is sovereignty? Third, What sort of relationship is it possible to establish between self and sovereignty? By the 1890s, Indian nationalism had evolved an indigenous term that captured the tripartite nature of the problem: swaraj. This term has two constitutive elements: swa, indicating "selfhood," a reflexive particle pointing back to the speaker, as well as raj, indicating "rule" or "sovereignty." The ligature of "self" and "sovereignty" in swaraj had a patent sense, namely, "self-rule," and this allowed nationalists to convey the imperative that India must be ruled by Indians, not by the British.

But swaraj unpacks in complicated ways, because one never knows what definitions of self and of sovereignty, and what conception of the possible relationship between them, compound into the apparent meaning upon any given iteration. Like many other terms in a vast nationalist lexicon, swaraj was a new coinage, a word whose life more or less coincided with the career of Indian nationalism, and one that did not seem to have either a history before the establishment of British rule or a future beyond the achievement of India's independence. Understood broadly, self, sovereignty, and their relationship form the shared semantic field of all these words. Other important members of this list include swadeshi (economic and cultural self-reliance), *satyagraha* (truth force/soul force), and *Harijan* (God's creature/child of God), while still other terms were used a great deal during the same period, but have either a prior existence, or an afterlife, or both: thus, *dalit* (crushed/ground down), *Pakistan* (Nation of the Pure), *azadi* (independence), and ahimsa (non-violence).

The East India Company began controlling most of India from 1757; the Crown Raj began in 1858 and ended in 1947. Throughout this time, colonialism, capitalism, and Christianity, the three most powerful weapons of the imperial state, severely threatened Indian political selfhood and Indian political sovereignty. In every corner of the subcontinent, colonized subjects experienced this threat, and responded by creating a range of new institutions, such as the Indian National Congress and the All India Muslim League, the Aligarh Muslim University and the Banaras Hindu University, the Brahmo Samaj and the Arya Samaj, the Hindu Mahasabha and the Self-Respect Movement, the Prarthana Samaj and the Satyashodhak Samaj. All kinds of entities sprang up across colonial India, from political parties to educational institutions, from religious sects to social movements, from reformist groups to militant outfits, seeking to capture and articulate identities and histories that would distinguish India from Britain, and endow Indians with a space of political self-confidence from which to challenge British rule. A complete description of these myriad measures to confront the loss and effect the recovery of the self under colonialism might constitute a perfect history of Indian nationalism. But that is not what I endeavor to write here.

Rather, I try to tell a few fragments of a vast and complex story, tracing the ideas of five persons only, from among a large number of Indian founding figures. Many generations of thinkers and leaders, men and women, Hindus and Muslims, upper castes and lower castes, brought India from the failed mutiny of Indian sepoys against the East India Company in 1857 to the birth of two new nation-states in 1947. I have selected five—mainly Gandhi, the Tagores, Nehru, and Ambedkar—partly because they are among the more self-reflexive, the most influential, and the best known of India's many founders. But partly I was drawn to these five thanks to the power of their own texts (i.e., because of the arguments that they made in their writings). When discussing Rabindranath, I consider also his nephew Abanindranath Tagore (1871–1951), who was a painter, a theorist, and a builder of art institutions, but I look at his paintings rather than his writings as the texts relevant to my argument.

In each of my protagonists I saw an ethical and epistemological engagement with self and sovereignty so profound and so sincere that I found myself able to reimagine India through their vision, as the place I name in the title of my book: *Righteous Republic.* This India arguably does not coincide with the nation-state born on August 15, 1947, at Independence, or even with the liberal republic born on January 26, 1950, at the promulgation of the Constitution. The righteous republic is a separate place, a repository of certain norms and values whose traces we may find even today in postcolonial India—norms and values without which it becomes impossible to either establish India's distinct historical identity in the world or justify its abiding claim to moral authority in the global community. Gandhi and others discussed in this book really created the ground upon which India stands—a solid plinth of moral selfhood and ethical sovereignty, absent which India is nothing more than the token of a type, a nation among nations, with no special contribution to human history.

Needless to say, Gandhi and his peers did not build a new India ex nihilo. They fashioned a number of political categories, most notably swaraj and swadeshi, with complex genealogies that braided Indian and Western thought. We know a great deal by now about what the Indian founders owed to liberal, Marxist, and socialist ideas; about what they took from the British, the Germans, the French, the Americans, the Russians, and the Italians (i.e., from all the major modern political traditions of England, Europe, and North America). We know less, however, about how these thinkers related to India's own rich intellectual history, which includes classical and folk traditions, Hinduism and Islam (besides other Indic religious systems, like Buddhism, Jainism, and Sikhism), an almost unfathomably large and multilingual literary repertoire, and the legacies of immediately precolonial polities that were variously Muslim (Mughal), Hindu (Marathas and Rajputs), Sikh, and tribal, and had developed an enormous taxonomy of institutional and symbolic forms never entirely trampled over or stamped out by the colonial state. India had lost herself and had to find herself again; find her way back to self-recognition, self-possession, self-mastery, and self-realization. The story I want to tell is of the quest of the five founders for an Indian selfhood hitherto obscured by foreign domination.

Indian anticolonial, patriotic, and nationalist politics had a number of distinct strands, all of them important to some extent—Hindu, Muslim, Communist, and Fascist, for example—and oftentimes these overlapped as well, so that it was possible to have Hindu Fascists, or Progressive Muslims, or extremists of a variety of persuasions. The figures I have chosen do not fall into any of these ideological camps. It may be recognized that perhaps one reason why these five attained preeminence was because their imaginings of a possible India were the least exclusionary, the most capacious. They worked with the fact that India's diversity was a given as well as a goal. To envision a set of norms and values that could further the flourishing of millions upon millions of human beings, across incommensurable cultural differences, was not within the power of any but very few of India's founding generations. I am not suggesting that none but these five men had the breadth of imagination needed to make India, but certainly these five did have it. Whatever else they might be accused of, pettiness was not an intellectual or ethical flaw that any of them suffered from.

Hannah Arendt posited a Western political tradition from Plato and Aristotle to Karl Marx.[11] Is there an Indian political tradition in quite the same way? Political ideas, texts about politics or with political themes, and a variety of state forms together with more or less explicit ideologies and practices of rule may indeed be found aplenty in Indic premodernity, in India's vernacular millennium, in its early modernity, and in the colonial period. But do these quanta of a broadly political character cohere into a self-conscious and roughly continuous tradition, of which India's moderns like Gandhi and his cohort are a recent instantiation? This question cannot easily be answered in the affirmative. Nevertheless, the founders had some sense of the past, and of their political inheritance. They turned, from time to time, to whatever it was they understood as being available to them by way of a classical legacy of ideas and ideals, seeking thereby to bolster the authority and legitimacy of the political claims they were making in the present.

A foundationalist turn in a time of political crisis and cultural conflict is not at all uncommon in modern history. Indeed, every significant democracy has sought to ground itself in a political tradition receding backward from the moment of its founding to a hoary antiquity: from France to the United States, from the United Kingdom to Italy, from Turkey to Israel. In many cases, there is no geospatial connection between the presumed ancestors and their present-day descendants: thus classical Greece and Rome become the political progenitors of the entire Western world, from the United States and Canada, to all of Western Europe, to Latin America, to Australia and New Zealand.[12] In other cases, physical proximity or even overlap means very little, so that the very same Greece and Rome are not claimed by the nearby countries of Muslim North Africa (notably Egypt, which was in fact the seat of Mediterranean civilization in the ancient world), as their political forbears.

For India's founders, the beginnings of polity lay in the life of the Buddha; in the Mauryan imperium, with its Aśokan edicts and the *Arthaśāstra* of Kauṭilya; in the Sanskrit epics, the *Rāmāyaṇa* and the *Mahābhārata,* and especially in the *Bhagavad Gītā* embedded within the latter; and in the Gupta imperium and its cultural artifacts. Why these moments of political history and textual production were included in the modern imagination of India's ancient foundations, while other, equally impressive moments were not emphasized much or at all, is a question that many readers will want to raise. Why are the sultans of Delhi and of the Deccan, the Dravidian dynasties from the Cholas to the kings of Vijayanagara, the rulers of Kashmir, the Rajputs, the Marathas, the Sikhs, the Nayakas, and so many other ruling formations of the east, west, north, and south not factored into the core narrative of India's political tradition? What about the borrowings and exchanges that characterized numerous cross-cultural formations involving India (or some parts thereof), for example, the Indo-Greek, Indo-Sinic, Indo-Persian, Indo-Arab, Indo-Tibetan, Indo-African, and Indian Ocean cultures—after all, isn't so much of India's political history best understood within these hyphenated frameworks, and aren't so many of the key texts of India's political premodernity the products of such border crossings?

As it happens, some elements of India's long and heterogeneous political past were left out because they are relatively recent (or, more precisely, less ancient); others because they are regionally constrained; some because they are affiliated to Islam or to minority religions; many on account of their uncertain or supposedly low-caste status; some because they are miscegenated with "foreign" cultures; and yet others because they do not bear a strong relationship to any of the subcontinent's languages that were transregionally powerful prior to English: Sanskrit, Pali, Tamil, and Persian. This catalog of reasons for omission makes the political tradition, when it is implicitly or explicitly invoked, narrow, selective, biased, and discontinuous in both space and time. I return to these defects below.

* * *

In every one of the past five decades, the academic literature has seen at least one major return to the problem of tradition with regard to India: Lloyd and Susanne Rudolph's *The Modernity of Tradition* (1967), Louis Dumont's *Homo Hierarchicus* (1970), J. C. Heesterman's *The Inner Conflict of Tradition* (1985), and Ronald Inden's *Imagining India* (1990). In the past decade, the most significant intervention on the question of tradition has been that of Amartya Sen in *The Argumentative Indian* (2005).[13] Unlike its four predecessors, Sen's book is not mainly concerned with caste and its structuring role in Indian society; rather, it is concerned with democracy. (It could be that we are ready to talk about Indian democracy only now that it has been in place for over six decades.) For Sen, India's knowledge tradition, broadly construed, is characterized by such features as rationality, debate, heterodoxy, skepticism, pluralism, toleration of difference, and the practice of public reasoning. Because of these characteristics, he calls it an "argumentative tradition." Further, he sees this long tradition as laying the necessary historical groundwork for the eventual adoption, by the Indian nation founded in the mid-twentieth century, of democracy and secularism. If India, after it has gained its freedom from British rule, becomes a secular democratic republic, this is because it has, from its earliest political beginnings, been engaged in a cultural conversation that flourishes in the clamor of many voices and through the disagreements between them.

The beginnings, for Sen too, lie in the Buddhist, Mauryan, epic, and Gupta formations, with later highlights that include the Mughals, especially the Emperor Akbar; medieval dissenting poetic traditions affiliated with bhakti radicalism and Sufi Islam; traditions of science and mathematics, especially in the first millennium; and particular schools of ancient Hindu philosophy, ranging from the metaphysical (Upaniṣads and Vedānta), to the epistemological (Nyāya), to the materialist (Lokāyata/Cāravāka). He also notes and underlines the continuous presence of religious plurality on the subcontinent, which embraces large and small, old and new, major and minor, Indic and foreign groups at every juncture. Indians have been arguing with one another throughout their recorded history: this made them a raucously accommodative people, naturally receptive to and prepared for democratic self-rule. India adopted democracy not because it was taught democratic theory by its colonial masters, but because it had engaged in what was effectively democratic practice throughout its intellectual history, up to and including the nationalist struggle against colonial rule. As Indian politics began to develop authoritarian and exclusivist tendencies in the 1990s, with the rise of the Hindu Right, Sen made a powerful appeal to his countrymen that they recognize their real history of argumentative coexistence in a welter of intellectual, political, and cultural differences.

In a situation of felt political crisis (such as the Hindutva takeover of Indian politics in the 1990s), to what idea of an Indian political tradition (such as "the argumentative tradition") can we have recourse? What is the backstory of Indian democracy, that is to say, what history of thinking about self, sovereignty, and their ligature in Indian traditions of political thought has the power to weave disparate and discontinuous phenomena of a broadly political description from India's past and present into a coherent narrative? Arguably, today, in the seventh decade of their republic, Indians may lean on their founders, like Gandhi, Nehru, Tagore, and Ambedkar, among others, to provide the banisters of political thinking that make contemporary Indian politics legible, comprehensible, and meaningful. But who did the founders themselves have to support them in their arduous ascent toward swaraj? Where had their norms and values to come from, when the past had yet to be deciphered as a story that made sense, that led toward a future of freedom, that produced in its readers the self-knowledge that is the true purpose of all effective storytelling (and hence history writing)?

Several features of the default Indian political tradition constructed in modern times are problematic: the emphasis on ancient India, with its Hindu and Buddhist elements, at the cost of medieval India and Islam; the preference for texts in transregional and classical languages like Sanskrit, Pali, and Persian, over regionally limited but nonetheless highly influential vernaculars; an implicit division of kings, warriors, writers, and saints from the Indo-Islamic past into "good Muslims" and "bad Muslims," and the accommodation of the former into an account that otherwise excludes all Muslims in general; a bias toward polities, societies, and ruling classes that fit within not just the caste system, but its upper echelons, and a concomitant neglect of low-caste, outcaste, and tribal identities that nevertheless have played a huge part in the political life of the subcontinent; pervasive and persistent gender bias; the bias toward literate elites and their texts and practices over the bulk of history as made, lived, and experienced by unlettered subalterns; the unbalanced interest in religion, literature, and philosophy over physical, natural, and social sciences, and so on. Sen does not try to explain away these distortions and lacks: where possible, he tries to correct them, and where historical data are missing and thus no correction is possible, he acknowledges that the narrative as it stands has serious problems and limitations.

But it is Sen's systemic solutions rather than his attempt to rectify specific problems in the idea of an Indian political tradition that are most useful. Without repeating his arguments, I would summarize them to state that both "India" (or "Indian") and "tradition" (as in "Indian political tradition") have to, perforce, function as heuristic devices rather than categories with definite and determinate extensions. Both entities are meaningful, make sense, allow people to talk about them despite disagreements over particulars, have a long historical life, and persist in their conceptual core over and across terminological variations. Secular-minded liberals may object to what the Hindu Right means by "India" or "an Indian political tradition," and vice versa, but this does not mean that India does not exist or that an Indian political tradition does not exist. These are not categories that can be argued out of existence, no matter what the magnitude of the conflict over their meaning on a given occasion. We can quarrel—pretty much ad infinitum—about where exactly an Indian political tradition begins (for instance, I happen to think it begins with the life of the Buddha), or how far back in time it is possible to speak reasonably about India or an India-like category (I am with Sen in going back to the early Greek, Arab, and Chinese identifications of the land and people of the subcontinent, south and west of the Indus and the Himalaya, extending into the peninsula to its southernmost limits). But even to quarrel in a non-absurd way, we need to agree first on a working definition of the things we are fighting about.

Sen concatenates Yājñyavalkya, Buddha, Kauṭilya, Aśoka, Krishna, Kalidasa, Khusrav, Akbar, and Kabir, for example, into a chain of moments in India's moral imagination, articulated variously through mythical, literary, and historical persons, all of whom had something valuable to say about self and sovereignty, about ethics and rationality, about the psychological and social aspects of human experience that preoccupy us even today when we engage in politics. Sen accepts that he chooses these moments and these voices and that someone else might choose other moments and other voices instead. He grants that his choice is driven by his agenda, which is that of promoting Indian democracy, and that a separate agenda, such as the construction of a Hindu nation, would result in quite different choices. He acknowledges that his "argumentative tradition" as a construct is neither perfectly unambiguous, nor entirely continuous, nor impervious to improvement.

However, he does not grant Ramachandra Guha's claim that the "proximate past" has more to teach us than the "distant past," simply because one is closer to us, in a strictly chronological sense, than the other.[14] The worth of Akbar lies in what Akbar had to say about the peaceful coexistence of religions and the role of the state in managing religious differences, not in his having lived a mere 400 years ago; we continue to think about Aśoka because Aśoka seems to have invented, in the Indic political world, the idea of ethical sovereignty, and we cannot discard him just because he lived and died 2,200 years ago. We don't know anything, and we may never discover anything, about the historicity of a figure like Yājñyavalkya, or indeed even the very humanity (as opposed to the divinity) of figures like Krishna and Rama. But because entire traditions of inquiry into the human condition come down to us through the voices of speakers who carry these names, we are prepared to set aside that which we do not and perhaps cannot know about them, and focus instead on the seemingly perennial interest of these characters. What is close and what is remote, what is attractive and what is repugnant, what is to be cherished and what is to be rejected in the historical record has reference to our values and our struggles in the present. Gandhi and Tagore wanted India to be free of British subjugation. Many Indians today want their nation to remain strong, stable, plural, and inclusive. The dialogue between the moderns and the ancients must be guided, Sen argues, by "positional objectivity" and "practical reason."

From about the mid-1890s, Gandhi and other nationalists faced a political crisis that led, in my reading, to their quest for what we could call "the sources of the self"—an Indian self. A cogent tradition of Indian political thought was not to hand, certainly nothing on the order of Arendt's Plato-to-Marx type of proposition, which would have made perfect sense to a European contemporary of Gandhi's who might have been trying to think about a Western political tradition at that very time. Indian religious, political, philosophical, and social traditions did offer ways of thinking about self, sovereignty, and self-rule, especially through categories like dharma (normative order), *ātman* (self), *nīti* (policy), artha (political economy), *nyāya* (justice—though also logic), *daṇḍa* (retributive justice), ahimsa (non-violence), rājya (rule/kingdom), *śakti* (power), *yuddha* (war), *rāṣṭra* (nation), and *rājadharma* (the ethics of rule). In addition, an entire vocabulary was built from the roots *śas-* and *śam-* that capture the sense of "control," "cutting," "quenching," and "quelling": *śāstra* (authoritative text or textual tradition), *śāsana* (the practice of rule), *śastra* (weapon), *anuśāsana* (discipline, both discursive and physical), *ānṛśaṃsya* (compassion), and so on. The categories of the four ends of man (*puruṣārthas*): dharma (good works), artha (material prosperity), *kāma* (bodily pleasure), and *mokṣa* (liberation from the cycle of rebirth), as well as the four orders of society plus the four stages of life *(varṇāśramadharma),* are relevant as well. So too are the three ontological tendencies (*guṇas*): the veridical *(sattva),* the dominant *(rajas),* and the unyielding *(tamas).* All of these, and other such categories, had an ancient provenance, and were definitely to be found in the congeries of texts already listed above as favorite sources for India's modern political thinkers: the life of the Buddha, the *Arthaśāstra,* Aśoka's edicts, the epics, the *Gītā,* and so on. A nationalist like the early Aurobindo, in his radical phase, drew heavily from this traditional repertoire to suggest new political categories like *rājshakti* (capacity for rule) and *ātmashakti* (inner strength), and to endorse a category like swadeshi that his peers were using very widely in anticolonial politics.

What makes the founders treated in this book so interesting and important is that even when they were aware of old categories of Indian political thought, they did not seek to recuperate or revitalize them as such. Rather they invented and worked with new categories like swaraj, swadeshi, and satyagraha. In retrospect, we cannot reconstruct the course of Indian nationalism without these words. They were central to the nationalist project. But it turns out, oddly, that they were also evanescent. Only two of the period's many coinages really have any sort of postcolonial life in India—*dalit* (crushed/ground down), which indicates the political identity of groups formerly considered untouchable in caste orthopraxy and particularly conveys the emotions of righteous protest and empowering anger against social discrimination and historical injustice; and *azadi* (freedom/independence). Both these terms are associated with as-yet-incomplete political projects, which may explain their survival and continued usage in Indian political life. The first, *dalit,* is nowadays conjoined with *bahujan* (literally: the majority of the people, the masses), and the hyphenated *dalit-bahujan* is used to indicate the totality of lower caste and untouchable groups in caste society who now have a common platform in the identity-based politics of representative, electoral democracy. The second, *azadi,* is now used only in Kashmir and not in any other part of India.[15]

Parenthetically it should be noted that ahimsa is an archaic term found in Jain and Buddhist thought, and given political valence by Aśoka through the drama of his turn to pacifism in the aftermath of carnage. Its importation into the modernist political lexicon is probably initially result of Gandhi's personal engagement with Jain philosophy, through his spiritual preceptor in his early years, Raychandbhai Mehta (1867–1901), though later, as Chapter 1 shows, it was the *Bhagavad Gītā* that helped the Mahatma to understand the true meaning of ahimsa. For Gandhi and his followers, it was perhaps the hardest of all concepts to integrate into either the theory or the practice of modern politics, whether Indian, Western, or of mixed descent. Nonetheless Gandhi made ahimsa an inalienable part of his idea of ethical action in both political and personal life. He insisted that swaraj could never be achieved without adherence to ahimsa and *satya* (truth). Although it was awkward to have to enshrine ahimsa in the middle of a vast, difficult, and mainly realist project of nation building, statecraft, and political governance, Nehru, who led India in the first years of its independence, never really challenged the importance or efficacy of this Gandhian tenet. The founding violence of Partition, which reached catastrophic proportions in 1947, not to mention the considerable violence used to integrate recalcitrant princely states, and the wars fought to defend Indian interests against Pakistan and China throughout Nehru's three successive administrations, from 1947 to 1964, all unfolded within the prevalence of the notion that the Indian nation was bound to ahimsa. Indeed, as the righteous republic, India could not but be unswerving in its commitment to this most ancient of political categories.

* * *

Unlike a dozen major European political philosophers between Hobbes in the mid-sixteenth century and Marx in the late nineteenth century, Gandhi, Nehru, and Ambedkar were neither theorists nor historians. They were thinkers and practitioners of politics, leaders of mass movements, and at various times the heads of parties, states, or ministries. The Tagores, Rabindranath and Abanindranath, were also not political philosophers—they were primarily artists. So it might be better to compare the Indian founders considered in this book, as a group, to nineteenth-century Americans like President Abraham Lincoln and his contemporary poets and philosophers, Ralph Waldo Emerson, Walt Whitman, and Henry David Thoreau, than to the intellectuals who constitute a European tradition of modern political thought. My protagonists all lived in the hurly-burly of political life, or in the crucible of creative genius. All five of them built or ran institutions, whether educational, communitarian, or political. While they needed to find or fashion ideas about Indian self, sovereignty, and self-rule, and in search of such ideas they might have turned to a variety of historical sources, they were not primarily in the business of discovering, constructing, or resurrecting a political tradition.

I would go so far as to say that they both sought a tradition and belonged in a tradition, but the historical completeness or logical structure of that tradition, its robustness as an intellectual construct, its explanatory power at every stage of its articulation with respect to an eventual Indian modernity, its internal cogency and external longevity, are really more our concerns and the concerns of contemporary scholars. Sen worries that in forgetting their argumentative tradition, Indians are losing the will to be democratic. Khilnani is concerned that we have insufficient information about which parts of India's multiplex knowledge tradition were genuinely open, tolerant, and confrontational, and wonders what went on in long periods of historical time and in enormous swaths of India that stretched between the flashes of unorthodox thinking spotted and deservedly lauded by Sen.[16] Guha questions Sen's criteria for selecting some texts and not others as worthy of notice. His point is that if we are including in our idea of a tradition only those texts that appear to lead up to democracy, then we cannot very well claim that democracy was inevitable based on the prior existence of those texts.

A progressive thinker like Ambedkar insisted that the Indian tradition—by which he meant a Brahminical, Sanskritic tradition—was the opposite of argumentative; that it was authoritarian, and this was responsible for modern India being intellectually conservative, socially reactionary, and politically oppressive, with or without British rule. Ambedkar was not wrong, even if Sen is right. But while they were all able to devote some time to reading, research, writing, and polemics of a broadly historical character, the founders, including Ambedkar, had more pressing work to attend to in achieving Indian swaraj, such as identifying a set of norms and values that would both make the argument for and give concrete shape to the righteous republic.

These norms and values drew strength and inspiration from ideas of ethical sovereignty, just rule, and non-violence that had long circulated in the intellectual traditions of the subcontinent, some political and some not. But these norms and values also had to take cognizance of the real world, as it were, in which Indian selfhood was unfolding: a world in which the dominant political form was (and is) the modern nation-state, and all politics was (and is) suffused with violence. My focus, in this book, is on the moral imagination of the founders and on the relationship of their moral imagination to a longer-term moral imagination that I would like to call "Indic," with all of the empirical, analytical, and ideological purchase of that term. Using "Indic" instead of "Indian" allows us to displace the nation from the center of our understanding of the political tradition in which we are locating India's founders, while at the same time differentiating this political tradition from a Western political tradition (especially in its liberal, socialist, and Marxist strands), which also had a deep impact upon Indian political modernity. "Indic" has the advantage of capturing the fluctuating geospatial unit we intend, in the *longue durée,* with a broad array of languages, religions, and cultures, without restricting our reference to the most recent phase of Indian history, defined by the colonization of the subcontinent, followed by the creation of the modern nation-states of India and Pakistan upon the end of British rule. "Indic" does not in principle exclude Indo-Islamic history, although it is not covered in this book.

The Indian Constitution recognizes two names for the country: the English word "India" and "Bharat," the Hindi word, traceable to Sanskrit and found in most Indian languages. In Indian languages, it is now standard practice to use both India and Bharat, and no difference is made or understood between them. Both words are equally old and have ancient roots. The adoption of one or both gives away the foundationalism at work in the making of the Constitution: I say that to note a fact, not to pass a judgment. "India" belongs in a family of words from Sanskrit, Greek, and Arabic, including the nouns *Al-Hind,* Hindu, Hindustan, Indus, Hindi, *Indika,* Sindh, *Sindhu,* and *Hindavi,* denoting a variety of entities—land, ocean, river, country, people, religion, language, history, region, and so on. There isn't really much doubt as to where, in the wide world, any or all of these might be found. Bharat is a term that comes out of the Sanskrit epic the *Mahābhārata,* but was seen to coincide to such a great extent with the geophysical expanse of India at the time of Independence that the makers of the Constitution treated the two words more or less uncritically as synonyms. The equivalence, once so determined, appears to have become pretty widely accepted by Indians in both official and informal usage. When ordinary folks say "Bharat," today—incidentally, this is also the word that occurs in the Indian national anthem, written by Rabindranath Tagore in 1912 and adopted by the Constituent Assembly at Independence—except in specialized contexts, the reference is to India and not to epic geographies (the space of Bhāratavarṣa), epic genealogies (the Bhārata clan), or epic narratives (the Mahābhārata war).[17] When I use "Indic," in this book, I mean an adjective or a qualifier that includes rather than excludes both the historical and the contemporary senses of "Bharat" as well as "India." For me, the value of "Indic" is heuristic rather than definitive.

In Chapter 1, I consider Gandhi's tract of 1909, *Hind Swaraj* (translated by him as *Indian Home-Rule*), since it set the agenda that Indian nationalism was to follow for the next four to five decades, until Independence. I am concerned substantively with Gandhi's definitive reinterpretation and reactivation of the category swaraj, and formally with the place of *Hind Swaraj* in an Indic political tradition. I argue that this text resolves the "epistemological crisis" in political thought to which Indian nationalism before Gandhi was an early response, and that it does so precisely by reconstituting the meaning of swaraj from simply political independence to genuine self-mastery, with a crucial deepening and expansion of the idea of the self (swa-) already embedded in this concept. Where there is true swaraj, the stance of ahimsa, absence of the desire to harm, is what regulates and reorganizes the relations between any two selves, or between self and other. When ahimsa becomes the norm of norms *(ahiṃsā paramo dharmaḥ),* the abstinence from violence and the eschewal of violent intent become the basis of a new social contract.

In Chapter 2, I read a cycle of poems by Rabindranath Tagore, all of which engage with the fifth-century Sanskrit poet Kalidasa, who was very possibly attached to the court of the Gupta Emperor Chandragupta II "Vikramāditya." I am especially interested in a number of poetic symbols that Tagore evolves over the course of his literary career to signify classical India, ancient Indian history, and the disjuncture and pathos that characterize the relationship between India's present and her past. I also look at a set of paintings by Rabindranath's nephew Abanindranath, that show Shah Jahan contemplating his most famous architectural legacy, the Taj Mahal, at different stages of its construction. I examine these paintings in close connection with a poem by Rabindranath that also frames the Mughal emperor and his monument to love, again to reflect on the gulf that separates us from our history, fracturing and dispersing the self, and on the inconsolable yearning of the human imagination for an integration between time present and time past.

Chapter 3 also examines Rabindranath's famous essays against nationalism, delivered as speeches in America, Japan, and India during World War I, in conjunction with Abanindranath's famous painting *Mother India* that provided a sort of mascot for Swadeshi politics in Bengal in the early twentieth century—a movement that Rabindranath at first supported and later repudiated in his Bengali novel of 1916, *The Home and the World (Ghare Baire).*

Chapter 4 frames a series of national symbols: the state seal, the anthem, and the flag, chosen for India at the time of Independence, and suggests that their semiotics establish a strong lineage for the new republic going back to the first state of a subcontinental scale: the empire of the Maurya dynasts in the fourth–third centuries BCE. I look carefully at Nehru's affinity for the Mauryans, especially Aśoka, and at the Aśokan conception of ethical sovereignty as being underpinned by a normative order *(dhamma),* non-violence (ahimsa), and institutionalized religion (the Buddhist *saṃgha*) that Nehru found so appealing. If Nehru was drawn to values like pacifism, compassion, justice, and tolerance that are extolled in Aśoka's edicts, I also trace how India's first prime minister may have been influenced to embrace the contrary elements of strategy, surveillance, punishment, and war elaborated by the political philosopher Kauṭilya—a founding father for the Mauryans—in his text the *Arthaśāstra.* The mixture of realist and idealist elements in the political thought of the Mauryan imperium quite closely adumbrates Nehru's own dual ideology, or rather, anticipates the tension between his beliefs as a political thinker and his compulsions as a political leader.

My fifth and final chapter is devoted to B. R. Ambedkar, the foremost leader of the Dalit community in the twentieth century, a nationalist with special concern for the rights of social, religious, and cultural minorities in both the colonial and the postcolonial dispensations, chairman of the drafting committee of India's Constitution, the first law minister in Nehru's cabinet, and a political thinker with perhaps the most juridical and legislative imagination of all his peers. I ask why Ambedkar, in the last year or two of his life (he died in 1956), converted to Buddhism, taking many of his followers with him. For the founder who did the most to move Indians out of hierarchical understandings of identity (centered around caste, religion, gender, region, and language), into the modern form of political subjectivity (i.e., equal citizenship), to turn at the end of his journey to the very first historical person, the original dissenter, and the most long-lost figure, as it were, in an incipient Indian tradition of protest, suggests his longing for alternative genealogies of political thinking to those he had learned from the West. Ambedkar's last work, published posthumously, was titled *The Buddha and His Dhamma,* and this retelling of the Buddha's sermons begins with a remarkable disavowal of the Four Noble Truths. In what sense, then, was Ambedkar really a Buddhist? The answers to this question return us to the heart of the intertwined problems of past and present, self and sovereignty, as well tradition and modernity, that form the sinews of this inquiry.

* * *

In the course of my research I wondered if the founders felt any affinity for premodern, Indic categories of political thought, given that they were, one and all, very modern—Westernized, Anglophone, secular, and rationalist—in their educational and professional profiles, and in their intellectual trajectories. Except the Tagores, most Indian nationalists studied the law, and many practiced before or alongside their political careers. They carried out most of their political work through well-known categories, as already pointed out, of new vintage: swadeshi, swaraj, satyagraha, Harijan, Dalit, and so on. Swaraj turned out to be the master category in this book and in my own thinking. My inquiry into the political foundations of modern India began with swaraj. It is in swaraj that both elements that I seek in the writings of the founders occur simultaneously—self and sovereignty. Swaraj was important to Indians agitating against colonial rule across the board, from the Maharashtrians, Tilak, Gokhale, Ranade, and Savarkar; to the Bengalis, Aurobindo, Vivekananda, the Tagores, and Bose; to the North Indians, Gandhi, Nehru, Azad and Lala Lajpat Rai; to South Indians like C. Rajagopalachari and S. Radhakrishnan.

But it was Gandhi who made swaraj central to a pan-Indian nationalist endeavor. He was the one to take it on in its early meanings from the 1890s, and transform it into the main item on the agenda of the Indian National Congress. His first major announcement of what swaraj would eventually come to mean was contained in his 1909 tract, *Hind Swaraj,* which was banned, translated, circulated, and finally published in a big way over the following ten years. Even though he titled it, in translation, *Indian Home-Rule,* in fact the book outlined how swaraj was to move *away* from the idea of home rule and become something totally different, a novel category closer to self-rule or "the sovereignty of the self." The English phrase "home rule" still meant that while Indians could eventually rule India, they would do so on sufferance, because of the magnanimity of the British Raj. It meant India's continuing subordination to the British monarchy; its partial, dependent autonomy within the protective and unshakable umbrella of empire. In Gandhi's interpretation, swaraj was to be something else entirely.

Like swaraj, swadeshi too was widely adopted in different parts of India, especially in the earlier stages of Congress-led nationalist agitation. The idea of swadeshi (economic self-reliance) seemed to go into a sort of recession after the Partition of Bengal and the communal violence following upon it in the first decade of the twentieth century. But after his formal entry into mass politics in about 1919, Gandhi kept swadeshi alive in another form, through his campaigns for *khadi* (handspun, handwoven cotton) and *carkhā* (the handheld spinning wheel), symbols of India's industrial self-reliance, artisanal base, and domestic manufacturing sector as well as local markets. For Gandhi, they ought to have been more than symbols—they ought to have led the way to an economic and social revolution, which of course was not to be, given Nehru's and even Tagore's differences with Gandhi on questions concerning technology. But the failure of a Gandhian economic model aside, in my understanding, swadeshi as an economic and developmental ideology became very deeply ingrained in the Indian political imagination and continues to manifest itself in government policy and public debate even today, over six decades after Independence. This is because swadeshi means not just a preference for indigenous over foreign goods, but in its widest sense the self's reliance on all that is its own, all that is proper to it, its property. Broadly construed, swadeshi signifies the self's ownership. At its most capacious, the concept of swadeshi encompasses the meanings of "self-reliance," "self-possession," and "the ownership of the self," which bring it quite close to the "self-mastery" and the "sovereign selfhood" conveyed by swaraj. If these meanings were pertinent a hundred years ago during colonialism, they are all the more so today, during globalization, when India's economic and technological porosity to the rest of the world poses some serious questions for its cultural identity and political freedom.

While I knew to look for swaraj and swadeshi as central to the founding of the righteous republic, I did not have a clear idea, at the start, where else the founders other than Gandhi might take me. After several years of reading for this book, I felt I was ready to isolate five categories, each one associated with one of the thinkers I had chosen to write about. Except for swaraj and swadeshi, all of these categories are in fact very old—that is, they can be found in Indic thought from its earliest stages, with histories long preceding India's colonization by the British. For Gandhi, the relevant category is ahimsa, the self's benign orientation toward others, devoid of the desire to injure or harm, that makes collective life possible in the first place and allows human beings to think further about political forms and the structures of their coexistence with one another. For Rabindranath, the category I discovered to be key is viraha, the longing produced by separation, the self's yearning, a yearning that is coeval with being in time and does not end in a futurity of closure and union, which to my mind gives us insight into his skeptical attitude toward history and his counterintuitive stance against nations and nationalism.

For Abanindranath, the category I felt best conveyed the ontology of his art is samvega, aesthetic shock, the self's shock of self-recognition, its ability to know the truth about itself when it comes face to face with powerful aesthetic representations of itself. But for samvega, we cannot make sense of Abanindranath's search, and with him that of the entire Bengal School, for a truly Indic art. For Nehru, the category guiding his politics, both anticolonial and postcolonial, is dhamma/dharma, usually understood as "normative order" or "law," but for our purposes in this book really the self's calling, its aspiration at all times for the highest possible good, for the greatest possible weal, its intrinsic buoyancy that leads it ever upward in search of the truly political society, the perfect moral commonwealth. Nehru was equally invested in artha, "purpose," "substance," or "goal" that gives to the self its motivation, its capacity for purposive activity, and in some cases its instrumental nature. And last, for Ambedkar, the category I think underlies his stupendous effort in trying to remake stubbornly hierarchical India as an egalitarian polity is not, as expected, the coinage Dalit (meaning a former Untouchable), but deeper below that, the bedrock, as it were, which is duḥkha, suffering, the self's burden, its gravity, the enormously strong force field that is caste society, in which every self crashes into every other till they are all smashed to little bits. In converting to Buddhism shortly before his death, Ambekdar made one last attempt to allow the self to escape the deadly pull of the gravitational field of duḥkha, whether read as social or metaphysical suffering, as a collective or an individual burden.

That a genealogy of Indic morals should lead back to Indic categories ought not surprise us as much as it in fact does. Why are we so surprised to discover traces of millennia-long debates and traditions in the thought of modern India's founding fathers? Did we think that they had irretrievably forgotten their own intellectual past? Did we think that colonial rule of barely a few decades had undone centuries of careful inquiry and reflection into every aspect of selfhood? That knowledge of the self, the central concern of Indic civilization for the entire length of its existence, had simply been erased from Indian minds by the late nineteenth century? Or did we become so distracted by how Indians dealt with Western categories—capital, reason, justice, race, nation, citizenship, science, democracy—that transformed Indian political life between the mid-eighteenth and the mid-twentieth centuries that we lost track of continuities in Indic political thought from a long precolonial history? It's true that the founders had to devote most of their attention and energy to negotiating with the British on their terms. As the ruling side, the British controlled the lexicon of politics; Indians, subjected, could not insist that the conversation go on in a vocabulary that would have made cultural sense to the people. What is remarkable is the extent to which Gandhi did, actually, force the imperial adversaries to speak his language. But even he could not very well bring back into fashion modes of understanding and talking about sovereignty, violence, law, freedom, authority, and other fundamentals of politics from discourses that had long ceased to have any real manifestation in the instantiations of power, the forms of the state, the practices of rule, and the personalities of rulers. Indic political categories did not disappear, but they did, under colonialism, become fugitive.

* * *

There may be some concern that the six categories I am associating with the five founders—ahimsa, viraha, samvega, dharma, artha, and duḥkha—don't seem to be primarily political, at least at face value. Aesthetic, yes; spiritual, yes; universal, yes, that is to say, having to do with the human condition as such—but not political in particular. We are concerned with the self, granted, but we are also, thanks to the basic blueprint of swaraj, interested in sovereignty at the same time. So how is sovereignty to be rediscovered via these six seemingly apolitical or non-political categories?

Ranajit Guha, in his pathbreaking book *Dominance without Hegemony: History and Power in Colonial India* (1998), which brought together arguments he had built up over two decades, carefully compared British and Indic categories of domination and subordination, coercion and persuasion. He argued that in every instance throughout the eighteenth and nineteenth centuries, British categories found their Indic counterparts, so that the two political idioms worked in tandem to produce Britain's "dominance without hegemony" in India. Thus the British idea of "order" was reinforced by the corresponding Indic idea of *daṇḍa* (punishment); "improvement" by dharma (normativity); "obedience" by bhakti (devotion); and "loyalty" by *dāsyabhāva* (servitude). Even "protest" was domesticated into "dharmic dissent" (dissent that nevertheless remained within the bounds of dharma). The combined effect of these categories was to ensure that the British dominated India, but for various reasons this dominance stopped short of being hegemonic.

In the gap between the very real dominance of the British and their never-to-be-achieved hegemony, Indian elites found a space for their power, and used it both to oust the British and to establish their own dominance over Indian subalterns. Thus the subalterns, India's ordinary people, her laboring classes, peasants, and workers, were twice subordinated, both by foreign rulers and by native elites. When Western categories at work during colonial rule proved unintelligible to the masses, the ready availability of a corresponding Indic political idiom allowed a translation into concepts that were already a part of subaltern experience. Altogether, a fear of punishment and a desire for improvement led to greater obedience and loyalty toward whoever happened to be the masters—white skinned or brown skinned, it did not make much of a difference. Independent and democratic India, in this reading, was really a neocolonial state, continuing the British Raj under a different name.

Besides Guha, other major scholars of the Subaltern Studies school also read nationalist intellectuals and political leaders, like Bankim, Gandhi, Tagore, Nehru, and others, along the same lines—as members of what Partha Chatterjee identifies as a "comprador bourgeoisie."[18] Marxist and Gramscian understandings of the relationship between class conflict, nationalist movements, and the "passive revolution" underlie these interpretations of Indian nationalism. Indic, especially precolonial, political categories here fail to help subalterns to overthrow either the yoke of colonialism and imperialism or the hegemony of native ruling classes. The main purpose of Indic idioms of power, consent, and even dissent, according to Guha, Chatterjee, and Shahid Amin (to name just the most prominent members of this school of historiography), is to translate unfamiliar, foreign forms of politics, on the one hand, and on the other hand, to permit native upper classes and castes to reinforce their age-old sway over the Indian subcontinent.

Amin analyzes Gandhi's charisma, the source of his tremendous personal appeal for India's masses over the course of almost three decades, as a function of the simpleminded religiosity, the almost childlike faith, of the subalterns who comprised the Mahatma's audience and following.[19] The premodern or the precolonial, in this narrative, stands not for a separate tradition of political thought that Gandhi might have been drawing on and embodying in his person, in order to reach the people of India, but rather for the inability of peasants and villagers to think like modern, rational individuals. Gandhi's followers were superstitious, gullible, susceptible to rumor, and prone to looking upon Gandhi as a holy man, a miracle worker, a saint, a mystic, or even an avatar. Gandhian nationalism then, cannot be regarded as the triumph of an Indic political tradition over the British Raj. For Chatterjee, whose book *Nationalist Thought and the Colonial World: A Derivative Discourse* (1993) is too important and complex to summarize here, Indian nationalists were ultimately defeated by what he calls "the cunning of reason," so that India was forced, despite Gandhi's best efforts, to accept a "derivative" political modernity and the primacy of the nation-state form. There is no political or economic space, as it were, that escapes the logic of capital in the modern world, and India, though it aspired to be the exception, did not achieve that goal. The gap between "political swaraj" and "true swaraj" was confirmed at Independence, understood subsequently as the difference between the Nehruvian and the Gandhian paradigms.

What I am suggesting, in this book, is that our investigation into the fate of Indic political thought should not stop at "derivative discourse" and at the mutually mirroring and reinforcing character of Western and Indic categories of power. If *daṇḍa* and bhakti, punishment and devotion, function in a colonial regime to reinforce the message of order (to be provided and maintained by the British rulers) and duty (to be followed and fulfilled by their Indian subjects), then these categories were clearly co-opted into the dominant ideology of rule. But the categories I found to be important to the founders are not so easily usurped by or useful to a polity thoroughly Western in its conception and form. In fact, to return to the point I anticipated might cause the reader some concern, they are not political categories at all. All six of them originate and flourish in discourses that are strictly speaking outside the realm of politics. To my mind, this is what makes them so germane, and this is also the reason for our surprise at the role they play in shaping the political thought of the founding fathers. (It has to be noted though, four out of the six—ahimsa, dharma, artha, and duḥkha—cross over into the territory of the political very early on in their historical life, largely thanks to Jain and Buddhist intellectual traditions and histories of political power.) In other words, I am asking that we pay attention to these categories precisely because they break the mold of Western reason, and thereby loosen its hold as well, on ways of being, thinking, and writing in colonial India. The appearance of these categories in the thought of the Indian founders suggests that there were yet ways in which these men were not, intellectually, Europeans.

* * *

Muslim leaders and intellectuals in India during the relevant period, between the 1880s and Independence/Partition, arguably also faced more or less the same questions as their caste Hindu or other compatriots. But in many ways their predicament was peculiar. Islam's careers on the Indian subcontinent in the millennium leading up to British rule had left behind at least two traces that modern Muslims could both claim for themselves and hope to construe as a legacy for all Indians—one, a political tradition represented by the relatively recent memory of the Mughal Empire, and two, a religious tradition (or a collage of smaller traditions) of Indic and Indo-Persian Sufism, which in practice often attracted adherents from Muslim and non-Muslim communities. But while both the Mughal and the Sufi inheritances were potentially inclusive, in reality their power had long been attenuated by the colonial state and its forms of domination. Simultaneously, Indian Muslims also found themselves having to refashion their relationship to larger communities of Islam outside India, from Iran to Turkey to West Asia to Arabia to Egypt, regions that themselves were undergoing the great transformations necessitated by modernity. The poet Iqbal (1877–1938) and the theologian-politician Azad (1888–1958) were peers in every way of the five figures I write about here.

The men who assumed the political and cultural leadership of India's Muslims in the very phase under discussion—principally Sir Syed Ahmad Khan, Allama Mohammad Iqbal, Mohammad Ali Jinnah, Maulana Abul Kalam Azad, the Ali Brothers, Dr. Mukhtar Ahmed Ansari, Sheikh Mohammad Abdullah, Khan Abdul Ghaffar Khan, and perhaps a few others—also searched for an authentic selfhood. But whether that self could only be appropriate for Muslims or would work for India as a whole must remain a question for another book. In markedly different ways, these thinkers—admittedly some more intellectual than others—all confronted the fact of decisive and irreversible Muslim defeat at the hands of the British in 1857. They grappled with the twin tendencies in the Zeitgeist, toward religious reform on the one hand and a renewed fundamentalism on the other. They tried to think about their community in the old frames of faith, custom, practice, region, and ethnicity that they could foresee would not necessarily make a successful transition into the new order of secular nation-states and modern legal-juridical regimes. As the national movement reached its crescendo, and communal violence increased all across the subcontinent, Muslims had to choose between the dark unknown of the two-nation theory and the even more depressing prospect of being rendered a perpetual minority in post-Partition India. Could all of India's Muslims, diverse and scattered, be pulled into a single unified shape? Where did they stand relative to other segments of the *ummah* (community of the faithful) in different parts of the world, especially in the homelands of Islam further west in Asia? Indian Muslims had long coexisted with Hindus, but could they share political power with them in the emergent postcolonial dispensation? Wherein lay the wellsprings of a hyphenated "Indian-Muslim" identity—in the "India" part of that ligature, or in the "Islam" part of it?

For some years in the late teens and early 1920s, it seemed as though the logic of Khilafat—a struggle that appeared to be about restoring the religious authority of an Islamic caliphate but in reality was the last gasp of the Ottoman Empire—would give Indian Muslims a raison d'être, a sense of political direction, and internal cohesion as a community. The Indian National Congress under Gandhi's (then) new leadership encouraged this campaign and threw its weight behind the Pan-Islamic ideology of the Khilafatists. But when Turkey itself, led by Mustafa Kemal Atatürk, rejected and finally destroyed the stranglehold of the Ottoman dynasts and made a resolute turn toward secular modernity and European nationalism, Muslims in India needed to pause. It became increasingly obvious that their future had to be worked out in an Indian context, with regard to players and elements within the subcontinent: secular and sympathetic Congress leaders like Gandhi and Nehru, antithetical Hindu communal forces, the lingering-departing British, and Islamic theology and traditions of innovation and reflection within it, as well as a broad, diffuse historical narrative that encapsulated Islam's trajectories in India over the course of a thousand years. India offered a rich repository of resources for self-examination and self-renewal, as well as the ever-present threat of fragmentation, dissolution, and assimilation that had obstructed Islam from becoming the sole, dominant idiom of religious life in the subcontinent from the very beginning and throughout medieval and early modern history. In the early twentieth century, anti-imperialist movements in India (as elsewhere) were often imbued with religious sentiment, which was not necessarily a problem when religious and national communities coincided; however, for Indian Muslims, the enormously challenging task was to triangulate their feelings of domestic patriotism (as Indians) with transnational *jihad* (the struggle for righteousness decreed by Islam) on the one hand, and Hindu-led but on the surface non-sectarian, anodyne anticolonial nationalism on the other.

Muslims in South Asia had over the centuries written their learned texts and popular poetry in Bangla and Braj, Punjabi and Saraiki, Sindhi and Gujarati, Kashmiri and Malayalam, Dakhni and Urdu, Farsi and Hindavi. By contrast, Arabic and Turkish, although they were supposed to signify origin, apotheosis, and authenticity in Muslim identity discourse, remained essentially foreign languages. In other words, the Muslim quest for a self had to turn inward, into the soul, and into India. In their distinct ways, Iqbal, Azad, and Jinnah all pursued these options, though none of them succeeded perhaps, in settling once for all the conundrum of whether there could really ever be a selfhood for Muslims that might weld the pious individual, the community of believers, the pluralistic nation, and ultimately all of humanity into one integrated structure with spiritual depth and political resilience. Or else the failure might equally be attributed to India's non-Muslim thinkers. There is no point in apportioning blame, but by the end of the nineteenth century, colonial prejudices combined with Hindu fears and Muslim defeat resulted in a thoroughly communal view of Indian history, which over time became so naturalized that by the mid-1940s even a mind like Nehru's, as can be seen at work in his classic *The Discovery of India* (1946), could not but read the present (with Partition looming) back into the past (as a long saga of conflicts that constantly had to be dealt with through India's particular genius for reconciling differences).

Yet today, long after the passions of Independence are quieted, is it possible to conceive of a reconciled Indian self that admits both Hindus and Muslims, taking as its basis some third, non-sectarian foundation that has yet to be imagined? (A federalist solution, parenthetically, had it worked itself out, would nonetheless still have avoided the question of how to arrive at a transcendent Selfhood beyond Hindu and Muslim selves—perhaps one reason why such a road found no takers, whether among Jinnah's followers or his opponents.) Can there be coexistence, unity, mutual tolerance between Hindus and Muslims, rather than the inequality between a "majority" and a "minority" that seems to be the fate of these two entangled communities in South Asia? Can Islam ever be perceived as anything other than trauma and interruption, intrusion and invasion, the unwanted guest who must be absorbed and overcome—the Self's inevitable Other? These unanswered questions continue to haunt us generations after the founders made India, Pakistan, and Bangladesh, and left us their deeply flawed legacies. Even India's vaunted secularism, sadly, has turned out to give credence to the two-nation theory in surreptitious ways, victimizing minorities within independent India as though they deserved punishment for surviving the Partition and coming out on the other side as "Indians" rather than as Muslims, Christians, Sikhs, Dalits, or tribals.

In the long run, a complete intellectual history of modern South Asia must take on the elephant in the room, which is the place of Muslim traditions of inquiry into self and sovereignty in the making of India—and Pakistan. Leaders like Sir Syed, Azad, and Jinnah, and poets like Ghalib, Hali, and Iqbal are perhaps as poorly understood in their capacity as founding fathers in Pakistan as they are in India—an omission that is equally inexcusable in the historiography of either nation. Nor do we have a strong sense of the role played by non-religious but nonetheless sectarian institutions like the Aligarh Muslim University (f. 1877), Jamia Millia Islamia (f. 1920), and the Muslim League (f. 1906) in making possible a modern Muslim identity or a modern identity for Indian Muslims (even acknowledging that those two categories are potentially distinct from one another would be a step in the right direction). It's almost as though the Indians left these figures to the Pakistanis to memorialize, critique, or forget as they thought fit, because in India they came to be seen, retrospectively, and for the most part unreasonably, as preparing the ground for the creation of a separate Muslim homeland all along, while the Pakistanis did not really take them on wholeheartedly because they seemed to be too rooted and caught up in an Indian problematic (with the exception of Jinnah, and that too only after 1940).

Was there an "epistemological break" in Muslim knowledge traditions on the subcontinent any time in the window, say, between 1857 and 1947—something on the order of Gandhi's *Hind Swaraj* (1909), that we could clearly identify as marking a before and an after in Muslim political thought? Faisal Devji has suggested certain parallelisms between on the one hand Gandhi and Jinnah (Gujarati lawyers from trading communities, and fathers of their respective nations, both), and on the other Nehru and Iqbal (Westernized Kashmiri aristocrats, and writers of key texts, both). Such preliminary intuitions need to be explored, debated, fleshed out, and if necessary discarded, before we can claim to have a proper history of the political foundations of the twin nations.

Partha Chatterjee has discussed how modern thinkers do not posit two unequally long, yet symmetrical and parallel traditions, one Indic, one Indo-Islamic, that lead up to, respectively, India and Pakistan. I do not have the wherewithal, in this book, to try to understand the intellectual antecedents of modern Muslim political thinkers, like Sir Syed Ahmad Khan (1817–1898), Mohammed Iqbal (1877–1938), Mohammed Ali Jinnah (1876–1948), or Maulana Azad (1888–1958). Nor am I able to follow what is made of an Indo-Muslim political tradition (if such a thing is ever constructed) in the founding of the nation of Pakistan. But certainly within modern India's genealogy for itself, the Islamic heritage is not handled in any meaningful way: it is neither aggressively assimilated nor violently expunged; neither claimed nor refused for whatever its contribution to India's political thought through the ages. Needless to say, this is both intellectually and ethically a highly dissatisfying state of affairs. It means that no one in India has come up with a reading of the past that properly accounts for all kinds of political phenomena springing from Islam that have affected, indeed shaped, the course of Indian history from the seventh-century Arab conquests of the Sindh to the defeat of Bahadur Shah Zafar, the so-called last Mughal, in the debacle of 1857. When it comes to India's political tradition and its underlying puzzle of self, sovereignty, and their ligature, the rule of Muslim kings in the subcontinent for over a thousand years remains the blind spot.

Gandhi via his solidarity with the Khilafat Movement in the early 1920s and his complete opposition to Partition in the 1940s, Nehru through his special brand of secularism developed and strengthened over the full course of his political career in colonial and postcolonial India, Ambedkar through his larger engagement with the question of minority and minorities (again, like Nehru, a matter he dealt with both before and after Independence), and Tagore via the question of Bengali Muslim identity that came up early in the first iteration of Swadeshi politics at the turn of the twentieth century, all undertook serious engagements with Indo-Muslim culture and politics. But none of them had any systematic place for the Islamic past in their idea of an Indian political tradition and of the political foundations of the new republic. Indian secularism, in the aftermath of Partition, made the gesture of inclusion toward all that was Muslim and still remained in India. (At the time, the significant part of the subcontinent's Muslim population, as well as a great deal of the territory that had ever been under Muslim rule, remained in India rather than going over to Pakistan. Muslim-ruled or Muslim-majority princely states like Junagadh, Hyderabad, and Kashmir were integrated into the Indian union using varying amounts of force and to varying degrees of "success.") But as the history of independent India has shown, particularly since the early 1990s, this gesture was for the most part a hollow one. Had Gandhi lived and actually moved to Pakistan as he had proposed to do just prior to his assassination (by a Hindu fanatic) in January 1948, the idea of an Indian political tradition, particularly with respect to Indian Islam, might have been very different from what it became. We cannot know.

* * *

Studying India between 1885 and 1947 harbors the danger of not seeing what is staring us in the face. We are so accustomed to regarding this period through the lenses of nationalism and colonialism, liberalism and imperialism, religious revival and social reform that we are more than likely—in fact we are almost certain—to miss the most extreme flux, the unprecedented soul searching, the radical reinvention of the idea of India, the sheer existential chaos of this period. The founders looked in every direction, for a way out of the darkness, or, as Rabindranath called it in an unforgettable line of his Bengali poem "Shah Jahan": "the ever-falling darkness of history" *(atīter-cira-asta-andhakār).*

One of the reasons, I believe, for our blindness, for our inability to perceive the seriousness of the crisis of self and sovereignty that overwhelmed India not one century ago, is the mundane reality that our scholarship proceeds in English, for the most part. So much of the newness of founding discourses is contained in and revealed by the lexicon that emerged in the 1890s and in the decades following. Very little of this lexicon is in English—barring a few exceptions, like "home rule," "dominion status," "separate electorate," or "partition," all British bureaucratic jargon that Indians were more likely to resist than accept. I want to show through this book, among other things, that the novelty and inventiveness of the work of the founders cannot be recaptured unless we are attentive to the words they retrieved from the past or made up afresh and used to express their struggles.[20] Philological attentiveness is essential in the method I advocate and also attempt to follow myself. If this discussion were to take place in an Indian language—Hindi, Marathi, Bengali, Gujarati, or whichever vernacular—such philology would be fundamental and inescapable; it would be the very default of our reading and writing. It is because Indian history and social sciences carry on largely in English that we have to take extra care not to miss all that is right before our eyes.[21]

For the entire length of their public careers, India's founders meditated on and grappled with the problem of an Indic selfhood. For Gandhi, the self both expands into the civilizational self and contracts into the individual self; in thinking about the self at these two very different scales, he displaces it from its usual location in Indic political life, which is the community *(samāj/jāti)*. If swaraj is "the dominion of the self," then it is a realm whose extension cannot be measured within the bounds of history. Neither territorial nor temporal measures as understood historically, nor the form that the state might take, are relevant to swaraj. This is why it is not important whether Rama really lived in Ayodhya or fought in Lanka; whether a war like the Mahābhārata actually occurred on the battlefield of Kurukṣetra; whether Krishna was a cattle-herding boy or a peace-broker king, a god or a man; whether a *satyāgrahī* resisting the British today by making salt, weaving cotton, or fasting to protest injustice becomes a citizen of an egalitarian and democratic nation-state called India tomorrow, or not. Rather, for Gandhi, at one level, swaraj is *Rāmrājya* (Rama's reign)—a civilizational norm of ethical sovereignty, just rule, and the ideal ruler; on another level, swaraj is when I overcome fear in the face of danger, or when I face my enemy without the desire to harm him. In this understanding of swaraj, nationalism has no contribution. Chatterjee has developed this point at length and with great subtlety—he distinguishes "political swaraj," the limited, and finally achieved, goal of Indian independence from British rule, from "true swaraj," the mastery of the self or the self's dominion that Gandhi was after.[22]

For Rabindranath Tagore, the self may only be signified through symbols in either poetry or (abstract, non-mimetic) painting—it cannot be captured in the discursive or analytic language of social science, philosophy, or politics. The self is a palimpsest of traces *(saṃskāra)*, an elusive presence in dream, memory, and reverie, an entity both immemorially old and absolutely momentary, subject to instantaneous decay, evanescent and yet marked by experience. It is as absurd to construct a history for this self as it is to historicize it in the present. The self does not yield itself up in the mirror of history. The self for Rabindranath is the self found in the thought of the Upaniṣads: infinitesimal *(sūkṣma)*, concealed *(guhya)*, primordial *(purāṇa)*. Can this subtle, hidden, ancient self be entombed in gigantic, magnificent monuments? Is there a style of art in which it may be delineated accurately? Does it reveal itself through the relentless probings of history? No. History is the language of the nation, and history is far too ham-fisted to ever grasp the shy, secretive, evasive self. The only language proper to it is poetry.

For Abanindranath, however, the self is both the master and the subject of tradition. If the tradition—of art, of literature, of any of the forms of knowledge and imagination known in the Indic world—is carefully reconstructed, then we may obtain a more or less stable image of the self. This reconstruction itself is a challenging task, but in the face of the aggression of Western thought, Indians have no choice but to find and reclaim their traditions. The act of claiming is also the act of becoming. Krishna, at play and in love, in childhood and in youth, is a timeless face of the self, the self in playful engagement with others *(līlā)*. The large, heavy-lidded eyes, the sinuous limbs, and the glowing colors of the figures in the Ajanta Caves are windows into the self that is a repository of wisdom and peace. The passions and powers of the Mughal emperors are the self at its most expressive, its human apotheosis. The gentle, slightly indistinct landscapes of Bengal and Orissa, of the plains and the mountains, the rivers and the groves of east and northeast India, are the home of the self, its place in the world. Through his continuous experimentation with styles of painting, Abanindranath is pursuing the very same self, Rabindranath's will-o'-the-wisp, firefly self, and it has to be said that over the body of his artwork, some portrait of this self does emerge from the uncertainties of spatiotemporal flux *(saṃsāra)*, history *(itihāsa)*, and tradition *(paramparā)*.

For Nehru, the self is the center, the observer, the still point of reason and judgment in a turning world. This self can travel through the ages, watching history unfold; it can traverse the vast space of the subcontinent, taking in its vertiginous detail; it can converse with a multitude of other selves, if only it is prepared to listen. The self keeps its eyes and ears open, and keeps on moving. The self as conceived by Nehru is engaged in a constant process of discovery and discernment. Moreover, embedded in a totality of selves, it is the protagonist of democracy. The self is secular; it is rational; it is fair-minded. It aspires always to better its material and moral condition, as also that of its fellows—in this way, it faces out toward a future. It has a quickness to it, a vibrant intelligence; it is impatient with all that is dull and dour. As the leader of the Congress and the prime minister of India, Nehru endorsed a series of images and symbols to figure the self of India—some very old, like Aśoka's Lion Capital; some entirely new, like the modernist city of Chandigarh, designed by Le Corbusier. The national flag, which would identify the Indian republic in the global community, could have had at its center Gandhi's spinning wheel (carkhā) or, as it eventually turned out, the ancient Mauryan *dhammacakra* (wheel of law). Both kinds of wheels signified the perpetually dynamic as well as the ethically centered character of the Indic self that Nehru sought to articulate as the heart of his political vision. In a way his was the self easiest for his countrymen to grasp, and this is perhaps the reason that the Nehruvian self was the one that remained and flourished in postcolonial India, a self that now, long after Nehru's passing, is in need of a resurgence.

Last, for Ambedkar, the self had to be painstakingly carved out of the shackling dross of a violent, hierarchical, and unequal society—it had to emerge out of the darkness of premodernity into the light of the rule of law, social justice, and egalitarian citizenship. From its most crushed, the self had to rise up to its most emancipated condition. From its wellsprings of anger centuries deep, a great new edifice had to be built. Ambedkar rejected all interpretations of selfhood that subjected the self to rituals of humiliation, denied its intrinsic dignity, or resented its capacity for transformation and renewal. For him, caste was a jail; he demanded that all men and women be released from it, out into a state of potentiality—in the dual sense of power and promise—to make of their lives what best they could. The Indic self had too long been bound in the chains of caste, gender, religion, region, and custom—first it had to be returned to a zero state, shorn of all its imputed attributes, and then it could begin to fashion itself as it wished. To Ambedkar, political freedom (swaraj) meant precisely the freedom to make the self. Both *karma* (a theory of consequential action) and dharma (a totalizing normativity) were impediments to, and not the vehicles of, self-realization. Ambedkar did not follow the Buddha in the Buddha's renunciation of worldly power, only in his impulse to understand and thereby master suffering (duḥkha), the burden of the self, both personal and social. Of all the founders, Ambedkar alone envisaged a self that was radically modern, in that the ground of its being was neither ontology nor deontology, but the law. Save for his very last and most mysterious gesture, conversion to Buddhism, Ambedkar's "self" could almost be said to be one with and the same as "the citizen": not the predefined and overdetermined person of orthodox *varṇāśrama-dharma* (caste society), but the legal-juridical-constitutional citizen. The turn to Buddhism, however, complicates this story of the Ambedkarite self, and it is to this turn that I want to pay attention in this book.

* * *

As my chapters on Nehru and Ambedkar respectively show, Nehru drew a set of symbols and signifiers of ethical sovereignty from the Mauryan and especially the Aśokan imaginary, while Ambedkar created a new sect of Buddhism and converted both himself and hundreds of thousands of his Dalit followers. Does this mean that Buddhism, whether as sign or as substance, had some special purchase for the founders of modern India? Was the new republic implicitly supposed to hark back to the archaic blueprint of a Buddhist imperium? Were ideas of non-violence, just rule, an ideal ruler, and a normative political order, espoused not just by Nehru but also by Rabindranath and by Gandhi in various forms, together with Ambedkar's formal conversion into the religion taught by the Buddha and propagated by Aśoka, explicable as a broader Buddhist turn in modern Indian politics? Did a Buddhist third way, as it were, serve as some sort of acceptable alternative to either Hindu or Muslim political traditions, which were too different from and too opposed to one another, and therefore too divisive for the people of India? I think it might be tempting to raise these questions, but in fact the answer in all instances has to be in the negative. While it might look like Nehru and Ambedkar were both drawn to Buddhism qua Buddhism, my suggestion is rather that Nehru's engagement with Aśoka and his edicts, and Ambedkar's engagement with the Buddha and his teachings, were really explorations of different aspects of India's fugitive political selfhood. Buddhism as a historically defined and differentiated religion, originating in

India, encompassing a number of distinct schools and sects of doctrines and practice, scattered geographically over several modern nations, has little to do with what either Nehru or Ambedkar made of it.

As I explain at length in the body of the book, Nehru sought easily identifiable and appealing ways to marry the political life of the new nation with a set of norms and values that had an ancient lineage, a wide discursive availability, a degree of translatability into visual icons and tactile artifacts, and the imprimatur of contemporary thinkers like Gandhi and Tagore who commanded both prestige and popularity. What Nehru sought, in the Aśokan and Mauryan materials—that is, in the edicts, the pillars, the Lion Capital, the *Arthaśāstra,* and the *cakra*—were not the historical relics of an ancient Buddhist empire, but ways to represent and communicate the kind of nation he was hoping to build as the leader of free India. To put it strongly, had the conditions been right, he might just as easily have turned to Jain, Hindu, or Sikh texts, icons, and symbols. As a matter of fact, he was quite comfortable taking up his personal residence as the first prime minister of India in Teen Murti Bhavan, which had previously been occupied by the British commander in chief, and addressing his people at the very moment of Independence (midnight, August 15, 1947) from the ramparts of the Mughal-built Red Fort. As is very clear from Nehru's magnum opus, *The Discovery of India* (1946), for him, India could be represented by aggregating all manner of histories and traditions and by drawing, almost indiscriminately, on their symbolic resources. Nehru had no special attachment to Buddhism per se. The aspect of selfhood that interested him, I argue, was the self's aspiration—its buoyant, self-improving, self-clarifying tendency. The category that best encapsulates this ascending, soaring, *volant* capacity in the self is dharma/dhamma, beautifully conveyed through the national symbols that Nehru chose and approved from the excavations at Sarnath and the text of the *Muṇḍaka Upaniṣad.*

Similarly, even though Ambedkar founded a sect of Buddhism, the Navayana or "New School," my reading is that what drew him to Buddhism was neither the figure of the Buddha nor even the greater part of the Buddha's teachings, nor for that matter the various iterations of Buddhist doctrine in the extant schools of India, Nepal, Sri Lanka, Burma, Thailand, Tibet, Japan, or China (or any other country, for that matter). What worked for Ambedkar about the life and teachings of the Buddha was rather the centrality within those discourses of the category of duḥkha, which he understood as the self's burden—its heaviness, its gravitas, its undertow. And this oppressive weight upon the self, in Ambedkar's analysis, came not from a flaw, a fault or a forgotten debt that was peculiar to the individual self, but from the imbalances in the very structure of caste society that unjustly placed heavy burdens upon some while allowing others to fly high. In his interpretation, then, duḥkha was not one's own, proper, particular suffering, but the totality of social suffering as such, the ubiquitous suffering—arising from universal inequality and its concomitant injustice—endemic in a caste-based social structure like Indian and especially Hindu society.

Nehru was completely agnostic with respect to all religions (which is one way of explaining why he was not really interested in Buddhism); Ambedkar, on the other hand, systematically tested and rejected Sikhism, Islam, and Christianity before adopting Buddhism, which goes to show that he was in principle willing to go with whichever religion allowed him to address the social problems of violence, inequality, and humiliation that preoccupied him. Thus, strange as it seems, neither Nehru nor Ambedkar had any special investment in Buddhism, even while one picked out its hoary icons to symbolize the new nation, and the other apparently made conversion the very final gesture of his complex and symbolically powerful, meaning-laden political career. Something along the same lines can be argued also with regard to Gandhi's propensity to valorize *Rāmrājya* (the Kingdom of Rama), by which he meant not a Hindu Utopia derived from texts like the ancient *Rāmāyaṇa* or the medieval *Rāmcaritmānas,* but a type of polity that placed a high premium on truth, justice, courage, compassion, and dignity, and strove to maintain harmony and respect between different groups and classes within the society.[23] When Gandhi spoke of *Rāmrājya,* he was being no more religious and no more faithful to a specifically Hindu, devotional, Rama-centric construct than Nehru was wanting to act like a Buddhist emperor when he turned to the figure of Aśoka or than Ambedkar was being a devout Buddhist in any traditional sense of that term.

* * *

Subaltern Studies has been the most systematic and sustained engagement with the problem of colonialism in Indian history to date, and it has had the salutary effect of forcing historians of Indic premodernity and early modernity, also, in turn, to question and sometimes discard their premises, especially those that were holdovers from Orientalism and Indology. But it is now important to see not only the impasse between tradition and modernity in India, but also the relationship of some kind of complex and perhaps compromised continuity between them, mediated as that relationship was by colonialism. Certain roads were not taken but we can still discern them, up to a point, in India's past; we know that logics, categories, and forces were active in Indic premodernity that never had anything to do with capital in the first place, and that produced world systems, as Sheldon Pollock shows in his *The Language of the Gods in the World of Men* (2006), not assimilable to or commensurable with the blueprints of European history. The British did not do India in, nor did India shake off the cloak of empire and come out its original, untouched self onto the stage of world history. India is rooted in its own earth, like every other great living culture. It had a prolonged encounter, we might even say collision, with the post-Enlightenment West, but this did not mean that it ceded its difference *tout court*. If an examination of the origins and workings of colonial rule in India is going to place an emphasis on precisely the domination of the British and the subordination of the Indians, then a *longue durée* history of Indian democracy is going to show us other patterns and tendencies in India's past that made it possible for the country, despite caste, colonialism, imperialism, and great economic difficulty, to embrace democratic politics and representative government. Such a school of history has yet to clearly emerge.

Sometime in the late fifteenth or early sixteenth century, in that gulf of history between the deep past designated as "classical" and the crisis precipitated by colonialism, Kabir was a mystic poet who lived in Banaras and composed poems whose precise number or exact text we cannot really be sure of. What we know from hints in some of the poems attributed to him, from later hagiographic literature, and from the beliefs of a sect of his followers (the Kabir Panth), is that he was in all probability unlettered, a weaver, raised in a Muslim family, and either an initiated or a self-taught practitioner of both Nathpanthi Yogic as well as Sufi Muslim forms of discipline and devotion. He was considered low caste (on account of being a weaver). He did not establish his own sect or cult, and very likely he did not lead the life of a family man, although he did not renounce all worldly activity either—he kept on working his trade, at the very least. He challenged and ridiculed religious orthodoxy and social conservatism, whether Hindu or Muslim. His language was inventive, incisive, and highly eccentric. He was indubitably gifted with profound poetic talent. The poems of Kabir—or poems said to be by Kabir—are sung and remembered all across northern and central India even today, almost 600 years later. He is claimed by at least seven different poetic or devotional traditions, all of which continue to be active and to collectively attract millions of adherents: the eponymous Kabir Panth, the Sikh Panth in Punjab, the Varkari Sampradaya in Maharashtra, the Bauls of Bengal, generic pan–North Indian bhakti or devotionalism, and Indo-Islamic Sufism in North India and Pakistan, as well as contemporary radical Dalit poetry, especially in Hindi and Punjabi. He is undoubtedly one of the most widely known and best-loved poets to have emerged in South Asia in the last 1,000 years, which is saying a lot, because this has been nothing if not a millennium of vernacular poetry all across the subcontinent.

No intellectual history of modern India, and especially not one that is interested in the sources of the self for the makers of modern India, can afford to ignore Kabir. The world of Hindi literary history and criticism over the past 100 years has seen a sustained debate on the place, importance, and canonicity of Kabir, whose language, idiosyncratic and unstable as it is, can at the very least be taken as a collage of the multiple dialectal ancestors of modern Hindi. In the first half of the twentieth century, the two important interventions on Kabir both came out of Banaras, the city where he had lived—the first, an attempt to marginalize Kabir, from the critic Ramachandra Shukla, followed by a powerful restitution of Kabir to canonical status by the great Hindi intellectual Hazariprasad Dwivedi. More recent contributions have come out of Delhi from Namvar Singh and Purushottam Agrawal. The noted Dalit intellectual Dr. Dharam Veer has, in the past decade, attempted to capture Kabir exclusively for the Dalit community, its self-understanding and its self-respect, denying that caste Hindu, secular liberal, or any other kind of elite literary culture can have a legitimate claim to the oeuvre of this outcaste poet. Shabnam Virmani, a filmmaker based in Bangalore, has, through her multimedia "Kabir Project" (2003–), consisting of film, music, and text, documented living traditions of song, performance, devotion, and scholarship centered on Kabir all over North India and Pakistan. Most recently the scholar Milind Wakankar has published perhaps the first comprehensive analysis and critique, in English, of what Kabir, as a Dalit and as a Muslim, means for contemporary subaltern politics in India.[24]

This book does not contain a chapter on the reception of Kabir in the twentieth century, but I do want to flag his importance to the search for the self in modern India. Looked at in one way, Kabir was just another demotic poet—one of several whose oeuvre appears in many of the languages of medieval India from about the twelfth century, a period that Pollock, in *The Language of Gods in the World of Men,* refers to as "the vernacular millennium." The biographical details of his life are vague and we do not have even one authoritative compendium of poems that can be conclusively attributed to him and to him alone, as an individuated, historical author. Yet Kabir is pulled into the center of debates about canon, language, literary history, religion, caste, social change, and moral values throughout the twentieth century. Rabindranath Tagore translated some of the poems into English soon after he received his Nobel Prize in 1913, using as his source text a Hindi and Bengali anthology prepared by his friend Kshitimohan Sen (1910–1911), who in turn collected a number of songs from the Bauls and other minstrels who wandered about in Bolpur, the small village where Santiniketan had been established. Tagore seemed to take for granted the spiritual and mystic content of Kabir's poetry, as well as its popular provenance, but he failed to anticipate the storm of intellectual and political passions that would eventually envelop Kabir as the century advanced. (Hazariprasad Dwivedi, whose book *Kabir* [1940] made the boldest claim to establish Kabir as a founding father of Hindi letters and as the source of a certain modern energy in Hindi poetry, taught at Santiniketan from 1930 to 1950, where his own agonized relationship with Banaras as well as the immediate influence of Sen and Tagore fed into the making of this pathbreaking work.)

The reason Kabir became so contested, in my view, is that he took on a new life as a cipher for both his critics and his admirers, signifying many of the issues that animated the quest for an authentic and representative selfhood. Kabir relentlessly satirizes and ridicules organized religion of every kind; at the same time, he also attempts to fashion a highly personal creed that extracts and fuses the pith of both Hinduism and Islam. In some simple sense he is a Muslim, but he creates a poetic symbol for the highest truth that he names "Ram," a concept whose meaning and theology is equidistant, it seems, from the Rama of the Hindus and the Allah of the Muslims. He is a lowly weaver, perhaps even an Untouchable, but he does not give cognizance to any conception of inequality, whether physical, social, or spiritual. He is rebellious, iconoclastic, outspoken, and headstrong. He coins a wholly original idea of love *(prem)*. He invents a completely original, utterly intimate Ram: a Ram all his own, not to be found in the Sanskrit epic, in South Indian temples, or in the poetry of Tulsidas, his near contemporary and fellow inhabitant of Banaras. Kabir draws on vocabularies that treat body and word, corporeal experience and linguistic signification, as alternates for one another, and both as possible routes to ineffable states of ecstasy, knowledge, and transcendence—vocabularies that are found in a variety of Yogic, Saivite, and Sufi systems, which may or may not be in conversation with one another at different moments in the history of Indic religions.

Kabir is counted both with and above the great bhakti poets of the north—Mira, Surdas, Raidas, Dadu, Haridas, and others; the Varkari poets of Maharashtra—Gyaneshwar, Namdev, Eknath, and Tukaram; the Sikh poets—Nanak, Namdev, and other gurus; the Sufi poets of Hindustan—Khusrav, Bulle Shah, Shah Hussain, Shah Bahu, Baba Farid, Abdul Rahim Khan-i-Khana, and others; the medieval poets of greater Bengal—Jayadeva, Vidyapati, Candidas, and Caitanya; the Vacana poets of Karnataka like Basava and Akka Mahadevi; the Vaiṣṇava Alvars and the Śaiva Nayanars of Tamil Nadu; and the Kashmiri poets Lal Ded, Nooruddin Wali (or Nand Rishi), and Habba Khatoon. Kabir is appropriated primarily for the traditions associated with the conception of a formless God *(nirgun)*, but this does not mean that his name is not taken in close proximity with the traditions that worship a God with attributes *(sagun)*. He enjoys a transregional, multilingual, and cross-sectarian fame, and stands, literally, alone *(akela)*. The question I believe we have to ask is: What makes Kabir so peerless? What carries him across India, across time; what makes him the counterweight who keeps things in balance, without whom India's poetic traditions, whether of devotion or of dissent, would come crashing down under the burden, the incoherence, the heterogeneity of their collective corpus?

For modern India, Kabir represents the ultimate telos—an ability to simultaneously acknowledge irreducible differences and overcome them; an unflickering flame of faith that burnishes the gold of an equally precious skepticism; the strength to stand firm in a stance of confident rationality even while gazing unblinking into the abyss of violence. To proceed toward an enlightened, humane, inclusive nationhood even with its almost unbearable burdens of caste conflict, communal hatred, and sectarian prejudice, India itself has to approximate to the condition of Kabir—the coherent, charismatic, autotelic Self. It has to not be riven by its many schisms (Brahmin/Untouchable, Hindu/Muslim, *nirgun/sagun,* Yogi/Sufi, Ram/Rahim, god/God), but faceted by them into a glittering whole that reflects light in every direction. Modern India's literary thinkers—whose efforts of "criticism" and "interpretation," as Wakankar argues, are throughout closely braided with the work of anticolonial nationalism—keep circling around Kabir like blind men around an elephant, trying to comprehend this colossus in our midst—our greatest poet, our biggest conundrum, the scourge of our traditions, and the essence of our self.

* * *

So what is the "righteous republic"? How does it coincide with or differentiate itself from the Republic of India? How does it relate to Gandhi's "Hind Swaraj," India in a state of self-possession and self-mastery? Is it the same as, or different from, the nation-state called India that came into existence in August 1947? Is it an abstraction? Is it a reality? Is it any more or less imaginary than the "India" that constitutes the incalculably vast and varied aggregate of millions of such imaginings on the part of individuals who have participated in the life of India over the course of, say, the past century? The founders never ceased to ponder this question, of what it was that lay at the heart of their strivings. In 1905, Abanindranath paints a delicately-hued image of a young goddess who comes to be known as "Mother India." "What is Swaraj?" asks Gandhi in Chapter 4 of his *Hind Swaraj* in 1909. In a letter to his friend C. F. Andrews in 1921, Tagore coins the phrase "the idea of India." Jailed in Ahmednagar Fort at the height of World War II, Jawaharlal Nehru embarks on a historic "discovery" of India. From 1946 to 1949, Ambedkar and over 200 other members of the Constituent Assembly carefully deliberate upon a definition of India in the form of the text of its Constitution.

We have a sense of every twist and turn in the battle to regain the sovereignty of India that the founding generations waged against the British, clarifying over the course of many decades their final goal of self-determination and self-rule. But they saw that India's freedom is not just the freedom to *rule* itself. True freedom is in fact India's freedom to *be* itself. This being of India, its selfhood, is the ground of its sovereignty, and this being, for the founders, had to have both a substantial past and an indefinitely extending future, beyond the limited and limiting circumstance of subjugation. The Indian struggle for political independence became a mass movement, cutting across class, gender, region, and ethnicity, because it offered, simultaneously, many prospects that attracted, inspired, involved, and motivated ordinary people—the incorporation of long-running habits of knowledge and practice into the lived present; the integration of tradition and modernity; the possibility of an ameliorative modernization; the confrontation and resolution of a grave epistemological crisis; the invention of new ways of being, thinking, and acting in the world; the recentering of politics in a stable, confident, mature sense of self; the promise of putting into action a set of values that had deep histories as well as universal ethical appeal; the uplifting example of extraordinary men and women, like Mahatma Gandhi and his peers; and so on.

In other words, the project of Indian nationalism was overwhelmingly a moral project, one that sought to make India a better place and to give Indians a better life than they could ever have under colonial rule. An ideal of the time, "selfless service" to the nation—which the founders repeatedly enacted themselves and exhorted their compatriots to follow—was in fact paradoxically a kind of service that promised a much stronger, more enduring relationship between self and sovereignty than loyal servitude to the colonial master would ever yield. Swaraj is more than making India free; swaraj is the becoming Indian of the self of millions upon millions of people—it is one of the most profound exercises in collective transformation ever to be undertaken in human history. This study begins to look at the imaginative and interpretive work undertaken by five of the best known of India's many founding figures as, in an effort to harness the past and warrant the future, they read with care and concern some of the important texts that their rich intellectual traditions had put in their hands.

In 1912, as the British Raj moved its Indian capital from the imperial city of Calcutta to the old seat of Mughal power, Delhi, Rabindranath Tagore published what would become one of his best-known poems, quoted in Bengali and in English translation all over South Asia for the past century. The poem is a simple prayer for a different vision of India than the colonized, subjected, and defeated country that Tagore lived in:

> Where the mind is without fear and the head is held high;
> Where knowledge is free;
> Where the world has not been broken up
> Into fragments by narrow domestic walls;
> Where words come out from the depth of truth;
> Where tireless striving stretches its arms towards perfection;
> Where the clear stream of reason has not lost its way
> Into the dreary desert sand of dead habit;
> Where the mind is led forward by thee
> Into ever-widening thought and action . . .
> Into that heaven of freedom,
> My father, let my country awake.[25]

This is the very place I have called the righteous republic.

I

Mohandas Gandhi

Ahimsa, the Self's Orientation

India's political modernity is unimaginable without Gandhi. This is ironic, given Gandhi's objection to modernity along every significant vector: capitalism, biopolitics, technological development, industrialism, atheism, and pervasive, endemic violence. If India or indeed the world had followed Gandhian tenets in the twentieth century, nothing would be the way it is. Critics are therefore inclined to evaluate Gandhi in the idioms of the counterfactual: utopianism, nostalgia, antimodernism, saintliness, or, in the worst case, reactionary traditionalism. He has been accused of being everything from bourgeois to megalomaniacal, from unrealistic to plain crazy. But no one can deny that Gandhi altered the very language of politics in India; that without his influence, postcolonial India as we know it would not exist. This chapter is not concerned with revisiting Gandhi's long and eventful life on three continents; nor does it set out to evaluate his dealings with either the British imperial power or his nationalist colleagues in India at any stage of his fifty-year political career. In other words, unlike the greater part of the scholarly literature, this chapter is not concerned with Gandhi's biography, nor with his role—through a series of movements, agitations, mobilizations, talks, treaties, negotiations, travels, imprisonments, trials, fasts, marches, speeches, and other events of a political nature—in the long process of India's decolonization.

My purpose, rather, is to read two of a number of political categories used, redefined, or invented by Gandhi: swaraj (self-rule) and ahimsa (non-violence).[1] These are the two categories that lay the political foundations of modern India. The "self" is semantically central to both categories. The first, swaraj, literally means the sovereignty, rule, or mastery (raj) of the self (swa); here the self is named, it is presented at the very lexical surface of the word. The second, ahimsa, literally means "the absence of the desire to harm"; here the self is indexed by the concealed desiderative *(hiṃs-)*—harm is absent (negativizer *"a"*) from the will or intention of an implied agent, the self. Moreover, Gandhi frequently switched registers between the ideas of an individual and a collective selfhood, thus addressing both India and every person in it, as also potentially every human being anywhere. In this way he meant to investigate how one might purify one's being by removing from it the reflex of violence (the intention to harm another) and, simultaneously, how a non-violent political community might be constructed for the greater good of India and humanity at large.

A number of contemporary scholars have engaged with Gandhi's political philosophy, notably Lloyd and Susanne Rudolph, Bhikhu Parekh, Ashis Nandy, Anthony Parel, A. K. Saran, and Uday Mehta. This scholarly engagement is quite apart from the interpretations of Gandhians like Vinoba Bhave, Acharya Kripalani, Baba Amte, Sundarlal Bahuguna, Sunil Sahasrabudhey, and many others who have treated the Mahatma's ideas as a sort of practical philosophy in different areas of political, social, and economic life. A comprehensive understanding of Gandhi as a political thinker must take into consideration a vast lexicon of concepts that he worked with, mainly, but by no means exhaustively: swadeshi (economic self-reliance), satya (truth), satyagraha (truth force/soul force), Harijan (literally, "God's creature," an Untouchable), *sarvodaya* (universal welfare), khadi (handspun, handwoven cotton), carkhā (hand-driven spinning wheel), *aparigraha* (non-covetousness, trusteeship), and so on. Admittedly, Gandhian thought is best understood in its totality, with a proper sense of how he related non-violence with truth, truth with freedom, freedom with discipline, discipline with belief, and so on; how he advocated the correlation of religious practices with economic activity, of political mobilization with social change. It is indeed difficult to isolate this or that category from the complete Gandhian edifice—a difficulty increased, as Akeel Bilgrami points out, by the fact that Gandhi was not a systematic philosopher.[2]

If I have singled out swaraj and ahimsa, then, it is at least as much for positional as for substantive reasons. Both swaraj and ahimsa in their Gandhian iterations play a central role in defining an Indian politics from circa 1920 onward, and in conferring upon it both a long history and a truly modern quality. They root India's political modernity in a number of classical texts and discourses: Jain and Buddhist as well as Hindu. At the same time, they resolve a deep crisis in the political tradition that had made itself more and more obvious since the failed mutiny of 1857, and had reached a breaking point by the time of the Partition of Bengal and the failure of the Swadeshi movement between 1905 and 1908. In the first quarter of the twentieth century, these two categories stand between India's rapidly receding past and its yet-to-be-defined future. They permit Gandhian nationalism to ground itself in the idea of a political tradition that has, at once, historical continuity, pan-Indian resonance, and a creative capacity, responsive to the needs of a rapidly transforming present.

Gandhi's *Hind Swaraj* (1909) takes the swaraj already extant in Congress as well as extremist nationalist circles throughout the 1890s and 1900s, and completely redefines it so as to carry the anticolonial campaign into its next and final phase. His ahimsa, although highly innovative and original in his usage, very usefully reminds all Indians of the inaugural motifs of their political mytho-history: the renunciations of Jina Mahāvīra and Gautama Buddha, the conversion to pacifism of Aśoka the Maurya, the perfect kingdom of Rama at Ayodhya, and the struggle for ethical sovereignty of Yudhiṣṭhira and Arjuna, the Pāṇḍava princes. Gandhi's swaraj (self-rule, used very often to indicate political independence or liberty) resonates with existing Indic categories that denote transcendental freedom or spiritual liberation, like mokṣa, Nirvana, and *mukti*.[3] His ahimsa recalls and reinforces *karuṇā* (compassion, empathy), *dayā* (pity, generosity, kindness), *ānṛśaṃsya* (non-cruelty), *abhaya* (fearlessness), and *brahmacarya* (celibacy, sexual abstinence), all values and practices shared across the Indic religions as the basics of a life lived in accordance with virtuous normativity (dharma). Under Gandhi's intellectual leadership, swaraj and ahimsa, whose theater in Congress discourse was understood to be primarily political, became so thoroughly enmeshed with their sister categories already present in Indic discourses of transcendence that politics, ethics, and metaphysics began for the first time to share a common conceptual terrain. This Gandhian stroke of genius revitalized and revolutionized a tradition in crisis.

There are plenty of clues in Gandhi's own voluminous writings to warrant a thoroughgoing inquiry into Gandhi's classical sources: *Bhagavad Gītā*, Jain teachings, *Rāmāyaṇa, Mahābhārata,* Advaita Vedānta, *Manusmṛti,* the life of the Buddha, Vaiṣṇava bhakti poetry, and Tulsidas's *Rāmcaritmānas,* among others. Immediately it becomes clear that Gandhi was no theologian, nor a traditionalist, nor a sectarian with regard to any of the Indic systems. He took whatever he needed from different texts; he recognized no authority above his own interpretive prerogative. It is unreasonable, therefore, to expect rigorous and consistent schemata for an ethical politics to emerge from his thought. Nor can Gandhi be counted as one who orders and renders coherent a tradition of political thinking—he's not India's Hobbes, so to speak, nor its Hegel, nor its Marx.

However, precisely because ethical ideas are for him not just ideas but also guides for practice, his deployment of categories like swaraj and ahimsa has the salutary effect of reorganizing our entire vision of the norms and values that comprise an Indic politics, and making of it a conceptual structure that we can map and critique over an extended period of time, indeed, over the entirety of India's political history from the Vedas to the Constitution of India. Gandhi's intervention enables questions such as these: What are the contours of an Indic understanding of freedom? Why has Indic cogitation always considered categories of self and categories of violence closely together? Others, too, among Gandhi's contemporaries raised such questions, notably Sri Aurobindo, Sri Ramakrishna, and Swami Vivekananda, but for obvious reasons, Gandhi's answers, however unsystematic, were the ones to have the maximum political traction and the greatest importance for the very foundations of the new republic.

Gandhi's *Hind Swaraj* in 1909 made a Galilean breakthrough in the Indic political tradition. In order to flesh out this claim, I turn to the history of science in Europe and draw an analogy between Galileo's role in the Western tradition of scientific thought and Gandhi's role in the Indic tradition of political thought. Further, I want to show that what is crucial about Gandhi's ahimsa is neither its robustness as a philosophical category nor its effectiveness in the face of *raisons d'état*. In fact, most of the realities of the latter half of Gandhi's life—from the two world wars to the totalitarian regimes, from atom bombs to death camps, from British India's catastrophic communal Partition to the Indian adoption of the biopolitical nation-state as soon as the Raj is overthrown—take absolutely no cognizance of his endorsement of non-violence as the center of his political creed. Gandhi's ahimsa is so very significant because it references an insistent marriage of questions of being with questions of power that is at the heart of the Indic construction of the political.

* * *

The building in New Delhi where Gandhi was to hold his last prayer meeting, on January 30, 1948, and where he was shot dead at point-blank range by Nathuram Godse, is called Birla House. It now houses the Gandhi Darshan Samiti and the Gandhi Smarak, a museum-cum-memorial space. Abutting the grounds where Gandhi was assassinated, barely six months after India gained independence from British rule, is a small gallery, covered with a mural depicting the life of the Mahatma. This mural was painted in 1973, by Ram Kripal Singh, an artist from Shekhawati, Rajasthan, who belonged to the tradition of illustrated oral storytelling known as "Pabu ji ki Phaḍ."[4]

The mural shows the life of Gandhi from birth to death, and seems to draw heavily from both his autobiography, *The Story of My Experiments with Truth* (1929), and from dozens of famous photographs of Gandhi that were available during his life and are now, in many cases, housed inside the main museum at Birla House. In its reliance on the historical record, as narrated by Gandhi himself, and on documentary evidence like photographs, the mural is, on the one hand, meant to be true to life. But as any spectator can tell, it is also highly allegorical, painted in the style of the life of the Buddha, Christ, or even an epic character like Rama or Krishna. Mohandas Karamchand Gandhi, born in October 1869 and killed in January 1948, also appears as a timeless figure, the protagonist of a narrative that is as much moral as it is historical, its events and transitions marked by Gandhi's mistakes, realizations, epiphanies, and miracles—moments that bring together a man's mortal life, the history of India, and the greater quest of the human race for an ethical society.

The story of Gandhi's life is prefaced by an entire wall of paintings showing other episodes in the moral life of India, including scenes from ancient India, the epics, the *Gītā,* the Buddha's life, what appears to be Mughal history, and the history of Gujarat, where Gandhi was born. One figure is reminiscent of the cave paintings of Ajanta. Krishna speaks to Arjuna on their halted chariot, the god's body its characteristic blue and his hand raised in a gesture of address, Arjuna's head drooping and his eyes downcast with anguish and doubt, his back turned to the horses who are rearing and impatient to rush into the battlefield. The move from the mythic and the historical panorama into the particularities of Gandhi's mortal career is quite abrupt, but perhaps this is because the earlier glimpses are meant not to provide an actual account of how India came to have Gandhi as its moral protagonist, but to suggest a certain context of ideas and to establish its temporal depth, as also its thematic stability.

Kripal Singh's mural is oddly true to how Gandhi understood his own life and work, and to his understanding of the life story, as it were, of an Indic self: a self in search of the higher truth, of liberation from the cycle of birth and death, of spiritual evolution and psychic freedom. The mural shows Gandhi as a young lawyer in England and South Africa, and later as a *satyāgrahī* back in India, slowly but surely becoming the Mahatma. Over time his clothes change from Western to Indian, and he ages. He is shown talking to Nehru, in a dialogue that has an unhurried quality, being a perennial exchange of knowledge between wise men: *satsang* (the company and conversation of the good). He is also shown deceased, though his body bears no signs of violence, no bullet wounds, no flowing blood—Gandhi seems in repose, rather than brutally killed. The mural is truly a *māhātmya,* a narration of the greatness of Gandhi, an illumination of his inner qualities, his virtues, intended to extol the normative value of his life for a moral history of India. The mural may not give us a chronologically accurate, positivist, verifiable account of what happened in British India as a result of Gandhi's actions, but his character, and along with or through it the selfhood and self-knowledge of India, are successfully conveyed to the viewer.

Gandhi wrote his *Hind Swaraj* onboard the ship *Kildonian Castle* in November 1909, and by all accounts did his writing in the throes of an epiphany. He wrote continuously in Gujarati for ten days, on the ship's stationery, first with his right hand and then with his left. He made very few changes and corrections to the text he wrote, apparently getting most of it right the first time. The contemporary editor of *Hind Swaraj* in English, Anthony Parel, notes that several critics have compared Gandhi's burst of inspiration to other epiphanies, in the biblical tradition (St. Matthew, St. Luke, St. Ignatius Loyola), as well as in Western political thought (Rousseau).[5] Certainly Gandhi's time on the ship between London and Johannesburg seems to have been characterized by what W. G. Sebald called the "facets" that qualify epiphanies, namely *claritas* (lucidity) and *veritas* (truth).[6]

In an incisive reconstruction of the history of Western science, the philosopher Alisdair MacIntyre has described the role of Galileo in making an "epistemological break" that entirely reoriented a tradition in crisis and gave it a new lease on life.[7] Galileo's text of 1632, *Dialogue Concerning the Two Chief World-Systems, the Ptolemaic and the Copernican,* in MacIntyre's view, resolved the epistemological crisis that had beset Europe's scientific tradition after Copernicus's discoveries rendered prior theories incoherent and inadequate as descriptors or predictors of reality. An epistemological crisis, according to MacIntyre, may afflict not just a tradition but also an individual; in fact, an excellent example is the tragic figure of Shakespeare's Hamlet, whose inability to reconcile his original knowledge with his new knowledge, and whose failure to realign his beliefs based on what he subsequently learns, results in his unhappiness and death. To resolve such a crisis, one must be able to break with the past and move on, as it were. For Western science, Galileo made possible the realization of error, and the transition into a new phase of thought, better in tune with the structure of the real world. MacIntyre suggests that it isn't only scientific traditions but also religious and political traditions that are from time to time plagued by crises and require decisive reorientations if they are not to lapse entirely into incoherence—he mentions Luther and Machiavelli as shapers of epistemological traditions whom we may usefully compare to Galileo in their respective spheres.

I would like to propose that we think of Gandhi as precisely someone who, through his text *Hind Swaraj* in 1909, resolves a crisis in the Indic political tradition, and makes possible an epistemological break with the type of political thinking that had defined Indian nationalism from at least the founding of the Congress in 1885, if not incipiently for most of the nineteenth century. In this sense, Gandhi is a Galilean figure. He confronted the crisis of political thought manifested in the Partition of Bengal in 1905, the creation of the Muslim League in 1906, the decisive split between moderate (constitutionalist) and extremist (violent) factions of the Congress at the Surat session of 1907, and the popular failure of the first iteration of swadeshi ideology after 1908. Further, he took the definitive step toward solving the problem by striking out in new directions in his little tract, as indicated by his coinage of novel terms like satyagraha and Harijan, and his completely original interpretation of existing categories like swaraj and ahimsa. Gandhi's revolutionary position in an Indic tradition of politics should not be underestimated.

But it is not just the analogy to Galileo that is useful in our analysis of the trajectory of foundational political ideas in modern India. Gandhi is Hamlet-like too, given the ironic dimensions of his own psychosexual and spiritual narrative, especially as revealed in his difficult, lifelong struggle with celibacy *(brahmacarya),* as well as the tragedy inherent in his relationship to the larger history of independence, partition, communal violence, and the formation of the nation-states of India and Pakistan. For Gandhi, then, the epistemological crisis was both in his personal journey and in the tradition of political thought that he inherited. With *Hind Swaraj,* he was able at least to resolve some of the feeling, for himself and for others, that Indian nationalism was stuck in a rut, degenerating into incoherence, losing its intellectual momentum, and unable to either accurately describe or concretely affect the course of the political reality defined by British domination and Indian subordination.

Over the next ten years, between 1909 and 1919, the text was banned, circulated underground, translated into multiple Indian languages and English, and widely disseminated not just in India but all across the British Empire, as the agenda of a possible politics and the manifesto of the coming community. By then Gandhi had returned from South Africa to live permanently in India, traveled the length and breadth of the subcontinent, visited Rabindranath Tagore in Santiniketan, established his ashram at Sabarmati, Gujarat, and positioned himself to take over the leadership of the Indian National Congress, in addition to witnessing the horrors of World War I and attempting to support the British war effort. After gestating for a decade, by 1920, when the Congress adopted Gandhi's program of non-violent non-cooperation against British rule, *Hind Swaraj* was recognized all over India for its revolutionary reconstitution of the political tradition and its achievement of an epistemological break relative to the previous three to four decades of Indian nationalism.

In MacIntyre's account, one way to understand an epistemological crisis as suffered by an individual (like Hamlet) is as a crisis in the self. When our beliefs about the world no longer account for our experience, and we need new knowledge in order to make sense of our experience, then it is really our sense of self, our idea of who we are, that comes under massive stress. The failure to acquire the knowledge necessary for understanding and explaining the world as it now presents itself to us (differently than it did before) and, moreover, the inability to construct a narrative that can clearly define the difference between what we believed earlier, and why, and what we now believe, and why, results, according to MacIntyre, in madness.

In other words, the self is in danger of completely collapsing and disintegrating under the strain of an epistemological crisis. But a crisis in the self, for MacIntyre, is ultimately traceable to or concomitant with a crisis in the tradition that has formed the self.[8] In this way, an epistemological crisis that affects any given individual is related to a larger epistemological crisis that affects a tradition as such, for traditions and selves are mutually constitutive. By this ontology, selfhood is embedded in a tradition; a tradition must have its protagonists—as Galileo was for European science in the seventeenth century—who both experience and resolve any epistemological crisis threatening the tradition (and other selves grounded in it) with dissolution.

For an Indic tradition of political thought, to my mind, Gandhi is exactly such a protagonist. The crisis in the Indic political tradition is something he experiences viscerally, personally, at various moments in his own life. A number of such moments may be garnered from his extensive autobiographical and confessional writings, and from the accounts of his contemporaries, but let us think particularly of his extreme guilt and self-flagellation at his father's death in 1885 at the exact moment when he was away from his father's sickbed having sex with his wife, Kastur; his extreme struggles with meat eating and vegetarianism throughout his early youth in both Gujarat and England; his awful humiliation at being thrown off a train in South Africa because of racial prejudice against him, and his long night of soul searching at the Pietermaritzburg Station in May 1893; and most crucially, though perhaps not finally, the epiphany on board the *Kildonian Castle* in November 1909 that led to the writing of *Hind Swaraj*. (The Mahatma's desperate plea for a cessation of the killing, rape, and strife between Hindus and Muslims in Noakhali, a part of Bengal horribly affected by pre-Partition violence, in January 1947 is another such moment of acute, almost catastrophic crisis.)

Gandhi experienced many profound crises, often related either to his own sex life, or to the use of force and the outbreak of violence in political campaigns that he tried to conduct in the spirit of ahimsa, or indeed to his disagreement with other prominent political leaders, like Nehru, Tagore, Ambedkar, and Jinnah, over a range of issues, from caste to technology, from religion to secularism, from abstinence to marriage. But the crisis of greatest interest to us for the purposes of our argument is that which resulted in his frenzied writing of *Hind Swaraj* in just ten days, with both hands, without pause and without error, as though driven by a new knowledge of the meaning of swaraj without which India's self, India's polity, and India's sovereignty would all lapse into utter incoherence: the political equivalent of madness.

The most important claim in the entire work is surely the last line of chapter 4, "What Is Swaraj?," in which Gandhi as the "Editor" claims to the "Reader" that he is "endeavouring to show that what you call Swaraj is not truly Swaraj."[9] In Gandhi's persona, at that moment, the crisis of the self and the crisis of the tradition that formed the self find a perfect convergence, and this convergence is perfectly articulated by him in stating that what he is after is a redefinition of the category swaraj: the sovereignty of the self. Without a narrative that accounted for the difference between the old, wrong way (what in Gujarati Gandhi called *kudhāro*), and the new, right way *(sudhāro),* the Indic political tradition, and with it any sense of a viable Indic selfhood, would cease to be possible in the world.

I believe that in November 1909 Gandhi had a clear apprehension—this is why the word "epiphany" is repeatedly invoked—of the epistemological crisis at hand, and of the epistemological break that would be necessary for India to survive and flourish as a political entity. The Galilean hinge connecting past and future, the gateway between old and new knowledge, the text that actualized the reconstitution of the tradition of political thought in

India, was Gandhi's *Hind Swaraj.* Gandhi himself was the subject of the crisis in India's selfhood and in its sovereignty, the revolutionary of an Indic political tradition, and, in some ways and at certain moments, also the tragic hero in a historical narrative that was not always coherent, especially around the twinned issues of violence and non-violence, given that India's peaceful independence came at the cost of its bloody Partition. The Birla House murals somehow capture the revolutionary quality as well as the tragedy that mark the narrative of Gandhi as a historical character—indeed, as the moral protagonist of India's modernity.

Before Congress's nationalism in the last decade or two of the nineteenth century, the term *svarāj* or *svarājya* had only ever been used in Maharashtra, in the context of Shivaji's attempt to establish an independent kingdom in defiance of Mughal authority in the mid-seventeenth century. The idea of Maratha self-rule and, stemming from that, Hindu self-rule, defined as against Muslim domination, were traces that remained in the political imagination of this region and surfaced again, long after the British had overthrown the Mughals, among Maharashtra's nationalists like Tilak, Gokhale, and Ranade, around the turn of the twentieth century. But when Gandhi wrote *Hind Swaraj* in 1909, although he did have the Indian National Congress very much on his mind (as we can see from the opening chapters), he was really reinventing swaraj in much the same way that he reinvented ahimsa: both categories had had long historical lives, yet neither category had ever meant exactly what he got them to mean during the anticolonial struggle.

After Gandhi had (re)introduced the term "swaraj" into the public sphere, as it were, it continued to be hotly contested by several different parties. Hindu nationalists as well as Muslim nationalists still defined freedom in terms of the self-mastery of religious communities, rather than of a single, unified India as such; the colonial government pushed in favor of partial and segmented autonomy, a kind of continued subordination of India by Britain; conservative nationalists, the so-called moderates or Constitutionalists, could not conceive of the absolute independence of India from British rule; and even the Congress at the height of its influence, under Gandhi and Nehru's leadership in the 1920s and 1930s, did not insist on 100 percent self-determination. Nehru began speaking publicly in favor of freedom from the late 1920s; the

Government of India Act of 1935, followed by provincial elections in the late 1930s, set in motion the move toward self-representation and democratic self-government. But not until the early 1940s did the idea of *pūrṇa svarāj* or complete self-rule for India by Indians gain salience. As Partha Chatterjee has argued, even after *pūrṇa svarāj* was achieved, in 1947, there was still a shortfall in India's freedom, because of the distance between "political" swaraj and "true" swaraj as Gandhi had originally envisioned it.[10] This gap has yet to be filled, six and a half decades after Independence.

Mithi Mukherjee has traced the genealogy of Gandhian swaraj to related but different categories of mokṣa and Nirvana, which are ethical categories, connoting freedom, but coming out of the discourses of transcendence rather than the discourses of politics.[11] Mukherjee argues that this makes sense because Gandhi himself thought of "freedom" equally in political and in transcendental terms; or, to put it in another way, in Western and in Indic terms. If we are willing to look at the semantic umbrella of "swaraj," then the *Bhagavad Gītā*—in which Krishna explains to Arjuna the three equally valid paths *(mārga)* to ultimate liberation (mokṣa), namely, knowledge *(jñāna),* action (karma), and devotion (bhakti)—can be read as a source for Gandhi's swaraj as much as it is a source for Gandhi's ahimsa (as I argue below). The discipline of detachment *(anāsakti yoga)* and action free of the desire for its outcome *(niśkāma karma),* are taught by the god as the means for a soul to be released from the cycle of rebirth and from the bondage of bodily existence, suffering, ignorance, and mortality. Mukherjee shows that Gandhi sought this final freedom for his soul as much as he sought political emancipation for India, and that his various exercises in self and sovereignty were all along simultaneously oriented toward both these ends. A purely political conception of "liberty," as learned in India from France, Britain, and America, constituted one register of Gandhi's swaraj but was by no means the entirety of its semantic burden.

* * *

In order to understand precisely how innovative Gandhi was in bringing ahimsa squarely into the discourse of modern politics, it is important to be attentive to the primary contexts in which this term occurred in India. As the vast Indological scholarship on this subject attests, ahimsa—together with its opposite, *hiṃsā* (violence/injury/the desire to harm)—may be found principally in Jain doctrine, in the *Mahābhārata,* and in the edicts of Aśoka. Scattered references also exist in the wider Brahmanical as well as Buddhist literature. Occasions for the use of the term "ahimsa" seem to be limited, so far as we can tell, to four or five topics of debate, corresponding to significant areas of collective life in early premodern society: war, ritual sacrifice, asceticism, hunting, and vegetarianism. Two or three thousand years after these first discussions of ahimsa, Gandhi is thinking about war as well as vegetarianism, and to some extent also certain elements of ascetic practice, principally *brahmacarya*. But all the rest of the social reality in which ahimsa was originally embedded has vanished from view.

Most Indic cultures have long moved on from the hunting-gathering stage; the principal doctrinal struggle of our age is no longer between Brahminical and renunciative traditions; the world of Vedic sacrifice has receded to the remotest past, on the verge of becoming unintelligible to us. A striking feature of ahimsa in its primordial sense is its reference to human life in connection with other aspects of nature, notably animals and plants. Numerous episodes in the *Mahābhārata* where ahimsa and its sister category ānṛśaṃsya (non-cruelty) come up have to do with birds, beasts, and trees. By the late nineteenth century, man's place in the natural order is not on top of the list of issues agitating Indian thinkers, not even Gandhi, although in *Hind Swaraj* Gandhi presciently critiques the ecological costs of the industrial society. Still, the problem of violence against living beings other than humans is not a major priority for Indian nationalists, unlike their distant ancestors of whichever faith. Within Indic civilization, ahimsa has been the concern mainly of particular schools of ascetically oriented religion, notably certain types of Jainism and to a lesser extent other streams, Buddhist as well as Yogic. Even the epics have recognized that for ordinary people, the laity as it were, as well as for rulers and warriors (i.e., those involved in politics), ahimsa strictly speaking is impossible to live by. It is an ideal; nobody is expected to be able to follow it and still remain alive.

Two major exceptions to the overwhelmingly non-political or apolitical extension of ahimsa in Indic antiquity are the figures of Aśoka, an emperor of the Maurya dynasty, and Yudhiṣṭhira, one of the protagonists of the *Mahābhārata*. Let me say right away that it is absolutely meaningless to object that one of these is a historical person while the other may or may not be. As far as we are concerned, both have an equally complicated relationship to historicity. To the extent that both figures are indispensable to any history of moral life in the Indic world, both "exist" in the exact same way. The Aśoka who has come down to us through his own edicts or the Aśoka in Buddhist texts, say the *Aśokāvadāna*—which of these is more historical? Where had Aśoka gone for the hundreds of years before the 1830s when no one, apparently, paid any attention to his rocks and pillars scattered all across the subcontinent—can the historicity of a truly historical person simply be suspended for centuries? What if the literary character named Yudhiṣṭhira were based on the historical king Aśoka, as some modern scholars have suggested?[12] Or what if Yudhiṣṭhira really was a scion of one of the ancient war-mongering clans—Bhāratas or Bhārgavas, Yādavas or Pāñcālas—that many historians believe populated the earliest, almost mythic phase of India's unknown and unknowable history? These questions and others like them have yielded no useful answer for at least the past two centuries, if not more, during which European historiographic protocols have been foisted on India.

Better that we begin with the premise that what interests us is the role played by the moral personalities called Aśoka and Yudhiṣṭhira—ethical sovereigns and anguished individuals, both—at the time when India's founders were engaged in their search for an Indic selfhood and an Indic sovereignty. For it is these two figures who are associated centrally with a discourse that connects power and violence, a king's prerogative to rule versus his duty to protect, the compulsions of order versus the demands of care. Both yearn for peace and rectitude in near-apocalyptic circumstances. Both embody the extreme moral dilemma *(dharma-saṅkaṭa)* that produces narratives marked by irony and tragedy. Both are portrayed through tropes like the riddle, the curse, and the change of heart—archaic "experiments with truth." When Aśoka or Yudhiṣṭhira consider ahimsa or ānṛśaṃsya, therefore, it is the closest thing to Gandhi's "non-violence" that may be found in the Indic political tradition. This is not about the consumption of meat, sacrificial victims, hunted animals, "collateral damage" in war, or renouncing the pleasures of the flesh—all serious but not insuperable ethical problems. It is about non-violence as the norm of norms *(ahiṃsā paramo dharmaḥ);* indeed, it is about the very ground of normativity itself *(dharmo rakṣati rakṣitaḥ)* that allows for the upholding *(dhṛ-)* of normal life. What Gandhi has in common with his historical and mythical forefathers Aśoka and Yudhiṣṭhira is the instinct to find the *axis mundi:* to grasp the very principle that upholds the world and makes possible ordered human existence.

As an idea in religious discourses, ahimsa is part of a family of concepts, including *kṣamā* (forgiveness), *dayā* (pity), *karuṇā* (compassion), *tyāga* (renunciation), *anukrośa* (commiseration), *dāna* (charity), *sevā* (service), and *maitrī* (goodwill). These occur widely in lists of virtues prescribed for ascetics as well as for laypersons, across Jain, Buddhist, and Hindu traditions. Other values are also usually present in the same lists: *asteya* (avoiding theft), *aparigraha* (eschewing covetousness), *satya* (truthfulness), *brahmacarya* (sexual abstinence), *śauca* (cleanliness), *santoṣa* (contentment), *abhaya* (fearlessness), and so on. Traditionally, all these virtues are meant to regulate the relationship between self and other, and produce harmony between our material existence and our moral life. They contribute to both general social betterment and the likelihood of personal liberation from the bonds of karma. In his writings, Gandhi evinces an interest in every one of these qualities, a propensity that his readers have attributed to his innate religiosity. Gandhi believed that if one is able to cultivate some combination of these values, and do so in a disinterested, dispassionate, routine way, then it lessens one's suffering and that of others. A general state of welfare for all may be called, in Gandhian lexicon, *sarvodaya* (universal improvement). His early vegetarian activism in England, as well as the alternative communes (ashrams) that he founded in South Africa and in India later in his career, together with his lifelong obsession with chastity, show that Gandhi took these ideas very seriously indeed.

The fact that ahimsa originally belonged in this catalog of virtues and rules of conduct, one among many different kinds of self-control and self-discipline that have been part of an everyday moral vocabulary in India for centuries, makes it even more difficult to revamp the concept, as it were, in order to get a meaning out of it that is political rather than personal. As a ruler, Aśoka had no trouble being tyrannical *(caṇḍa),* it seems, until the massacre at Kalinga pushed the violence of his reign over a threshold surpassing even his own tolerance. Yudhiṣṭhira, always agonizing about the ethical compromises necessitated by power, named *ānṛśaṃsya* (literally, the opposite of being murderous) as the highest type of normative compulsion *(paramo dharmaḥ)* when quizzed by his own father, Dharma, in the guise of a riddling Yakṣa. Translating ahimsa as "non-violence" and treating it as a political virtue, Gandhi reminded his fellow Indians of these characters (Aśoka, Yudhiṣṭhira) and these contexts of utterance (edicts, epics), thereby creating a political tradition in the very act of recalling it. This Indic tradition, which attempted to remove harm and the desire to harm *(hiṃsā)* altogether from the equation between any two persons, stood in contrast to the Western tradition as defined by Machiavelli and Hobbes, where the social contract is premised on the capacity for mutual harm held in check and traded for interests.

As I see it, ahimsa contains three latent tendencies. When I say "tendencies," I mean semantic properties that yield distinct types of action in the world—all three of which have been attested historically. The first is renunciation *(sannyāsa)*. This is the tendency that orthodox Jain thought emphasizes. For reasons that I do not have the wherewithal to elaborate here, it seems to me that *sallekhanā* (voluntarily allowing oneself to die), considered the apotheosis of ascetic practice in some schools of Jainism, is to take ahimsa in this sense to its logical limit. Better to die than to live by inflicting ceaseless, unavoidable violence upon other sentient beings. The second tendency I find inherent in ahimsa is service *(sevā)*. This may be seen in all types of charity and good works recommended in both traditional and modern creeds, and may extend without difficulty from humans to plants, animals, and every other kind of living creature. If the idea of non-violence appeals not just to Jains, Buddhists, and Hindus, but also to Christians, Muslims, Jews, and Sikhs, it is because some version of an ethics of service is understood and valued in all religions.

The third tendency in ahimsa is indeed normative conduct in political life (dharma/dhamma). This was the meaning of ahimsa for figures like Aśoka and Yudhiṣṭhira. Phrases like *dharmarājā* (just king) and *dharmarājya* (normative sovereignty) that pervade political discourse in the Sanskrit epics as well as in the Buddhist literature have reference precisely to a type of rule by a type of ruler where sovereign violence is strictly bound by limits *(maryādā)* and used with extreme care, only to maintain order and never to oppress the weak. We might say that the Indic world produces a strong theory of violence, but no strong theory of evil, so fundamental is the belief in the ethical rationality of human affairs even in the midst of a cosmic order *(daiva)* that is profoundly mysterious *(guhya)* in its workings and overwhelmingly likely to give us suffering (duḥkha). Gandhi's brilliance, in my reading, lies in his ability to harness all three potential significations of ahimsa at once, to use it to suggest the possibility of renunciative freedom, promote the ethic of social service, and hold up the ideal of a righteous republic.

* * *

It is no simple matter to unravel the genealogy of Gandhi's ahimsa. We know that ahimsa is a prominent category in Jain thought. Gandhi's father was a Vaiṣṇava Hindu, a *bania* by caste, and a local aristocrat of sorts in his own community. Gandhi's mother gravitated toward the Pranami sect, which incorporated elements of Hinduism, Islam, and Sikhism, and was peculiar to and popular in certain parts of Gujarat in the nineteenth century. Gandhi himself had a close association over about a decade of his young adult life with a diamond merchant named Raychandbhai Mehta (1867–1901), who became well known in the course of his relatively short life for his interpretation and teachings in Jain doctrine. In matters concerning Jainism, Mehta, better recognized as Srimad Rajchandra, seems to have been Gandhi's preceptor, although they were almost exactly the same age.[13]

Nevertheless, Jain ahimsa is not really Gandhi's ahimsa. Gandhi is not obsessed with the incidental and unavoidable violence involved in merely staying alive as a human being, nor does he advocate the voluntary embrace of death, *sallekhanā*, in order to be consistent with the Jain doctrine of the absolute eschewal of creaturely violence. True, he wishes to minimize physical as well as psychic violence in his everyday life, and sexual abstinence as well as vegetarianism are important steps in that direction, but his is never the life of a Jain *muni* (monk). Nor could the more extreme ascetic aspects of strict Jainism translate into a political creed that Gandhi might then advocate successfully to an entire country.

The Jain faith has always been a minority religion in India, even though there have been powerful Jain rulers and dynasties in premodernity. Gandhi in any case was born into a Hindu *bania* family in Gujarat, which, like countless other prosperous families belonging to the trader-merchant-commercial classes in western India, practiced either the Vaiṣṇava faith or the Jain faith at home, including a basic repertoire of social conservatism, vegetarian diet, personal as well as collective and public piety, the glorification of celibacy and bodily self-control even in thriving households, and a fundamental religious literacy permitted by upper-caste status. The ecstatic, even orgiastic extremes of practice otherwise known in Gujarat Vaiṣṇavism and the drier, more ascetic manifestations demanded by Jain doctrine found a middle ground that Gandhi, like others of his caste, class, and religious background, no doubt inherited and inhabited. It was not unusual in this cultural milieu to think of ahimsa as a virtue, without then becoming marked as either strongly Jain or strongly Hindu as a consequence. But from this sort of a diffuse—one might even say vague—adherence to ahimsa as one of several ethical values, to Gandhi's ahimsa that is absolutely central to his construction of an ethical politics, is a long and rather complex path, and one that we have to work hard to follow.

As far as I am able to decipher, Gandhi actually gets his ahimsa not from Jainism but from the *Bhagavad Gītā*.[14] This may appear at first to be counter-intuitive. How is a text about the necessity of fighting a war and about the correct mental attitude required of a warrior supposed to teach Gandhi or anyone else how to be non-violent? To some extent, the trouble lies in our use of the term "non-violence" as the preferred translation of ahimsa—a usage I would advocate phasing out in the long run. The conclusion I have come to after reflecting on Gandhian ahimsa over a period of time is that the word "non-violence" confuses rather than clarifies the concept. In developing the category of ahimsa, Gandhi rather wanted to work through a range of corporeal, emotional, psychological, and political stances toward the problem of violence, to make it possible for a thinking person to live with and in the midst of violence even while hewing close to his moral center.[15] Gandhi's idea was not that people shouldn't fight for justice, or that they should meekly bear injustice, or should hide from the violence that is both within themselves and all around them. At no point does he intend to generate passivity in the practitioners of ahimsa—far from it. Cultivating ahimsa is itself a mighty struggle, even, on occasion, a violent struggle—this is the first thing we need to understand about the Gandhian category, and the term "non-violence" obscures this primary meaning from view.[16]

What complicates our task further, is that even within the *Gītā,* ahimsa in and of itself is neither prominent nor elaborated as a category.[17] Rather, its occurrences in the text are innocuous, as merely one in a schedule of practices that characterize an awakened, steadfast, and ethical man *(sthita-*

prajña), one who is virtuous in the sense of possessing both virtue and virtuosity. For example, in chapter 13, verses 7–10, Krishna lists a number of habits of mind, ahimsa included, that count as knowledge *(jñāna),* while everything other than these constitutes ignorance *(ajñānam).*[18] In chapter 16, verses 1–5, the god enumerates what he calls "divine property" *(saṃpadaṃ daivīm),* including ahimsa, which Arjuna possesses, in contrast to "demonic property" *(saṃpadam āsurīm)*—the former is emancipatory *(vimokṣāya),* while the latter is binding upon the soul *(nibandhāya).*[19] In chapter 17, verses 14–16, Krishna spells out austerities that constitute bodily, linguistic, and mental restraint *(tapa):* ahimsa is part of the first list, one of several kinds of corporeal austerity *(śarīraṃ tapa).*[20] In all these instances, ahimsa does not stand out in any way as being the definitive trait of a wise man *(jñānin),* a warrior *(kṣatriya),* an individual in search of liberation *(mumukṣu),* a fighter *(yoddhā),* a disciplined person *(yogī),* or indeed of someone who is—or aspires to be—all this rolled into one, such as Arjuna. Rather, ahimsa is generally a good quality to have, along with many others. Gandhi, like every other reader of the *Gītā,* would not have any reason to be especially attracted to ahimsa when it appears within catalogs like the ones quoted above.

Instead, Gandhi understands ahimsa to be precisely the relationship between self and other that Arjuna must achieve in order to be able to do what he has to do but is feeling impeded from doing, namely, to take up arms against his Kaurava kin in the battlefield of Kurukṣetra. For Gandhi, ahimsa is the relationship between self and other that the Indian must master in order to be able to do battle against colonial rule. Indeed, any individual must cultivate ahimsa in order to tackle an intimate enemy, whatever the particular conflict at hand, whosoever the parties at war, and regardless of the nature or degree of violent force involved. In this sense, Gandhian ahimsa is not just another one of a long list (nor one of several lists) of assorted positive values to be got from the *Gītā;* it is in fact the essence of the entire *Gītā,* the text's full import distilled into a single category.[21] Without a will disciplined by ahimsa—absence of the desire to wantonly harm another just for the sake of harming him—Arjuna may not advance into Kurukṣetra, the battlefield of the Kurus filled with armies, generals, chariots, and weapons. Likewise, unless we too adhere strictly to ahimsa, we may not enter into *dharmakṣetra,* the very ground of normativity upon which ethical action unfolds in the world.[22] If the heart of Krishna's message is *niśkāma karma*—action untainted by desire for its outcome—then ahimsa—absence of the desire to harm—must equally qualify all of our dealings with others, even our adversaries (and in some ways, most especially our adversaries). The only kind of action we may recognize as ethical is that which equally avoids becoming instrumental on the one hand (driven by desire, kāma), and irrational on the other (driven by blind violence, *hiṃsā*).

One way to construct politics is to delineate an ideal type of political action. In constructing the politics of swaraj around the central category of ahimsa, the habit of mind, the relationship between self and other, the nature of action, and the type of person that Gandhi intends can be glimpsed in the text of the *Gītā* even when the word itself is not used. Thus in chapter 6, verse 32, Krishna says to Arjuna that one who regards all others equally, by analogy with himself, in both joy and sorrow, is a *yogī* of the highest order.[23] These two qualifications of a *yogī,* namely, the ability to look fairly upon others *(samaṃpaśyati)* and to analogize both the gladness and the pain of others to one's own experience *(ātmaupamyena)*—in other words, the capacity to put oneself in another's shoes—here we are very close to what Gandhi understood by ahimsa. Similarly in chapter 11, verse 55, the god says, "O Pāṇḍava, one who is devoid of ill-will towards other beings, he alone comes to me!"[24] Again, Krishna is eulogizing someone who lacks hostility *(nirvairaḥ yaḥ, saḥ)* toward all creatures *(sarvabhūteṣu),* not so different from one who might have the mental posture of ahimsa. The metatext of the *Mahābhārata,* in which the *Gītā* is embedded, returns again and again to noncruelty (ānṛśaṃsya), and this too is akin to ahimsa, enfolded into Gandhi's understanding of the category upon which he seeks to build an ethical politics. In my view, we need ahimsa also to interpret Gandhi's word for the Untouchable—Harijan (literally "God's Creature")—an appellation premised on his capacity to see and address even the most despised of human beings, the untouchable, by analogy to the self (ātmaupamyena), with non-hostility *(nirvāira),* absent cruelty (ānṛśaṃsya), and free of the desire to harm (ahimsa). The name "Hari," in Harijan, of course, is another name of Krishna.

The various lists of physical and psychological states in which ahimsa occurs, in the *Gītā* as well as in Jain, Buddhist, and Yoga texts more widely, include a number of virtues that Gandhi fully endorses. A complete taxonomy of peaceable and empathic orientations of the self toward others and of forms of self-discipline available from Indic ethical traditions would be very long, so let me just indicate here the main values that Gandhi referred to most often, under various names in Gujarati, Sanskrit, or other languages: *brahmacarya*, *śauca* (purity of mind and body), *śānti* (peace), *dayā* (compassion), *kśamā* (forgiveness), *satya* (truthfulness), *abhaya* (fearlessness), *ātma-vinigraha* (self-control, which would include a range of dietary, sexual, sartorial, and expressive checks upon the self, a general tendency to restrain the appetites, that Gandhi pursued throughout his life), *vairāgya* (indifference toward sensual pleasure), *mārdavam* (gentleness), *amānitvam* (humility), *anahaṅkāra* (the lack of egotism), *samacittatvam* (equanimity), and *sthairyam* (steadfastness, stillness).

One way to understand Gandhi's ahimsa is as metonymically indicating some or all of these characteristics of the self that he wanted to fashion. While all of these properties may characterize the self of a *yogī*, especially as the *Gītā* defines such a person, for Gandhi many of them besides ahimsa had political valence as well. Not only in *Hind Swaraj* and *The Story of My Experiments with Truth*, but all across the vast body of his articles, letters, speeches, and discourses, in the context of private as well as public actions as disparate as toilet cleaning, fasting, abstinence, spinning the carkhā, unarmed protest, civil disobedience, vegetarianism, wearing khadi, fighting untouchability, and taking the name of God in prayer *(haribhajan, rāmanāma)*, ahimsa and its sister virtues permeate Gandhi's thought through and through.

Gandhi's reliance on the *Gītā*, on Tulsidās's *Rāmcaritmānas*, on Jain precepts, and on the Vaiṣṇava devotional poetry of Gujarat, Maharashtra, and other parts of North India all demonstrate at least two things simultaneously: first, he was intimate with these texts, comfortable with them, and immersed in them in a way that suggests long-term commitment rather than momentary interest; second, his method of quotation, citation, learning, and "use" of the concepts found in these texts was eclectic rather than systematic, and in a sense thoroughly independent. A famous verse in the *Mahābhārata* runs as follows:

> Doctrines are unstable
> Scriptures diverse,
> There isn't one scholar
> One may call an authority.

The essence of dharma
Is hidden in a cave—
Let us tread the path
Taken by the great multitude
Gone before us![25]

Gandhi exemplifies this attitude: call it skeptical, antiauthoritarian, autonomous, self-reliant, democratic, populist, or simply non-traditional.[26] The line "The essence of dharma is hidden in a cave" *(dharmasya tattvam nihitam guhāyām)* may be read as saying that dharma is elusive, concealed, obscure, and inaccessible—or that it is hidden in "the heart's cave" (an inflexion of "cave," *guhā,* that is found in the Upaniṣads), that is, is deeply personal and must be discovered by each person for himself or herself. At the same time, the fact of each one finding his or her own dharma adds up to a vast multitude *(mahājana),* and in the ultimate analysis we only ever go the way of all flesh, follow our innumerable ancestors down the path of self-discovery and self-knowledge that is entirely universal and absolutely particular at the same time. The path is, paradoxically, trodden by one and all, and to be discovered afresh by each one—such is the difficulty of dharma.

It is significant that Gandhi does not seem to rely on or respect any kind of scholastic, interpretive, or commentarial tradition when he reads Indic texts, and yet I am claiming that he resolves a crisis in the Indic political tradition and reconstitutes such a tradition for modern India. This is indeed the case. The analogy with Galileo is once again useful. The revolutionary reconstitution of a tradition in crisis must come about at the hands of someone who is able to see the tradition and see beyond it or see through it; who is unafraid to question it and indeed realizes that it must be challenged if it has to be preserved and revivified. For Gandhi, the essence of dharma is at once recessed deep in his own conscience and elaborated by the uncounted generations before him who have pondered Krishna's message and sung the songs of the bhakti poets, practiced Yogic austerities, and muttered under their breath the many names of God.[27] Gandhi has no need for tradition in the sense of a concatenation *(paramparā)* of authoritative texts *(śāstra),* or a doctrinal position *(siddhānta)* based on the serial interdependence of a truth claim *(sūtra)* followed by its commentary *(bhāṣya).* It is Gandhi's eclecticism, his independent thinking, his originality—always already a profound engagement with what has gone before and what has come down to the present—that makes it so hard for us to lay out the genealogy of his ancient innovation, ahimsa. The ahimsa we know today both precedes the historical Gandhi (and exists for a long time prior to him), and is his invention, a characteristic of selfhood that he wants to fashion concretely and purely in response to the crisis of the self that besets colonized India.

To be able to reflect and critique so freely, to think for oneself, to take or leave the past, to find solace in one's own heart, or to take comfort in the popular texts and well-known practices that have sustained countless multitudes, with or without the endorsement of learned authorities, organized religions, and systematic traditions, this already is a kind of swaraj. As Krishna says to Arjuna:

> *Evaṃ buddheḥ paraṃ buddhvā,*
> *Saṃstabhy' ātmānam ātmanā,*
> *Jahi śatruṃ, mahābāho,*
> *Kāmarūpaṃ durāsadam.*
>
> Understanding, thus,
> That which is beyond understanding,
> Steady yourself by yourself.
> O Powerful One,
> Slay your enemy Desire,
> So hard to defeat![28]

The key here is the god's exhortation, early in the *Gītā*, to the nervous and demoralized prince that he steady himself using himself as his support, or that he establish himself in himself by himself, find and fix his identity. Gandhi takes this lesson to heart.[29] India's desire (kāma) for the West, for a Western politics, Western civilization, Western modernity, is its worst, and most powerful, enemy *(śatru)*. India has to find its own center, its selfhood, and this is a struggle in which self-reliance (swadeshi), or a founding of the self in its indubitable selfhood, is the only way to achieve swaraj.

* * *

Mahatma Gandhi was not alone in reading the *Bhagavad Gītā* during the anticolonial and nationalist period in India, stretching from the late nineteenth to the mid-twentieth centuries. An astonishing number of prominent political leaders and intellectuals wrote about this text: Bankim Chandra Chattopadhyay, Swami Vivekananda, Sri Aurobindo, Vinayak Damodar Savarkar, Lala Lajpat Rai, Bal Gangadhar Tilak, S. Radhakrishnan, and even B. R. Ambedkar, besides Gandhi of course. Their writings on the *Gītā* spanned Sanskrit, modern Indian languages, and English, which suggests a wide readership ranging from a highly specialized scholarly community to general audiences, whose interests might have varied from the religious to the political. With the exception of Gandhi, readings of the *Gītā* by these thinkers all exhibited, to different extents, one or more of three aspects: traditional exegesis, modern historicist criticism, and the effort to locate the text in a canon of political thought. (Gandhi stands apart, as I discuss below.)

First, as traditional exegetes, our modern readers behave exactly like commentators and analysts in the Indic literate traditions, both Sanskrit and vernacular, engaging with the philosophical substance of the text—its theories of self, agency, mortality, divinity, discipline, and knowledge, among other subjects. Thus, very much like premodern Brahmins, they dwell on ideas of self *(ātman),* disinterested ethical action *(niśkāma karma),* war *(yuddha),* violence *(hiṃsā),* sovereignty *(*rājya*),* moral order (dharma), and the agentive path *(karma mārga)* to liberation (mokṣa)—questions that have invited sustained reflection and debate throughout the existence of the *Gītā,* over two millennia of Indic intellectual history. Second, as colonial subjects, the Indian nationalists sometimes adopt historicist and philological methods of reading. Depending on their individual scholarly training and inclination, they address problems such as the date of the *Gītā,* its relationship to the complete text of the *Mahābhārata,* the date of the *Bhārata* war, the historicity of the characters in both the epic and the long dialogic poem embedded within it, the flawed human being and/or perfect god figured in Krishna, the positioning of the *Gītā* relative to the life of the Buddha and the Buddhist canon, questions about the text's authorship, and the difficulties of translation between the original Sanskrit and modern Indian as well as European languages.

Third, as political thinkers, India's modernists turn to the *Gītā* because it seems to them to be extraordinarily rich in its allegorical possibilities. The

Gītā's positioning within the *Mahābhārata,* the epic of war; its setting on a battlefield, as a conversation between a hero who balks at his duty to kill his kinsmen and a god who is his friend and advisor; and its ethical teachings about self, sovereignty, violence, and normativity all made this text deeply resonant for Indian intellectuals searching for a tradition of political thought in their struggle against colonialism. A recent collective effort by several scholars to write a history of the *Gītā*'s reception in modern India emphasizes the attraction of the text for the construction of a modern political theory with clear-cut Indic antecedents.[30] This presumed attraction is based on two elements of the *Gītā:* one, the problem of fraternal conflict, and two, the idea of a founding moment of the political, in which Krishna, the god, reveals himself as supremely violent, utterly exceptional, and entirely sovereign when he shows his universal form *(viśvarūpa)* to a terrified and trembling Arjuna. Both ideas—of fratricide as a civilizational concern in an India consisting of many castes and many religions (all supposedly separate but all closely related to one another), and of the Indic counterpart to the West's political theology, as illuminated by thinkers like Benjamin, Schmitt, Derrida, and Agamben—are certainly suggestive, and undoubtedly draw the colonized student to the *Bhagavad Gītā*.

Because all three types of concerns are to be found intertwined in the approach of the Indian intellectuals of the nationalist period, it is not possible to claim, in any simple sense, that they read the *Gītā* as a piece of political theory: rather, it both is and isn't seen as that. For Savarkar, for example, it is a source of support and solace during long years in prison; for Gandhi, it is very simply a guide to life in the everyday sense, whose lessons he both meditates on for himself and reflects on together with his ashram associates; for Tilak and for Aurobindo, it is a text whose doctrinal contents must be engaged with all the seriousness of any scholastic exegete in the Sanskrit *bhāṣya* tradition—and this quality of close, informed engagement and substantive commentary is not undermined in any way by their readings being in, respectively, Marathi and English. All four of these readers, despite their serious differences as both political thinkers and textual critics, are what we could call practicing Hindus, and in this they stand in marked contrast to Ambedkar, who reads the *Gītā* with the very same angry iconoclasm he directs at a range of texts in the Sanskrit systematic traditions. Radhakrishnan is a philosopher, an Indologist, a Brahmin, and a statesman all at once: his interpretation of the *Gītā* is no more an exercise in political theology exclusively than is that of his anti-Brahmin, anti-Hindu, historically minded, and fiercely modernist colleague Ambedkar.

What is significant is that when we think of the *Gītā* in the context of colonial rule and Gandhian nationalism, we imagine that it must have spoken to modern minds at the time because of the very nature of its themes: the necessity and propriety of violence versus non-violence, the dilemmas surrounding righteous conduct in an unjust and unstable world, the conundrum of fraternal conflict and fratricide, the mysteries of duty and responsibility in wartime, the fundamental human fear of death, and so on. In other words, we get carried away by the potential for allegory contained in the text. Contemporary readers, however, went to the *Gītā* for a number of heterogeneous reasons: because it counted as scripture, because it had historical interest, because it had pedagogical value as a text of morality, and because it provided a language in which to talk about political issues, especially inasmuch as politics has to do with violence, sovereignty, and war. But this last feature of the text was by no means its unique draw for nationalist-era thinkers.

In postcolonial India, the *Gītā* came to be seen, increasingly, as a sacred text, a holy book for Hindus, like the *Guru Granth Sāhib* is for Sikhs, the Bible is for Christians, and the Qur'an is for Muslims. Hindutva ideology had a role to play in slanting the *Gītā* thus, for one community, and for purely religious purposes. But in the late nineteenth and early twentieth centuries, leaders and intellectuals were reading the *Gītā* as part of a widespread cultural moment of self-criticism and reconstruction. Movements of social reform, religious revival, and the quest for a political tradition were all equally responsible for the renewed interest in this text, on the part of readers as different as Tilak and Aurobindo, Gandhi and Ambedkar. This is not an unreasonable focus, since modernist readers were indeed situating the *Gītā* relative to historical conditions in their immediate environment, mainly issues surrounding colonialism, violence, and political responsibility. But this was not their only agenda, nor is the *Gītā* itself so monochrome a text as to lend itself exclusively to the construction of an Indic political theory. Gandhi's idiosyncratic appropriation of its complex and multilayered message is proof of the fact that the *Gītā* could be made to do different work for different readers in modern India.

Gandhi knew the *Gītā* from an early age (under twenty years), and his familiarity with and admiration for the text grew continuously throughout his political career. By midlife he was spending time on it on a daily basis, completing a full reading of all eighteen chapters every week and then starting again at the beginning.[31] Chapter 2 ("Sāṅkhya Yoga"), especially, he claimed to know by heart and to meditate upon constantly, as his personal spiritual guide helping him through countless big and small crises. It is noteworthy that Gandhi engaged with the *Gītā* in Sanskrit, in Gujarati, in English, in Marathi, and in Hindi. We should not doubt that his simultaneous facility in the original classical language of the text, as well as in multiple Indian vernaculars, besides English, allowed him access to a range of lexical details and semantic nuances.[32]

That he was linguistically adept also meant that he could relate to a number of literate traditions of reading the *Bhagavad Gītā* in different parts of India and at different times in Indian history. Gandhi was thus comfortable with forms of Indic commentarial, critical, and pedagogic praxis whose tendency had always been to take texts like the epics, the *Gītā,* Tulsidas's *Rāmcaritmānas,* Jñāneśvara's *Jñāneśvarī,* and many others known to Gandhi out of the domain of specialist theology and into the realm of popular debate, performance, and retelling. He used his ashram routine, as well as his journals like *Harijan* and *Young India,* as open forums where followers, dissenters, and curious onlookers could ask him questions about the *Gītā.* He would explain his position in a manner reminiscent of traditional didacticism: Gandhi addressed the public essentially like a village elder, a canny old family member, or a local wise man, sometimes all of these rolled into one.[33] This quality of approachable, adaptive, context-sensitive, and basically unorthodox commentary also makes his "philosophy" not very systematic or doctrinally consistent at all. Gandhi managed to be, at the same time, a traditional-looking figure and something of a very modern reader, in keeping his relationship to a text like the *Gītā* both close to the parameters of moral pedagogy and firmly planted in the space of creative interpretation.

For Gandhi, especially, the *Gītā* does not become a primer for violent action on the part of subjugated Indians against the British Empire, nor does he ever use it to justify fratricidal violence between Hindus and Muslims, say, or caste Hindus and Untouchables, or any other dyad of intimate enemies.[34] For him, the *Gītā* was the best possible guide to self-knowledge, ethical action, psychic discipline, and transcendental freedom in any circumstance, every single day throughout one's life, and not just a dramatization of moral crisis and its resolution within a political framework.[35] This was why Gandhi took very little interest in the *Mahābhārata* as a whole, or even in other texts in the discursive neighborhood of the *Gītā,* such as those coming out of Buddhism or Mīmāṃsā. He was simply not excited by the narrative and allegorical possibilities of the *Gītā* on the one hand, nor by its historicity on the other. Its science of the self was Gandhi's mainstay, and something that he returned to on a daily basis.[36]

Gandhi approaches the *Gītā* in a very different way than we would expect. He reads the text from the perspective of a conventional Hindu, a devout reader, one might say, wanting to learn from Krishna about the disinterested commitment to duty *(niśkāma karma),* the cultivation of detachment *(anāsakti),* the relative merits of the pursuit of devotion to God (bhakti), knowledge of the human condition *(jñāna),* and ethical action in the world (karma) as the three potential paths *(mārga)* or disciplines *(yoga)* leading to ultimate freedom (mukti) from mortality and causality, the eruption of the transcendental in the mundane *(avataraṇa),* the manifestation of divinity *(avatāra),* the full expression of the divine principle *(viśvarūpa),* the playful and changeable character of reality (līlā), and the possibilities for intimacy and mutual recognition between constrained physical being *(jīva)* and limitless universal being *(ātman).* Gandhi is focused on the substantive teachings of Krishna to Arjuna.[37]

He is also devoted to the literary-linguistic aspects of the poem that is the *Bhagavad Gītā,* reciting it daily, knowing its verses by heart, dwelling on the beauty of the poetic language and the power of the words that the poet thought fit to put in the mouth of God. To a non-skeptical reader, the *Gītā* is indeed beautifully composed, worthy of being called "The Song of the Lord." Its rendering of strictly philosophical discourse in a narrative setting, via metrical language, as a dialogue between two characters who are thoroughly rounded and believable, and through tropes with truly magnificent poetic force is something unique in the vast corpus of Sanskrit philosophy. Gandhi remains fascinated with this work for over fifty years of his adult life, more and more immersed, he tells us, with the passage of time and the increase in his understanding of what it means.

Less important, from Gandhi's point of view, is the frame of war.[38] He is willing to take the poem at its word—the battlefield Kurukṣetra is a metaphor for the space wherein dharma unfolds as a conflict between options, a perpetual drama of what to do and what not to do, opposing forces, like enemy armies, bearing down on the individual in a relentless battle called life.[39] What Arjuna must prepare himself to do, with Krishna's help, is not a choice between fighting and not fighting: fight he must; the key is to fight with the right attitude, fully cognizant of causes, consequences, and constraints. Kinsmen and cohorts are to be attacked; a kingdom is to be defended; strategies devised; foes outwitted. There will be blood and mayhem. Any method is unjust; any outcome will cause pain; suffering is ineluctable; and the undeniable truth of all our experience is that the living, inevitably, die. Can Arjuna steady his nerves, by keeping his eye on the far side of the battle, by remembering that in the greater order of time, a human life is frail, fleeting, and forgotten?

We don't need the *Mahābhārata* in all of its verbose complexity to make Arjuna's depression *(viśāda)* comprehensible. Every morning we gather our troops, so to speak, steel ourselves to go up against unknown and unimaginable and often insupportable odds. Gandhi comes to the paradoxical conclusion that to put up a fight in one's right mind, with fearlessness, with clarity, with purpose and concentration, without a desire to harm others but with the determination to get beyond the here and now, this is ahimsa. If ill-intentioned or thoughtless violence is *hiṃsā,* and paralyzed, cowardly non-violence is *glāni,* then what Krishna is exhorting Arjuna to do, to pick up arms in a courageous and conscientious manner, is, however counterintuitive it may seem, ahimsa. Gandhi wants to learn the techniques to make up one's mind, to face the unavoidable, to cultivate the correct inner poise as one fares forward into the field of human endeavor, which is the staging ground *(kṣetra)* of dharma, expecting to be buffeted and sometimes battered by the unpredictable vagaries of life on earth. Mainly one seeks to free oneself of unreasonable expectations; of ill will toward others; of wearying attachments. But such a state of mind is not achieved except by daily effort: this Gandhi knew.[40]

In a new reading of Gandhi, Uday Mehta shows that Gandhi's ahimsa takes him outside the binary of both war and peace, of security and order, of violence and the political society in the Hobbesian sense.[41] His non-violence is as incommensurable with peace, order, and politics as it is with war, security, and violence. I think Gandhi's position with respect to the *Gītā* reinforces this claim. To return to the *Gītā* literally thousands of times and remain unmoved by fact that the location of the dialogue between Krishna and Arjuna is a chariot parked in the midst of two armies *(senayor ubhayor madhye)* is to reject the Bhārata war *(yuddha)* as well as the terrible, desolate peace *(śānti)* that will follow it; to keep a distance from the councils where war is planned, the battlefield where it is fought, and the kingdom where its fallout must be lived through by those that remain. The *Mahābhārata* itself transcends the immediate aftermath of the conflict that it describes, its narrative continuing on to Krishna's strange and lonely death (here is a god, who survives Armageddon by remaining a non-combatant, but is killed by a hunter's stray arrow), and the death march of the five Pāṇḍava princes and their surviving kith and kin in the high Himalaya many years after hostilities have ceased, and almost all the protagonists are dead. Gandhi too, has this bigger picture in the forefront of his interpretation of the *Gītā*. Not the orgy of violence, not the wasteland of peace, not the stratagems of battle, not the structures of a *kṣatriya* society whose central concern is making war, but the training of the will such that a person—Everyman—is able to behave conscientiously, consciously, and correctly in any challenging life situation: this is the *Gītā* according to Gandhi.

Gandhi, more than any of his colleagues, veered completely off the nationalist track, reading the *Gītā* as a text of ahimsa. Mehta goes so far as to suggest that not only is Gandhi outside the framework of war and peace, his thinking does not actually square with modern politics at all, not even with democracy (and certainly not with nationalism and the nation-state), so far-reaching are the implications of his alternative theory of non-violence. To me, Gandhi's understanding of the *Gītā* is more symptomatic of his being a radically antipolitical thinker than it is revelatory of his quest for an Indic political theory.

The economy of violence leaves no room for the sovereign self as Gandhi reconceptualizes it. In premodernity, it is still possible for the poet of the *Gītā* to pause the overwhelming and relentless violence of the saga of the Bhāratas, to depict a hiatus where Krishna and Arjuna may consider and reflect upon their options as god and man, as peacemaker and warrior, as friends, as brothers-in-law, as guru and disciple, both confronting the same prospect of the annihilation of their shared world and all those who populate it. But modern violence is increasingly total: it permits no breathing room, no second thoughts, no transcendence. Gandhi cannot imagine freedom—self-rule—in either Britian's parliamentary democracy or in its colonies, whether South Africa or India or any other. For him, swaraj is not mere "dominion status" nor "home rule," bureaucratic terms devised by the Raj to keep India under colonial rule even while granting Anglophone Indian elites limited roles in government. Unless there is freedom from fear *(abhaya),* the achievement of true non-violence (ahimsa), and the adherence to the truth (satyagraha), all India can hope for is "English rule without the Englishman," as Gandhi writes in *Hind Swaraj.*[42] This view is completely consistent with his reading of the *Gītā,* which is concerned neither with Kaurava victory nor Pāṇḍava defeat, nor the death or survival of this or that hero or general, nor even with the winning of the kingdom of Hastināpura, but with the clarification of Arjuna's will, the purification of his self, and its cleansing through the dialogic process of self-examination under Krishna's guidance.

* * *

Very close to ahimsa in meaning, but not identical, is the category ānṛśaṃsya, literally, "the absence of injury to man" or "the opposite of hurting a man." This term occurs extensively in the *Mahābhārata,* and is usually simply translated as "non-cruelty."[43] In the *Gītā,* Krishna doesn't expound on this quality for Arjuna's benefit; perhaps the reason for this is that ānṛśaṃsya is really a virtue needed more by a king aspiring to be ethical, like Yudhiṣṭhira, or failing to be ethical, like Duryodhana: it is not so much the prerogative of a warrior who is not a king, like Arjuna. But in the *Mahābhārata,* with a character like Yudhiṣṭhira who is entirely obsessed with the maintenance of dharma, and an enveloping, inescapable atmosphere of war in which every dharma is definitely going to be violated by one and all, ānṛśaṃsya becomes really important as a value. A good way to understand it today is to think of torture in modern warfare, usually treated as being beyond the pale, violating the laws of war, exceptional, unlawful. To try to adhere to the norm of ānṛśaṃsya is to refuse to cross over to the zone of exception where torture is acceptable as a legitimate part of conflict. The Mauryan emperor is supposed to have had a prison known as Aśoka's Hell where inmates were cruelly tortured; after his conversion to ahimsa, Aśoka is said to have destroyed this terrible place.[44] In the new Aśokan dispensation, we could say that ānṛśaṃsya became enshrined as part of the imperial dhamma. Gandhi took both ahimsa and ānṛśaṃsya seriously, though perhaps he regarded them as categories oriented toward spiritual and bodily violence respectively, similar but not the same, related but not identical to one another.

The locus classicus of the category ānṛśaṃsya is an episode in the *Mahābhārata,* in the Book of the Forest, where Yudhiṣṭhira meets his father, Dharma, in the guise of a Yakṣa, and must answer a series of the Yakṣa's questions in order to get back the life of his four temporarily deceased brothers. Dharma poses dozens of riddles, and Yudhiṣṭhira guesses each and every one of them correctly, but he really wins his brothers back by answering, in response to the question "What is the highest dharma?": "The highest dharma is ānṛśaṃsya." Further, Yudhiṣṭhira is under the impression that only one of the Pāṇḍava brothers may be revived; when asked which one he chooses, he says Nakula, who is actually only his half brother. His choice is an instantiation of his belief in ānṛśaṃsya: he picks Nakula in order to be non-cruel and fair toward his stepmother Mādrī. Explaining himself to the Yakṣa, he says that if Nakula is returned, then each of his father Pāṇḍu's two wives, Kuntī (his own mother) and Mādrī (his stepmother), will have had at least one son saved. The Yakṣa is so pleased with this reasoning that he revives all four brothers, Bhīma, Arjuna, Nakula, and Sahadeva. While Yudhiṣṭhira has named ānṛśaṃsya as the highest dharma, in fact it turns out to be the difference between life and death.[45] We may understand from this story that non-cruelty in human affairs is so important that it makes the difference between being alive and being dead. Yudhiṣṭhira's legendary fairness, his deep sense of justice, which remains unshaken even in the face of terrible (and potentially irreparable) loss, is powerfully conveyed through his exchange with his disguised father.

This short but crucial episode, known in the literature as the *Yakṣapraṣṇa,* "The Yakṣa's Question," both establishes ānṛśaṃsya as the supreme virtue or the norm of norms *(paramo dharmaḥ)*, and suggests that in its absence, we may as well all be dead. It also reinforces Yudhiṣṭhira's identity as Dharma's own son and as an ethical sovereign *(dharmarājā, dharmaśīla rājā)*. But most crucial is the lesson that non-cruelty has to be cherished—and can effectively be practiced—even in the face of adversity; there is something tractable and achievable about it, something realizable in a single gesture or decision that is entirely within a mortal man's control. Yudhiṣṭhira could just as well have chosen Arjuna or Bhīma, the brothers closer to him by kinship, affection, and temperament, and more valuable on account of their central roles in the fortunes of the Pāṇḍava princes and of the kingdom of Hastināpura.

Surprised by his answer—"Do revive Nakula, O Yakṣa!"—the Yakṣa asks him why he did not choose either of his blood brothers.[46] It turns out that Yudhiṣṭhira is thinking not of himself, or even of his brothers, but of the two mothers who would be the most aggrieved by the death of their children. As a warrior and a ruler, Yudhiṣṭhira cannot follow ahimsa consistently, or even in an intermittent way; he does not really have the option to be non-violent when his entire life is driven by the logic of war. But as a kinsman, and as a son, in that instance, as he stands by the poisoned lake looking at the corpses of his beloved brothers and negotiating with the Yakṣa in hopes of getting at least one of them back from the dead, Yudhiṣṭhira does still have it in his power to be cruel and selfish, or kind and just. Because of who he is, he must follow the ethical call to ānṛśaṃsya. Any reader of the didactic epic, any protagonist of a moral dilemma may feel inspired to follow suit.

Different scholars note the significance of the divergence between Aśoka's ahimsa (non-violence) and Yudhiṣṭhira's ānṛśaṃsya (non-cruelty) to different extents. Some find the two concepts to overlap so much as to count as one and the same. In this view, they are effectively synonyms. Others think that the subtle distinction between the two has greater implications for how we read the ethical message of the Aśokan proclamations versus that of the many narratives embedded in the *Mahābhārata*. But the fact is, the edicts and the epic belong in different genres of historical material; they differ along every axis, of authorship, form, purpose, date, language, and intention. Aśoka had the edicts carved after his conversion to pacifism at Kalinga; through them, he tried to publish the law of the land far and wide over his territories and beyond. He wanted to convey to his subjects that in his kingdom, dharma/dhamma prevails and ahimsa is a valued category: this is the imperium of righteousness. He provided detailed guidelines to do with prisons and punishment; meat and vegetarianism; cooking and hunting; war; permissible livelihoods and occupations; hospitals; and the protection of forests and wildlife and all matters to do with the preservation, care, and continuance of natural and social life.[47] His edicts are life affirming, we could say.

The epic, by contrast, is all about war. War is the backdrop and the foreground; war is the past, the present, and the future. In this unremittingly grim scenario, with its relentless suffering, betrayal, and death, that one of the lead characters (Yudhiṣṭhira), who stands to win and eventually rule the kingdom, should want to limit cruelty and keep alive some notion of violence that is not, ought not be, excessive is already a sign that he is struggling to remain moral in a dark and terrible universe.[48] The *Mahābhārata* is the world's longest meditation on violence. No aspect of violence, whether physical or psychological, individual or collective, human or non-human, karmic or irrational, routine or tortuous, is left unexplored. In such a bleak vision as pervades the epic, ānṛśaṃsya, with its relatively smaller purview, makes a lot more sense than ahimsa, which is simply unthinkable within the terms of the poem.

The figure of the ethical sovereign *(dharmaśīla rājā),* a ruler who bears an agonistic, conflicted relationship with his own sovereign power *(rāja-śakti),* with his prerogative of violence *(hiṃsā),* with his material interests (artha), with the punitive force at his disposal *(daṇḍa),* and with the rules of politics *(rājnītī);* a king torn between truth (satya) and power *(sattā);* one who would just as soon renounce the world as rule it—all the individuals considered as heroes in the Indic political imagination share these qualities. Gandhi's public persona, especially after 1920, when he entered and dominated mainstream Indian nationalist politics, conformed to this type. He resembled Rama and Aśoka, Yudhiṣṭhira and Siddhartha Gautama; he revered them; and he reminded his Indian followers of the most recognizable traits of their ideal ruler. That Gandhi never took office only reinforced this image in the exact way that made him beloved to the Indian people. Gandhi's fluency in a peculiarly Indic idiom of ethical sovereignty, his self-presentation as a renouncer *(sannyāsī, satyāgrahī),* and his espousal of ahimsa as a core political value contributed in a big way to his extraordinary success as India's leader despite never holding any official position as such.

Gandhi's lifelong love for the *Gītā,* and his relative indifference toward the *Mahābhārata,* may be traced to his interest in cultivating the selfhood of one who is spiritually and physically disciplined *(yogī),* a renouncer *(sannyāsī),* a warrior *(kṣatriya),* or a fighter *(yoddhā)*—all the ideals held up by Krishna for Arjuna, and his concomitant lack of interest in the selfhood of an ethical sovereign *(dharmaśila rājā),* like Yudhiṣṭhira. Gandhi was engaged in the search for a strong and virtuous Indic self, not so much in the quest for normatively exercised political power *(rājadharma).* The protagonist of ahimsa and swaraj, for Gandhi, was to be a genuine *satyāgrahī,* not an Indian ruler who might replace the British crown. This was the reason why not only did Gandhi not assume political office himself; he also could never bring himself to support the Congress's aspiration to assume political control and form a government after India's independence from British rule.

Psychic and bodily discipline, renunciation of material desires, courage in the face of violence, non-violent resistance to injustice, unflinching truthfulness, and ethical action regardless, without attachment to the outcome—such were Gandhi's desiderata. All of these are most clearly and directly articulated in the *Gītā,* whereas in the *Mahābhārata,* complications of narrative, character, plot, and aesthetic effect keep the self enveloped in layer upon layer of uncertainty, ambiguity, and often outright contradiction. In a sense, the long epic resembles life itself, relentlessly changing and infinitely complex, whereas the short poem unfolds in a hiatus, with the god talking to the man as the war is momentarily in suspension. In the midst of the constant high drama of the nationalist movement, the tumult of history all around him, Gandhi created for himself and others in his ashram the few minutes of calm every day in which the *Gītā*'s lessons could be read and pondered afresh. Its values provided a constant point of reference, quite apart from the success or failure of a given civil disobedience campaign, or of a political mobilization that Gandhi and the Congress were engaged in at any particular juncture.

* * *

An important series of "episodes" in this life of Gandhi—by "this life," I mean his life understood thus, as the Birla House murals render it—has to do with his relationship to Rabindranath Tagore. Tagore is shown in conversation with Gandhi in a tableau of murals that is clearly based on a painting by Abanindranath Tagore made around 1921, showing a meeting between Tagore, Gandhi, and C. F. Andrews in Santiniketan in 1915. Tagore and Gandhi were hardly ten years apart in age, and in their generation, among a galaxy of stalwarts in the national movement, they were probably the two most eminent leaders. It was principally the two of them who called one another "Gurudev" and "Mahatma," epithets picked up and echoed by the entire country and eventually much of the world. The details of their many meetings, extensive one-to-one correspondence, public writings (articles, polemical pieces, letters) addressed to one another, and the complexity of their interaction over the course of three decades have been reprised by a number of historians.[49] What is so interesting for our purposes is that both were unequivocally opposed to violence; both rejected the nation as the telos of the struggle for independence; neither one believed in nationalism; both had an aversion to the bureaucratic, institutionalized, militarized state; both were suspicious of political parties; both are considered India's founding fathers over and above all their contemporaries; both evidently held one another in genuine affection and respect—and yet they repeatedly staged these elaborate arguments in the national press. It's hard to think of two figures who were more on the same side in the complicated politics of their times, and yet they thought they disagreed, often vociferously. What does this mean?

Most of their disagreement apparently centered on Gandhi's views about the carkhā, khadi, mechanized production processes, and new technology as a whole.[50] There were other opinions of Gandhi's too, usually those that seemed more superstitious than rational, more religious than scientific, and more traditional than modern, that irritated Tagore. In the long run, Ambedkar and Nehru shared the poet's annoyance, and thus Gandhi was rather isolated, among his fellow founders, for his radical ideas, which at the time appeared to be retrograde rather than advanced. Tagore did not approve of the edges of Gandhi's thought that could be read as not progressive, though in hindsight we are forced to wonder whether the lack of progressivism lay in Gandhi's ideas or in the perception of his contemporaries. Certainly in his lifetime, few, even men as sympathetic and devoted as Tagore and Nehru, could relate to Gandhi when, for example, he claimed that an earthquake in Bihar was a direct punishment from God for the Indian sin of practicing untouchability; when he advised Jewish victims of Nazi atrocities to embrace suffering and use ahimsa to wage war against totalitarianism; when he launched and called off various non-cooperation movements depending on whether the Indian freedom fighters were able to be non-violent in the face of British force or not, regardless of the political success of such movements or the timing of his responses.[51] Throughout the 1920s, 1930s, and 1940s, the Congress's leadership, besides influential but non-political actors like Tagore, were frequently driven to their wits' end trying to understand why Gandhi did what he did, in the first place, and moreover, why the Indian public always seemed to follow him no matter how irrational he appeared to be to his colleagues in politics.

The controversy between Tagore and Gandhi around the carkhā, especially, is very difficult to reconstruct today. Gandhi saw virtue in the spinning wheel from a number of different angles—as a form of low-cost, indigenous, sustainable technology; as an aid to meditative practice; as a beacon of India's self-reliance, and a reminder of the power of swadeshi. Eminent Gandhians like J. B. Kripalani and J. C. Kumarappa took the humble wheel to be the key artifact of the symbolic system of Indic civilization as well as the backbone of an alternative economics.[52] Contrarily, Tagore saw the carkhā as a sign of India's tendency toward technological backwardness, as a loss of human effort, as an alarming indication of the Indian people's blind belief in a figure like Gandhi, as the fetish of an unreasoning mass politics, as the glorification of unthinking labor over genuine creativity, as a wasteful, repetitive, backward device if there ever was one. Gandhi felt liberated and uplifted by it; Tagore felt stifled by it. Gandhi valued its simplicity and humble character; Tagore found it demeaning and deadening. In the event, after Independence, the public as well as the postcolonial state steadily lost interest in both carkhā and khadi, so that they became mere mementoes of a social ideology and a political movement of the past but had no place in the economic policy of the new India. Ironically, it is not that Tagore won out over Gandhi; both men, rather, were forgotten by an aggressively capitalist futurity.

The quarrel about the carkhā between India's two most original founding thinkers, and our difficulty now in following the nuances of the arguments that they presented to one another, whether for or against this archaic device, are indicative of the abyss that has opened up between the search for an Indian self a century ago and the place where that self has arrived today. Some of the best recent scholarship on Gandhi, by Tridip Suhrud, Suresh Sharma, Ajay Skaria, and Leela Gandhi, exemplifies how far Gandhi's use of language—or languages, like Gujarati, English, Hindi—has receded into obscurity, and requires the utmost philological care, sometimes even deconstruction, in order to become clear to us a few decades on. What Gandhi intends by his determined advocacy of the carkhā, what he means when he prescribes the repetition of the name of Lord Rama *(rāmanāma),* why it is significant that he died with Rama's name on his lips, how we are to interpret his vegetarianism in England, the logic behind his public fasts and his use of fasting as a mode of satyagraha, how to explain the strong imagery he used in *Hind Swaraj* to deride the British Parliament as a "prostitute" and a "barren woman," why he clashed with Tagore, otherwise his admirer and friend, over issues of labor and technology: these are some of the questions taken up by a new generation of Gandhi scholars. Common to all their endeavors to better read the Mahatma is an attention to language that literally necessitates prizing apart his sentences and searching for the lost world of ideas from which his words emerged and in which they made sense. Ever elusive, Gandhi turns out to think and speak sometimes as a Jain, and other times as a Sanatani Hindu; as a Gujarati *bania* or a Victorian intellectual; his vocabulary as genealogically complex as it was inventive and protean, as rooted in interpretive traditions as it was entirely intuitive and eccentric.

As Khilnani writes:

> Gandhi, at the close of his *Autobiography,* explained the relationship between his spiritual quest, his pursuit of truth by means of *Ahimsa* or non-violence, and his involvement in public life . . . an important formulation . . . which makes no sense if read solely in terms of the grammar of traditional Hinduism, or the lexicon of modern politics. . . . Gandhi steers our attention to the profound unconventionality of his ethical sense: its existence as a product of radical, original, and deeply personal choice. The necessity of choice, and the discovery—by means of experience

and constant experiment—of the capacity of judgment that allows right choices to be made: that is the core drama of Gandhi's *An Autobiography.* As such, it is a very modern drama; and Gandhi's was a very modern life—perhaps, most of all, in its judgment that there was more to life than just being modern.[53]

2

Rabindranath Tagore

Viraha, the Self's Longing

For theorists interested in the relationship between politics, poetry, and modernity, it would be natural to turn to certain poets when considering the conceptual foundations of their respective nations: Whitman for America, Yeats for Ireland, Iqbal for Pakistan, Nazrul for Bangladesh. It would seem that India's poet in such a series would be Rabindranath Tagore, but it is not so. Four of the most significant critics of Bengali modernity all sense that he is a misfit. Amit Chaudhuri reminds us that Tagore was a lyric poet, not an epic poet; Dipesh Chakrabarty points out that Tagore was deeply interested in the prosaic as an appropriate subject for poetry; Ranajit Guha suggests that for Tagore, history was personal rather than public, and that time, for him, unfolded idiosyncratically in the mind rather than chronologically in the world; Partha Chatterjee uses Tagore's categories of "home" and "world" as the key for a larger division of private (inner, spiritual, social, traditional, Indian) and public (outer, material, political, modern, Westernized) spheres in colonial Bengali culture.[1] In his own writings following the failure of the Swadeshi movement in Bengal, Tagore disavows nationalism and patriotism in no uncertain terms, remaining stubbornly recalcitrant even after Mahatma Gandhi emerges as the leader of

India's freedom struggle and becomes his close personal friend. How monumental an error of judgment occurred in designating Tagore as India or Bengal's national poet can be judged from the fact that both India in 1947 and Bangladesh in 1971 adopted two of his songs as their respective national anthems.[2] These gestures consolidated the misreading of Tagore as a poet of nationhood when he was in fact anything but that.[3]

To be sure, some reasons for this gigantic misunderstanding lie in Tagore's oeuvre. He was indeed one of the principal modernizers of the Bengali language, stabilizers of its script, and systematizers of its grammar. He regarded modern Bengali literature—of which he single-handedly produced a significant proportion, in every major genre—in light of its medieval traditions and its links to an even older Sanskrit literature. In other words, he put forth a strong conception of a Bengali literary history stretching back a millennium and more. Moreover, he was markedly a poet of place. His landscape and his poetry become imaginatively conjoined for his readers in such a definitive way that Bengali poets after him find it almost impossible to reimagine Bengal in a manner acceptable to their audience. As William Radice, one of his most gifted contemporary translators, notes: "Tagore is near to his people."[4] Modern Bengalis to this day literally see their country through Tagore's eyes. The generation of Bengali poets immediately after him was the most beleaguered, in a sense, by his monumental legacy.

In 1913 Tagore won a Nobel Prize for literature, the first in Asia, which of course made him forever after liable to nationalist appropriation, not just by Bengal, but also by India as a whole. He belonged to a wealthy, influential, didactic, cultivated, and creative family whose status, over four to five generations, made every aspect of Bengali cultural life tractable to its conspicuous talents, ambitions, experiments, and criticisms. The family was closely associated with the Brahmo Samaj, the reformist sect that loomed large in late nineteenth-century Bengal. Indeed, the Tagores were Bengal's first family throughout most of Rabindranath's lifetime (1861–1941), and he himself became its most famous member. He founded an arts school (Santiniketan), a humanistic university (Visva-bharati), and a rural development institute (Sriniketan). He wrote around 200 books and made close to 3,000 paintings, drawings, and illustrations, besides composing music, with an entire musical style named after him (Rabīndra Śaṅgīt). Standing thus in an extraordinarily intimate and uniquely powerful relation to Bengal's language, literature, landscape, and culture (especially its print, literary, educational, artistic, and social culture), how could he not be mistaken for a national poet? Tagore would seem to be Benedict Anderson's dream come true.

But Rabindranath turns, and recedes into a horizon far from the modern nation-state. One of his songs, "Eklā Calo Re," beloved of Gandhi, has a haunting refrain: "If no one heeds your call / O luckless One / Walk alone! Walk alone!" I want to follow Tagore down this lonely path, away from his fame, fortune, and family, into a place where he struggled with what I read as an aporia: a silence in the stream of language, a gap in memory, a break in the imagination, a radical undermining of narrative logic that renders the text untenable. In this place that Tagore went to by himself, something was missing and could not be supplied, not even by the tremendous creative power that this man—a polymath, a genius, a visionary, a public intellectual—had at his command. This aporia, from the Greek "without passage," this chasm over which no bridge could be built, this absence that Tagore knew to be concealed in the multitudinous effervescence of the phenomenal world, is figured, in my understanding, at two points in Rabindranath's work: one, a small group of poetic and prose writings in which he engages with the fifth-century Sanskrit poet Kalidasa and his long poem *Meghadūta* (The Cloud Messenger), and two, the modernist style of his paintings, made in very large numbers in the last two decades or so of his long life.

In Tagore's *Meghadūta* corpus, five poems written over fifty years, the category that signifies this aporia is called "viraha," Bengali/Sanskrit for the longing produced by a separation between lovers, a longing that may or may not end in the sundered lovers reuniting.[5] This longing, taken from Kalidasa, becomes the mode in which Tagore relates to the deep past. The India of the past, then, becomes a place that he loves and from which he is, as a representative of modern man, sundered, perhaps irremediably. The affect of viraha permits—in fact, in the protocols of classical Sanskrit poetry, it necessarily accompanies—the endowing of the longed-for object with remembered beauty, but it does not enfold within itself a promise of reunion. In positing a relationship with the historical past of the nation through an aporetic category like viraha, Tagore is able to meditate upon notions of memory, loss, and beauty in conjunction with the beloved country, but he does not put forth the suggestion that this country could be the goal of any sort of praxis, any act motivated by human will, including politics. An idea of India that resembles a separated lover for whom one longs in perpetuity is very different from the idea of India as a nation-state, the object of political desire, subject to political will, attainable through political action.

In Rabindranath's paintings, by contrast, the aporia is figured not through anything he paints but rather through the very things he does not paint, does not depict. The state of separation is enacted on the canvas, as it were: that from which he is separated is not there; it is precisely where he is not; he is precisely where it is not. In order to see the absences in his paintings (as it were), I compare his paintings to those made by his nephew Abanindranath as well as his disciples and acolytes, who together formed a distinctive school of art right out of Rabindranath's home, Jorasanko, and his school, Santiniketan, and came be to regarded as the vanguard of a Bengali/Indian artistic renaissance throughout the first quarter of the twentieth century.[6] These artists vigorously and programmatically painted the India of the past as a way of building a road—the highway of history—leading to the India of the future. Art for them was a form of praxis, and their political project—the making of an Indian nation—could and did have its visual correlative. The longing they felt for India held every hope of fulfillment, union, attainment: it did not share the logic of viraha. I will read what Rabindranath writes in the *Meghadūta* poems and essay, and also read what he does not depict visually in his paintings, both as reflexes of the very same aporetic impulse in him, his gesture of turning and walking away rather than passing through, or crossing over, to the far side where the nation (possibly?) awaited him and his fellow colonial subjects.

The political significance of the Tagorean aporia, to my mind, is that he is unable to or refuses to articulate poetry/art and nationalism with one another. Unlike Whitman, Rabindranath the poet does not sing democracy; unlike Yeats, he does not sing the homeland; unlike Iqbal, he does not sing the nation of the faithful. As an artist, unlike Abanindranath, he does not paint "Mother India." We cannot apply to him any of the usual monikers—he was not a cultural, religious, political, or aesthetic nationalist. In his capacity as a literary historian, critic, and theorist, Tagore used an inventory of categories, such as *samāj* (society), *sāhitya* (literature) and swadeshi (indigenous), all of which, both etymologically and philosophically, emphasized community, togetherness, and belonging.[7] Such categories undoubtedly have a moral dimension and are relevant primarily in the context of collective human life. But Tagore was never able to square these ideas with political praxis, especially with Swadeshi nationalism as it was unfolding all around him immediately before and after the Partition of Bengal (1905). He wrote extensively about the Sanskrit epics the *Rāmāyaṇa* and the *Mahābhārata* in relation to what he called the "soul," the "soil," and the "heart" of India. But he never composed a work in this genre, as Chaudhuri notes, preferring to write the poetry of "implication and inquiry."[8] In fact Tagore regarded the epic poem as archaic poetry, and the epic poet as an archaic author, both extinct, he claimed, like the race of giants.[9] Certainly he made no attempt to connect this ancient literary form with the political project of founding a modern Indian nation.

The aporia that characterizes Tagore's political consciousness stands in vivid contrast to the constructivist stance of his older contemporary, Bankim Chandra Chattopadhyay (1838–1894). Bankim adumbrates many of the ways in which Tagore becomes emblematic of as well as a creator of Bengali modernity, to the extent that we want to associate global phenomena like "modernity" with particular individuals, as is common in the West, for example, with Walter Benjamin or Charles Baudelaire. But Bankim's thought, cumulatively, becomes a source of ideas and images for Hindu nationalism, while Tagore is not available to the Hindu nationalist imagination. Bankim's Utopia, Anandmath; his god, a warlike classicized Krishna; his slogan, "Bande Mātaram!" (Hail Mother/Motherland!)—all meet with Tagore's criticism, both textual and practical, in his novels *Ghare Baire* (The Home and the World) and *Gora,* in his critique of Bankim's *Kṛṣṇacaritra,* and in the way he ran his own Arcadia, Santiniketan.

War, or the myth of war, is important to Bankim, as Sudipta Kaviraj shows in the best study of Bankim so far.[10] His imagined community is hostile to the British (or to whites more generally) and violently excludes Muslims. His deity Krishna is the warrior-statesman of the *Bhagavad Gītā,* not the cowherd lover-boy of Bengali Vaiṣṇava poetry and theology. His heroines command the passions of the soul and the rigors of the body. Whether as a novelist, a historian, or a political thinker, Bankim is utterly unlike Rabindranath, and as the younger of the two men, the latter has every opportunity to critique and distance himself from both the opinions and the style of the former. Another way to put it is to say that in the imagination of

Rabindranath, war does not figure: in the state of separation *(viccheda)* there is no possibility of conflict. The yearning of viraha is neither the desire to harm the other nor the thirst for victory over the other: it is a longing unbounded by a teleological futurity, devoid of both the facticity and the fatality of war.

Bankim and Rabindranath both make Bengal; they both love Bengal; they both stand for Bengal. Together with their predecessor Raja Ram Mohun Roy (1774–1833), they are after all its founding fathers. But when it comes to thinking Bengal as a nation, or as a metonym for the Indian nation, Bankim is a nationalist, while Rabindranath, as I will show, is not. For both of them the land is green and gold, and its people are beloved, and its tongue contains all of the potentiality necessary for poetry as well as politics. But as soon as Mother Bengal begins to assume the shape of a nation, Tagore repeats his solitarist refrain, his conscientious objection: "Walk alone . . . speak alone . . . tread alone . . . burn alone!" In 1917 Tagore famously declared, "I am not against one nation in particular, but against the general idea of all nations."[11] Here he is the opposite of his contemporary and peer Muhammad Iqbal (1877–1938), who provided an argument and a myth that literally conjured a nation of South Asian Muslims out of thin air. As a (proto-)Hindu nationalist and a (proto-)Muslim nationalist, respectively, Bankim and Iqbal resemble each other more than either of them does Rabindranath. (None of the three, of course, lived to see the birth of India, Pakistan, or Bangladesh.)

Tagore is a national poet who does not believe in the very form of the nation-state, and who is avowedly against nationalism in both of its meanings—as the aspiration of subjugated peoples for political self-determination, and as the pride of already free nations in their nationality. He flatly opposes nationhood as the telos of politics. Rabindranath died in August 1941, almost exactly six years before India's independence, but it would be hard to imagine that had he lived to see the day, he might have been easily co-opted into the rituals of nation making, as was the case with, say, Sarojini Naidu. In his creative work, as a poet, painter, musician, dramatist, and fiction writer, Tagore is highly individualistic. In his essays and speeches he concerns himself primarily with the social, never directly with the political. His one sustained and direct engagement with politics—via the Swadeshi movement—ends very badly. In exploring the aporetic moments in his oeuvre, in retracing his solitary path, we may perhaps begin to understand the paradox (another meaning of the Greek "aporia") at the center of his dramatic, illustrious, and truly significant life.

If it is not accurate to characterize Rabindranath as India's national poet, nor to think of him as a poet of nationhood, democracy, or indeed any other form of modern politics (unlike other poetic peers, such as Whitman, to whom he would seem, at first, to compare), then we may be confronting not just the uniqueness of this man, this poet, but rather through him, some larger truth about the very nature of the relationship between aesthetics and politics in modern India. Sheldon Pollock has shown how *kāvya*—the Sanskrit term for "poetry"—is central to any account of Indic premodernity and, most significantly, to a history of power in premodern India.[12] It's not clear how kāvya could be the key category for an entire civilization for close to two millennia, constitutively entangled with ideologies and practices of rule, and suddenly, as a sort of surgical operation performed by colonialism, disappear overnight from the body politic.

One way to put the problem is to ask: What becomes of kāvya in India's modernity? How are sovereignty, violence, law, right, and justice on the one hand, and value, beauty, meaning, imagination, and representation on the other—two sets of concepts that were married to one another in historically determinate ways via the premodern literary category of kāvya—connected to each other in modern Indian literature?[13] What genres, what configurations of the linguistic sign and of the representational economy are there in the past 200 years that tell us about the flow of the aesthetic in the arteries of the Indian modern? If modernity changes the way in which the poetic and the political are imbricated with one another on the Indian subcontinent, what is the new mode in which the two remain connected? In the enigma of Rabindranath Tagore lies our answer, or at least the beginnings of one.

* * *

If India could be a poem, that poem would be the *Meghadūta*.

A lonely Yakṣa, exiled from his home to a place called Rāmagiri, upon seeing a cloud on the first day of the season of Āśāḍha, begins talking to it.[14] He describes his beloved, from whom he has been parted, and begs the cloud to travel to her with his message of love and his assurance that he will soon be reunited with her. The Yakṣa tells the cloud how to reach his city, Alakā, what the route there is like, what the city is like, how to identify his house, how to find his beloved, what state she is likely to be in, and what to say to her. The cloud listens silently, but, says the Yakṣa, he will not take this silence for refusal. He knows that the cloud is his brother and his friend. The poem ends with the Yakṣa bidding farewell to the cloud, hoping it will never be separated from its spouse, lightning. We have no doubt that the cloud, thus entreated, indeed has embarked on its journey, bearing its sweet burdens of rain and a lover's missive, accompanied by its flashy but faithful wife.

At the sight of a cloud,
the mind of even a happy man takes a turn—
how much more so a man at far remove
longing for an embrace![15] (*Megh-K.* 1.3)

A cloud is a conglomeration
of vapour, light, water and wind,
and messages must be conveyed
by living beings with keen faculties.

Ignoring, in his enthusiasm, this incongruity,
the Yakṣa made a request to the cloud—
those consumed by love
petition the sentient and the dumb
indiscriminately. (*Megh-K.* 1.5)

Everything about Kalidasa's poem, dated roughly to the court of Candragupta II, called Vikramāditya, in the first half of the fifth century CE, is lovely. The language is polished to perfection; the premise is charming; the voice of the lovelorn Yakṣa rings true; and even the vaporous water-laden addressee assumes an entirely believable personality, by turns kindly, playful, stately, and sonorous. Kalidasa recalls to us a time when to our eye a cloud, a mountain, and an elephant all shared certain properties; a time when animals, humans, semidivine beings like Yakṣas and Siddhas, and the great god Śiva all inhabited the same spaces: a time of human naïveté, natural plenitude, and poetry of a kind that is no longer possible.

The entire work, metrically perfect, is permeated by a deep empathy for both human predicaments and the rhythms of the natural world. We sense that the poet knows the emotions of love and longing, and has also observed keenly every aspect of nature by which he may be surrounded. At the same time he is urbane, describing the social, sexual, and romantic pursuits of the inhabitants of several cities that the cloud will pass over. His Sanskrit has the sophistication that is itself an index of a flourishing literary culture. The mountains, plains, forests, rivers, cities, and kingdoms that make up the cloud's imagined passage northward have names and locations that match those found in ancient history. Moreover, they conjure up a land so filled with beautiful people and places, so exquisitely and lovingly delineated from the cloud's aerial perspective, that it is hard to imagine a listener or reader who would fail to be enchanted by this India.

Rabindranath Tagore, the bard of India's modernity, was one such reader. His Bengali poem *Meghdūt,* written in 1890, is not a retelling of the Sanskrit *Meghadūta,* but an ode to Kalidasa, to his poetry, to the emotions stirred by his poem even 1,500 years later, and to the glimmering landscape he created in verse, whose contours remained beloved even in the depths of a colonized present. As Dipesh Chakrabarty has shown, Tagore himself was the poet who imagined Bengal into existence: his poems not only became national anthems—of Swadeshi Bengal in 1905–1908, of free India in 1947, and of Bangladesh in 1971—but for many Bengalis throughout the late nineteenth and twentieth centuries, provided the very idiom in which their country and their attachment for their country could be brought into words.[16] Tagore conjured up a golden land as deftly as his predecessor Kalidasa did, in poetic images inspiring a particular type of attachment that needs to be correctly characterized. This much is clear: it is not patriotic love. The notion of "patriotism" makes no sense with reference to something a modern reader might feel on account of the words of a poet like Kalidasa, who lived centuries ago; it is also inappropriate in connection with Rabindranath, who did not work with territorial, geopolitical, cartographic, and exclusionary conceptions of space in indicating either Bengal or India.[17]

Yet, for the modern poet, what mars the beauty and power of his own creation is its rupture, its separation, from the past. Like the Yakṣa from his beloved, like the hermitage in Rāmagiri from the city of Alakā, like Rabindranath from Kalidasa, India too is in a state of separation, viccheda, not from some different place, but from its own past self, which may as well have been another country.[18] Amit Chaudhuri is the one to understand this, in one of the more important insights of contemporary Indian literary criticism: "In his poem, Tagore brilliantly reworks Kalidasa's tale of separation from the loved one into a narrative of the separation of the self from history; the beloved pining in the city of Alakā becomes a figure of the past, intimate but distant, beautiful, but not quite recoverable."[19]

At the sight of a cloud,
the mind of even a happy man takes a turn—
how much more so a man at far remove
longing for an embrace! (*Megh-K.* 1.3)

meghāloke bhavati sukhino'pi
anyathāvṛtticetaḥ
kaṇṭhāśleṣa praṇayini jane
kiṃ punar dūrasaṃsthe

How much more so a man at far remove! Tagore figures himself as this very man, at a far remove *(dūrasaṃstha),* literally, situated at a distance. But at a distance from what, or from whom? At first he speaks for "all separated lovers," for "every exile in the world," for "each lover," for "companionless people" sitting in "loveless rooms."

Their voices come to me from your poem;
They sound in my ear likes waves on the sea-shore. (*Megh-T.* 16–17)

Alongside and emanating from the *Meghadūta,* then, Rabindranath senses, like the waves of the sea, the murmur of all the separated lovers who ever pined for their loved ones. What Tagore hears in Kalidasa's poem is an intimation of disembodied, continuous, cumulative longing; the longing of everyone, ever, who might have been tormented by separation (viccheda). In excess of its own constitutive words, what sounds through the poem is viraha itself. Rabindranath can hear it, like the sound of thunder or of the ocean. For forty-five lines, Tagore tells of how Kalidasa's poem makes, for all time, and for all people, a perduring connection between the pain of separation in love, viraha, and the rainy season *(Āśāḍha).* Thanks to the *Meghadūta,* a mood and a season have become forever conjoined in the Indic imagination, and at each of its countless iterations, the poem at once articulates, heightens, and assuages the complex sensation of viraha for its readers through the ages.

> Ah, supreme poet, that first, hallowed day
> Of Asarh on which, in some unknown year, you wrote
> Your *Meghaduta!* (*Megh-T.* 1–3)
>
> Since that day, countless first days
> Of the cooling rainy season have passed.
> Every year has given new life to your poem . . . (*Megh-T.* 35–37)

Tagore is in awe of Kalidasa's power as a poet, for his poem gives voice to all lovers both before and after him. He is the "supreme poet" because his poem alters and marks time and space both, "breaking time's bonds," journeying "through land after land" (*Megh-T.* 13, 24). By contrast with Kalidasa's transcendent poetry, Tagore is acutely aware of his own very specific, very limited, location:

> In the easternmost part of India,
> In verdurous Bengal, I sit. (*Megh-T.* 48–49)
>
> In a gloomy closed room I sit alone
> And read the *Meghaduta.* (*Megh-T.* 58–59)

Tagore is alone, in a room, with Kalidasa's Sanskrit poem. At this moment he is primarily a reader, not a poet himself. This room is not just any room: it is a room in India, in its easternmost part, in Bengal. Moreover, it is not just the rainy season, or the verdant natural beauty, or even the emotional landscape of the place that connects Tagore to Kalidasa, but a specific poetic tradition, in which Jayadeva, the medieval poet and author of the *Gīta Govinda,* is both Kalidasa's descendant and Tagore's ancestor. Jayadeva is equidistant in time from both poets (one before him, one after), but he is joined with them in a common horizon of poetry that surpasses the rules of historical temporality:

> Here too the poet Jayadeva watched on a rainy day . . .
> The density of a sky in full cloud. (*Megh-T.* 50, 52)

Tagore is already in the extraordinary double position of being able to identify intensely with both the poet who wrote of love in separation and the pining lover he created in his poem. But then he, Tagore, enters into a third position, that of the cloud, also a creation of the immortal poet. As soon as he has brought us up to the present moment, he is also ready to leave the present for the timeless time of the poetic flight of fancy:

> Today is a dark day, the rain is incessant,
> The wind is ferocious . . .
>
> My mind leaves the room,
> Travels on a free-moving cloud, flies far and wide. (*Megh-T.* 53–54, 59–60)

Rabindranath is overwhelmed by multiple emotions: his own dark mood on a rainy day, the ancient poet's creative impulse, the memory of Jayadeva, the Yakṣa's pain, the cloud's exhilaration, and finally, the identification of every lover who ever read the poem and subsumed his own feelings to those of the nameless Yakṣa in Rāmagiri long ago. Tagore's poem is a vortex of these different emotions; their incommensurable temporalities fuse into a single structure of feeling. His wonder—for perhaps the predominant rasa of Tagore's poem is *adbhuta*—grows as his heart travels "thus, like a cloud, from land to land" (*Megh-T.* 92).[20]

> Who but you, O Poet . . .
> Could take me there? (*Megh-T.* 96, 98)
>
> Poet, your spell has released
> Tight bonds of pain in this heart of mine.
> I too have entered that heaven of yearning . . .
> Beyond all the rivers and mountains of this world (*Megh-T.* 106–108, 122)

This is the poem's crescendo. Rabindranath is in Alakā, "Heavenly, longed-for city . . . that heaven of yearning" (*Megh-T.* 94, 108). He has entered the celestial city with the Yakṣa's bereaved beloved, with the Yakṣa "at far remove," making a fevered entreaty to his insentient friend, with the cloud who has yet to go there, with Kalidasa, who, as the master of his own poetic universe, was everywhere at once, with Rabi who loved and missed his dead Kadambari,[21] with Jayadeva, who wrote of the viraha of Radha and Krishna, and with every lover who has ever asked:

> Why does love not find its true path? (*Megh-T.* 118)

After such a climax, inevitably, a return to reality:

> The vision goes. I watch the rain again
> Pouring steadily all around. (*Megh-T.* 111–112)

For a while the pouring rain and the poem in front of Tagore had melded into a profoundly affecting experience. Of what order was this experience? Was it emotional, psychological, imaginative, sensory, literary, or historical? What was the ontological character of this experience? It would seem that it had a distinct ontology, which is the ontology of the poetic. What Tagore's poem describes is poiesis itself.

* * *

The word "poiesis" is Greek, like aporia. The philosopher Giorgio Agamben provides a thumbnail genealogy for the term.[22] Originally Plato defined poiesis as the bringing of something into existence that was not there before. In Aristotle's gloss on the Platonic *sūtra* (as it were), the transition from non-being to being necessarily involves taking on a shape. Agamben himself combines these two archaic definitions to state that poiesis is the production into presence of a form. This iteration therefore emphasizes bringing something from concealment and non-being to the light of presence. Further, Agamben usefully differentiates between poiesis and praxis, a distinction important for my reading of Tagore's stance on poetry and on politics, to which I return later in this chapter. For Agamben, poiesis has to do with making visible, with unveiling; it is a mode of expressing the truth. Praxis, on the other hand, is concerned with doing, with acting; it is a mode of expressing the will. "[What] the Greeks meant with the distinction between *poiesis* and praxis was precisely that the essence of *poiesis* has nothing to do with the expression of a will (with respect to which art is in no way necessary): this essence is found instead in the production of truth and in the subsequent opening of a world for man's existence and action."[23]

Buddhadev Bose, twentieth-century Bengal's leading poet and critic after Tagore's passing, is not impressed by the *Meghadūta*.[24] He is critical of Sanskrit poetry as a whole, of Kalidasa's entire oeuvre, but especially so of the *Meghadūta*. This is because the *Meghadūta* alone, in his opinion, of all of Kalidasa's work, comes even close to conveying what a modern sensibility would regard as genuinely poetic meaning. Here at last is a poem that is not stifled by the extremely conventional and rule-bound nature of Sanskrit poetry; a poem that has a hint of natural power, as opposed to artificial ornament; in other words, a poem that despite being in the Sanskrit language is closer to the organic poetry of medieval and modern Bengali. It is not entirely *saṃskṛta*.[25] But the *Meghadūta*, too, fails to break out of its time, its language, or its very historicity as a literary object.

Bose is scathing, complaining, chiding, frustrated, and downright nasty about this poem. To some extent, one can understand that in questioning Sanskrit kāvya, Bose seeks to unsettle all poetry considered canonical in Bengali literary criticism, up to and including Tagore. His iconoclasm is at least partly motivated by his desire to establish his own modernity, his departure from hidebound tradition, whether classical or vernacular. But I disagree with his reading both of the features of Sanskrit poetry in general and of Kalidasa's *Meghadūta* in particular, so I do not reprise it here. Simona Sawhney undertakes such a reading at some length, in her excellent book on the relationship of Sanskrit literature and literary theory to modern Indian literatures and literary critical practice.[26] Suffice it to say that the principal rasa of the poem, the *karuṇa* rasa, moved Tagore so much that he wrote his own poem about Kalidasa's poem.[27] By contrast it did almost nothing for Bose.

Surely what gets in the way is Bose's theory about the absolute difference between premodern and modern poetry. To my mind his theory precedes his reading of, say, Kalidasa, Jayadeva, Jibananda, Candidas, Tagore, and other Bengali poets (some of them his own contemporaries), as well as numerous ancient, medieval, and modern European poets, including Homer, Shakespeare, Dante, Coleridge, Rilke, Baudelaire, and T. S. Eliot. He is so fixated on his theory of this difference that he literally does not read the *Meghadūta*. He does not understand what Tagore understands, that when Kalidasa compared Mount Kailasa to Śiva's laughter, it was not a question of this or that kind of simile authorized by the canons of Sanskrit poetics, perfect or not so perfect, but the very image of the sacred mountain through which that mountain, that god, and their relationship would ever after be figured in the Indic mind.[28]

Mount Kailasa . . .
stretching across the sky

with its lily-white lofty peaks,
looks like the wild laughter
of the three-eyed god
piled up night after night. (*Megh-K.* 1.58)

śṛṅgocchrāyaiḥ kumudaviśadair
yo vitatya stithaḥ khaṃ
rāśībhūtaḥ pratiniśam iva
Trayambakasy'āṭṭahāsaḥ

Tagore, meanwhile, transported by this and many other utterly breathtaking metaphors that are graven in the Indic imagination, feels a visceral affinity for Kalidasa; he senses for one wild, euphoric moment, if you will, the possibility of his own inclusion in the tradition. He has almost ascended into a sky where India's poets are arranged in a luminous constellation, like stars, from time immemorial. Thus he cannot stop thinking about the poem, even after he has finished reading it, and even after his vision of Alakā, "Heavenly, longed-for city," has passed:

The darkness thickens; the solitariness of night approaches.
Far across the plain, the wind moans aimlessly.
I am sleepless half the night, asking—
Who has cursed us like this? Why this gulf?
Why do we aim so high, only to weep when thwarted? (*Megh-T.* 113–117)

Tagore's questions raise other questions for his readers: Who exactly does he mean by "us"? The "gulf" he mentions—who is separated, from whom, by this gulf? Does he mean himself and his unmentioned, unnamed beloved?[29] Who are the "we," who aim high, and thwarted, as we must be, weep? Nothing in the poem clarifies the references. Yet they make Tagore sleepless with anxiety.

We return to the question we began with: if Tagore, like the Yakṣa, is a man at far remove, then what is it that he is removed from? Amit Chaudhuri is quite right to see that the object arousing Tagore's pangs of separation, the referent of his viraha, is no woman, alive or dead, nor even the idea of a separated beloved, but rather a certain vision of the past, the past that has become another country, a country from which he is exiled and to which he will never return, unlike the Yakṣa (who will go home once he has served his sentence). Tagore has, in a stroke of genius, rendered the particular affect of a sundering between the self and the past in terms of *viraha*. This self—the self of modernity—yearns for the past like a lover, indeed, like Kalidasa's Yakṣa for his separated beloved.[30] What traverses the distance in time bearing the message of longing is not a cloud, but the poem itself, Tagore's own *Meghdūt*.

⋆ ⋆ ⋆

The real object of Tagore's apparently unascribed yearning becomes clear only when we read his poem in conjunction with one of his short essays, also titled "The *Meghadūta*" (1891).[31] In the poem, his mind "leaves the room, / Travels on a free-moving cloud, flies far and wide" (*Megh-T.* 59–60). It goes to all the places named by Kalidasa, and so traverses the geography of classical India, stretching between the river Narmada at the southern limit (where the Yakṣa is serving time for a minor transgression against his lord, Kubera), and Mount Kailasa in the northern reaches of the Himalayas, on whose slopes stands the celestial city, Alakā, home to the Yakṣa and his—currently miserable and solitary—beloved. Many rivers and cities are met along the way, from the forests of central India, to the river valley of the Ganga, to the plains of the Punjab, to the foothills and the high passes of the Himalaya mountains. Most notable are the city of Ujjayini, "gazing at her own great shadow in the Shipra river" (*Megh-T.* 83), where the Gupta emperor Vikramāditya had his court and Kalidasa himself likely lived, and Alakā, the imaginary dwelling of gods and semidivine beings, which is the final destination of the cloud, and eventually of the Yakṣa himself.[32] For Tagore, Alakā is the name given to "that heaven of yearning" that Kalidasa built:

> When, o wanderer at will,
> you see her in the lap of the mountain
> as if in that of a lover,
> her shawl the Ganga slipping off,
> you will not fail to recognize Alaka:
>
> at the time of your coming,
> she wears in her soaring palaces

a mass of clouds raining water,
just as a lady in love wears her hair
entwined with strings of pearls. (*Megh-K.* 2.63)

In his essay "The *Meghdūta,*" Tagore says of the country described in the *Meghadūta:* "From Rāmagiri to the Himalayas ran a long stretch of ancient India over which life used to flow to the slow, measured *mandākrānta* metre of the *Meghadūta*. We are banished from that India, not just during the rains, but for all time" (Tagore, 222). This banishment—who is it who gives the orders, the equivalent of the Yakṣa's lord? Who banishes us from "that India"? Tagore does not say. "It was the India of the poet," Tagore writes. "We are banished from that India. We have only the poet's cloud to send there as a messenger" (Tagore, 223). The names given to cities, mountains, forests, and rivers in that India are beautiful. "There is a comeliness, a dignity, a purity about those names," totally unlike "the vulgar cacophony that surrounds us today" (Tagore, 222). We have some sense of the lay of that land, thanks to the hints—the glimpses, the scents, the shadows—conveyed by Kalidasa, but no details are available to us.

Tagore tries to convey the insurmountable temporal gulf between now and then, us and them, the present and the past, this India and that India, through spatial imagery: "From this narrow sea-girt present, when we look at the shores of that ancient land described in the poem . . . we feel that between them and us there ought to have been a bond. Our common humanity binds us intimately together, but remorseless time separates us" (Tagore, 223). Tagore seems to yearn for "that India," the India of an inaccessible past, as the Yakṣa for his beloved. He wishes that a "common humanity" shared between people in the past and people in the present could somehow enable them to bridge "this gulf" (*Megh-T.* 116) that separates them from one another, but history is all about a viraha that never ends in a sweet union of sundered lovers. In Kalidasa's poem, Tagore finds a symbol for the unattainable past, and this is Alakā, "Heavenly, longed-for city" (*Megh-T.* 94): "Thanks to the poet, *that distant past has been transformed into the city of Alakā,* an everlasting visionary land of beauty. From this present world of ours, overcast by the grief of separation, we send out to it this cloud-messenger, our imagination" (Tagore, 223; emphasis added).

In Rabindranath's *Meghdūt,* what is it that is being brought to expression? What was it that was separated from the reader—the reader of Kalidasa's poem, as well as the reader of Tagore's poem—and is now being produced into presence? It is "the India of the poet." Rabindranath thus creates an allegory of the modern self's encounter with the past, which means both a historical world consisting of places and persons (lovingly delineated in ll. 61–91) and a poetic tradition, begun by Vyasa and Valmiki, continued by Kalidasa, and carried further forward by Jayadeva, Vidyapati, and Candidas. Poiesis—the production into presence of a form that was thus far hidden—allows there to be such an encounter. But Tagore's modern consciousness is also painfully aware of the separation between, on the one hand, the exiled brooding self in the present and, on the other hand, the vitality and fullness of the past, with its lovely landscapes, beautiful figures, and poetic traditions.

To confront this separation is to feel viraha (longing, yearning), which is of course also the very *bhāva* (emotion) that Kalidasa's poem itself is about. Reading about the Yakṣa's viraha vis-à-vis his separated beloved induces in Rabindanath (i.e., in the reader) his own viraha, his own yearning for the past, for tradition, for the lost celestial city, as it were, of a truly Indic poetry. But after a sort of delirium of identification, a tantalizing moment of arrival in that India, that wondrously beautiful place conjured by Kalidasa's verses, Rabindranath snaps back to reality: here, now, night, the falling rain, Bengal. The vision is at an end and only a lingering wretchedness, a cascade of distraught questions remains: Why are we apart? Why must we weep? Why can we not be reunited? *Meghdūt*—together with all the poems of this cycle—is an allegory for the modern sensibility's exploration of the tradition, and an attempt to come to terms with the slip-sliding of the self that occurs as a result of this encounter. The self oscillates between memory and forgetting, *euporia* (plentiude) and aporia (privation), poiesis (expression as form) and aphasia (the lapse into language-less-ness).

Ranajit Guha remarks that even in the midst of a nationalist milieu, wherein history and historiography were at the very center of the struggle for power between the colonizer and the colonized, Tagore stood apart. His historical vision was

> original . . . distanced no less from the colonialist historiography propagated by the Raj and the ideologues of imperialism than from the narrowly sectarian Hindu view of the past that had been influential in nationalist thought since its formulation by Bankimchandra Chattopadhyay in the 1870s. Tagore overcame his early inclination in favor of the latter to settle eventually on a strong anti-imperialist, secular, and liberal-democratic interpretation of Indian history. This was to serve as a basic source of ideas for the freedom movement in its climactic phase between the two world wars. Both Gandhi and Nehru, as well as their followers, drew profoundly on it in order to educate and mobilize the people in the campaigns for independence. One would have expected such a writer, an eminent historian in his own right, to speak well of historiography and its practitioners. But that turned out not to be the case.[33]

Guha is right that Tagore had a genuinely "original" historical vision. What is so remarkable is that even as he sat at the very nerve center of nationalist discourse—and in his own person came to embody, for Bengalis, for Indians more generally, and for the founding fathers (as Guha points out), a particular strand of humanist cultural nationalism—Tagore was thinking about history in terms that make sense only in the framework of poetry. The world-making activity of the creative mind, in his vision, is poiesis and not politics; the characteristic affect of history is viraha, the pain of separation; and the way to connect to the past is not, say, through the revivalism and indigenism of his Swadeshi nationalist colleagues, but rather through the poetic imagination. Rabindranath was not merely "original" in his thinking. To my mind he was on an entirely different path than any of his peers, whether Orientalists or Modernists.[34] According to Isaiah Berlin, reading Tagore from the outside, it seemed that he veered neither toward "radical modernism" nor toward a "proud and gloomy traditionalism." In Berlin's estimation, this moderation on Tagore's part constituted "the rarest form of heroism."[35]

It is worth noting that the space to be traversed by the Yakṣa's cloud, and retraced by Tagore, is indeed a space that to modern readers suggests classical India, but it is not the same as the "epic space" evoked by the travels of various characters in the *Mahābhārata*.[36] Kalidasa's India is not the Bhāratavarṣa of *itihāsa* and *purāṇa* literature: it is not the zone to be conquered by a king, to be pervaded by sovereign power. Indeed it is not a political space at all, not a space of conquest or of rule, not territory to be won in war and subdued by force. The cloud passes over cities but has no inkling of their rulers. To the extent that it can see figures from its passage in the sky, all the people that it sees are women. The Yakṣa makes no mention of thrones, armies, or kings, of the battles that might be going on in the countries that the cloud will traverse. Rivers, mountains, forests, and flowers find as much mention as human settlements. Tagore chooses Kalidasa's aesthetic and natural interpretation of geographical space over the space of power and conflict that is available from the epic and mythic genres.

His *Meghdūt* meditations have as little to do with the Gupta Empire of the fifth century as they do with the British Empire of the nineteenth century: India, for him, in this corpus and in his paintings, is simply not subject to political will, indigenous or foreign. He sees it through Kalidasa's poetry as a land of love and of beauty, human as well as natural; in his paintings he makes no effort to map or visualize it at all, whether as archaic or as modern. Meanwhile, nationalist historians, artists, and ideologues, Tagore's contemporaries in Bengal, Maharashtra, and other parts of colonial India, were busy imagining India as a continuation of a mythopoeic Bhāratavarṣa, a powerful Indic polity of subcontinental dimensions. The rolling wheel of the premodern Buddhist/Hindu ideal ruler, the wheel-turning king *(Cakravartin)*, or the wandering horse of the ancient horse sacrifice *(Aśvamedha Yajña)*, or the rock and pillar edicts proclaiming an imperium of righteousness (dhamma) planted all across India by the emperor Aśoka (ca. 250 CE)—these symbols of political and territorial sovereignty (rājya) participate in an entirely different semiotic than Kalidasa's airborne tourist.

It is symptomatic of Rabindranath's resistance to the nationalist imagination that when his mind leaves the room and travels from land to land in the classical past, it does so on the back of a cloud messenger *(meghadūta)*, not a royal steed *(aśva)* or the wheel of power (dhammacakra). The place produced into presence by Kalidasa's poiesis, "the India of the poet," is neither the space of history, nor the space of power, nor epic space. It is rather the space of the Indic imagination, the space of poetry and of an Indic poetic tradition, from which Rabindranath feels exiled, as indeed the Yakṣa is from Alakā, and the modern self is from "that India." In Rabindranath's poems dense with symbols, all of the different meanings of exile, and all of the different sensations of yearning, are piled up one on top of another *(rāśī-bhūta),* like the mass of clouds that he sees outside his window in verdurous Bengal—like the ones the Yakṣa himself saw long ago in his lonely spot in Rāmagiri.[37]

* * *

In another, very late poem, titled "Yakṣa" (1940), Tagore, now almost eighty years old, returns to his beloved *Meghadūta.* His translator William Radice complains that this is a particularly difficult poem to translate from Bengali into English.[38]

> A huge separation dwells at the heart of onward time
> That tries door after future door,
> Life after future life
> In an endless attempt to close its distance from perfection.
> The world is its poem, a rolling sonorous poem
> In which a remote presage of joy annotates vast sorrow. ("Yakṣa," 11–16)

Separation, now, for Rabindranath at the end of his life, dwells at the very heart of time; it is the essence of futurity. History, then, is asymptotic. There will always be a "distance from perfection"—like the distance of the Yakṣa and his cloud friend from the city of Alakā—and the attempt to close the gap (which he had already, in his essay "The *Meghadutam,*" called "this gulf") is "endless." Tagore's asymptotic and aporetic history is entirely different from Hegel's teleological history: the latter promises closure, the former, infinite extension. Even more subtle, and difficult to grasp, is the fact that Tagore is trying to understand our relationship to the future by analogy with our relationship to the past. Both past and future are perfect; hence, neither one is available to us imperfect beings. Were we, mere mortals, to actually be in the unattainable past (or the unattainable future, for the two are interchangeable), then like the Yakṣa's beloved, we too would be miserable, petrified, passed out of history into an eternal stupor, without recourse to either words or actions.

The poet has given her pining no language,
Her love no pilgrimage—
For her, the unspeaking Yakṣa city
Is a meaningless prison of riches.
Permanent flowers, eternal moonlinght—
Mortal existence knows no grief as great as this:
Never to awake from dreams. ("Yakṣa," 24–30)

It is the "huge separation . . . at the heart of onward time" that makes us yearn, and this yearning that creates, as it were, the panorama and the narrative of human history. It was the "blessed Yakṣa" ("Yakṣa," 17) whom Kalidasa endowed with viraha, the pain of separation, and this pain produced his message, addressed to the distant and silent beloved, to be delivered via the insentient but presumably benign cloud. In this sense, were it not for the viraha troubling the Yakṣa, the poem would not exist. The stanzas of his poem, Tagore says to the "supreme poet," are like "dark-layered sonorous clouds" (*Megh-T.* 4):

As the thunderclouds clashed, their booming released
In a single day the heart-held grief of thousands of years
Of pining. Long-repressed tears,
Breaking time's bonds, seem to have poured down
In torrents that day and drenched your noble stanzas. (*Megh-T.* 10–14)

Kalidasa's stanzas about the address of the Yakṣa to a cloud are themselves like rain clouds; the poem itself is like an object in nature.

Your stanzas are themselves
Like dark-layered sonorous clouds, heaping the misery
Of all separated lovers throughout the world
Into thunderous music. (*Megh-T.* 3–6)

Here human emotion (misery), nature (clouds), and poetry (stanzas) are all three fused into a single composite poetic symbol in an instance of mind-boggling synesthesia. Kalidasa's poem is comparable with "the Ganges in full monsoon flood" (l. 27) that becomes, eventually, through the alchemy between streams and mountains, earth and sea, "a great mass dominating the sky" (l. 34). His *Meghadūta* is like a river in spate or a massive bank of clouds; it both overruns the landscape, and dominates the horizon, of poetry. While the rainy season has always stirred fresh pangs of grief in the hearts of separated lovers, once Kalidasa has written his poem, for the first time in "thousands of years" a palpable form is given to that "heart-held grief." The poem brings to language the entirety of the experience of viraha that preceded it, and gives voice to all the viraha that will, inevitably, follow. The poem is at the vanishing point of history, where past and future converge.

In his *Meghdūt* poem(s), Tagore seems to work out several themes, strands, and insights. His essay, though, is more ambiguous. Neither his subject (the self), nor his addressee ("you"), who together form an "us" or a "we," is ever clearly named. All pronouns are indexicals, but these pronouns in Tagore's essay somehow evade their function, which is to point at particular persons.

> We stand, each one of us, on a lonely mountain peak, gazing northwards. Between us, the sky, the clouds, and the fair earth with its Reva, Shipra, Avanti, Ujjayini, its beauties, wealth and delights, stretch out like a painting. They arouse memories, but do not let us approach nearer. Desires are stirred but never satisfied. Two human beings, and so far apart! (Tagore, 225)

Again: which two human beings does he mean? An Indian present and one past? Kalidasa and Tagore? The poet of the ancient world and the poet of the modern world? The landscape now is no longer like a living thing; it is rather a painted scene. We have memories of it, as though we had been there, but we cannot approach it any longer. We yearn for it, but our yearning is and will remain unfulfilled. We are both (the two of us) human, yet we are far from one another, each one on a lonely mountain peak, and far from the vista that stretches between us that is marked like a real map with names of actual places, and yet wholly imaginary. Tagore is aware of the almost dreamlike quality, the illogical nature, the reference-less syntax, of his prose. It makes emotional sense but doesn't really stand up to analysis. Who is he talking to? Who is he talking about? What is he describing? (Does his long-lost Kadambari haunt him, still, she who passed away in his youth, at the very beginning of his married life?)

His last sentence acknowledges that he has sidestepped common sense, much like the Yakṣa, because of being in the state of separation, of being at a far remove: "Who knows, you may also have lost the distinction between reality and imagination" (Tagore, 225). The only place where the order of reality and the order of imagination may productively fuse to yield an object with a third, distinctive ontology is poetry. In the logic of poetry, Rāmagiri and Alakā, Ujjayini and Santiniketan, the Yakṣa and his beloved, Kalidasa and Tagore, you and I, that India and this India, all enter into a shimmering structure of interconnection whose meaning is above the rules of history, and certainly beyond its orderly syntax.

Ranajit Guha reads and translates Tagore's late essay, "Sāhitye Aitihāsikatā" (Historicality in literature, May 1941) to indicate that Tagore located history not in the public and the political, but in the personal and the literary. The "events" that for Tagore counted as historically significant were not political upheavals and economic changes, but deeply personal moments in an individual's memory, occurrences in the natural world, and other such shifts and breaks in the life of the soul, the self, and nature. In this essay he personalizes the "self" of history even more sharply, to the poet himself, to Rabindranath (whom he names as though he were a third person). I would take Guha's reading a step further and locate Tagore's understanding of history squarely in the domain of the poetic. Tagore opens his very last meditation on history and literature by declaring as much ("very last" because he died a few days later):

> I have heard it said again and again that we are guided altogether by history, and I have energetically nodded, so to say, in my mind whenever I heard it. I have settled this debate in my own heart where I am nothing but a poet. I am there in the role of a creator all alone and free. There's little to enmesh me there in the net of external events. I find it difficult to put up with the pedantic historian when he tries to force me out of the center of my creativity as a poet.[39]

* * *

Chaudhuri brings to our attention another poem by Tagore, titled "Dream," written in 1897 and published in 1900.[40] In this poem, which is related to but slightly different from both the essay and the poem named after Kalidasa's *Meghadūta* that were written six or seven years earlier, the poet or the figure of the poet, who speaks in the first person, goes to visit his beloved:

> . . . in the city of Ujjain,
> by River Shipra . . . ("Dream," 2–3)[41]

The signs marking her house are all very similar to the signs that would indicate the Yakṣa's house to the cloud, but the poet's beloved ("my first love," l. 4) in this poem lives in Ujjayini not Alakā; she is not nameless, but named Malavika (l. 45); she lives not on Śiva's mountain, Mount Kailasa, but near a Śiva temple; the poet goes to visit her himself, instead of sending a messenger, and he makes his visit in the spring (the season of love), not the monsoon (the season of separation). In one way this poem appears to be about union, not separation. However, crucially, as the title of the poem suggests, the meeting of the lovers takes place in a "dream-world" (l. 2) or in "a previous life of mine" (l. 5). Moreover, when the two lovers are face to face, language fails them. The beloved is beautiful, of course, and has the limbs, clothing, and ornaments of a female figure from Kalidasa. But the Yakṣa's beloved, as we know, never got any speaking lines.

> Seeing me, my love . . .
> slowly . . . without words
> asked with her tender eyes,
> "Hope you're well, my friend?"
>
> I looked at her face,
> tried to speak,
> but found no words.
> That language was lost to us:
> we tried so hard
> to recall each other's name,
> but couldn't remember.
>
> We thought so hard
> as we gazed at each other,
> and the tears streamed from
> our unflickering eyes. ("Dream," 65–79)

This scenario has the unmistakable air of a dream: the loss of memory, the wordless encounter, the emotional intensity that finds no outlet in language, the moment of address which is also the precise moment of amnesia, the unasked and unanswered question that hangs in the air, the beloved named Malavika whose name he cannot recall, eyes that stream but are "unflickering." The meeting of these lovers is no meeting at all. The end of viraha is not perfect union but an utter inability to unite, even in speech. The present and the past are divided by absolute aphasia: "That language was lost to us" (l. 72). Yet, paradoxically, after a passage of time whose extension we cannot guess,

> Keen with yearning,
> they mingled quietly—
> her breath and my breath. ("Dream," 91–93)

Buddhadev Bose reads "Dream" ("Svapna") as Tagore's homage to Kalidasa in which, after a string of borrowed images: the city of Ujjayini, the river Shipra, the overdetermined house, the overdetermined beloved, suddenly, "we are startled and halted—we get the electric feel of a modern poet's sensibility."[42] The poem has, up to a point, the *lakṣaṇas* (the defining attributes, the characteristic features) of any reiteration of the *Meghadūta*, past or present. Yet it produces in its readers a frisson, which comes from our recognizing in it a modern sensibility concealed beneath the garb of classicism. The telltale "modernity" of the poem underlies the beloved's unuttered question (in Bose's rendering, and Mukherjee's translation): "Is all well with you, friend?"[43]

For Bose this question cannot be asked in Kalidasa's world, or indeed in Sanskrit poetry at all. Only Tagore, coming as he does after an entire age of medieval Vaiṣṇava poetry, may put such a question in the beloved's eyes—and even he cannot put it in her mouth. Modernity flares up in this one moment, then recedes again: "It may be noted that the protagonist of the poem 'Swapna' seems to forget how to speak as soon as the query is posed, the heroine has no answer to offer (no answer is possible). . . . The darkness of the poem is not that of night but of separation and forgetting, a viraha without beginning or end. This thirst will never be slaked; this beloved will always disappear . . . as soon as she is touched."[44] Thus even for Bose, who sees "Dream" as a poem that takes a sharp, brief, but significant modern turn, as it were, Tagore cannot render the conundrum of recognition across the gulf of time, the impossible union of self and other over the separation of history, except in this way:

> Night's darkness swallowed
> the city of Ujjain.
>
> In the Shiva-temple
> on River Shipra's bank
> the evening service
> came to an abrupt end. ("Dream," 94–95, 98–101)

Again and again, Rabindranath hits the wall:

> Night's darkness swallowed
> The city of Ujjain. ("Svapna," 94–95)
>
> The vision goes. (*Megh-T.* 111)
>
> The evening service
> Comes to an abrupt end. ("Svapna," 100–101)

These are the moments "without passage"; these are expressions of aporia. Rabindranath does not participate in the classicization of tradition (whether Hindu or Islamic) common to Bankim and Iqbal. He can float, like a cloud, over the city of Ujjain, Kalidasa's city, the seat of the Gupta imperium, fifth-century India's cosmopolitan capital, vanished metropolis of the ancient world; he can see the clouds gather about its tall turrets, see its great shadow reflected in the River Shipra: he does not enter it. He can come to Alakā, the heaven of yearning, but the moment he arrives, the vision vanishes. Rabindranath does not, cannot, and will not inhabit the past. He cannot be present in the past.

When he does go to Ujjain, to meet his lover, it is in a dream, and in the dream he loses his language, and his lover is wordless too, and then in the dream temple by the dream river in the dream city the evening service comes to an abrupt end, and the dream breaks. It was a dream of another lifetime. That language is lost. This is not revivalism, not reconstruction, not historical fantasy, not nostalgia. It is an inconsolable yearning for the past whose only property is its mute and absolute pastness. The past affords no passage to Rabindranath. Those who want to classicize the tradition, like Bankim, who seek to reenter and reinhabit and recreate and recapture a classical past, must be able to imagine it, to not feel blinded by aporia. For them it cannot be that a huge separation dwells at the heart of onward time; they do not experience that irreparable separation from the past that for Rabindranath causes such longing, such anguish, such viraha. No nationalist may harbor an aporetic relation to the past.

We are here; the past is there. Between the two, aporia. No passage. A huge separation. A nation must subsume within its temporal horizon the past, the present, and the future. To the nationalist, daylight would flood the city of Ujjain—it would not be swallowed forever by night. To Rabindranath, only this mortal world, here, now, the present, has light, is dappled with shadows. Worlds of past and future are on the other side of a separation which makes us long for them but which we cannot overcome in either direction to close the distance from perfection. We try door after future door, life after future life, and yet, always, this gulf, this weeping when we are thwarted. Aphasia: the loss of language. Amnesia: the loss of memory. Aporia: the loss of a way through. All we may recognize is the fact of separation, and its characteristic pain, viraha.

If nationalists felt viraha they could not busy themselves about nation building. If the masters of tradition felt viraha, they would stop trying to make the modern in the image of the classical. They would watch the clouds gather, the sky grow dense, the darkness thicken, the treetops rise, the rain pour steadily all around, night follow evening, wind moan across the plain. Here is Bengal, which is what it is, away from the motionless mounts of heaven; there is Alakā, beyond all the rivers and mountains of this world. No narrative of Indian nationhood can bridge the gap, for Rabindranath, between here and there, Bengal and Alakā, present and past. Poetry may allow a journey between here and there, but poetry will not weave the two into a unity of perduring form, which is the nation. Who but you, O Poet, could take me there? Kalidasa can take Rabindranath there. Mahatma Gandhi cannot.

* * *

In an early article on Kalidasa's *Meghadūta*, Sudipta Kaviraj offers an interpretation of the Sanskrit poem that comes to him, as he indirectly acknowledges, via Tagore.[45] Kaviraj reads the *Meghadūta* as simultaneously a love story, an account of a journey (implausible and yet believable), and, most powerfully, a poem about "alienation." At one level of meaning, the poem does have the quality of "a romance with the land."[46] We love it for this reason, but in the final analysis this is not what makes the poem immortal. The real pull of the *Meghadūta*—and we might add, the source of its mood of *karuṇā* (sadness provoking compassion; the sort of melancholy that elicits our empathy)—is that it traces a "dream return of man to his home, to himself."[47]

In the first part of the article Kaviraj appears to be using the term "alienation" in a Marxist sense, and this is odd, jarring, not quite convincing, given that the subject is a poem from the fifth century CE. (References to the "feudal" character of society in Kalidasa's time, or Kalidasa's own "democratic" inclinations, are similarly incongruous.) But it turns out Kaviraj is unmistakably reading Kalidasa through Tagore; in fact, one might say that his reading is Tagorean through and through, as can be seen in the final lines of his essay. The lack of clarity about what exactly alienation means is Tagore's, not Kaviraj's; Kaviraj is merely inheriting Tagore's unease, his stance of one who is alienated, at a remove, dūrasaṃstha, far from something, someone, some place, some state (but we do not know what, precisely), and projecting this alienation onto the Yakṣa.

More than three decades later, I suspect today Kaviraj himself would not want to approximate viraha to alienation, even while it is clear that both terms share a common provenance in the idea of separation. The conceptual burden of each of these two words is simply too specific for us to use one as a translation of the other, and their histories hardly overlap at all. And yet like other modern readers before us—Tagore, Bose, Kaviraj—we too grasp the pathos of the Yakṣa's predicament in a visceral way. The journey in a future that will never come about is meant to take us back to a past that is gone forever. This journey mapping the distance from the present to a time (gone or yet to come) that is unattainable is by necessity an imaginary journey—hence a journey that can only be made by an imaginary traveler (a traveler who is no traveler at all, an impossible or made-up traveler, here, a cloud):

> The individual problem of this particular yaksha has a solution; but the universal problem of those others like him has not. A

> separation for one year, does not, after all, justify this abysmal sense of sorrow. There is a strange sense of fatality about this grief. This specific yaksha might reunite with this love and with his unbroken life, his nonalienated self. . . . This specific yaksha might earn his private reprieve. But alienation will still be the human condition. So the poem would stand, though its occasion, its accidental subject may desert it. There will always be enough men to substitute for him.
>
> One might go even further. The sadness comes because one knows that [the] yaksha himself—the symbolic representative of mankind—does not really believe in a reunion. The yaksha himself knows that he is banished forever. He still carries on the tragic pretence that it is only for a while. . . . That is why he must build that dream-world against his suffering. It is the "fortress of his soul." He will never return. That is why he must transcend his exile. He must forever return. In dreams.[48]

It seems increasingly likely that Indian literatures, whether classical or modern, will be read by focusing on the categories proper to them. Sawhney's careful reading of Kalidasa's *Abhijñānaśākuntalam,* for example, proceeds through a deeply perceptive and moving treatment of *bhaṅga,* a term in Sanskrit that indicates at once a backward glance, a turning head, and a broken neck—thus, fear, longing, and death, all intertwined and superimposed in the same corporeal gesture.[49] She is also attentive to *smara* in Kalidasa, another complex term, meaning simultaneously love (or passion) and memory (or remembrance), and *atithi,* as well as its related *ātithyam,* that is, the figure of the guest and the notion of hospitality. Since *atithi,* guest, literally means someone who is "without a date"—that is, unprecedented, unexpected, unannounced, someone who arrives suddenly, without warning—*ātithyam* or hospitality also opens up the possibility of relationships set apart from the routines of everyday life, in a time outside time, as it were. Sawhney develops this idea and I do not have space to reprise her argument here, just as I cannot condense her strikingly beautiful analyses of *bhaṅga* and *smara.* Sawhney does not discuss viraha.

Most significantly, for our purposes, she reads Kalidasa as Kalidasa, and Kalidasa via his modern readers, not only Tagore but also other twentieth-century Bengali and Hindi writers like Buddhadev Bose (1908–1974), Hazariprasad Dwivedi (1907–1979), and Mohan Rakesh (1925–1972). The advantage of Sawhney's approach is that it rings true to the primary (Sanskrit) texts but also cleaves to a tradition of reading these texts without which they would be unintelligible to us, namely, a tradition that is distinctly modern, with all of the presuppositions and entailments peculiar to Indian modernity. The moral of the story seems to be that it is very difficult, if not impossible, for us to relate to Kalidasa without Tagore as our mediator. What is true of Rabindranath is true also of a number of other moderns—Sawhney traces, just as a small demonstration of the modernity of tradition, the figure of the Yakṣa in Hindi poems by Srikant Verma and Dharamvir Bharati, from the mid-twentieth century.[50]

Simona Sawhney and Prathama Banerjee both demonstrate the viability, nay, the necessity, of reading Indic texts through Indic critical categories.[51] Banerjee brings to bear a number of categories from Sanskrit literary and philosophical discourse on her analysis of Bankim and Rabindranath, such as *kalpanā* (imagination), rasa (the affect produced in the course of an aesthetic experience), *svapna* (dream), *darśana* (vision/manifest form), *itihāsa* (history, but literally, "veridical account of a historical nature"), *sāhitya* (literature; but literally, "togetherness"), *sahānubhūti* (empathy; but literally, "shared experience"), līlā (play/playfulness), *bhāva* (emotion), and so on. Banerjee does not impose or import these categories from Sanskrit poetics out of some sort of whimsical indigenism; rather, she finds them very much in use in the Bengali, especially that of Rabindranath the historian, essayist, and critic. I cannot reprise her argument here, but I do want to note, with appreciation, that it is by the willingness to work with categories used by Rabindranath himself that Banerjee arrives at her important understanding of the relationship between time, history, the literary imagination, the idea of the primitive, and competing conceptions of nationhood in colonial Bengal. In his theoretical claims articulated in Bengali, Rabindranath undoubtedly relies on Sanskrit literary and aesthetic theory; Banerjee therefore must engage this genealogy in her own work and does so with remarkable intellectual and historical acumen.

* * *

Returning once again to our primary texts:

> A huge separation dwells at the heart of onward time . . .
> The world is its poem, a rolling sonorous poem
> In which a remote presage of joy annotates vast sorrow.[52]

Let us paraphrase these lines from "Yakṣa" into two propositions:

1. At the heart of time is separation.
2. The world is time's poem.

We have already considered the theme of separation continuously throughout this chapter, via the categories of viraha and aporia. Let us turn now to the second proposition: that the world embodies the poiesis of time. The activity of time, in other words, is to produce the world into presence *(poiein)*. In the very heart of this presence, of this being-present-of-the-world, dwells a huge separation that cannot be overcome, despite the fact that time tries door after future door, life after future life, to close the distance from perfection. A remote presage of joy—the attainment of perfection—annotates vast sorrow—insurmountable, eternal, repeated, separation.

> O blessed Yakṣa—
> The fire of creation is in his yearning.[53]

The "fire of creation" in the Yakṣa's yearning for his beloved is nothing other than the urge to produce into presence *(poien)* a world—a "many-colored, shadow-dappled mortal world"—that he and his beloved may inhabit together, overcoming their separation, "away from the motionless mounts of heaven." Presence is the end of yearning. To be present is to cease to yearn. But since the logic of time is premised on separation, presence is always deferred, and the deferral of presence to futurity leaves us, inevitably, yearning. At best this yearning may be voiced rather than dumbly, hopelessly endured. Compare the clamor of poiesis, whether of time or of the Yakṣa—

> The world is . . . a rolling, *sonorous* poem . . .
> God has granted that the Yakṣa may *pound her door* with yearning
> ("Yakṣa," ll. 15, 31; emphasis added)

—with the asignifying hush of the beloved's viraha:

Where *silently* his beloved waits . . .
The poet has given her pining *no language* . . .
For her, the *unspeaking* Yakṣa city
Is a *meaningless* prison of riches. ("Yakṣa," ll. 19, 24, 26–27; emphasis added)

Seeing me, my love . . .
slowly . . . *without words*
asked with her tender eyes,
"Hope you're well, my friend?" ("Dream," 121; emphasis added)

When Rabindranath reads the Sanskrit *Meghadūta* aloud to himself, what he hears in Kalidasa's poem is poiesis itself:

All this time, companionless people have sat in loveless rooms . . .
In the faint lamplight, the have slowly read aloud that verse . . .
Their voices come to me from your poem;
They sound in my ear likes waves on the sea-shore. (*Megh-T.* 42, 44, 46–47; emphasis added)

But this ability to hear poiesis as it unfolds, in poetry, in the world, is not consistently available to Rabindranath—in his dream, which is really his nightmare of confronting the aporia he fears, the huge separation at the heart of onward time—in his dream:

I looked at her face,
tried to speak,
but found no words.
That language was lost to us . . . ("Dream," 121)

The work of the poet is poiesis; the work of the politician is praxis. Poiesis is about expressing the truth. Praxis is about expressing the will. Poiesis is the domain of art, especially poetry. Praxis is the domain of politics, including nation building. Rabindranath, as a poet and artist, is concerned only with poiesis; praxis he leaves to those who are directly involved in political life. The Yakṣa's yearning, his inability to close the distance to perfection, ever fuels his creativity, produces in him an outpouring of poiesis. His address to the cloud, his imaginings and descriptions of the cloud's journey, these come about on account of his separation from his beloved and his unfulfilled longing to return home. On the other hand, his beloved, who is already at home, is silent, struck dumb, locked into an uncreative passivity. Her love has no language because it is not love felt at a far remove from the perfect city of Alakā. The beloved's aphasia is the opposite of the Yakṣa's poiesis. Quite apart from the separated lovers and the expression, in poetry, of their love and longing for one another, is the praxis of nationalism, which seeks to annex the past, claim history for the nation, and assert the power of the human will over time, nature, and circumstance.

Past, present, and future have all to be made tractable to the nation, attainable for it. The celestial city is to be conquered, its soaring palaces regained by those who were wrongfully sent into exile. In Rabindranath's imagination, by contrast, it is a cloud that must go out to Alakā, not an army. Moreover, we will never know whether the cloud actually made it to its destination, or whether the Yakṣa ever returned home. Ambiguity is the human condition; the past is irreparably sundered from us; the future is always open; the questions that torment us are just as likely to remain unanswered as they are to be resolved. All we may know is the bittersweet taste of viraha and the state of creative unrest in which our unfulfilled desires keep us. We cannot do better than talk to the clouds, pound the gates of futurity with our yearning, try door after future door, life after future life, to close the distance from perfection. This vision is irreconcilable with the certainty, the closure, the fulfillment that nationalism expects and demands. The myth of praxis is the myth that the world may be shaped by the human will; Rabindranath, giving voice to a poiesis that belongs to Kalidasa, to the Yakṣa, to Rabindranath himself, and to all mankind, does not subscribe to the myth of praxis.[54] He believes only in the truth of poiesis. Many years ago, Isaiah Berlin saw the value in Tagore's unique position: Indians, he wrote, ought to be proud of "the rarest of all gifts of nature, a poet of genius, who, even in moments of acute crisis . . . unswervingly told them only what he saw, only the truth."[55]

* * *

A vision of the world in which at the heart of onward time lies "a huge separation" (in Bengali: *bipul bicched*), a difference/distinction/distance *(bhed)* relative to perfection or completeness *(pūrṇotā),* is fundamentally premised on the idea of the ever-unfulfilled nature of human yearning, and the ever-incomplete character of human effort. Humanity may strive to keep on striving; it may learn to rejoice in its restless, creative energy; it may burn, like the Yakṣa, in the fires of creativity *(sṛiṣṭīr agun);* it may annotate, like Kalidasa, the world *(bishvo)* that is time's poem *(kābyo)* with a small gloss *(ṭīkā)* of beauty, like the *Meghadūta;* it may make a gesture of poiesis, fashion a poetic work in a lovely meter like the one used by Kalidasa *(mandākrānta)* that counts as a remote presage *(śudūr bhūmikā)* of the eventual bliss *(ānanda)* that comes after vast sorrow *(birāṭ dukkha)*—but it is not for mortal men to "close the distance from perfection" *(pūrṇotār śāṭhe bhed miṭāte).* The beloved—for whom the Yakṣa yearns, toward whom he strives, with whom he seeks reunion, to whom he sends the cloud messenger—that beloved does not and cannot answer back. The poet, Kalidasa, has given her no language *(bhāṣā)* with which to bridge the gulf of viraha, to ford its hazardous waters, to make the pilgrimage across the divide *(bhed)* and close the separation *(bicched)*—no language that might have reunited the sundered lovers in a message and an answering message, a call and its reply. *Kobī tāre deye nāi biroher-tīrtha-gāmī-bhāṣā.*

But this is the way of the future: the future never answers us back. We do not know what it wants to say to us. It remains mute, frozen in whatever image we have cast it in, even if it is an image of great splendor—unfading flowers, eternal moonshine *(nityapuṣpa, nityacandralok).* The riches of the future are voiceless *(bānīhīn),* and thus meaningless *(arthahāra).* We pound *(āghāt koriche)* on the door *(dwāra)* of the future; we desire to sweep our beloved away, back into our wonderful *(bicitro)* mortal world *(mortyobhūme),* into its chiaroscuro *(chāyā),* its varicolored *(nānāborṇo)* tumult, its flowing, vital cascade of presence and change *(toroṅgito prāṇer probāho).* Rabindranath has no conception to offer of a future time that can be attained, whose shape we may know, whose language we may understand.

The reason I have dwelt at such length on these poems, especially *Meghdūt* and "Yakṣa," is because I find that they reveal Rabindranath's metaphysics, and without an understanding of this metaphysics, we cannot really decipher his rejection of nationalism. Nationalist struggle, indeed any kind of political struggle, is future-oriented action par excellence. Rabindranath cannot conceive of the future except as a place where the human proclivity for incessant movement is arrested *(stabdhagati),* a place where human striving is stupefied by or rapt in dreams *(svapnamugdha),* a place that does not offer a way forward *(śommukhe colār poth nāi)*. For him, the future is not the celestial city *(svargapur)* that it is imagined to be—it is rather the greatest grief imaginable in our existence in the mortal world *(astitver eṭo boḍo śok nāi mortyobhūme)*. The future is the graveyard of human aspiration, the tomb of our desire.[56] The nation we place in the future is not something that Rabindranath can endorse; it's likely that at some very deep level, he does not even understand what it means for his countrymen.

Through the cycle of poems we have considered in this chapter, Rabindranath develops the category of viraha, the longing born of separation, and the figure of the Yakṣa, transformed into a poetic symbol, as constant factors in his theory about the past, and about the relationship of the Indic self to history. To those versed in Indic literature, music, and art, viraha is a familiar enough category, written, sung, and painted through the ages. It is difficult to think of representations or theorizations of romantic and passionate love in the Indic imagination, from Bharata in the first century to Bollywood in the twenty-first century, absent viraha, a perennial theme. In the Indic context, viraha is usually understood as an index of the beauty and evocative power of any work of art that takes love as its subject, be it the love of man and woman, of deity and devotee, of guru and disciple, of Nature *(prakṛti)* and Consciousness *(puruṣa)*, or of the universal soul *(brāhman)* and the individual soul *(ātman)*. Indeed, across a range of Indic aesthetic and philosophical systems, any dyad on the order of Self and Other, both separated from one another and yearning for a reunion that may or may not be possible, can be understood as being in the rubric of viraha. Rabindranath's *Meghadūta* treatments stand squarely within a deeply entrenched and widely appreciated semiotic that is ubiquitous in Indic cultures.

What I am suggesting in this chapter and in this book, however, is that we be prepared to take viraha in a different direction, as I believe Rabindranath himself intended to do. In placing the Yakṣa, a symbol for the Indic self that all the founders sought in their different ways, at a far remove from Alakā, the celestial city and his long-lost home, Rabindranath reconceptualizes the yearning for history as a narrative of irremediable loss and unfulfilled longing, a tale of viraha with the drama of a separation that is undeserved and the pathos of a reunion that is thwarted. In this reading, viraha unexpectedly becomes a political category, signifying—in a manner open only to a poet of Rabindranath's stature—the sundering of the modern Indian from his traditions, of the nation from its past, and indeed of the very self of India from a teleological notion of perfectible history.

Rabindranath is questioning all metaphysics based on the idea of closure and perfection. Nationalism, understood in its Western sense, is grounded in such metaphysics. For Rabindranath, the nation cannot logically enfold within itself both the past (the home that the Yakṣa is in exile from) and the future (the home to which he wants to return). The Yakṣa speaks, in an outpouring of poiesis; there is in fact nothing he can do, by way of praxis, to attain his heart's desire. What is permissible, at best, is a dream journey to a remembered homeland, made through an imaginary friend like the rain-bearing cloud, carrying a message to the distraught beloved in the form of a poem whose beauty itself is the closest thing to happiness available in the human condition *(birāṭ dukkher pote ānander śudūr bhūmikā).*

Only a few decades after Rabindranath's death (in 1941), a politics premised on such a fundamental rejection of the interdependence between nationality and historical time, along with an absolute privileging of poiesis over praxis, is so remote from the Indian nation's self-understanding as to be practically unintelligible. The figure that Rabindranath calls "the India of the poet"—where by "poet" we should understand both Kalidasa and Rabindranath himself—is utterly, incommensurably at odds with the India of the nationalist. Rabindranath seeks to find ways to express (especially in language, and most of all in poetry) the truth of this India: he is not willing to see India as the object upon which he, or the British Raj, or Indian nationalists, or even the Indian people ought to exercise the will to power. So where does his symbol for the Indic self (swa-), the Yakṣa—forever at a far remove (dūrasaṃstha) from the place/person/time of his longing, out of his head *(anyathāvṛtticetas)* because of his exile from home, in the throes of inconsolable viraha born out of separation (viccheda) from all that is beloved to him—where does this Yakṣa stand with respect to the idea of sovereignty (raj)?

In Kalidasa's *Meghadūta,* we are told nothing whatsoever about the Yakṣa's lord and master *(bhartā),* whom he neglected to serve, and whose punishment (in the form of exile from Alakā to Rāmagiri) he must now endure. In classical mythology, the ruler of Alakā is Kubera, the god of riches, so we may assume that it is Kubera who has banished the Yakṣa for being forgetful of his responsibilities *(svādhikārapramattaḥ).* But while the poem starts off with the premise that the Yakṣa is losing his mind slightly, and has taken to talking to the clouds as soon as the rainy season approaches, it does not in any way explore the question of the judgment behind the Yakṣa's predicament. Rabindranath, too, does not search for the backstory—he does not ask, what did the Yakṣa do wrong, exactly, and who is the cruel person who has punished him thus? In other words, it is not important to Rabindranath to ask: What power, what agency, what heartless authority exiled the Indic self from India? Who placed the Indic self at a distance from its home, a distance that it may never be able to cover again?

A nationalist would immediately answer: the British have captured the city of Alakā, seized its riches, laid siege to its soaring palaces, and ousted its rightful inhabitants, like the Yakṣa. It is colonialism that has sundered Indians from their India, driven them from their home in the world and captured the beloved country for a foreign power, while its true residents yearn from afar and dream of a reunion that is never to be. But Rabindranath does not assign blame. All history, in his vision, is infused with pathos, and the history of India's unfortunate colonization is simply another instance of loss, separation, and longing that characterizes the very being of man in time, the embedding of societies in temporal structures that are partly natural givens and partly of human making. All history is aporetic, not just the history of colonialism. Poetry is the only passage. His response to the problem of sovereignty is not to fight back, not to resist or defy power, not to treat the beloved as a possession that must be won by force, taken back as she was snatched away—that is to say, his response is not any kind of praxis that may be understood as nationalist, as defending the nation. His response is to make present into form *(poiein)* the wonder *(adbhuta),* the pleasurable affect (rasa), and the potential for sheer tumultuous creativity in the human heart (in Bengali: *toroṅgito prāṇer probāho*) when it is thrown into a state of separation (viccheda).

For Tagore, a lifelong meditation on Kalidasa's poem *Meghadūta* became an important means by which to establish some relationship with ancient India, with the past as such, with the future, and with the very nature of the human experience of history. This experience was figured in and through the beloved country, the longed-for city, the friendly cloud, the majestic mountain, the playful river, but all of these constituted a "nation" only inasmuch as the "nation" became a map of emotions, deeply felt, sensuously experienced, imaginatively rendered. Nothing properly "historical" happened, strictly speaking, in this lovely land—no wars or revolutions, no migrations or settlements, no treaties or partitions, no colonization or independence. The ornate fancy of a talented poet, the passing of a lightning-flashing cloud over a verdant storied landscape, the lament of a human voice far from home, the jagged laughter of a three-eyed god—these are the elements that lead Tagore to history, and beyond history, to the very mystery of time itself. Time is in essence separation; separation produces pain; pain, poiesis; and poiesis is what constitutes the unending stream of human life in this world:

> God has granted that the Yakṣa may pound her do-or with yearning.
> He longs to sweep his beloved
> Away on the surging stream of his heart,
> Away from the motionless mounts of heaven
> Into the light of this many-colored, shadow-dappled mortal world.
> (“Yakṣa,” 31–35)

3

Abanindranath Tagore

Samvega, the Self's Shock

In the opening years of the twentieth century, Abanindranath Tagore (1871–1951), Rabindranath's nephew and a prominent artist living at the Tagore palazzo in Calcutta, Jorasanko, made a trio of paintings depicting the Emperor Shah Jahan (r. 1628–1658) at different stages of his life, together with his great monument to love, the Taj Mahal. Abanindranath painted Shah Jahan thinking about the Taj, then supervising its building, and finally, on his deathbed, gazing at it from a distance. The paintings were shown at the Durbar in Delhi in 1903, and one of them, *The Passing of Shah Jahan,* won the silver medal in a contest there.[1] The Durbar itself was a Mughal institution—it meant, literally, "holding court"—eagerly inherited by the British crown that controlled most of India. The British defeated Bahadur Shah Zafar in 1857–1858 and symbolically took over the court of the Mughals. The Delhi Durbar of 1903 marked the coronation of Edward VII as emperor of India. Abanindranath's works, displayed on this occasion, should have read like an ironic commentary on the evanescence of power and on the pathos of mortality that afflicts all human endeavor, even the greatest architectural project of one of the most powerful monarchs ever to rule India. In giving Abanindranath the prize, however, the British authorities evidently missed the irony altogether.

In his essay on Rabindranath's relationship to Orientalism and the Orient, Amit Chaudhuri describes Abanindranath's paintings as "faux Mughal," with "their life-blood partly in the kitschy, the popular."[2] He claims that this is a historically accurate description, rather than a value judgment, but it's difficult not to sense Chaudhuri's disapproval of what he sees as the unreconstructed Orientalism of Abanindranath's art—even if he grudgingly admits that the artist is considered to be "the father of modern Indian painting."[3] Several major art historians writing about Abanindranath and the Bengal School of painting associated with him and his students have examined in detail how he was trained and promoted by his teacher, E. B. Havell (1861–1934), and appropriated by Sister Nivedita (1867–1911). He thus became drawn, willy-nilly, into both Orientalist and nationalist projects that were unfolding in tandem in colonial Calcutta between roughly 1895 and 1915. Even Chaudhuri's incisive reading of the complex lifeworld of the Tagores and of their prodigious creative output as a family, which leads him to identify Rabindranath's Orientalism as "revisionist," does not give Abanindranath his due—quite the opposite.

The consensus in the art-historical scholarship seems to be that Abanindranath was a preeminent figure in his cultural context, but that he cannot by any means be counted as a truly gifted painter. Too much about his art reflects the influence of those with whom he was in conversation, from the first systematic historian of Indian art, the Englishman Havell, to Indian intellectuals involved in or disillusioned with Swadeshi politics like his uncle Rabindranath, to the Japanese painter Kakuzo Okakura who was trying to theorize "Asian" art, to his colleagues and acolytes at the Calcutta Art School, at the Bichitra Club in Jorasanko, and at Kala Bhavan, the art department at Visva-bharati University, many of whom became increasingly enamored of the traditional arts of Bengal.[4] That such a diverse range of understandings about the importance of pictorial and sculptural arts for Indian nationalism could all converge at the Jorasanko house and in Santiniketan is a testament to Abanindranath's role as a magnet for vanguard thinking about art in his day and age. Alas, it is also a reason, in the eyes of most critics, for regarding his work as a clear glass through which to see the ideas of others, rather than admiring it as a fountainhead of original images reflecting a genius all his own.

Ananda K. Coomaraswamy (1877–1947), the part-British part–Sri Lankan thinker who pioneered the history of South Asian and Southeast Asian art, worked as a geologist and mineralogist in Sri Lanka, and collected and curated Indian art in Boston, as well as writing important works of philosophy, philology, and religious studies that ranged widely over Indian and European languages, was a close contemporary of Abanindranath. Coomaraswamy was a polymath of the kind that modern South Asia has had too few of—in this sense he is comparable, paradoxically, to his near-exact contemporary, the poet-philosopher-politician Muhammad Iqbal (1877–1938) on the one hand, and on the other hand to the much younger mathematician-historian-archaeologist-Marxist D. D. Kosambi (1907–1966). They had little in common with one another politically, to be sure, but they shared a scope and a depth of knowledge seen in just a handful of others in the first half of the twentieth century.[5] Interestingly, all three men—gigantic intellects and powerful shapers of the culture—are poorly understood in the intellectual history of modern South Asia.

It is fashionable nowadays to be wary of Coomaraswamy, to consider him a reactionary and thus keep a distance from him. This could be because of the knitting together, in his thought, of a number of strands, all of which make contemporary scholars uncomfortable: a frank exploration of forms of cognition and emotion that we may call religious, an impetus to define and theorize the classical, an approach to texts through words (i.e., through readings that are fundamentally etymological and philological), and a comparative virtuosity that post-Orientalist Indology simply does not engender in students of premodernity. It is likely our own inadequacy that makes us shrink from Coomaraswamy.[6]

Coomaraswamy did get involved, briefly, with the whirlwind of post-Swadeshi cultural politics in Calcutta, but much of his life was divided between England, Sri Lanka, and, after 1917, the United States. This made him only an indirect participant in the founding of India, else what he did for Indian art history as a discipline would surely qualify him to be counted as one of the founding fathers. He first visited India in 1907, returning again in 1909 to spend the next three or four years in the country, braiding his art-historical and nationalist agendas tightly together during one of the most exciting and productive phases in India's long battle against colonialism. (Coomaraswamy was not, strictly speaking, Indian, but this fact seems not to have hampered his sympathy for Indian nationalism in any way.) He died in 1947, or it would not be hard to imagine Nehru wanting to bring him back to the subcontinent to, say, head the Archaeological Survey of India or build up one of the major museums in Delhi or elsewhere. According to his son Rama Coomaraswamy, he had wanted to retire from the Museum of Fine Arts in Boston, return to South Asia and take *sannyāsa,* but death cut short his plans.[7]

Here I invoke Coomaraswamy not as an intellectual in his own right (well though he deserves in-depth scholarly treatment), but in a reconsideration and repositioning of the art of his contemporary Abanindranath, who to my mind has not received the critical attention due to him in any global account of the ideas that were key to the founding of the Indian republic.[8] In one of his numerous short essays, really not much longer than a note, published in a Harvard journal in 1943, Coomaraswamy explicates the Pali word "samvega" that he translates as "aesthetic shock."[9] I dwell below at some length on the meaning of samvega. To anticipate my larger argument, I want to suggest that Abanindranath's Shah Jahan paintings, in particular, are expressions of precisely the "aesthetic shock" he experienced—as a viewer, an artist, an ideologue, a Bengali, and an Indian—when looking at the Taj Mahal, when looking at Mughal miniature paintings, and when thinking, through the Taj as well as through Mughal miniatures, about the promise and the loss of a truly Indian art in light of India's colonization by the British. Parenthetically I read Rabindranath's poem "Shah Jahan" (1914/1916) as a companion piece to his nephew's paintings, though it appears to have been written ten to fifteen years after the artworks it resonates with.[10]

The existing scholarship in English takes Abanindranath seriously as an art theorist, an institution builder, a major nationalist (and yet never a chauvinist), and a hub for Bengali, Indian, Asian, and European art practice as well as for the exchange of ideas across significant cultures of modern art and artistic experimentation throughout the pre-Independence period. But his critics—Guha-Thakurta, Mitter, and even Banerji—are concerned, almost anxious, one might say, about the numerous influences upon Abanindranath, and the ripple effects of his being serially taken up with different kinds of art (Western, Japanese, Chinese, Persian, Buddhist, Rajput, Mughal, or tribal Bengali) upon his disciples and peers. He learned so much from so many sources, evolved so continuously as an artist and thinker, and painted in such a bewildering array of styles over the course of five decades that it might seem patently impossible to discover in his oeuvre a single answer to his search for an Indic "self": the search we are assuming underlies the efforts of all of the founders discussed in this book.

"From our reading of his oeuvre," writes Siva Kumar drily at the end of his monumental catalog-cum-commentary on Abanindranath Tagore, "it is evident that there is more than one Abanindranath."[11] Of course, the heterogeneous nature of his art means that we have difficulty placing him in any one tradition, even in an Indic tradition, one that is already imagined as being mixed, complex, and multivalent, thanks to the very nature of Indian history in which Indian art is embedded. Abanindranath tried his hand at a vast variety of techniques and ended up making all sorts of art, from landscapes to portraiture, from illustrations for children's books to nationalist icons, from grand historical tableaux to scenes depicting his family members in domestic settings, from ornate Orientalist fantasies to atmospheric glimpses of nature in Bengal and neighboring Orissa. Siva Kumar does much to establish Abanindranath as a leading, if not the foremost, narrative painter of the twentieth century, at least in India and possibly even in the entire British Empire.

* * *

Coomaraswamy defines samvega thus: "The Pali word *samvega* is used to denote the shock or wonder that may be felt when the perception of a work of art becomes a serious experience."[12] He goes on to list a number of related words in Pali and Sanskrit, found in Buddhist and Vedic sources, which together map a semantic domain that Coomaraswamy explains as an experience with two stages: the first emotional, the subsequent one cognitive; the first, whereby we have a sensation, and immediately thereafter the second, whereby we understand a meaning. He recounts a few stories from the Buddhist literature that gloss the family of words springing from the root *vij-*, denoting "agitation." He explains that it is somewhat like a horse being whipped—one moment is the physical impact of the lashing, and following that, the horse recognizes that it must do something, run faster, perhaps (which it does right away, if it has been properly trained). The term "samvega" integrates this staggered (and staggering) experiential moment:

> *Samvega,* then, refers to the experience that may be felt in the presence of a work of art, when we are struck by it, as a horse might be struck by a whip. It is, however, assumed, that like the good horse we are more or less trained, and hence, that more than a merely physical shock is involved; the blow has a *meaning* for us, and the realization of that meaning, in which nothing of the physical sensation survives, is still a part of the shock. These two phases of the shock are, indeed, normally felt together as parts of an instant experience; but they can be logically distinguished, and . . . it is with the latter aspect of the shock that we are chiefly concerned. . . . In the deepest experience that can be induced by a work of art (or other reminder) our very being is shaken *(samvijita)* to its roots.[13]

He goes on to speak of the self "being completely dissolved and broken up," of "the body-blow," of "the thunderbolt"—all as means to convey the samvega delivered to us by certain works, whether artistic or intellectual or musical. This same order of comprehension carries over into the domain of experience that we may call "religious"—hence the Buddhist *vajra* (thunderbolt), and St. Augustine, whom he quotes: "O axe, hewing the rock!"[14] Coomaraswamy does not elaborate, and we need not be detained here by the meanings of samvega in spiritual contexts. The important point he makes is that the real cause of this aesthetic shock—this sudden, hard-hitting, physically palpable eruption of knowledge produced in our minds when we encounter a genuinely significant work of art—is that we are, and we know that we are, in that moment, in the presence of truth. Only one who is ready may feel samvega, for "this shock can be felt only if we have learned to recognize the truth when we see it."[15] The word samvega, then enfolds the experience of beauty and the knowledge of truth, but in a manner that captures the jolt we feel when we come face-to-face with a beautiful, indeed perfect, intimation of that which is true. Anyone who has experienced art (or music, or mathematics, or language) in this way recognizes what Coomaraswamy is talking about. This is aesthetic shock.

Abandindranath's Shah Jahan triad, to my mind, is supposed to convey samvega: the aesthetic shock that the painter experienced in his encounter with Indian history, particularly the history of Indian art, as expressed through both the Mughal miniature form and the sublime architectural form of the Taj Mahal. As a matter of fact, Abanindranath went on to paint a number of works depicting the Mughals, specifically the great emperors Jahangir (r. 1605–1627) and Aurangzeb "Alamgir" (r. 1658–1707). He also painted the tragic figures of Dara Shikoh (1615–1659) (Aurangzeb's older brother and heir apparent, whom he had assassinated) and Bahadur Shah Zafar (1775–1862), the last Mughal, who was defeated and imprisoned by the British in 1857, and made to endure the execution of his sons in Delhi, eventually dying in captivity in a jail in Burma five miserable years later.[16]

Far from being an expression of kitsch, an Orientalist reflex, a programmatic appropriation of an especially high moment in precolonial Indian art, or an ideologically driven revivalism of the Mughal miniature form, Abanindranath's engagement with Shah Jahan and other protagonists of the Mughal dynasty is, in my view, at the very heart of his reaction to the history of India and its traditions of representational painting. *Shah Jahan Dreaming of the Taj Mahal, The Building of the Taj Mahal,* and *The Passing of Shah Jahan* all show us, not the Taj Mahal directly or in detail, nor Shah Jahan alone, but the emperor in the act of looking at the Taj—"looking," that is to say, with his imagination, with his memory, as well as with his physical eyes, at a structure that stands for a number of things at once: his undying love for his dead queen, Mumtaz Mahal; his own erstwhile prowess as a monarch, once able to commission and supervise the building of so magnificent a monument; the fleeting nature of human life contrasted with the abiding nature of beauty itself; the political power and aesthetic refinement of the Mughals, rulers of Hindustan such as were never seen before or since; and last but not least, the facticity, the the eternity, the intransigence, of Death.

Mitter recounts how a contemporary of Abanindranath made fun of his drawing skills, saying that Shah Jahan's horse, in *Shah Jahan Dreaming of the Taj Mahal,* looked rather like "a cross between a rat and a pig."[17] We have already noted that in our own time Chaudhuri calls Abanindranath's style "faux Mughal."[18] Mitter sees in the Shah Jahan trilogy more of an "archaeological" exercise on the part of Abanindranath, vis-à-vis Indian art, than an expression of genuine inspiration.[19] All the historians discuss the combination of Mughal form, Western humanism, a Sanskritic theory of *bhāva* or emotion, and Japanese wash techniques in these works, so that what stands out about them is their hybridity, not their intrinsic and integrated impulse, as it were.

Mention is made of the death of Abanindranath's young daughter in the Calcutta plague of 1902, an incident that by the painter's own admission had left him depressed and filled with thoughts of mortality as he worked on *The Passing of Shah Jahan,* showing the emperor's daughter Jahanara sitting at the foot of his deathbed. Mitter, Guha-Thakurta, and Siva Kumar also devote considerable attention to Abanindranath's historicism, to his nationalism, and to the ways in which his work was consistently drawn into the prevalent polemic about Indian art (re)discovering itself and finding its distinct identity in a colonial milieu. None of these readings is incorrect—we might even say that all of them are accurate—but, from the point of view of the significance of these paintings as indicators of a quest for the Indic self, all of the critics, I think, miss the point.

Abanindranath was shaken to his very roots (*samvijita,* in Coomaraswamy's explanation) by a vision, a panorama, an immense horizon of a possible art in which one could conceive of Indic understandings of power, death, love, beauty, and so on, conveyed via a system of signs and meanings proper to them, and standing apart from the overbearing conventions of European art. To judge whether Abanindranath's formative/transformative samvega came out of his ten years of study at the Calcutta Sanskrit College (1881–1890), or his engagement with E. B. Havell (whom he took to be his guru, between 1896–1897 and 1906, when Havell left India for good), or his first exposure to Mughal miniatures and to the Ajanta cave paintings, one would have to be a psychoanalyst. Whenever it was—and it could have been over a long period of time—that Abanindranath understood the very possibility of the existence of an Indian art even under colonial rule, he set about trying to create it. The Shah Jahan paintings are an early, and to my eyes rather pure, instantiation of this understanding. Both their technical shortcomings and their formal accomplishments are equally unimportant. They embody their maker's aesthetic shock and, by doing so, reveal to us that he was really after, and really onto, something else, something in the nature of an Indic imagination articulated in an Indic idiom: the contours, in other words, of an Indic self.

I would even go so far as to hazard that the reason that Abanindranath's work and that of his school of painting appealed so much to the general public was because people could recognize in it a truth that he and his disciples had glimpsed. The recognition of truth, as Coomaraswamy reminds us, is an integral part, the trigger as well as the lasting residue, of the experience of samvega. Although they could only express themselves through scholarly histories, in specialist language, Havell and Coomaraswamy too struggled to articulate the spirit, the separateness, the specificity, and the quiddity of Indian art. And because Abanindranath, Havell, Coomaraswamy, and many others—Nandalal Bose, Annie Besant, Asit Haldar, Sister Nivedita, and so on—were trying to say, for the first time ever, not just that there is an Indian art, but also what that Indian art had been through the ages, and what it could be once again in the present and future, their chosen task was by no means easy. Academic histories of the revolution in Indian art in early twentieth-century Bengal lose sight of the utter originality and hence sheer difficulty of the project at hand.

A 1915 issue of a Calcutta journal, *The Modern Review,* carries a small piece by the historian Jadunath Sarkar, titled "The Passing of Shah Jahan."[20] Abanindranath's work by the same title, painted thirteen years earlier, is the frontispiece of this issue of the magazine. Sarkar's account reconstructs the last seven years of Shah Jahan's life, from 1658 to 1666. In this period, Shah Jahan was imprisoned in Agra Fort by his son Aurangzeb, subjected to neglect as well as mental and physical abuse, divested of his considerable property, continuously spied upon, repeatedly insulted to his face and in writing, and forced to stand by helplessly as Aurangzeb had two of his brothers, including the crown prince and Shah Jahan's favorite son, Dara Shikoh, eliminated. He became very pious during his final years in captivity and was cared for by his daughter, Jahanara Begum (the female figure in Abanindranath's painting). When he passed away after a brief illness in 1666, his body was denied a grand funeral and instead buried very quietly and simply in the Taj Mahal, in a grave alongside his dead wife, Mumtaz Mahal. Not only did Aurangzeb not come to the burial; he did not even come to pay his respects to the grieving Jahanara until a month later.

Sarkar presents a chronicle of the aged and incarcerated Shah Jahan that is filled with pathos. We cannot help thinking, along with the historian: what a sad end to the life of a Great Mughal! While Sarkar's reconstruction of events is based on a number of contemporary records, it seems obvious that Abanindranath's image of the death of Shah Jahan directly influences the historian's view. The section that describes the passing of the emperor is titled "The Dying Scene":

> Early in the night of Monday, 22nd January, his condition was declared hopeless, and the end was expected at any moment. At the news that death was near, Shah Jahan thanked God for all the gifts and favours received in life and proclaimed his resignation to the will of the Maker. With perfect composure, he gave directions for his funeral, offered consolation to his surviving wives, . . . his eldest daughter Jahanara, and other ladies of the harem who were weeping round his bed, and asked Jahanara to look after her half-sister. . . . Next, he made his will, took leave of his family and servants, giving them his last presents and keepsakes, and ordered the *Quran* to be read. Finally, while the sacred verses were being solemnly intoned, amidst the wails of the women and the sobs of his attendants, Shah Jahan, retaining full consciousness to the last and gazing on the resting-place of his beloved and long-lost Mumtaz Mahal, repeated the Muslim confession of faith, and murmured the prayer,
>
> "O God! Make my condition good in this world and the next, and save me from the torments of hell-fire!"
>
> A moment later he sank peacefully into his eternal rest.
>
> It was quarter past seven in the evening. The body lay in the octagonal tower . . . where life had departed, in full view of the Taj Mahal, where he wished his mortal remains to mingle with those of his queen.[21]

The close correspondence between this word picture by Sarkar and *The Passing of Shah Jahan* need hardly be underscored. The scene in Abanindranath's rendering, after circulating for more than a decade in the public sphere, had become one with the historical truth as it was imagined by the leading historian of the times. The painting and the history were published together in *The Modern Review* as means of representing one and the same historical fact in two media: language and art. They illustrated one another, so to speak, and they were meant to convey the same—true—thing, in different ways. The sickness of Shah Jahan, the closeness of Jahanara, the view of the Taj, the time of evening, the winter's cold, the spare furnishings, and the helplessness of one who had been the emperor of Hindustan are essential, irreducible elements of both Abanindranath and Sarkar's reconstructions, and through them, of history itself, to the extent that the past can ever be known by those, like us, who live in a future time.

* * *

In 1916, as part of the collection titled *Balākā,* Rabindranath published a poem titled "Shah-Jahan." This poem was probably written in 1914, that is, soon after Rabindranath won his Nobel Prize for literature, the first in Asia. Abanindranath's painting, Sarkar's history, and Rabindranath's poem all return to the same subject: the passing of Shah Jahan, and each one of these is a work beautiful in its own medium and in its own way. According to Rabindranath's translator, William Radice: "The mixture of form and freedom in the verse of the poem is . . . the key to its meaning—indeed I can think of no other poem in which form is so completely wedded to content."[22] A little later he writes: "Perhaps it is necessary to have seen the Taj Mahal to appreciate fully a poem which so uniquely captures its beauty and atmosphere."[23] There can be no doubt that both Sarkar's historical account and Rabindranath's poem are in dialogue with Abanindranath's painting, so closely do the three works resemble one another, and such is the unity of mood between them.

Rabindranath's "Shah-Jahan" is addressed directly to the emperor and chides him for seeking "To conquer time's heart / Through beauty" (ll. 43–44). The Taj Mahal, radiant, pearlescent, is "one solitary tear" that the grief-stricken Shah Jahan hopes will "hang on the cheek of time" (ll. 15–16).

> How wonderful the deathless clothing
> With which you invested
> Formless death . . . ! (ll. 45–47)

> Poet-Emperor,
> This is your heart's picture,
> Your new *Meghadūta* . . . (ll. 59–61)

This beauty is your messenger,
Skirting time's sentries
To carry the wordless message:
"I have not forgotten you, my love, I have not forgotten you." (ll. 71–74)

But Shah Jahan cannot change the logic of human history, of human love, or of human memory, all of which follow the arrow of time. They go hurtling into a heedless futurity, as though borne along by a river in full flood: from *ghāṭ* to *ghāṭ,* as the poet says, in a memorable image that is hard to translate from the Bengali, although Radice comes as close as possible to the sense and the music of the original lines:

O human heart,
You have no time
To look back at anyone again,
No time.
You are driven by life's quick spate
On and on from landing to landing,
Loading cargo here,
Unloading there. (ll. 19–26)

The emperor's once awesome temporal power is powerless in the greater imperium of time. His armies are scattered, his throne shattered, his servants dead, his harem vanished; his empire "has dissolved like a dream" (l. 76). Rabindranath means to invoke the ages; of course we know from Sarkar's account that for Shah Jahan, things had come to such a pass even within his lifetime, right in front of his very eyes. But Rabindranath takes a further step away from this scenario of loss, death, and grief: in the ultimate reckoning, he says, not only does history escape Shah Jahan, but Shah Jahan, too, escapes the "ever-falling darkness / Of history" (ll. 100–101).[24] "You kicked this world away / Like a used clay vessel" (ll. 119–20). For Shah Jahan, like every being, is not his body, not his works, not his feelings, but a soul that cannot be shackled by emotion, remembrance, commemoration, space, time, or any of the constraints of creaturely existence. At the very end of the poem, it is the Taj Mahal that speaks, and it says of its maker:

"That traveller is no longer here, no longer here.

I remain here, weighted with memory:
He is free of burdens; he is no longer here." (ll. 140, 148–149)

Abanindranath, Sarkar, and Rabindranath all seem to be spiraling in ever-widening loops away from any kind of straightforward allegory about the mortality of the flesh, the immortality of a thing of beauty, the capacities and incapacities of power, and the persistence or the frailty of love. They seem also to be distancing themselves from an obvious commentary about the nature of the Mughal Empire or by analogy the British Empire—although such a commentary could indeed be read into these three meditations on the passing of Shah Jahan.

In Rabindranath's poem, the reflection is deeper than in Abanindranath's painting; it probes further into history's ever-falling darkness, until it comes out on the other side into an uninterrupted, eternal light where life "breaks / The knot of memory and runs / Free along universal tracks" (ll. 111–113). The nephew's painting lingers at the very last look that Shah Jahan casts toward the Taj Mahal, and thus toward his past, his earthly life, his love for Mumtaz Mahal who is gone, his empire, his might, all of which are behind him. We look at Jahanara, who looks at the emperor, who looks at the Taj, and there, at the world's most beautiful tomb, the line of sight stops. Death absorbs all visions that are directed toward the marble domes and minarets glimmering white in the moonlit distance. In the uncle's poem, however, the Taj too has a voice, it returns the gaze, it speaks back to us, and it tells us that Shah Jhan, emperor of Hindustan and world's most devoted lover, has transcended his memories, his mourning, his monument, and his mortal coil.

Tombs remain forever with the dust of this earth:
It is death
That they carefully preserve in the casing of memory.
But who can hold life?
The stars claim it: they call it to the sky,
Invite it to new worlds, to the light
Of new dawns. (ll. 104–110)

Abanindranath's focus is on Shah Jahan, while his Taj Mahal is a smallish, vaguely delineated form far away (across the Yamuna River?); Rabindranath gives equal attention to Shah Jahan and to the Taj, devoting to it some lovely lines—"The poignant gentleness of love / Flowered into the beauty of serene stone" (ll. 57–58), "your tireless, incorruptible messenger" (l. 89)—more musical and striking yet in Bengali than they are in English. For Sarkar, the historian, the Taj is merely the place where Mumtaz Mahal is buried and eventually her husband's body will also be placed, beside hers. Although the two Tagores and Jadunath Sarkar treat the same historical episode in different—if related—ways, in my view they all share the original aesthetic shock that makes them return to this moment, this scene, this center, each one in his own medium. It is Abanindranath who is first hit by the samvega; but the shock waves keep on traveling outward and are felt by Sarkar and by Rabindranath, one after the other, throughout a period of several years.

Abanindranath himself, too, made a number of paintings about the Great Mughals over time, processing historical events as well as the individualized characters of the emperors. One—rather disturbing—painting depicts Aurangzeb poking the head of his decapitated brother, Dara Shikoh, with the point of his sword.[25] Another shows Shah Jahan as an old—but not yet dying—man.[26] Two others, as already mentioned, show Shah Jahan on horseback imagining the Taj before it is made, and later gazing out at it, as it stands half-built in the distance. There is a painting of Jahangir (r. 1605–1627) walking in his garden, smelling a flower; and three of Aurangzeb at different ages in his life, young, old, and very old.[27] But though the Shah Jahan triad is moving as a whole, none of these other paintings really concentrate their meditative force, their mood, and the primacy of idea over image like *The Passing of Shah Jahan*. This one work, to my mind, works, as it were, because it embodies the painter's experience of samvega. No wonder it launched Abanindranath's career as a major painter, and launched, moreover, the entire Bengal School of Swadeshi painting that was to dominate Indian art for the next two or three decades.

* * *

Does it make sense, then, to think of samvega as a category in political theory, when we are trying to understand exactly what was going on in the world of art during the period normally characterized as Swadeshi Bengal? I think this the case. Coomaraswamy does not place samvega in a political frame: he is interested in the original contexts in which this word or its variants occur, and these all happen to be aesthetic or religious. But I am indeed advocating that we reconsider Abanindranath, the father of modern Indian art, and undoubtedly a major cultural nationalist of his time, as someone who, from the 1890s onward, was in the throes of a deep aesthetic shock, moved by a prescience, an intimation, and eventually, a certain knowledge of the *svatva* (selfness) of Indic art. Throughout his career as a painter he struggled to find the appropriate forms, the images, and the techniques as well as a coherent, objectively verifiable history of representational art that would allow him to put forward exactly what might be meant by the idea of "Indian art." Many of his paintings may be read (and have been read) for the signs of his quest for the Indic selfhood of art; I have chosen three in the Shah Jahan series both because they are relatively early and because they convey in a primordial, undiluted fashion the lightning bolt of truth felt by Abanindranath that he was able to subdue and channel more masterfully in later work.

In this search for an Indic tradition and an Indic idiom, Abanindranath inevitably turned to some of the best-known stories and characters that could be found in Indian literature, mythology, religion, and history, and set about illustrating familiar textual narrations with novel pictorial depictions. He also simultaneously relied upon his contemporary art historian friends and colleagues, who were during the same years writing the first accounts of Indian art through the ages, to supply a chronology as well as geography of styles and themes. His milieu in colonial Bengal was predominantly Orientalist, and Abanindranath, though brilliant in his own way, did not have his uncle Rabindranath's unique ability to withstand the force of Orientalism and to develop a highly individual, fiercely non-conformist approach to the Indic past. In fact many, if not most, Indian Indologist scholars, artists, and intellectuals in places like Calcutta and Poona in the early twentieth century were Orientalists to some degree or other: this does not mean we dismiss their historicism, their philology, or their politics as being in bad faith. Colonized nationalists are often Orientalists: this ought to be taken as a sort of *sūtra* of colonial history.

Abanindranath became the center of the renaissance in Indian art from about the turn of the twentieth century. He set the agenda in several ways:

thematically, because of the kinds of subjects that he chose to paint; stylistically, because of the techniques that he both used himself and taught to his students; institutionally, because of the schools and salons of art that he either headed or founded; theoretically, because of his writings and publicly expressed views on art; and finally, ideologically, because of his dealings with all of the major practitioners, historians, ideologues, and institution builders of the times who had anything whatsoever to do with Indian art. In addition to his prominent, indeed towering presence in the world of art and aesthetics, he was also directly involved in nationalist political activity, especially during the Swadeshi movement (c. 1900–1910). From about 1900 to 1925, Abanindranath and his mentors and disciples dominated the world of Indian art from Calcutta. Guha-Thakurta and Mitter have told his story in most excellent accounts, so I need not reprise here the details of his career as a painter, a teacher, and a "public artist"—by which I mean the counterpart to a public intellectual in the realm of art.[28]

Soon after *The Passing of Shah Jahan,* Abanindranath made the painting titled *Bhārat Mātā (Mother India)* that immediately became the very symbol of Swadeshi around the Partition of Bengal in 1905. Rabindranath endorsed this image, for in many ways he inspired its production. His poem "Dream" (1897; discussed at length in Chapter 2), for all its dreamlike abruptness, its lapse into silence, its abject sundering of lover and beloved, was part of an ongoing effort on his part, as well as one that on occasion overflowed from his own imagination and entered into the larger aesthetic and intellectual milieu surrounding him. Abanindranath often channeled some of his uncle's most powerful poetic images. In his painting *Mother India,* the figure depicted—a young woman, simply clad in a saffron-colored sari—has the four arms of a goddess, but in her four hands she carries grain, cloth, a manuscript, and a rosary, the signs of food, clothing, education, and religion. Not one of these is a weapon. Traditionally, the mother goddess in Bengal—Kālī, Durgā, Bhavānī, or Caṇḍī—would have four or eight arms and carry a different weapon in each hand, wear a necklace of skulls, ride a lion or a tiger, and tower over the bodies of slain demons or a prostrate Śiva.[29]

Abanindranath's goddess is far from bloodthirsty. She looks not only like a real woman, but also almost wifely, and the objects she holds all symbolize civic life and social goods. Her eyes are calm, not large and intense. Her tongue does not hang out of her mouth and her teeth are not bared, nor does her hair fly in all directions. She can be imagined in a home or in a monastery, not in a temple or on a cremation ground. There is nothing wild or ferocious about her—she conveys serenity, not power. Except for the color of her sari (saffron) and her two extra arms, she is quite far from Hindu iconography and Bengali Śākta semiotics. I would read the human proportions, the social orientation, the modesty, the youth, the simplicity, and the docility of this Mother India as indicative of a strong affinity between Abanindranath's image and Rabindranath's ideas.

Contrary to our expectations, what is sought to be depicted is a reformist rather than a powerful figure, a female who is familial or ascetic but not erotic or divine, a homely icon of social pedagogy and moral values, not a flamboyant deity of cosmic justice. When I say "contrary to our expectations," I mean our expectations of how a certain kind of militant nationalism might seek to express itself through art. Abanindranath's *Mother India* expresses what I take to be Rabindranath's overwhelmingly social concerns, his almost complete disregard for politics proper. She reminds her followers of the necessity to reform their *samāj* (social body), rather than change their *sarkār* (government). Her primary function is pedagogical and not retributive. The four items in her hands answer the material and moral needs of her devotees, but do not arm them against an oppressive colonial regime.

Readers today may compare the Bhartiya Janata Party's warlike images of the god Ram and his simian companion Hanuman with Abanindranath's placid *Bhārat Mātā* to see immediately the striking difference between the social affect of Tagore's Swadeshi and the political passion of Hindu nationalism in our own time. To my mind Abanindranath was deeply influenced by Rabindranath's understanding of Swadeshi, so that his slender and serene goddess seems to convey the same mood as his uncle's lyric poems, evoking a gentle, undulating land that will feed, clothe, educate, and spiritually nurture its people, without any reference to enemies or tyrants, without any need for fear or violence. During the rise of the Swadeshi movement, it was Rabindranath who led mass processions in which posters of Abanindranath's painting were carried, and Bankim's anthem, "Bande Mātaram," was sung on the streets. The poet and his associates reached out to the poor, to Muslims, to people perceived as being possible participants in social and political conflict, and tied friendship bands (known as *rākhī*) on their wrists, as if to seal a promise of mutual protection and care.

The Tagorean *Bhārat Mātā* does not trample anyone underfoot; she does not frighten anyone with her terrible wrath, nor slay anyone with her invincible weaponry. White lotuses are scattered at her feet; a glowing halo surrounds her face; a soft radiance envelops her. In fact, regarded correctly, she is not a religious nationalist symbol at all, at least not in the way in which we understand religion and politics to be connected with one another, via the ligature of violence, in post-globalization India. At most, she might be called an icon of cultural nationalism. Mother India assimilates neither to Hindu nor to Hindutva semiotics—she has a unique character that makes sense only in Swadeshi Bengal, only in a symbolic order that Rabindranath did so much to create single-handedly, with some help, in this case, from his talented nephew.

The Swadeshi interlude in Bengali politics, from 1900–1901 to 1911–1912, was one of the earliest political movements after the founding of the Indian National Congress in 1885 and before the launch of Mahatma Gandhi's nationwide agitations around 1919. Rabindranath was doubtless one, if not the major, protagonist of the Swadeshi movement until the outbreak of violence between Hindus and Muslims and the Partition of Bengal by the British authorities in 1905. It was he who first set Bankim's lyric "Bande Mātaram" (which Martha Nussbaum calls by the inadvertently amusing phrase "the Chatterjee anthem") to music and sang it at a session of the Congress in Calcutta in 1896.[30] The order for Partition was later rescinded, but by then Rabindranath had long recoiled from what he saw as the communally divisive nature of Swadeshi politics and from its inability to account for the interests of the poor and minority groups. The full complexity of his reactions to both the passions and the costs of Swadeshi is laid out in the love triangle of his novel *Ghare Baire* (The Home and the World, 1916), where the personal happiness of the heroine Bimala turns on her political judgment.[31] In the event, judgment comes to her too late. By the time she realizes that moral rectitude may not necessarily lie with the politics of anticolonial resistance, especially when such resistance comes at the price of communal strife and class conflict, she has lost both her marriage and her love.[32]

Rabindranath's nuanced view of human, social, and political ties at a moment when Bengal and India were clashing head-on with the British Raj was not greeted with appreciation and understanding from his contemporaries. In his novel, the Swadeshi radical Sandip is a demagogue, an adulterer, insensitive to and exploitative of the vulnerabilities of others, and ultimately a coward. The educated Westernized aristocrat Nikhilesh actually turns out to be a progressive husband, a real patriot, and a protective landlord for his dependent populations. It is Bimala who, like the author, like Bengal and like India, must learn, very slowly and painfully, to recognize wherein lies a true politics of nation making, resistance to oppression, and personal as well as national liberation. The marital/romantic dyad of man and woman, the family, the village, the community, the province of Bengal, and the nation of India, all form a series of concentric circles, and political life begins at the core before moving outward from the home to embrace the world. That Rabindranath was charting a political continuum at a time when Bengali *bhadralok* society practiced a strict division between public and private spheres, as Chatterjee has shown, naturally made him as well as his novel at the very least controversial, if not outright unpopular.[33]

All this is well known. What is significant, to my mind, is that Rabindranath's apparent change of heart with respect to the Swadeshi movement can be read back into many of his pronouncements even during the period when he was still directly involved with it. That is to say, from the very beginning, he was interested in Swadeshi less as a means to displace British rule and establish self-rule by Bengalis (or Indians more widely), less as a direct challenge to imperialism and colonialism, than as an alternative form of economics and politics. He saw Swadeshi as an occasion for elite Bengal to become involved with rural development, new forms of education, strategies for economic self-reliance at the village level, local governance reform, social pedagogy, the welfare of weaker sections, and the building of stronger ties between different caste and religious groups that lived together in traditional settings. In Rabindranath's vision, all of this was a way for India to take care of her social fabric regardless of the larger struggle for power between colonial subjects and imperial rulers. He was not taken up with the romance of the state, as it were. The real challenge, according to him, lay in the collective life of the *samāj* or society, not in the workings of the *sarkār* or government.[34]

The very word *samāj* is an indicator of how Rabindranath conceived of social relations. A *samāj* is not a unit of governance, not the entity over which the state exercises sovereign power, but rather an organic community structured according to rules internal to it—rules that have to do with hierarchy, affect, and the necessities of group survival and group flourishing. Literally, *samāj* means "[a group of people] arisen together," "coexistent," "coproduced," with connotations of harmony, integration, limits to and guidelines for personal conduct, and a collective destiny. A caste group can be a *samāj*. A professional group can be a *samāj*. A religious group can be a *samāj*. Even a multireligious, multiracial, and multicaste entity like India can be a *samāj*, provided that difference is subsumed under a principle of what Tagore calls "hospitality." Whatever community, organized according to birth, or work, or habitation, or belief, is relevant to an individual; whatever community is the reference, the frame, and the regulator of an individual's material and moral life; whatever community both produces and is produced by the individual in relation to other individuals; that community is the individual's *samāj*.

Tagore was interested in what Indians could do to improve their *samāj*, over and above what happened at the level of *sarkār*. His Santiniketan (literally, "Abode of Peace"), first established in 1901 and formalized in stages until the launch of the Visva-bharati University in 1921, should be seen as the Arcadian, apolitical social body that in many ways exemplifies Rabindranath's beliefs about *samāj*.[35] *Samāj* is hospitable; *sarkār* is disciplinary. *Samāj* is one's own; *sarkār* is imposed upon one. In a sense, the British Raj did not enter into organic social life at all. Since the Raj was removed from *samāj* and concentrated in *sarkār*, Indians were in fact already free to rule themselves by regulating and reforming the realm of the social.

> The seat of life of different civilizations is differently placed in the body politic. Where the responsibility for the welfare of the people lies, there beats the heart of the nation; and if a blow should fall thereon, the whole nation is wounded unto death. In England the overthrow of the state would mean destruction for the nation. But disaster can only overtake our country when its social body, its *Samāj*, is crippled.[36]

Just as a *samāj* has its modes of coming into being and of staying together—hospitality, integration, harmony—there are also forms of pedagogy, mobilization, and politics proper to it. These, for Tagore, include the village fair *(melā)*, the dramatic performance *(jātrā)*, the recitation of epics and moral narratives *(kathā)*, the chanting and singing of religious songs *(kīrtan)*, the Hindu sacrificial ritual *(yajña)*, and other forms of communal entertainment and mass praxis that connect people to each other, to other groups, to their shared religious and social beliefs and values, and to the very principles of collective coexistence.[37] The *melā* embodies the indigenous public sphere, as opposed to the English-style political "meeting" that educated Bengalis in Calcutta might call in order to gather together and debate political issues. The *melā* therefore is the most suitable platform for social and political pedagogy. It is a culturally appropriate space and time for conversation, communion, festivity, and, in the midst of all this, education. Tagore exhorts Swadeshi activists to visit the *melā* that occurs regularly in the countryside, and to disseminate their political message at this gathering of ordinary folk that is a natural form of associational life for them.[38]

Samāj and *melā* are categories that Rabindranath explicates at some length, because in his view, in recognizing and strengthening these native forms of social being, politics, and educational activity, India can develop her *śakti,* her inner strength, her moral fortitude, her vital force of unity and cohesion, which is ultimately the key to genuine liberation. Given that these were Tagore's ideas for what a political movement should be about—popular pedagogy, social uplift, rural reconstruction, the revival of village industries, and other forms of self-help—it begins to make sense that he was shocked by Hindu-Muslim communal violence, disillusioned with party politics among anticolonial Indians, and totally rejecting of the factional infighting between moderates and extremists in the Congress (institutionalized at the Surat session of 1907), as well as the emerging antagonism between the implicitly Hindu Congress and the newly formed Muslim League (founded in 1906).

After the Partition of Bengal, the dynamic between Lord Curzon's British administration and the Indian nationalists in the course of the Swadeshi struggle moved increasingly into a framework that took no cognizance of what Tagore felt was the Indian style of doing politics. It became more about *sarkār* than about *samāj,* more about political power than about moral *śakti*. The worst part, from Tagore's perspective, was that Indians complied with this foreign way of doing things, thereby losing the battle even before they had really begun to fight. His visceral recoil, figured so vividly in the tragedy of Bimala, Nikhilesh, and Sandip in *Ghare Baire,* is already adumbrated in his writings and speeches from the first decade of the twentieth century, where the Mother India that he is at pains to evoke for his countrymen is utterly at odds with the realpolitik that would, within a remarkably short time, bring Swadeshi to an abrupt and inglorious end.

Abanindranath painted Krishna. He painted the Buddha. He painted Tissarakṣitā, Aśoka's queen. He painted the Pāṇḍava brothers. He painted Pārvatī and Gaṇeśa. He painted the Mughals. These paintings were of a different order than *Bhārat Mātā,* which was originally supposed to be *Baṇga Mātā,* Mother Bengal, and only later became Mother India.[39] This is because Bhārat or Baṇga Mātā is an abstraction, a feminine embodiment of India or Bengal. She is not a deity, a figure from Hindu mythology, a character from Sanskrit literature, or a person out of Indian history. She is a modern entity, and her meanings, which are cultural and social, are most resonant during the Swadeshi movement. She immediately becomes a nationalist icon, but in fact the artist intends her to convey a certain kind of society: Rabindranath's nurturing, protective swadeshi *samāj* (indigenous community), not a political form of any sort, certainly not a *rāṣṭra* (nation).

When the British partitioned Bengal into Hindu-majority and Muslim-majority segments, when violence broke out between the two religious communities, when anticolonial politics became acrimonious, when Bengali nationalism became increasingly Westernized—that is, confrontational, divisive, assertive of incommensurable identities, and obsessed with the capture of power—Rabindranath went into internal exile. Siva Kumar says of *Bhārat Mātā:* "The image was clearly propagandistic and read as such. Its contemporary reputation rested squarely on its nationalist credential [*sic*] and was hugely disproportionate with its artistic quality."[40] Whether for artistic reasons, or for political ones, Abanindranath moved away, too, from his Mother India, gentle goddess of a conception of social relations that was rapidly vanishing from the horizon as a possible future for colonized India. But his travels into the past, and his search for an aesthetic register in harmony with the Indic self, continued for the rest of his long career as an artist.

* * *

Bankimchandra Chattopadhyay's slogan "Bande Mātaram!" in his novel *Anandamath* (1882), Abanindranath Tagore's painting *Bhārat Mātā*, and Rabindranath Tagore's novel *Ghare Baire* all have to be seen as part of an evolving conversation in colonial Bengal on the meaning, imagery, and value of a feminine, deified figure of the nation. To my mind, the three Bengali intellectuals here ought to be placed along a continuum, from militant religious nationalism in Bankim, to a qualified cultural and aesthetic nationalism in Abanindranath, to a rejection of nationalism altogether in the mature Rabindranath. In *Ghare Baire,* it is the villain, Sandip, who uses the cry of "Bande Mātaram!" to whip up divisive communal hatred in the peasantry and arouse the gullible heroine Bimala to a state of sexual and political excitement that will eventually ruin her marriage and her life. Sandip's brazen misuse of this slogan precipitates the disastrous turn of events that leads to the deaths of the young idealist Amūlya and the novel's noble hero, Nikhilesh.

Raw political passion, even in the guise of devotion to a goddesslike, nurturing motherland, is something that Rabindranath, after the failure Swadeshi and the Partition of Bengal in the first decade of the twentieth century, comes to regard as a fearsome and destructive force. Immediately after the novel, he delivers three lectures against nationalism in Japan and the United States (1916–1917), putting forth his doubts in no uncertain terms. By the time Tagore writes his extraordinary lecture "Nationalism in India," he has a full-blown critique of the ideology associated with the nation-state form. By "nationalism" he means both the yearning for nationality on the part of a colonized people, such as subjugated Indians, as well as the pride and assertiveness of nations like free America and the powerful countries of Europe. He is critical of nationalism in both its meanings. For the greatest literary voice of a nation to speak against nationalism, whether desired or achieved, when his country was still colonized, and when European imperialism had produced the most catastrophic global war ever seen, was completely unprecedented.

Tagore's lecture tour came after his Nobel Prize in 1913, during World War I (1914–1918), and before the first non-cooperation and satyagraha movements launched by Gandhi (1919–1921). Predictably, it did not make him friends in India, even as he came to be perceived as a prophetic voice in other parts of the world. Interestingly, though, there are remarkable similarities between Gandhi's *Hind Swaraj* (1909) and Tagore's "Nationalism in India." One appears well before World War I, while the other comes almost at the end of the largest armed conflict that the world had ever experienced up to that time. Both texts are extremely critical of Western civilization, materialism, wealth, competition, technology, violence, and political ideologies like nationalism, and thus both are utterly eccentric in their respective and shared milieux. In *Hind Swaraj* as much as "Nationalism," we find a critique of capitalism, especially of market- and profit-driven economics, together with a critique of colonialism. In Gandhi and Tagore's common view, Western prosperity, based as it is on the exploitation of nature and of other peoples, is not really a sign of progress—instead, it bespeaks a new kind of barbarism. Commercialism and machinery are not indications that the West is truly civilized. Both visionaries speak of India's distinctive character and think that for India to go the Western route would be cultural suicide. But Gandhi, perhaps the more radical of the two, advocates absolutely separate paths for India and the West; Tagore is rather for a more pragmatic "deep association" between them.

Notable in "Nationalism" is Rabindranath's critique of caste-based inequality. As compared to his Swadeshi-period writings, this account has a stronger conception of human rights that must, he feels, override caste hierarchy for Indian society to be genuinely humane. He attacks anachronistic tradition, which entrenches caste prejudice and reduces human beings to a state worse than beasts. He compares caste discrimination to the genocide of Native Americans and the enslavement of the blacks, but finds caste Hinduism in India to be preferable to the outright extermination and slavery of native populations in America and Australia. For all its flaws, in Tagore's opinion caste is the modus vivendi of a society as thoroughly permeated by difference as India.

He connects caste to a certain idea of federation, to toleration, to the peaceful—if problematic—coexistence of vastly different groups. The alternative, as seen in other highly diverse societies, especially of the West, is much worse. Caste prevents mobility and growth for particular groups, true, but at least it permits people to live together, as opposed to the survival of the strong at the cost of the weak seen elsewhere, especially in places where nationalism becomes the regnant ideology. He conceives of India as "the world in miniature," so great is its internal diversity. "It is many countries packed into one geographical receptacle."[41] Historically, the caste system, in his reading, has emerged as the least violent, most sustainable response to the extreme challenge of racial, ethnic, and religious integration across a completely heterogeneous social body.

A recurrent theme in Tagore's Swadeshi writings as well as the "Nationalism" essay is his idea of India's integrationist, assimilative character. In the latter text, he compares this feature of Indian history favorably to the genocidal violence underlying national unity in countries like the United States. Differences, both internal and external, are gradually accommodated into India from the very earliest stages of its history, through the twin modalities of hospitality and hierarchy. However, caste has its limitations for India too, "giving to her numerous races the negative benefit of peace and order, but not the positive opportunity of expansion and movement."[42] Rabindranath's argument is complex, since it both defends and critiques the caste system. His critique, however, is more powerful than his defense, because the defense in the end is only by comparison to Western societies where, according to him, racial and religious difference has been dealt with much more harshly and decisively than in India. Between the tyranny of inferiority and the terror of extermination, caste seems like the lesser evil.

In other words, his defense of caste oppression is not absolute—it is only comparative. He is outspoken in his condemnation not only of untouchability but also of the less extreme manifestations of the ideas of purity and pollution, the social ostracism, and the everyday humiliations associated with low-caste and outcaste status. Some of his criticism of caste comes from its inhumanity, some from its rigidity, and some from its effect of divisiveness on a society that already has to strain to hang together, so pronounced is its diversity. "A true unity is like a round globe, it rolls on, carrying its burden easily; but diversity is a many-cornered thing which has to be dragged and pushed with all force."[43]

In general Rabindranath seems very critical of any of kind of social division, political infighting, and the failure of a people to come together in a true unity of purpose. Looking back on the Swadeshi movement some years on, he comments on its political fallout, reiterating many of the views that he had held originally. He is especially scathing about internal divisions among Indian nationalists, and about the piecemeal demands of the various factions from the British government. He feels that Indian resistance to British rule has to be of a totally different order than nationalism—in fact, it has to take the hitherto unimagined form of a resistance to nationalism itself. If India won its political freedom from the British but then went on to model itself after the Western nations, then that would be no freedom at all—it would just be another form of slavery. He distinguishes between the fact of political power and true freedom, and insists that it is freedom that is worth pursuing, not power. Freedom and power are two different things. Moral and spiritual freedom, in his view, is incommensurable with political freedom that is built on social slavery. His is a strong indictment of the West and, in a different way, of India as well. Injustice and tyranny are not made acceptable by either material advancement or political power. These aspects of Tagore's argument are very reminiscent of Gandhi's *Hind Swaraj*.

He ends by clarifying that he is not advocating passivity for India, not calling for India to simply be an agricultural economy without the capacity to defend itself against foreign domination. India should be productive, should be strong, but not violent, not exploitative of its own or other people. He advocates a life of simplicity, contemplation, and the cultivation of the soul, an ethic of social cooperation and not economic conflict. These should be India's ideals, not a blind emulation of the misguided West. Again, in a prevailing climate of war and nationalist sentiments, both within India and in the world as a whole, Rabindranath's voice is absolutely unique.

Just as he walks alone during Swadeshi, he walks alone during a time when imperialism, capitalism, and nationalism are at their most bellicose and belligerent worldwide. He reiterates his firm conviction that the "real problem in India is not political. It is social."[44] And nationalism is not the answer to India's social problems—on the contrary: "Nationalism is a great menace. It is the particular thing that for years has been at the bottom of India's troubles. And in as much as we have been ruled and dominated by a nation that is strictly political in its attitude, we have tried to develop within ourselves, despite our inheritance from the past, a belief in our eventual political destiny."[45] It is this "political destiny" that Rabindranath questions, and ultimately rejects.

* * *

Shah Jahan and Bhārat Mātā were not the only tropes that Abanindranath and Rabindranath worked on and thought about in tandem. Another important figure to appear in both the uncle's poetry and the nephew's painting was the Yakṣa of Kalidasa's *Meghadūta* poem, discussed at length in Chapter 2. As I have already shown, the Yakṣa should be recognized as a major poetic symbol in Rabindranath's oeuvre, one that he returned to throughout his writing life, from its earliest beginnings to its very end. For Rabindranath, the Yakṣa was many things, from the poet's alter ego, to any lover longing for his distant love, to modern man in a state of separation from the past, to the Indic self, ever at a remove from its beautiful but unattainable history. If in order to understand Abanindranath's Shah Jahan we must have recourse to the category of samvega, then to understand Rabindranath's Yakṣa we must have recourse to the category of viraha. I am arguing that we cannot have a full account of the conceptual foundations of modern India without a willingness to accept what are apparently categories from aesthetics into the narrative of an Indic political theory. This is especially true for the two Tagores, whom I consider to be founding fathers of the Indian republic, seeing as they gave to India a literary and an artistic leg to stand on, as it were—two limbs without which the nation would quite literally be unable to move forward into its proper future as an ethical polity.

There is a hint in Rabindranath's "Shah Jahan" that he compares the Taj Mahal to the *Meghadūta* and thus the emperor Shah Jahan to the poet Kalidasa. He addresses Shah Jahan as *samrāṭ kobī* or "Poet Emperor," which could mean both "emperor who is a poet" and "emperor among poets," that is, the greatest poet of all. The figure of the Yakṣa does not enter into this set of metaphoric relations between Rabindranath's *Meghadūta* poems and his Shah Jahan poem. But Abanindranath paints the Yakṣa in his proper context of the *Meghadūta,* whether that of Kalidasa in the original Sanskrit, or that of Rabindranath, in multiple Bengali iterations. Tapati Guha-Thakurta, in her reading of Abanindranath's 1909 manifesto on art, *Bhārat Śilpa,* explicates very carefully his agenda for a new Indian aesthetics.[46] The work *Love-sick Yakṣa's Lament* (1904) seems to exemplify many of Abindranath's central concerns: a reference to ancient India, a character or theme from classical literature, identifiably (if broadly) "Hindu" subject matter, and the investment of the work with a certain emotional intensity, so that as viewers we are invited to feel empathy with the Yakṣa's pain rather than concerning ourselves with the artist's technical virtuosity or his adherence to the strict rules of painting.

Even the mixture of Japanese and Mughal styles that Mitter reads in this work fits in with Abanindranath's ideologically driven art: this hybrid Orientalism successfully references both the notion of an Asiatic tradition (including Indian, Chinese, and Japanese art) and a repertoire of indigenous Indian techniques (Mughal/Pahari). Abanindranath's painting is an extension, in a different medium, of his uncle's repeated engagement with the Yakṣa, and ultimately evidence of Rabindranath's success in transforming or translating this figure from classical Sanskrit literature into a modern poetic symbol. As Guha-Thakurta shows, Abanindranath's entire theory turned on the spiritual force and symbolic power of Indian art, and the Yakṣa, drawn from Kalidasa via Rabindranath, no doubt served as an appropriate vehicle for his idea of a native, and national, aesthetics.

Abanindranath's painting is followed by J. P. Gangooly's *The Banished Yakṣa* (1908), which shares its predecessor's qualities of lyricism and mood, depicting a lonely figure against a minimally delineated landscape.[47] Abanindranath's Yakṣa sits, with a stringed musical instrument, amid foliage, with monsoon clouds in the backdrop; Gangooly's Yakṣa stands on the edge of a cliff, holding a plate (of flowers? sweets?) in one hand, surrounded by clouds. In both paintings, the Yakṣa faces to the left, with his right hand raised and his index finger pointing upward, perhaps to indicate that he is in the midst of addressing the cloud messenger. Both are watercolors, and their overall effect is dreamlike, ahistorical, and awash with misty colors. The only element in either work that "speaks" is the Yakṣa's right hand, raised in a graceful *mudrā*-like gesture suggesting his timeless address to his vaporous friend. Interestingly, what emotional depth *(bhāva)* can be discerned in either painting comes from our prior knowledge of the identity and story of this figure, not from anything particular in the Yakṣa's facial expression or bodily posture as depicted visually. Given that Abanindranath and his disciples and acolytes systematically practiced literary illustration, these paintings were by definition to be read together with the (poetic) texts that they implicitly illustrated.

One of Rabindranath's early poems, the very short *Meghdūt* (1895, in the collection *Caitālī*), which is part of his cycle of *Meghadūta* treatments considered in detail in Chapter 2, ends with a line addressed to the Yakṣa:

Your separation-vīṇā sounds plaintively.[48]

This "separation-vīṇā" appears to be the very stringed instrument depicted in Gangooly's painting of the Yakṣa. (Incidentally, Gangooly too was related to the Tagores, on the maternal side.) It gives voice to the viraha experienced by the Yakṣa, and accompanies, in a tune filed with sadness, his poetic message to the cloud.

In a recent essay on the history of love in Bengali literature, Sudipta Kaviraj has traced the transformation in the language of love from a premodern, Sanskritic aesthetic of erotic love *(śriṅgāra)* to a modern aesthetic of emotional love *(prem)*.[49] In Kaviraj's reading, Bankim effects this transition, but does so in a way that suggests he is torn between these two different understandings of love, one centered on physical beauty, sexual allure, and bodily pleasure, the other on mental states, romantic attachments, and inner qualities of protagonists, particularly females. Once he becomes Bengal's leading litterateur, Tagore singlehandedly makes *prem* the dominant mode of love. For Kaviraj, Tagore's characters, especially his women, are all about individuation, interiority, and ordinariness, and their beauty lies in their emotional lives and ethical choices, not in their resemblance to Kalidasa's voluptuous heroines. Unlike Bankim's women, whose obvious (i.e., apparent) beauty makes them dangerous to those around them, the beauty of Tagore's women lies not in their faces and bodies but in their hearts and minds, in their words and actions. They are fashioned by Tagore as beings appropriate for love, not fear, nor desire.

Through close readings of Bankim and Tagore, Kaviraj is able to show how *prem* replaces *śriṅgāra* at the very level of the linguistic sign in Bengali, within a few decades toward the end of the nineteenth century. He also points to a similar transformation in the milieu of art:

> Such changes as outlined so far were not confined to literary creations alone. Literature after all describes physical beauty in language; and it is not surprising that these ideas come to influence the direct representational portrayal of beauty in painting. In this, Tagore's thinking runs closely parallel to the search for an emotional version of beauty in the work of painters of the Bengal school.[50]

Abanindranath's and Gangooly's wan solitary Yakṣa, wrapped in mist, talking to a cloud in a very private reverie, is thus the appropriate illustration for

Rabindranath's melancholy *Meghadūta* poetry, rather than for Kalidasa's original poem with its joyous celebration of the physical beauty of a country and its inhabitants, and of the erotic love suffusing this landscape.

All of the literature thus far focuses on two aspects of Abanindranath's Yakṣa: the technical details of the work or its formal genealogy in Japanese and Mughal art, and its place in a dialectic between tradition and modernity within Abanindranath's oeuvre as a whole. These are perfectly legitimate foci, because the painting warrants analysis along these lines. But I want to further draw the reader's attention to the dialogue between Abanindranath's Yakṣa and Rabindranath's Yakṣa, that is, to the relationship between the uncle's poetic symbol and the nephew's pictorial one. I also want to suggest that in addition to illustrating the *bhāva* of viraha, which comes directly out of Kalidasa's *Meghadūta,* this painting too bears traces, although fainter than *The Passing of Shah Jahan,* of samvega.

By this I mean that just as in meditating on Shah Jahan and the Taj Mahal Abanindranath seems to open a window into Indian history, by meditating on the address of the Yakṣa to the cloud he opens another window, into Indian poetry. In both these paintings, we witness some aspect of the Indic self suddenly becoming manifest to Abanindranath. The aesthetic experience condensed into these two works is so vivid that it produces, with a suddenness that in the Sanskrit is conveyed by the expression *jhaṭiti iva* (as though in a split second), a bolt of self-knowledge.

The emperor lies on the cusp of death, his head turned for a last look at his exquisite monument. The Yakṣa sits alone in the wilderness, his hand raised in an endearing gesture of conversational engagement, speaking to a dark cloud hovering over the treetops, so crazed by longing that he does not realize the hopelessness of his situation. Every civilization has its moments of clarity, mirrors for its soul, its memories that are never utterly lost, no matter how grave the crisis. Abanindranath, like Rabindranath, seizes on these epiphanies. Abanindranath's work is not nationalistic only because it uses Indian methods or relies on Indian art history, but also because it seeks to bring forth and give form to the very self of India, to that which is hidden, to that which is staggering under the weight of an occupation as much aesthetic and epistemological as it is political and economic.

When Mitter, Guha-Thakurta, and Siva Kumar call Abanindranath a nationalist, it is because he became involved with the Swadeshi movement, or because he experimented with styles taken from Indian art of the past, or because he created an image like *Bhārat Mātā,* or because he built new institutions of art education and art practice that ran parallel to and sometimes challenged colonial institutions. All of this did indeed happen, so that their assessment of his nationalism is not in the least inaccurate. What I am arguing is that the real evidence of his nationalism, of his love of his country and culture, lies in his search for the Indic self, articulated most clearly in the paintings that reveal his aesthetic shock, his realization of truth, his clear and certain knowledge of that which India is in danger of losing and must hold onto, defying the terrific power of colonialism.

But in reading Abanindranath thus, am I reducing India to a handful of essential symbols? One way of telling the story of Indian nationalism is precisely as the quest for an essence, something that makes India India, something that distinguishes India from Britain, from the British Empire, from European civilization, from the West, from the entire array of Others who were stifling the Indian imagination and destroying Indian traditions. In the next and penultimate section of this chapter, I turn to Rabindranath as a painter and examine why it was that unlike Abanindranath, he never tried to paint "India."

* * *

We cannot really get a complete sense of the early phase of Indian nationalism if we disregard the tremendous ideological effort made by Abanindranath and his group. These men (and some very few women) were among the foremost ideologues of the incipient Indian nation, giving to Bengali, Indian, and British audiences a repertoire of images with which to remember an India of old, and to imagine an India yet to come. In Bengal's nationalist art, the intended relationship between the viewer and the image was entirely different from Rabindranath's viraha, a longing arising out of irremediable separation. Rather, these images made the India of past and future visible, vivid, vital. Their purpose was to end the separation between India and Indians, between the past and the present, between the present and the future. Abanindranath's Mughals, his heroes and heroines from the *Rāmāyaṇa* and the *Mahābhārata,* from Jayadeva and Kalidasa, from the Buddhist canon, these and many other such characters in his paintings, including our

Yakṣa, were part of a project of making a national art, a self-consciously Indian aesthetic revival, powerful symbols in a public argument about the reality of precolonial India and the necessity for a new, postcolonial India.

By contrast, as a painter, Rabindranath was far more interested in individual talent than he was in tradition. Given everything we have now considered about his position on the nation and on history, perhaps this should not surprise us. His painting years came much later in his life, really only in the 1920s and 1930s, when he was already well over fifty. They coincided with the height of nationalist politics in colonial India, the decades dominated by Mahatma Gandhi. By this time Swadeshi art had run its course, and the Bengal School was no longer the cutting edge of the Indian artistic renaissance as it had once been. Rabindranath painted thousands of works in his sixties and seventies, deeply interested in, curious about, and open to trends in modernist art around the globe—Cubism, Futurism, Surrealism, Bauhaus, and Primitivism, most prominently. He also paid close attention to the mask-making and other premodern ritual arts of Africa, Oceania, and the Native Americans. His radar as a painter was pointed away from India, looking to and learning from the rest of the world, particularly high modernist Europe and the indigenous—so-called primitive—peoples of various continents. In addition to painting, he also practiced calligraphy, doodling, and "automatic" art, all strange and little-understood aspects of his multifaceted creativity that attracted a fair bit of attention from his international patrons and audiences.

It is astounding to recall that Rabindranath and Abanindranath lived in the same compound, in adjacent houses in Calcutta, for most of their lives; that they had the same friends and interlocutors; that their social, cultural, and political contexts were, for the most part, one and the same. When Rabindranath took Abanindranath's foremost pupil, Nandalal Bose, with him to head up the art department of his university in Santiniketan, he even managed to change Bose's trajectory as a painter, an educationist, and an institution builder, getting him deeply interested in tribal and folk art, in primitivist and experimental techniques, luring him away from the nationalist mainstream. Santiniketan's methodologies for art education were anything but conventional—needless to say, discipline was not at a premium, the free play of individual imagination was encouraged, and spontaneous creative impulses were emphasized. Much of the school's imprimatur as a vaunted site for artistic learning and practice came from Bose, but it was Rabindranath's overall aesthetic vision, and his authority as India's foremost creative talent, that ultimately gave it its special character.

Rabindranath's own works as a painter are primarily an exploration of his psyche, and almost never have any sort of historical content or mimetic form. His faces are masks, or unseen versions of the unseen self. His figures seem to arise from his consciousness; they do not inhabit the real world. Many of his designs are completely abstract, non-representational, irrational, oneiric, seeking to capture moods, memories, dreams, and buried impulses, taking us deep into the recesses of the poet's mind where reason and realism no longer prevail.[51] Sometimes his painting is childlike, deliberately resisting the craft and discipline he hones to the highest degree when he works with language or music. If Rabindranath writes for the world, he paints for himself. If his linguistic expression is about beauty, his art is free to express ugliness, cruelty, danger, and nightmare. In his painting he weaves a dense web of private symbols, charged with emotional, sexual, and psychic meanings that art critics have yet to properly decipher, interpret, or connect to the events surrounding him.

Abanindranath paints for the nation. He cares for Bengal, for India, for Asia, for the Orient. He worries about what is ours and what is not ours. He and other Swadeshi artists want to "salvage" the Indian past, in Mitter's account.[52] He fills his home, studio, and schools with artworks, as do his brothers, cousins, uncles, and nephews, creating an enormous collection that Coomaraswamy remarks upon for its size and quality, gradually emptying the estate of the European artifacts collected by previous generations of Tagores. He dreams of Swadeshi India as his Shah Jahan dreams of the Taj Mahal, a perfect structure arisen in an empty landscape, a thing of beauty contemplated in the mind's eye before it masses slowly to marble loveliness, across the river. The young prince on horseback thinks of the woman he loved, his queen, and envisions a form. The old emperor forlorn on his deathbed, his daughter at his feet, takes a last look before it vanishes, that testament to human pride, that signature of human folly. With death, the eyes close, the pearlescent Taj fades into a darkness from which there is no awakening. The Taj Mahal is the opposite of the love that caused its building. India too, when made, will elude its makers, betray their love, outlast their dreaming minds, enclose, like a tomb, their mortal coils and living spirits.

In Jorasanko, meanwhile, in the mansion of the Tagores and the "shrine" of cultural nationalism, Rabindranath paints for Rabindranath. Nationalist India and her ideological drives, her political objectives, her convictions, her passions, her desires, her imperatives, cannot colonize the art of Rabindranath Tagore, do not encroach on his canvas. He does not try to visualize what he called "the India of the poet" because the ontological condition associated with that India is viraha—"that language was lost to us." Rabindranath never paints Alakā, celestial city, where a friendly cloud, long ago, was begged to go by a Yakṣa, the banished one, forever at a far remove. Let us recall momentarily Kalidasa's gently comical but intensely moving lines quoted in Chapter 2:

> Meghāloke bhavati sukhino'pi
> Anyathāvṛtticetaḥ
> Kaṇṭhāśleṣa praṇayini jane
> Kiṃ punar dūrasaṃsthe

> At the sight of a cloud,
> The mind of even a happy man takes a turn—
> How much more so a man at far remove
> Longing for an embrace! (*Megh-K.* 1.3)

No nationalist can afford such an absolute loss of language, such irrevocable sundering, such a state of being out of his head *(anyathāvṛtticetas)* or at far remove (dūrasaṃstha), relative to the object of his striving. How can you build a nation when you are against nations? How can you dream an India when your imagination refuses the hubris, the incalculable abstraction, the forcible harnessing of millions of individual wills to a collective project of certain violence and dubious beauty? How can you depict an idea you do not believe in? No brooding Mughal emperor, no lovesick Yakṣa, no dancing Krishna, no wise Buddha ever appeared on his canvas. Rabindranath left behind no "nationalist" painting, not even one.

In some of his poetry and writings that we have considered, Rabindranath might refer to a painting or a painted image, in words. Thus:

> Poet-Emperor, this is your *heart's picture* ("Shah Jahan")

> There is Ujjayini
> Gazing at her own *great shadow* in the Shipra River *(Meghdūt)*

Suddenly there opened up, *as if drawn on a picture*
Asarh's tear-soaked beautiful world *(Meghdūt (b))*

We stand, each one of us, on a lonely mountain peak, gazing northwards. Between us, the sky, the clouds, and the fair earth with its Reva, Shipra, Avanti, Ujjayini, its beauties, wealth and delights, stretch out *like a painting.* They arouse memories, but do not let us approach nearer. Desires are stirred but never satisfied. Two human beings, and so far apart![53]

This kind of word picture and reference to paintings/pictures, however, does not translate into actual images in Rabindranath's paintings. In his longer *Meghdūt,* following Kalidasa's original poem, there is a descriptive section that is more than thirty lines long; similar is the case in "Jana Gana Mana," the poem that eventually became India's national anthem.[54] But he never gave visual form to these landscapes. They were always meant to be notional and evocative, not accurate, not cartographic in a strict sense. The way that India is rendered through these images suggests a geo-moral or a geo-aesthetic space, not a nation whose map we may try to locate somewhere on the globe. In these moments when Rabindranath's visual imagination is most clearly expressed in his poetry, we are reminded of the ancient Indic definition of a poet *(kavi)* as someone who is simultaneously a seer *(draṣṭā)* and a creator *(sraṣṭā),* one endowed with the power to see, with vision *(dṛṣṭi)* as well as the power to make, fashion, or create *(sṛṣṭi).* Even though later in his life Rabindranath took to painting, however, he did not give his vision *(dṛṣṭi, darśana)* of India any visual form.

Abanindranath was concerned with very concrete questions surrounding Indic traditions of painting (Buddhist/Mughal/Rajput, etc.), Indian historical and literary themes as fit subjects for modern appropriation, and canons of beauty and truth as understood from within a framework of Indian aesthetics. In a different work, already mentioned, he depicted the last Great Mughal, Shah Jahan's son Aurangzeb (r. 1658/1659–1707), examining the decapitated head of his apostate brother, Dara Shikoh, whose throne Aurangzeb had usurped.[55] The execution and usurpation were episodes in the history of India, and thus fair game for a properly Indian painting. If they contained or conveyed political intrigue and psychological drama, so much the better for the narrative power of the new nationalist art. For Rabindranath, by contrast, the Taj Mahal is no more a national monument than the Yakṣa is a teacher of ancient Indian geography; Shah Jahan was no more the ruler of medieval India than Kalidasa was the court poet of the Gupta emperor. The very same object is given a thoroughly historicist treatment by Abanindranath, and a thoroughly aporetic treatment by Rabindranath. This follows perfectly from the claim I have been making: Abanindranath was a nationalist; Rabindranath was not.

Rabindranath the painter doodled the tunes in his head, drew the ghosts that haunted him, sketched the fleeting remembrances that flitted across the firmament of his mind, gave faces to his innumerable alter egos, his shadow selves, the child and monster that lived in his heart. His personal torments and his intimate reveries, of which we know nothing, guided his brush. He resolutely ignored the Bengal School of art that took root and flourished in his own home, perched like a bird in the branches of that great tree, singing a song when he wished, taking wing when he liked, unfettered by ideology, unbound by tradition. If Indians wish that the clearest note in their aesthetic should be the note of freedom, then perhaps it would make sense for them to adopt as their national poet, their national painter, Rabindranath Tagore.

In his *Meghadūta* poems and writings, Rabindranath figures "the India of the poet" as the place to which one never goes, a place one may relate to only through a very particular affect, namely viraha. This India, Rabindranath's India, is like Kalidasa's Alakā, a place yearned for in the full knowledge that the yearning is limitless; it will never end in union or reunion. Such an India is exactly the opposite of the India that forms the telos of nationalism. All nationalist politics is premised on the faith that ultimately a certain vision of India—free, self-governing, and self-reliant—can and will be realized. In his poetry and essays examined in Chapter 2, Rabindranath has already set himself apart from such a political project. He does not believe that at the end of a long struggle defined by various nationalist ideologies and their concomitant practices—swadeshi, swaraj, and satyagraha—stands the Indian nation-state.

A huge separation dwells at the heart of onward time
That tries door after future door,

Life after future life
In an endless attempt to close its distance from perfection.
The world is its poem, a rolling sonorous poem
In which a remote presage of joy annotates vast sorrow. ("Yakṣa," 11–16)

Since he does not believe in India as a nation, as the perfection that will seal the process of political struggle, he does not, in his work as a painter, make any attempt to visualize India. Rabindranath does not show us what he cannot see. Abanindranath, as a Swadeshi painter, as a nationalist artist, is able to give form to many of his uncle's imaginings, like the Yakṣa or Bhārat Mātā, as also to characters and narratives from the historical and mythic past that he believes provide the basis for a specific type of political future, one of political self-determination. Abanindranath therefore stands very much within the nationalist mainstream (at least for a few years) while Rabindranath seems to go against the grain right to the very last.[56]

Through his *Meghadūta* treatments Rabindranath makes the argument that the relationship between us and perfection, whether past or future, is one of absolute separation, a separation that can produce in us a deep longing, a longing that leads us to make efforts to attain the unattainable, efforts that constitute our work but nonetheless do not bring us any closer to perfection. "India of the poet" is one such perfection, the irrecoverable archaic; the Indian nation, a sovereign power, is another such perfection, the impossible telos. In his *Meghadūta* cycle, Tagore repeats the image of an engulfing darkness (*andhakāra:* literally, "blind making"): in "Shah Jahan," it is "the ever-falling darkness of history"; in "Dream," "Night's darkness swallowed the city of Ujjain." This category of *andhakāra* is proximate to separation (viccheda) and to viraha. What cannot be imagined cannot be depicted; hence the absence of "India" in the paintings of Rabindranath.[57] With regard to these past and future entities Indians may feel viraha; in the present, in their life as it is given to them, Indians may only exert themselves to reform the social body, nurture their *samāj.* The politics of viraha militates directly against the politics of nationalism.

Rabindranath is India's national poet and perhaps also her national painter because he articulates through his poetry and through his art the most precious of all possible credos: a fundamental rejection of nationalism. He walked a lonely road, the road of resistance to nationalism as an ideology, and this was the road not taken by Indians in 1947, the road that remains only as a reminder of what might have been, what never came about: a properly Indian modernity. Such a modernity would circumvent the form of the nation-state as the only political form, and find some other, as yet unimagined politics, a politics premised on the assumption that people are "arisen together," as a moral and material community whose citizens are "co-produced." The boundaries of such a community would be forever extended through a principle of hospitality; its shape rounded into a proper unity through the constant work of integration. Its borders would not be policed by the exclusionary principles of race, ethnicity, religion, or caste; nor would it extend itself through violence toward others. But beyond these very general outlines of the republic, we know very little of what Rabindranath's India might have been, might have become.

* * *

The distinctive nature of Indian reality has become more and more difficult to talk about. Partly this is because India is becoming more and more like the rest of the world, thanks to globalization. Partly this is because of two centuries of the English language on the subcontinent. Partly this is because academic discourse has gone so far in the direction of diagnosing Indian modernity as being essentially derivative, and has developed such an extreme fear of Hindutva, that it is now next to impossible to find the scholarly language to say what is actually said quite eloquently in other media, like music, films, and literature, even so-called Indo-Anglian literature.

No one attending a Hindustani music recital, or watching a Bollywood film, or reading a novel (in English) by Pankaj Mishra or Arundhati Roy, can doubt for a moment that the experience is distinctly and particularly Indian; that the context from which these artifacts emanate is that of Indian culture, and not any other culture in the world. But history, theory, and criticism, in our time, have as intellectual practices ceased to share the imagination that still animates the arts in India. Indian intellectuals switch mental gears without even realizing what they are doing, so that they use one set of critical yardsticks, emotional responses, and aesthetic judgments in the concert hall or movie theater, and a whole other epistemological apparatus when addressing their students, peers, and reading audiences. This discursive schizophrenia is now pervasive in the academy. I believe it hurts scholarship in and about India.

I am well aware that putting forward ideas like samvega and viraha in this intellectual environment is a hazardous undertaking, all the more when I ask that they be taken up in the field of political theory and in a history of the ideas that give India its political foundations. But if we are to comprehend what it was that men like Rabindranath and Abanindranath were thinking, what conceptual categories helped them to make sense of the world and create the canons of modern Indian literature and art, why it was they who gave to India the image of Bhārat Mātā and the lyric that is India's national anthem, then we have to retrain our minds to enter an imagination from which we are almost terminally estranged.

We know infinitely more about Rabindranath's lifeworld than we do about Kalidasa's lifeworld. And yet things have come to such a pass that both Kalidasa, who lived a millennium and a half before our time, and Rabindranath, who lived hardly half a century ago, seem equally indecipherable, equally strange—talking to a cloud, dreaming of a celestial city, pining after an ethereal beloved, moved to meter by the mysteries of time and the pathos of mortal existence. We can still, today, grasp that a certain raga is appropriate to sing in the monsoon, but not that the monsoon, with its presence in the poetic and pictorial imagination of India for centuries, is an inalienable part of the Indic self. It is not that objects in nature, in and of themselves, a priori, belong to this or that culture, but that the monsoon, or the Himalaya, or the Ganga, for example, long ago ceased to be objects in nature, ceased to merely exist out there as objective data. They have been systematically, iteratively, and insistently incorporated into a symbolic order that is Indic. This symbolic order we have forgotten, and this we have to learn to recapture. Kalidasa, an ancient, and Rabindranath, a modern ancestor, both belong squarely within that symbolic order.

When Abanindranath started his career as a painter, he had read Sanskrit treatises on representation, mimesis, pleasure, semiotics, and the technical aspects of art. This scholastic understanding of aesthetics from classical Indian sources was at odds with what he studied in the studio with his European painting and drawing teachers. Then E. B. Havell came along and opened up to Abanindranath the whole history, as it was then possible to know, of Indian art, sculpture, architecture, and crafts; this astonishing historical knowledge was further augmented by others like Coomaraswamy. In time he was exposed to Chinese, Japanese, and Persian art, which he believed must have some bearing on Indian art because of a shared "Asian" quality in them all. But no matter how brilliant and synthetic Abanindranath's intellect, he could not very well throw all these disparate elements together on a canvas, like the ingredients in a salad, and expect to produce paintings with some integrity, some truth value. Without a profound veridical experience on the order of samvega, infusing his vision and guiding his brush, Abanindranath could never have become the painter that he was, the first modern artist in all of India, the figure who brought modernity to Indian art.

That the locus, as it were, of Abanindranath's samvega is the scene of Shah Jahan looking at the Taj Mahal ought to silence all those who object to invocations of tradition, fearing the overwhelmingly "Hindu" nature of tradition in an Indian context. Here is a character not out of antiquity; he is a medieval emperor. He is not Hindu; he is Muslim. He is not a god; he is a man. He is not mythical; he is historical. He did not build a place of worship; he built a tomb. His life does not have to be left to conjecture; his life is thoroughly known through documents. But Shah Jahan is the protagonist Abanindranath chooses to represent his quest for the Indic self. Flesh-and-blood Shah Jahan, Islamic king of Hindu India, one who wrongfully deposed his father Jahangir and was wrongfully deposed in turn by his son Aurangzeb, an aesthete and royal patron of the arts to surpass many of the world's richest and most powerful monarchs of the seventeenth century. The facts of Shah Jahan's reign and works cannot be gainsaid, need not be concocted.

But we are interested less in what Shah Jahan did than in what Abanindranath made of him, as a consequence of his own whiplash of aesthetic shock. In all three paintings—*Shah Jahan Dreaming of the Taj Mahal, The Building of the Taj,* and *The Passing of Shah Jahan*—we see the relationship between, on the one hand, the human imagination and the thing of beauty, and, on the other hand, the open-ended sweep of human aspiration and the impassable closure of death. We see both the potential and the limitation of worldly power. We see that yearning may produce something beautiful, but after that beautiful thing has come into existence, yearning exceeds it still, exceeds bounded being and continues on into the eternity of signification. Some of these meanings we understand more clearly when we read Rabindranath's poem in conjunction with Abanindranath's paintings.

I began this chapter with a comment on the irony of the British administration giving Abanindranath an award for painting an aged emperor looking at his prize possession—the Taj Mahal, India's contribution to the seven wonders of the world—even at the very moment when it slipped out of the view of his dying eyes, about to close forever. As the Mughals disappeared into the ever-falling darkness of history, so would the British, if they but knew it. Perhaps the first step toward regaining India's lost sovereignty was the intuition of the finitude of sovereignty; the knowledge that the self transcends even the most awesome capacities of sovereign power, remains beyond the reach of all historically known or as-yet-unimagined forms of power, articulates itself in its quest for a limitless freedom. The certainty that power ends is only a reminder that the self does not. The Tagores sought more than India's liberation from British rule. They sought self-knowledge: in the harness of poetry, in the protocols of painting, in the strains of music, in the intimations of a tradition that for thousands of years had pursued nothing if not to know that, the very One that knows.

4

Jawaharlal Nehru

Dharma, the Self's Aspiration, and Artha, the Self's Purpose

Birla House, the residence in New Delhi where Gandhi was staying at the time of his assassination on January 30, 1948, has a small gallery abutting the lawn where the Mahatma was to hold his last prayer meeting. This gallery contains a long mural covering three walls, depicting Gandhi's life in the context of India's history, from the very beginnings of the Indic world in myth and legend, to the day of his tragic death. As already described in Chapter 1, the mural was painted in 1973 by Ram Kripal Singh from Shekhawati, a region in Rajasthan known for its particular art of making long scrolls depicting stories from the epics.[1] There is of course no bard to unfurl and roll up the mural, which is permanently painted on the walls of the gallery, nor is there an accompanying text to recite, unless we understand the life of the Mahatma itself as a kind of epic saga, nested within the epic of India's freedom struggle, which is itself set within the long panorama of Indian civilization from the hoary antiquity of Rama and Krishna, Vedic rites and the religion of the Buddha, to Gujarat in the mid-nineteenth century, the scene of Gandhi's birth. We then travel via Gandhi's youth in England and South Africa, and his maturity in India, to Partition and Independence, to the postcolonial present that begins with his slain body and extends into an unknown future, beyond the limits of the wall and of the artist's vision.

One panel in this mural shows Gandhi in conversation with his principal protégé and heir, Jawaharlal Nehru. The two men face one another, and Gandhi speaks, his arm raised in a gesture of address, while Nehru listens, a smile on his face. They are sitting on the floor, on a raised platform inside a hutlike structure, under a thatched conical roof, in what could be Gandhi's ashram. Each one wears his most recognizable garb—the Mahatma a white unstitched *dhoti,* his chest bare, and his signature round metallic glasses; Nehru a gray *sherwani* (a kind of long buttoned coat with a Chinese collar that he was known to favor), and white pajamas, with a white khadi (handspun, handwoven cotton) Congress cap on his head. This scene, like the rest of the Birla House mural, has faded and peeling paint; a long crack runs diagonally across from top to bottom, cutting through the Mahatma's upper body. There is a timeless quality to this image: it is a dialogue between good and learned men in which their exchange of ideas benefits not only the two of them but all of India, and potentially the entire world.

This tableau of Gandhi and Nehru in perennial conversation, painted in a brightly hued, rough folk idiom that makes no stylistic distinction between gods and men, historical and mythical characters, epic heroes and contemporary leaders, provides an excellent figuration of the kind of political tradition that the founders inhabited as the heirs of an old culture, and fashioned anew as they struggled against colonialism. What makes this image so striking, however, is the fact that it represents, in a highly condensed and allusive fashion, one of the most important conversations that unfolded in India in the twentieth century, which took place over more than three decades between 1916, when the two men first met, and 1948, when Gandhi was killed. These two interlocutors—one older, one younger; one traditional, one modern; one who never held office, the other independent India's first prime minister for seventeen years—shaped, through their thirty-two-year engagement with one another, two positions that have come to define India's conflicted relationship with modernity. At the same time, this type of talk, the frank dialogue and mutual pedagogy of the virtuous—the *samvad* (literally: "simultaneous speech")—is supposed to have come down to us from time immemorial. Earlier in the mural are scenes from the *Bhagavad Gītā,* which is exactly such a conversation between Krishna and Arjuna, and the life of the Buddha, who continuously spoke to his disciples and followers in a series of sermons and interviews from his enlightenment until his death. Knowledge arises and is preserved, augmented, and propagated through this kind of utterance. Nehru, by his own admission, learned more from Gandhi than from any other individual he came into contact with in the course of his very eventful, very public, very talkative life.

Unlike Abanindranath, discussed in Chapter 3, Nehru has never lacked for the attention of historians and critics. The long history of writing about and critically assessing Nehru began with Nehru himself, as he crafted some of modern India's best prose in the English language. Not only was Nehru endowed with a prodigious literary gift, but his intellectual style was self-consciously dispassionate and philosophical, which makes reading Nehru a very distinctive experience, different in all kinds of ways from reading Gandhi, Tagore, and Ambedkar. In this chapter, I want to consider as a sequence three texts by Nehru: first, his celebrated *The Discovery of India* (1946), and last his less well-known but nonetheless extremely important *Letters to Chief Ministers (1947–1964)* in five volumes, a compilation of fortnightly epistles to the ministers heading up different states in independent India throughout the seventeen years of Nehru's three consecutive administrations as prime minister.[2] These letters were published more than two decades ago, between 1985 and 1989, but for some reason they have yet to be properly studied as an integral and essential part of Nehru's massive oeuvre, or as indicators of his political or intellectual style. (So far, Ramachandra Guha appears to be the unique exception to this neglect of the *Letters*.)[3]

The second "text" in the sequence that I want to consider is a body of fragments that are not actually collected into a single book or series, which consists of everything that Nehru had to say, in writings or in speeches, about the symbols he chose and approved as the Indian state's regalia. These were the Aśokan Lion Capital from Sarnath, which became India's state seal; the Buddhist dhammacakra (wheel of law) that adorns the center of the national flag; and the mantra from the *Muṇḍaka Upaniṣad* (*satyameva jayate:* "Truth Alone Triumphs") that became the national credo. Nehru wrote about Aśoka, the Mauryan emperor of the third century BCE, both in his letters to his daughter Indira, anthologized as *Glimpses of World History: Letters from a Father to His Daughter* (1934), and in *The Discovery of India;* he also spoke about Aśoka in the Constituent Assembly debates (1946–1949), when the national symbols were being proposed and adopted as part of the process of transforming India into a republic with its own constitution (1950). In addition, in both *Glimpses* and *Discovery,* Nehru also discussed Chanakya/Kauṭilya, a minister to Candragupta (Aśoka's grandfather and the founder of the Maurya dynasty), who wrote the very first Indic treatise on statecraft, the *Arthaśāstra.* The second in my sequence of three Nehruvian texts, then, encompasses everything that Nehru wrote or said about Aśoka, about Chanakya/Kauṭilya, and about the heraldry of the Mauryans that became free India's official regalia 2,300 years later.

Nehru's search for the self, I will argue, was structured around not one but two categories of selfhood—categories that are extremely old in Indic discourses of self as well as in Indic discourses of sovereignty—these being dharma (norm) and artha (purpose). Across the three texts that I consider—*Discovery,* his writings on the national symbols, and the *Letters to Chief Ministers*—there is a gradual transition: the emphasis in the earlier writings rests mainly on dharma; it then shifts to a tense equipoise between dharma and artha, and finally the burden of signification comes to rest on artha. I translate "dharma" as the self's aspiration and "artha" as the self's purpose; that is, I read Nehru as torn between the normative and the instrumental aspects of selfhood. The triad of texts overall illustrates this dichotomous sense of self in Nehru; however, my own focus will be on what Nehru has to say about the national symbols, since his views on them so far have not been seen as a proper part of his textual corpus (where in fact they squarely belong).

Another way to characterize the dilemma between dharma-based and artha-based conceptions of the self is to see the tension between Aśokan and Kauṭilyan paradigms of sovereignty in Nehru's own ideas of rule—Aśoka being the cruel emperor who had a change of heart and gave up violence; Kauṭilya being the theorist who saw security and surveillance as essential elements of state power, "long before Clausewitz," as Nehru himself wrote. Nehru's choice of national symbols marries these opposing vectors in his thought and practice, and is therefore worthy of our interpretive attention. It is of course important for the larger argument of this book that Nehru found both aspects of selfhood in the same historical formation, the Mauryan imperium, which displays all of the complexity that characterizes the relationship between tradition and modernity for the founders—it is a temporally remote moment of a political nature in Indic antiquity; it comes to life, as it were, through colonial philology, archaeology, and art history in the nineteenth and early twentieth centuries; it appears to be a repository of norms and values that can be reconstructed and accessed through a set of texts; and it ultimately yields, at the hands of a thinker like Nehru, political categories that he wants to use innovatively in defining India's future.

Because every prior reader of Nehru has noted the contradiction between an idealist and a realist Nehru, a Nehru who values dharma and one who prioritizes artha, Nehru as a Gandhian and Nehru as a Nehruvian, I will try to explore a way to understand and perhaps overcome this series of oppositions. In this effort I turn once more to Alasdair MacIntyre, this time to his essay "Poetry as Political Philosophy," which discusses Edmund Burke, William Butler Yeats, and Irish nationalism.[4] Following on Marx's insight in *The Eighteenth Brumaire of Louis Bonaparte* that the poetic fervor of revolution gives way to the prosaic reality of the bourgeois state in both England and France, MacIntyre proposes that the modern state in and of itself is a contradictory entity. It has one face turned toward the political imagination, and the other toward bureaucratic rationality—one aspect that appeals to our emotions and claims our imaginative allegiance, versus the other aspect that entails nothing more than cold cost-benefit analysis and a practical calculation of self-interest. The Janus-faced modern state provides a key to the split between Nehru's dharma-oriented and artha-oriented tendencies: on the one hand, a massively popular freedom fighter—passionate, ardent, eloquent, and principled—and on the other, a beleaguered elected administrator—scientific, systematic, deliberative, and compromising. The advantage of adducing MacIntyre's dualist schema regarding the modern state is that it not only helps us to grasp why Nehru, unlike other founders addressed in this book, necessitates the use of two equally important categories of selfhood rather than one. It also returns us to the relationship between self and sovereignty, swa and raj, which is the foundational dyad that drives this inquiry—as indeed it did the nationalist movement as such in modern India.

The fragments in the Nehru corpus addressing the national symbols provide a convenient stopping place where both dharma and artha, and the entire series of structured oppositions within Nehru corresponding to these two poles, may be examined in depth. The symbols have poetic force as well as workmanlike qualities—they function both as suggestive images conjuring up the idea of India as a haven of ethical sovereignty, reminiscent of the Aśokan polity, and as concrete seals of state power that will literally stamp every currency note, legal order, and official document from the very inception of the postcolonial state—an idea proposed by Kauṭilya in the distant antiquity of India's first imperial state. In *Discovery,* especially in its crucial third chapter, tellingly titled "The Quest," we get one of the last glimpses of Nehru in his high nationalist mode as the paragon of normativity and aspiration. By the time he has begun writing his fortnightly letters to fellow administrators and bureaucrats, barely three years later, the Nehru we see at work, day in and day out, is of necessity mired in purposive and instrumental decisions and actions: the poetry is almost entirely gone. Nehru managed to remain cognizant of the fracture within himself and to communicate rather compellingly the agony this caused him—what Khilnani on one occasion describes as the gap between his reflective and active selves, and on another occasion as the "chronic tension" between his "philosophical conceptions" and his "political conceptions."[5]

* * *

Nehru's *Discovery of India,* written in Ahmednagar jail between April and September 1944, appears on its face to be a history, but incorporates both poetic elements and the author's political philosophy. Here are three historical moments quickly sketched, but with the deft mingling of past and present, the events and persons of another time interlaced with the author's own role as a witness, and the deployment of cinematic technique (sounds, images, actions), they instantly become iconic scenes:

> At Sarnath, near Benares, I could almost see the Buddha preaching his first sermon, and some of his recorded words would come like a distant echo to me through two thousand five hundred years. Ashoka's pillars of stone, with their inscriptions, would speak to me in their magnificent language and tell me of a man who, though an emperor, was greater than any king or emperor. At Fatehpur Sikri, Akbar, forgetful of his empire, was seated holding converse and debate with the learned of all the faiths,

> curious to learn something new and seeking an answer to the eternal problem of man.[6]

It is this kind of writing, no doubt, that allowed the contemporary filmmaker Shyam Benegal to transform Nehru's *Discovery* into a long television series called *Bharat ek Khoj* (literally: "India—a Quest") in the late 1980s, with many such scenes filled out and converted into entire episodes.[7] Soon after this passage, however, we find that the author has snapped out of this reverie that so captivates our imagination and reverted to the idiom of political philosophy:

> Old established traditions cannot be easily scrapped or dispensed with; in moments of crisis they rise up and dominate the minds of men, and often, as we have seen, a deliberate attempt is made to use those traditions to rouse up a people to a high pitch of effort and sacrifice. Traditions have to be accepted to a large extent and adapted and transformed to meet new conditions and ways of thought, and at the same time new traditions have to be built up.[8]

Sometimes Nehru's tone is rousing, because it expresses such a single-minded, self-denying, altruistic pursuit of the loftiest goals that we cannot help being seduced and inspired by it:

> Behind the past quarter century's struggle for India's independence, and all of our conflicts with British authority, lay in my mind and that of many others the desire to revitalize India. We felt that through action and self-imposed suffering and sacrifice . . . we would recharge the battery of India's spirit and waken her from long slumber. Though we came into conflict continually with the British government in India, our eyes were always turned toward our own people. Political advantage had value only in so far as it helped that fundamental purpose of ours. Because of this governing motive, frequently we acted as no politician moving in the narrow sphere of politics, only, would have done, and foreign and Indian critics expressed surprise at the

> folly and intransigence of our ways. Whether we were foolish or not the historians of the future will judge. We aimed high and looked far.[9]

At other times, Nehru speaks rather more prosaically of practical politics that the Congress must undertake; here, for example, he simply reiterates what was by the 1940s an old adage of Gandhi's, drawn from *Hind Swaraj* almost four decades earlier, that the meaning of swaraj is not merely English rule without the Englishman:

> Individuals did not count, though we wanted good and true individuals to represent us; it was the cause that counted, the organization that represented it, and the nation to whose freedom we were pledged. I analyzed that freedom and what it should mean to the hundreds of millions of our people. We wanted no change of masters from white to brown, but a real people's rule, by the people and for the people, and an ending to our poverty and misery.[10]

In the context of Yeats's poetry and his political philosophy, as well his poetry as a vehicle for his political philosophy more narrowly, MacIntyre turns to the more general importance of the poetic imagination in the very construction of nationhood. MacIntyre states, in very broad terms:

> There are both human relationships and objects of attention in nature that could not exist without the constitutive work of the imagination. . . . So too with the community of a nation: to be Irish or English, I must be able to imagine myself as Irish or English, something achievable in part by participating in the shared poetic utterance of the nation. Take away shared songs and poetry, shared monuments and architecture, shared imaginative conceptions of what is for this nation sacred ground and you at the very least weaken the bonds of nationality. So nations to be real must first be imagined. And so too the loss of a coherent imagination can transform the kind of society that a nation is into something else.[11]

The real purpose of MacIntyre's essay is to illustrate a conflict between Edmund Burke (1729–1797) and W. B. Yeats (1865–1939), Irishmen both, in their attitudes to the Irish nation and to nationalism more generally. MacIntyre sees something of the very nature of the modern state revealed in the ideological and methodological differences between the liberal statesman and the modern poet, the former who made himself into an English gentleman and the latter who remained an Irish patriot to the very end:

> Burke's imaginary England was a prototype in and for the modern world in the way in which it seemed to provide a much-needed mask to be worn by the modern state. The modern state and those who inhabit and seek to uphold it confront a dilemma. It has to present itself in two prima facie incompatible ways. It is, and has to be understood as, an institutionalized set of devices whereby individuals more or less effectively pursue their own goals, that is, it is essentially a means whose efficiency is to be evaluated by individuals in cost-benefit terms. Yet at the same time it claims, and cannot but claim, the kind of allegiance claimed by those traditional political communities—the best type of Greek polis or of the medieval commune—membership in which provided their citizens with a meaningful identity, so that caring for the common good, even to the point of being willing to die for it, was no other than caring for what was good about oneself. The citizen of the modern state is thus invited to view the state intellectually in one way, as a self-interested calculator, but imaginatively in quite another. The modern state presented only in the former light could never inspire adequate devotion. Being asked to die for it would be like being asked to die for the telephone company. And yet the modern state does need to ask its citizens to die for it, a need that requires it to find some quite other set of images for its self-presentation.[12]

The genealogy of this insight—that the modern state has to look sometimes like a revolutionary dream and at other times like the telephone company, and that its two aspects, the imaginative and the bureaucratic, are opposed but inseparable—MacIntyre traces back to Karl Marx:

> The first great classic statement of these two aspects of the modern state was that by Marx in *The Eighteenth Brumaire of Louis Bonaparte,* who saw in the English revolution of the seventeenth century and in the French revolution of the eighteenth a sequence in which a stage of imaginative heroism . . . was followed by one of "sober reality," the prosaic reality of bourgeois society. The politics of poetic imagination gave way to a quite other politics. Marx . . . thought that he was describing the genesis of the peculiarly bourgeois state, when in fact it is the modern state as such that clashes with any politics of the imagination. And he failed to see that the "sober reality" of the modern state in good working order still requires an appeal to imagination, if only by way of disguise, an appeal which claims for the modern state that it is entitled to the same kind of imagination-formed allegiance appropriate for some at least of its antecedents and predecessors. Of course the continuing need for that appeal generates the incoherence that Burke disguised and Yeats diagnosed.[13]

The third chapter of *The Discovery of India* shows us Nehru explicitly appealing not only to the political imagination of his audiences, voters, and constituents, but also, in the process, willing himself to imagine India into existence. He describes in great detail and very vividly his election campaigns in 1936–1937, when he traveled the length and breadth of India, canvassing votes for congressional candidates, most of whom, he admits, he neither knew personally nor had the time or inclination to get to know. Nehru journeyed thousands of miles and came into contact with millions of people. He used every conceivable mode of transportation, ate very little, and hardly slept at all while he was on the road for weeks on end. From the mind-boggling heterogeneity of what he encountered—human beings, landscapes, languages, ethnicities, religions, cultures, and political inclinations—he needed to construct, both for the crowds who turned up to see and hear him, and perhaps more urgently still for his own satisfaction, a coherent entity, the nation called India.

Sometimes for this purpose he drew on an existing stock of images bequeathed to him as well as to his listeners by the preceding half-century of the nationalist movement: hence, the name of Gandhi, the invocation of the

Congress, and the symbol of Swadeshi nationalism first popularized by the Tagores in the early twentieth century, "Mother India." All three were potent and effective signs of the imminent nation. Nehru, whose attitude toward the masses was pedagogic at best and paternalistic at worst (or rather, can be interpreted in either way, depending on how sympathetic the reader wants to be), used these widely understood signals to drive home some basic lessons in imagining the coming community:

> Sometimes as I reached a gathering, a great roar of welcome would greet me: *Bharat Mata ki Jai!*—Victory to Mother India! I would ask them unexpectedly what they meant by that cry, who was this *Bharat Mata,* Mother India, whose victory they wanted? . . . The mountains and the rivers of India, and the forests and the broad fields, which gave us food, were all dear to us, but what counted ultimately were the people of India, people like them and me, who were spread out all over this vast land. *Bharat Mata,* Mother India, was essentially these millions of people, and victory to her meant victory to these people. You are parts of this *Bharat Mata,* I told them, you are in a manner yourselves *Bharat Mata,* and as this idea soaked into their brains, their eyes would light up as if they had made a great discovery.[14]

In my view, this kind of equivalence that Nehru is seeking to make, and to teach his audience to make in a routine way—an equivalence between two abstractions, the Nation and the People, Bhārat Mātā and the collective "you" of his mass address—is perfectly consistent with what MacIntyre calls the "politics of the imagination" that is one of the two faces of the modern state. Partha Chatterjee has a rather different reading, however, of "this remarkable passage" in *Discovery,* which, he suggests,

> tells us a great deal more about the ideological presuppositions of the new nationalist state leadership. To this leadership, the representation of the nation as Mother carried little of the utopian meaning, dream-like and yet passionately real, charged with a deeply religious semiotic, with which the nationalist intel-

> ligentsia had endowed it in its late 19th century phase of Hindu revivalism. . . . We do not have here a Bankim of *Anandamath* or a Rabindranath Tagore in his Swadeshi phase. We have instead a state-builder, pragmatic and self-conscious. The nation as Mother . . . does not figure in his own "scientific" vocabulary of politics. But he can use it, because it has become part of the language which the masses speak when they come to political meetings. So he interprets the word, giving it his own rationalist construction: the nation was the whole people, the victory of the nation meant the victory of the whole people, "people like them and me."[15]

For Chatterjee, Nehru is already—in 1936–1937, at the time of the election campaign described in this passage, or in 1944, as he writes about it in *Discovery*—thinking and acting like a state leader, which he will not in fact become for several more years. (That India would be free, that Nehru would be its first prime minister, were not outcomes that could be seen as set in stone any time between the mid-1930s and the mid-1940s, not even by Nehru himself.) Nehru's use of an image like Bhārat Mātā, then, is merely rhetorical, pragmatic, and perhaps even a bit cynical, because he deploys this figure—of the imagination, and of speech—not out of conviction and felt emotion, but because it can be used to work a crowd, a crowd that Nehru needs to win over but does not personally identify with in the least. In fact, Chatterjee goes on to say in the very next line following the paragraph above: "Men like Jawaharlal Nehru were acutely conscious of the immense cultural gap which separated the 'them' from the 'me.' "[16]

By contrast, in this instance, I would read Nehru as quite genuinely trying to conjure Bhārat Mātā as the body politic, composed of the bodies of millions of Indians, as an image that can convince and carry both himself as the speaker and the crowds that he addresses into a future of independent nationhood. As MacIntyre, following Marx, intuits, this sort of imaginative and symbolic appeal is very much a part of the discourse of the modern state, and a necessary part, without which the state cannot draw in the emotional allegiance of its citizens, cannot ask them to die in its name. Nehru here is not speaking as a calculating rationalist, distant from and condescending to the enormous gatherings that he addresses day after day for months. Had he lacked the nationalist fervor of a Bankim or the poetic appeal of a Rabindranath, had he spoken merely as the future talking back to the past, the bureaucratic head of a planned economy calling out to his backward countrymen in their language of mawkish sentiment and familial attachment, had he lacked conviction, in other words, then it seems very doubtful that he would have enjoyed the immense popularity that he did, for a good thirty years up to his death in 1964. Indians loved Nehru: this is an undeniable truth about India in the mid-1930s, the 1940s, the 1950s and even the early 1960s, until perhaps the disastrous war with China in 1962. They turned out to hear him in the millions during the nationalist era, and they voted him and his party into power consistently over three elections in the post-colonial era.

I think it is not correct to claim, as Chatterjee does, that Bhārat Mātā "comes to him as part of a political language he has taught himself to use; it is just another political slogan which had gained currency and established itself in the meeting grounds of the Congress."[17] To my mind, Nehru is using exactly the language of the poetic imagination, of revolutionary passion, of dream and idea and utopia, of a futurity that is forever attractive because it is forever receding, beckoning us forward, on and on into the unknown, fired by the very human propensity to aspire, to realize what we imagine, to achieve what we have not already, to become what we could be. Far from being detached and cynically manipulating his audiences, Nehru is himself caught up in the subtle alchemy that transforms him into the leader of all Indians and all Indians into the People of India. The body politic is not a lifeless cadaver, being prepared by a ruler-as-surgeon for the anatomical operations of a scientific state: it is a living, breathing, thinking, dreaming entity, with the energy of nationalist desire pulsing through it and joining all if its countless parts into a vital whole. It teaches Nehru as much as Nehru teaches the people; he feels connected to them for psychological strength and political sustenance as much as they look up to him to show them the meaning of the struggle for swaraj:

> I knew my people and I liked them, and their million eyes had taught me much of mass psychology. . . . My eyes held those thousands of eyes: we looked at each other, not as strangers

> meeting for the first time, but with recognition, though of what this was, none could say. As I saluted them with a namaskar, the palms of my hands joined together in front of me, a forest of hands went up in salutation, and a friendly, personal smile appeared on their faces, and a murmur of greeting rose from that assembled multitude and enveloped me in its warm embrace. I spoke to them and my voice carried the message I had brought, and I wondered how far they understood my words or the ideas that lay behind them. Whether they understood all I said or not, I could not say, but there was a light of deeper understanding in their eyes which seemed to go beyond spoken words.[18]

This is a moment of perfect communion between Nehru and "my people," the "assembled multitude": the "thousands of eyes" that hold his gaze; the "forest of hands" raised in a gesture of acceptance; the "murmur of greeting" rising up to fill the air; the "light of deeper understanding" suffusing all those present, leader and led alike. It is impossible to regard this scene with cynicism, to remain unmoved by its imaginative power, untouched by its ineffable emotion. Nehru is nothing here if not a poet of nationhood—the very sort of poet that Rabindranath decided not to be, retreating instead into a very different space, as a man ever "at far remove" (dūrasaṃstha) from the object of his desire. And as for Nehru's alleged consciousness of the "cultural gap" between him and his addressees, let me adduce the very passage from *Discovery* that Chatterjee takes as proof of Nehru's elitist alienation, and see in it an honest effort, carried out over decades, to overcome the constraining prejudices inculcated by class, caste, and education, and to build solidarity with other less-privileged Indians on the basis of thorough and critical self-knowledge:

> India was in my blood and there was much in her that instinctively thrilled me. And yet I approached her almost as an alien critic, full of dislike for the present as well as for many of the relics of the past that I saw. To some extent I came to her via the West and looked at her as a friendly Westerner might have done. I was eager and anxious to change her outlook and appearance and give her the garb of modernity. And yet doubts

> rose within me. Did I know India, I who presumed to scrap much of her past heritage? There was a great deal that had to be scrapped . . . but surely India could not have been what she undoubtedly was, and could not have continued a cultured existence for thousands of years, if she had not possessed something very vital and enduring, something that was worthwhile. What was this something?[19]

Indeed, Nehru's determination to discover the India that he was kept from in Harrow and Cambridge and in the wealthy Allahabad home and expensive legal practice of his aristocratic father, Motilal, has the character not of curiosity but of obsession. Nehru brings not just political ambition but all of the intellectual means at his command—journalistic reportage, anthropological fieldwork, electoral campaigning, the intimate and affectionate tutelage of Gandhi and Tagore, the reading of literature, the writing of history, and spells of deep personal reflection, especially over the ten years or so that he was locked up in jail in the course of his career—to construct India as an object that he and his compatriots can relate to in some fundamental way:

> As I grew up and became engaged in activities which promised to lead to India's freedom, I became obsessed with the thought of India. What was this India that possessed me and beckoned to me continually, urging me to action so we might realize some vague but deeply felt desire of our hearts? The initial urge came to me, I suppose, through pride, both individual and national. . . . What is this India, apart from her physical and geographical aspects? What did she represent in the past; what gave strength to her then? How did she lose that old strength, and has she lost it completely? Does she represent anything vital now, apart from being the home of a vast number of human beings?[20]

Nehru seems to have grasped something that the colonial state did not grasp: that without an appeal that was fundamentally directed at the imagination of ordinary people, no modern state could survive and hold on to popular allegiance. And further, this imaginative appeal, in order to be effective, would have to be made on the basis of shared images of the beloved nation—shared, that is, between the people and their rulers. The symbolic vocabulary, the repertoire of symbols signifying the nation, had to speak to and make sense to not just those in charge of running the state, but those in whose name the state existed. As he traveled the length and breadth of the land, Nehru was attentive to the elements of this lexicon, not merely so that he could blandly and instrumentally ventriloquize on behalf of what Chatterjee calls "the new nationalist state leadership," but because without discovering this common register of signification, without learning the rules of this language, neither Nehru nor the Congress could ever hope to communicate effectively with the people, nor involve them in a political project for which they would be willing to live and die. Gandhi had not only mastered this idiom; arguably he had singlehandedly invented a great deal of it, and what preexisted him, he used with consummate artistry and creative genius.

Nehru understands that even if the sources of popular wisdom and his own specialist knowledge are not the same—people learn from telling each other stories and passing them down the generations; the nationalist intellectuals learn from reading, often in English—nevertheless there has to be a shared content: he and his voters need to be talking about the same aspects of their beloved India:

> Often I was surprised by some such literary turn given by a group of villagers to a simple talk about present-day affairs. If my mind was full of pictures from recorded history and more-or-less ascertained fact, I realized that even the illiterate peasant had a picture gallery in his mind, though this was largely drawn from myth and tradition and epic heroes and heroines, and only very little from history. Nevertheless, it was vivid enough.[21]

The Discovery of India is an elaboration on this "picture gallery" in the mind of India that Nehru manages to enter and see, a vast storehouse of images from history that Nehru builds so that like the Irish or the English whom MacIntyre describes, Indians too could participate in "the shared poetic utterance of the nation." It is the last of his major texts—followed perhaps only by his address to the Constituent Assembly on the day before Independence, and his address to the nation at Independence—when we will see

Nehru as that face of the modern state which is turned toward the political imagination. From August 15, 1947, the very real business of governance must begin, and with it Nehru's language will become completely different, as can be seen in his *Letters to Chief Ministers*. But first, the middle stage, as it were, of the national symbols.

* * *

In the heady summer of 1947, the symbols of colonial rule were to be banished from Indian soil, and the India that Nehru was about to lead had to choose her own emblems. The national symbols were supposed to signify the birth of a new nation-state. They also figured the rupture between India's immediately prior identity as a mere colony under British rule and its new identity as a country with a long and prestigious history of its own, quite apart from the humiliating episode of colonization. Every idea, every law, every symbol that would be chosen to build a new, independent India was being debated in the Constituent Assembly.

As far as I am able to tell from the records of the Constituent Assembly, it was principally thanks to the polemical efforts of Nehru and Dr. S. Radhakrishnan, another prominent founding father, that Aśokan imagery came to occupy center stage in the Indian state's symbolism of nationhood. Nehru's heartfelt attachment to Aśoka and Radhakrishnan's patent admiration for Nehru seem to be the factors most responsible for the choice of symbols ultimately adopted. Except for a discussion preceding the adoption of the national flag, I have not been able to find an actual debate in either the Constituent Assembly, or later on in Parliament, on any of the other symbols. My guess is that through Nehru's writ and Radhakrishnan's influence, they were simply taken on board without much argument from others in the Assembly or the legislature.

But the Aśokan artifacts are more specialized and esoteric, in a sense. Art historians and archaeologists were more likely to have known about their origins and meanings than those who were involved in India's political life. Were experts consulted? If so, when, and at whose behest? Was there any contact between, say, the Constituent Assembly and the Sarnath Museum or the Archaeological Survey of India? I have not been able to locate any trace of such a correspondence, if indeed it did take place, nor have I been able to spot any remarks by either proponents or opponents about these choices, anywhere in the written record.[22]

The author of every one of these choices, at the time of Independence, was none other than Jawaharlal Nehru. At least this is what I am led to surmise, with a reasonable expectation of being true to the historical sequence of events, based on what we find of Nehru's statements about these symbols to the Constituent Assembly, as well as the fact that as the executive head of state, he must have given his final approval before any of these representations could be accepted as a part of India's official regalia.

Dr. S. Radhakrishnan (1888–1975), independent India's first vice president (1952–1962) and second president (1962–1967) as well as its ambassador to the Soviet Union (1949–1952), an academic philosopher, Sanskrit scholar, vice chancellor of the Banaras Hindu University and sometime Oxford don, and a close associate of Nehru's especially from about 1946 onward, seems to have encouraged and facilitated the choosing of these emblems, as far as we are able to determine, both from the Constituent Assembly debates and from his own scholarly writings. That Nehru and Radhakrishnan consulted art historians, Sanskritists, or staff (whether British or Indian) at the Archaeological Survey of India and/or at the Sarnath Museum, I am unable to claim definitively, although it can be said that much of the information that could conceivably have been obtained from such experts was already by this time available in a vast scholarly literature out in the public domain. While the Aśokan artifacts are in some sense esoteric, requiring both historical knowledge and art critical interpretation in order for them to make proper sense, nothing really prevented these two highly erudite and patriotic men from doing the archaeological and philological homework on their own.

The national symbols I focus on are three of several, and of these three, I really focus mainly on just two: the state seal (the Sarnath Lion Capital) and the dhammacakra (wheel of law) at the center of the national flag. The third, the national credo or national motto, *satyameva jayate* ("Truth Alone Triumphs") is taken from the *Muṇḍaka Upaniṣad,* which was one of the eighteen principal Upaniṣad texts translated and commented upon by Radhakrishnan in his capacity as a scholar of Sanskrit philosophical systems. While the credo too is important, I do not devote as much attention to it because it is adopted less directly at Nehru's initiative, I suspect, and is more clearly attributable to Radhakrishnan. The Lion Capital and the dhammacakra, on the other hand, seem both explicitly to communicate Nehru's vision of what free India's state regalia ought to look like, and implicitly to embody his consistent fascination with the Mauryan state and its ecumene. The Lion Capital is taken from the Aśoka Pillar found in Sarnath, as is the dhammacakra, though the latter motif is ubiquitous in Buddhist art and architecture all across the subcontinent, from the earliest period (which is the Mauryan) right into the middle of the first millennium.

For reasons that will become clear, I do not discuss the entire flag, whose three colors—saffron, white, and green—have various acknowledged significations, but only the wheel of dharma at its very center. I am treating the dispersed body of Nehru's statements about the Mauryan Empire, Aśoka, Kauṭilya, and these two national symbols taken from the Mauryan state (i.e., the Lion Capital and the wheel of law) as a core text in my reading of Nehru, following *The Discovery of India* (1946) and preceding his *Letters to Chief Ministers* (1947–1964). To me, these writings and speeches of Nehru's capture both the faces of the modern state that MacIntyre points out—the imaginative and the practical—as well as both the aspects of selfhood—its normativity (dharma) and its instrumentality (artha)—that I want to argue represent the outcome of Nehru's search for the self (the swa of swaraj), in keeping with the larger quest of the founding fathers that we are following in this book.

The Lion Capital consists of the frontal figures of four seated lions on a chiasmus, of which three are visible at any time, one facing the viewer and two in profile with their backs to one another. In January 2010, I traveled to the archaeological museum in Sarnath, Uttar Pradesh, where the original Lion Capital is displayed. The lions are carved in a stylized Achaemenid manner, with curly manes and open jaws. They sit atop a circular plinth, carved with four animals: a bull, an elephant, a horse, and a lion yet again, interspersed with four wheels or cakras. The entire design originally rested on a base shaped like an inverted bell-shaped lotus, but that floral portion is not included in the emblem. The original Lion Capital is imposing, but not enormous; two and a half millennia later, its texture remains smooth; the stone used is a kind of granite, chocolate brown in color, flecked with black.

The four lions point in the four cardinal directions, and the entire foursome sits atop a pillar, thereby surveying a landscape defined by the lions' lines of sight—a landscape whose circumference is literally as far as these leonine eyes can see. Following symbolic conventions used by Achaemenid and Persian rulers of the third and fourth centuries BCE, Aśoka planted several pillars with such leonid motifs all across the expanse of his empire: some with single lions, others with four. Pillars mounted with lion capitals functioned as the ancient world's signposts, skyscrapers, and broadcast towers all at once, indexing power by pointing both upward (via the stem of the pillar) and radially (via the eyes of the lion), and physically dominating any space in which they were placed. Aśoka's empire did not literally cover the huge swath of South Asia that is sometimes depicted on so-called historical maps of the Mauryan territories; rather, the pillars (as well as large rock faces carved with edicts, about which more later) were strategically located at crossroads and outposts, on borders and in peripheral regions, so as to suggest territorial capture and deep penetration where none or very little such control might have existed in the hinterlands. The lion capital had the capacity to endow a mere pillar with both greater height and a radius of influence as it were, besides its intrinsic aesthetic appeal and connotations of ferocity and strength associated with the figure of the lion.

State seal of the Republic of India, depicting the Sarnath Lion Capital and the national credo, *satyameva jayate*

The Sarnath structure originally had three parts: a cylindrical pillar, mounted by a quadruplex lion capital, in turn surmounted by a vertical dhammacakra. Broken fragments of this artifact were found by Sir John Marshall and F. O. Oertel of the Archaeological Survey of India in excavations conducted around the turn of the twentieth century. A photograph published around 1905 shows the freshly excavated archaeological site, a pit of dirt surrounded by low walls, with several key finds arranged like set pieces on a stage: fragments of the broken pillar, the lion capital, and the shattered wheel, as well as an image of the Buddha in a pose known as *dharma-cakra-pravartana-mudrā* ("Pose depicting the Buddha setting into motion the Wheel of Dharma").[23] It's amusing to think that the entire regalia of the future state of India, which was not even a gleam in Gandhi's eye in 1905, is laid out like stage props in this photograph—the different elements were probably so arranged by the archaeological team only so that they could be conveniently photographed, and not because anyone could possibly have had an inkling of their future uses to Nehru's nationalism. In all events, the dhammacakra, a symbol that occurs widely in Buddhist art and literature, when set atop a pillar would suggest that the worldly empire of the Mauryan dynasts and the ethical imperium of dhamma (dharma) were coextensive: they extended over one and the same territorial/abstract space.

The Republic of India took on the Sarnath Lion Capital as the state seal and put the dhammacakra at the heart of the national flag because of exactly the same meanings, and exactly the same logics of signification, that these two symbols had in their original context in the Mauryan world. They connoted simultaneously the concrete, historically specific, territorially defined power of a state and an abstract realm of ethical sovereignty, where dhamma/dharma, or in modern terms the rule of law, prevailed. Nehru's formal announcement to the Constituent Assembly on July 22, 1947, went as follows:

> Resolved that the National Flag of India shall be a horizontal tricolour of deep saffron (kesari), white and dark green in equal proportion. In the centre of the white band, there shall be a Wheel in navy blue to represent the Charkha. The design of the Wheel shall be that of the Wheel (Chakra) which appears on the

> abacus of the Sarnath Lion Capital of Asoka. The diameter of the Wheel shall approximate to the width of the white band. The ratio of the width to the length of the flag shall ordinarily be 2:3.[24]

A Home Ministry note dated August 24, 1956 (nearly ten years later) states that the Cabinet approved on December 11, 1947, Nehru's proposal that the Sarnath Lion Capital be adopted as the basis of the state seal, and that its design would conform closely to the Aśokan original, excluding only the inverted, bell-shaped lotus plinth on which the four lions sat. Several colleagues of Nehru in India's Constituent Assembly sought to attribute a range of meanings to the national symbols like the cakra. Other more or less viable interpretations of the cakra were also tabled:

1. It is associated, as a most ancient, basic, and yet indispensable form of technology, with ordinary people and their work—thus, for a primarily agrarian country like India, the lifeworld of the peasant and the villager.
2. An extension of this meaning is to take the wheel as a symbol of revolution *(krāntī)*.
3. Its purpose, onward movement, suggests the continuously mobile, dynamic nature of reality—in this sense the cakra stands for the law of life itself, which is perpetual change.
4. The iconography of the god Vishnu, especially in his avatar as Krishna, on the battlefield of Kurukshetra in the great Bhārata War, shows him carrying a disclike weapon called the *sudarśan cakra* (literally: "beautiful wheel-weapon").
5. The idea of balance, since a wheel will not stand upright or roll forward unless an appropriate set of forces is in play, thus indicates that without the law, a political system would not only fail to progress, but would simply collapse and fail.
6. This religious symbol is popular in Orissa, where Krishna is worshipped in the form of the deity Jagannātha, who is

associated with a blue wheel called the *nīla cakra*. Orissa—ancient Kalinga—was where Aśoka had his change of heart with regard to war and violence.

7. Yet others saw in the cakra the federal character of the state: the thirty-two spokes of the wheel all stood in an identical relationship to the center.

The emergent Indian nation-state was as expansive as the Aśokan empire and the cakra reminded the nation of its constituent parts as well as of its center that aspired to be strong and controlling. One by one, different participants in the debate on the flag put forward these readings, and they were duly noted in the record of the Constituent Assembly, but it was Nehru's interpretation of the meanings of the national symbols that India adopted.

In its specifically Aśokan iteration, which is the one I believe really clinched the argument for Nehru, the cakra has two mutually opposed but nonetheless doubly attractive significations. On the one hand, it stands for the entire congeries of Buddhist values present in the umbrella term dhamma: righteousness, law, peace, non-violence, and universal, normative order. On the other hand, it also symbolizes the rule of the wheel-turning sovereign, *cakravartī rājā,* who is responsible for the propagation and maintenance of dhamma throughout his territories. The cakra thus stands for both the abstract principle of dhamma and the temporal power of the wheel-turning ruler, *cakravartin*. It has one face turned toward eternity and the other toward the world, signifying a special kind of dominion that is at once impersonal and ubiquitous, as well as concentrated in the person of the king, in this case, Aśoka. The cakra, in this way, signifies the imperium of dharma/dhamma. Nehru too, I think, would have wanted it to convey simultaneously righteousness and sovereignty, the rule of law that prevails over the entire space of politics as such, and the authority of a very concrete, real, and particular dispensation—in other words, an actual state. "But what type of wheel should we have? Our minds went back to many wheels but notably one famous wheel, which had appeared in many places and which all of us have seen, the one at the top of the capital of the Asoka column . . . That wheel is a symbol of India's ancient culture, it is a symbol of many things that India had stood for through the ages," Nehru told the Constituent Assembly.[25]

The reason for Nehru's enthusiastic sponsorship of the capital and the wheel, and for his alacrity in carrying them through the Constituent Assembly, was really his abiding fascination with Aśoka, of all the ancient monarchs of India (apart from possibly Akbar the Great Mughal, r. 1556–1605) the one premodern sovereign with whom he personally identified most closely:

> For my part, I am exceedingly happy that . . . we have associated with this Flag of ours not only this emblem but in a *sense the name of Asoka, one of the most magnificent names not only in India's history but in world history. . . .* Now because I have mentioned the name of Asoka I should like you to think that *the Asokan period in Indian history was essentially an international period of Indian history. It was not a narrowly national period. It was a period when India's ambassadors went abroad to far countries and went abroad not in the way of an Empire and imperialism but as ambassadors of peace and culture and goodwill.* (Cheers).[26]

Some of the members of the Assembly brought up other Aśokan as well as Kauṭilyan ideals in connection with the cakra, using a kind of free association method, hence Panchsheel or "five virtues," principles of diplomacy to further the good relations between two states.[27] Nehru eventually was to sign an agreement that incorporated the idea of Panchsheel with India's northern neighbor, China, in 1954.[28] These virtues or principles were: (1) respect for one another's territory and sovereignty; (2) mutual non-aggression; (3) mutual non-interference; (4) equality and mutual benefit; and (5) peaceful coexistence. In its treatment of the Tibetan people throughout the 1950s, as well as its aggression against India in 1962, China violated every aspect of this fivefold doctrine that Nehru held so dear. But it is significant that the cakra itself was, to many Indian eyes, including very possibly those of Nehru himself, evocative of what history memorializes as Aśoka's desire for friendly relations with rival polities and neighboring states.

As Tagore kept on returning to Kalidasa and especially to his *Meghadūta* throughout his life, Nehru returned to Aśoka and to the Mauryan Empire numerous times in his writings. We find him using the examples of Candragupta, Chanakya, and Aśoka to wax eloquent about nationalism as a sort of

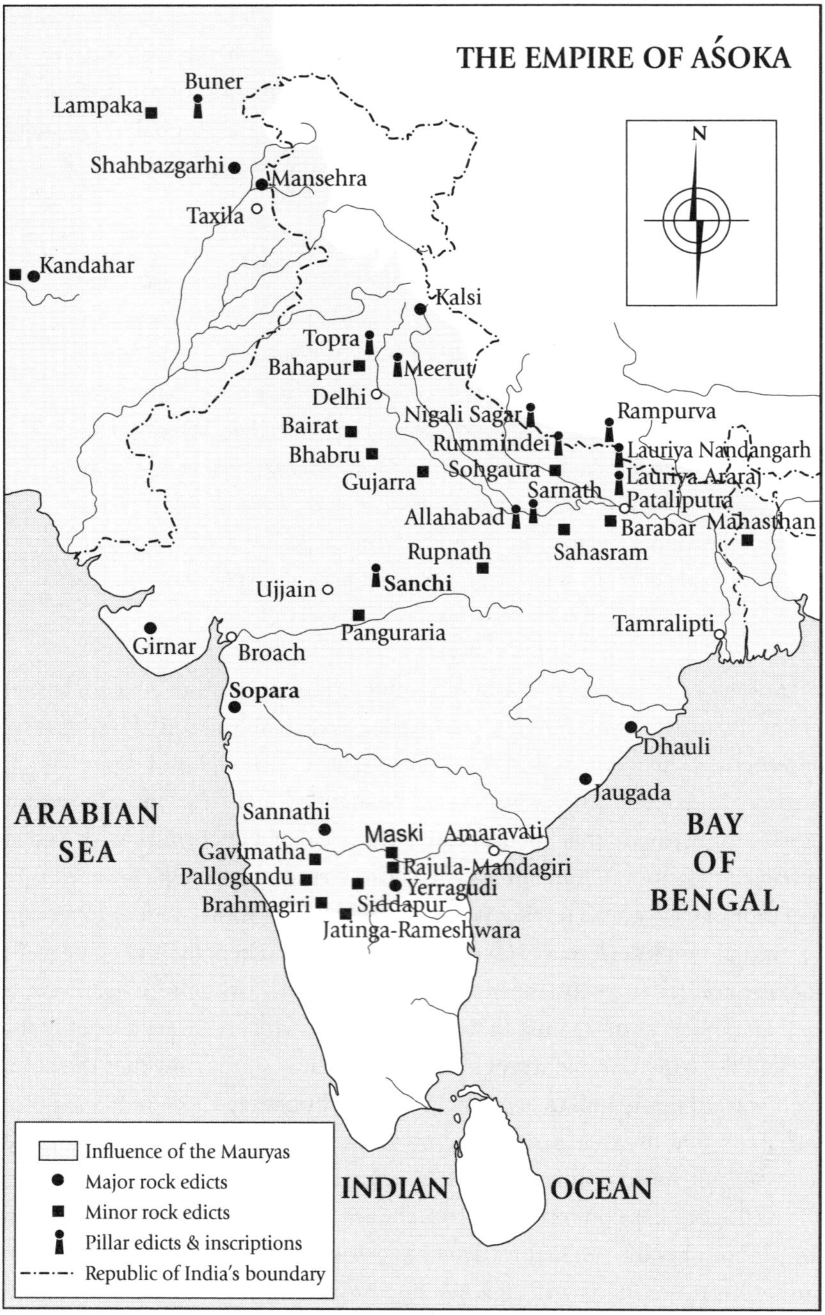
THE EMPIRE OF AŚOKA
N
Buner
Lampaka
Shahbazgarhi
Mansehra
Taxila
Kandahar
Kalsi
Topra
Bahapur
Meerut
Delhi
Nigali Sagar
Rampurva
Bairat
Rummindei
Lauriya Nandangarh
Bhabru
Sohgaura
Lauriya Araraj
Gujarra
Sarnath
Pataliputra
Allahabad
Barabar
Mahasthan
Rupnath
Sahasram
Ujjain
Sanchi
Girnar
Panguraria
Tamralipti
Broach
Sopara
Dhauli
Jaugada
ARABIAN
SEA
Sannathi
Maski
Amaravati
BAY
OF
BENGAL
Gavimatha
Rajula-Mandagiri
Pallogundu
Yerragudi
Brahmagiri
Siddapur
Jatinga-Rameshwara
INDIAN
OCEAN
Influence of the Mauryas
Major rock edicts
Minor rock edicts
Pillar edicts & inscriptions
Republic of India's boundary

primordial drive among all peoples, blithely resorting to anachronism and an ideological overreading of history:

> Soon news came of Alexander's death at Babylon in 323 B.C., and immediately *Chandragupta and Chanakya raised the old and ever-new cry of nationalism and roused the people against the foreign invader.* The Greek garrison was driven away and Taxila captured. The appeal to nationalism had brought allies to Chandragupta and he marched with them across north India to Pataliputra.[29]

> Ashoka succeeded to this great empire about 273 B.C. . . . *The old dream of uniting the whole of India under one supreme government fired Ashoka* and forthwith he undertook the conquest of Kalinga on the east coast. . . . This astonishing ruler, beloved still in India and in many other parts of Asia, devoted himself to the spread of Buddha's teaching, to righteousness and goodwill, and to public works for the good of the people. . . . He laboured hard at public business and declared that he was always ready for it.[30]

The dream of "uniting the whole of India under one supreme government" of course was not old, it was new, and it was not so much Aśoka's dream as Nehru's own. The "foreign invader" who provokes the "old and ever-new cry of nationalism" is not Alexander so much as John Company; the "appeal of nationalism" is what the Congress makes to modern Indians subjugated by British rule, and is imputed by Nehru to Candragupta completely without historical basis or political context. That Nehru's own preoccupations are squarely in the present can be seen as he tries to understand who Chanakya was through the modern figure of Clausewitz, the early nineteenth-century Prussian theorist of war:

> Kautilya is another name for Chanakya. . . . Chanakya has been called the Indian Machiavelli, and to some extent the comparison is justified. But he was a much bigger person in every way, greater in intellect and action. . . . Long before Clausewitz, he [Chanakya] is reported to have said that war is only a continuance of state policy by other means. But, he adds, war must always serve the larger ends of policy and not become an end in

> itself; the statesman's objective must always be the betterment of the state as a result of war, not the mere defeat and destruction of the enemy. If war involves both parties in a common ruin, that is the bankruptcy of statesmanship.[31]

But while Nehru cannot but praise Kauṭilya, given both his reputation as the brain behind Candragupta's throne and the antiquity of his treatise on statecraft, the *Arthaśāstra* (the manuscript of which was rediscovered and published in India in 1909), his real hero is Candragupta's grandson, Aśoka. Kauṭilya may have theorized war, and Candragupta may have waged the wars necessary to found the Mauryan Empire, but Aśoka surpassed them both in actually renouncing war and making non-violence his state policy. A particularly bloody slaughter in the eastern province of Kalinga sickened Aśoka to such a degree that he permanently gave up on warfare as a necessary element of rule. Nehru is riveted by both the political implications and the psychological drama of the Aśokan turn:

> Asoka succeeded to this great empire about 273 B.C. . . . The old dream of uniting the whole of India under one supreme government fired Asoka and forthwith he undertook the conquest of Kalinga on the east coast, which corresponds roughly with modern Orissa and part of Andhra. His armies triumphed in spite of the brave and obstinate resistance of the people of Kalinga. There was a terrible slaughter in this war, and when news of this reached Asoka he was stricken with remorse and disgusted with war. Unique among the victorious monarchs and captains in history, he decided to abandon warfare in the full tide of victory. The whole of India acknowledged his sway, except for the southern tip, and that tip was his for the taking. But he refrained from any further aggression, and his mind turned, under the influence of Buddha's gospel, to conquests and adventures in other fields.[32]

In a letter to his daughter from prison, included in *Glimpses of World History,* Nehru unequivocally express his disregard of kings and princes. Yet he makes a single exception for an emperor who he admired, whose life and ideas had moved and inspired him: Aśoka. In that letter to his daughter he writes:

> I am afraid I am a little too fond of running down kings and princes. I see little in their kind to admire or do reverence to. But we are now coming to a man who, in spite of being a king and emperor, was worthy of great admiration. He was Ashoka, the grandson of Chandragupta Maurya . . . and for an Indian it is an especial pleasure to think of this period of India's history. . . . Nearly the whole of India, except a tiny tip in the south, was under him; and it was easy enough for him to complete the conquest of this little tip. But he refrained.[33]

The story of Aśoka has at least seven elements that I think account for why he becomes a major symbol in Nehru's quest for an Indic self. The first is Aśoka's espousal of non-violence as a guiding value in his ideology of rule, following his change of heart after the destructive war in Kalinga. In the letter mentioned earlier, Nehru speaks of Aśoka, with relish: "According to H. G. Wells, he is the only military monarch on record who abandoned warfare after victory."[34] The second is Aśoka's decision to protect non-Buddhist communities, famously the Ajivika sect, from persecution. Nehruvian secularism owes something to this precedent. In *Glimpses of World History,* Nehru is effusive about the tolerant and non-sectarian Aśoka:

> The whole of history is full of religious persecution and religious wars. . . . It is good therefore to remember how a great son of India, intensely religious, and the head of a powerful empire, behaved in order to convert people to his ways of thought. It is strange that anyone should be so foolish as to think that religion and faith can be thrust down a person's throat at the point of a sword or a bayonet.[35]

The third element is Aśoka's stated intention, as a ruler, to both protect and propagate dhamma—which may be read narrowly in the sense of Buddhism, or broadly in the sense of normative social and personal conduct—all over his empire and beyond. The fourth is Aśoka's practice of sending diplomatic as well as monastic emissaries to other civilized parts of Asia, bearing both messages of political goodwill and Buddhist religious teachings to near and far kingdoms. The fifth is the institutional infrastructure of the Aśokan state: the fact that the emperor built roads, rest houses, public kitchens, and hospitals; planted trees and protected animals; and appointed officers with a special designation *(dharma-mahāmātra)* to oversee the implementation, so to speak, of dhamma throughout the land. The sixth is the caring, benign, and paternal orientation of the ruler toward the people, which makes him beloved to the gods *(devānāmpriya)* and the sinecure of all eyes *(priyadarśī)*. And finally, for Nehru, the seventh attractive element about Aśoka was his radial understanding of sovereignty, figured through the vast spatial scatter of the rock and pillar edicts.

In a way, Nehru saw himself as the new Aśoka. If India had to keep its "tryst with destiny," then only an ethical sovereign who was also a creative historian could be the keeper of that tryst—a mantle that Nehru was fully prepared to assume at Independence. Gandhi did not see himself as the new Krishna, nor did Ambedkar see himself as the new Buddha, but Nehru certainly saw himself as the new Aśoka. This strong, confident sense of a historic mission, purpose, and role was present in Nehru to a degree not seen in any of his contemporaries, not even those gifted with a comparable or perhaps superior understanding of history, a lively political imagination, and a position of leadership in the nationalist movement. Nehru proved to be first among equals in the impressive array of India's founders because he had what was in fact the clearest, least conflicted idea of India's foundations.

Nehru was not only a nationalist politician who became free India's first prime minister. He also played a significant role in international politics, providing leadership to decolonizing nations across Asia and Africa. He was launched on the world stage as a statesman of global stature when the Non-Aligned Movement came into its own in Bandung, Indonesia, in 1955. NAM, as it was called, provided a space for the new nations of the so-called Third World to maintain a political, ideological, and economic distance from both of the superpowers that had emerged after World War II—the capitalist United States and the communist USSR. Nehru, together with the leader of

Egypt, Gamal Abdel Nasser, and the leader of Yugoslavia, Josip Broz Tito, as well as other leaders like Indonesia's Sukarno and Ghana's Kwame Nkrumah, played a defining role in laying out NAM's position on various international disputes. Nehru promoted ideas of freedom, democracy, self-determination, goodwill, interdependence, peace, cultural exchange, and equality, not just within but also between countries, especially those outside Europe, emerging from the shadow of decades if not centuries of Western colonialism and imperialism.

Nehru wanted friendly and positive relations between India and China, as well as between India and other nations in the South Asian region, especially given the constant warlike tensions between India and Pakistan over Kashmir that extracted such high costs from both fraternal twins throughout Nehru's tenure as prime minister. In the 1950s, when the Chinese invaded Tibet and systematically assaulted Tibetan Buddhist culture, culminating in the exile of the Tibetan leader, the Dalai Lama, in 1959, along with thousands of his persecuted countrymen, it was Nehru who gave the Tibetan refugees a safe haven, in Dharamshala, a small hill town in northern India. He tried to support the fleeing Tibetans even as he struggled not to allow matters to come to a head in India's growing distance and discomfort with Mao's China. Nehru was unsuccessful in juggling these contradictory impulses to keep the peace with both the Chinese aggressors and their Tibetan victims. In 1962 the Chinese made aggressive incursions into Indian territory at multiple points all along the long Sino-Indian Himalayan frontier, so that the aged Nehru, against his deepest convictions, had to go to war with China. He lost this war, and died soon after in 1964, a broken man.

Nehru's charismatic global outreach through NAM, his behavior during India's wars with Pakistan (1947–1948, 1965) and China (1962), and his conflicted attitude toward the Kashmiris and the Tibetans, as well as several other episodes in the Indian northeast where Nehru had to consolidate the reach of the Indian state against popular resistance, reveal a leader who wanted to follow Aśokan ideals of welfare, friendship, pacifism, trust, and compassion, for the citizens of his country as well as for other countries, but who faced a world more given to strife than reconciliation.[36] In a foundationalist impulse that he shared with many of India's leaders, Nehru projected a personality, as a ruler, that converged with the real or legendary

Aśoka in the popular imagination of modern Indians. He even named his only child, Indira (born in 1917), after Aśoka's title "Priyadarshini," literally, "beloved of the gods and pleasing to the eye."

Aśoka provides a template for Nehru for a number of different reasons: his capacity to command and expand an empire, topped by his even greater ability to exercise restraint and eschew the possibility of realizing unbridled power; his intense religiosity—Aśoka converted to Buddhism and acted as a propagandist for this (then) relatively new faith—combined with his decision to refrain, once again, from forcing others to follow him; his professed care for his subjects and for all life—human, animal, and vegetable; and last but not least, his reflexivity—his thoughtful, honest, self-critical style of communication, so clearly imprinted on the rock and pillar edicts that he had planted all over the Mauryan sphere of influence.[37]

I suspect what Nehru found most compelling about Aśoka was that Aśoka, of all the sovereigns of ancient India, wrote down his ideas and took the trouble to make them comprehensible to people everywhere, by having them either translated or transliterated as appropriate by region. Aśoka was a ruler, a pacifist, ethical, ecumenical, and literary—a veritable Jawaharlal *avant la lettre.* Nehru's own life-long propensity to both write to and talk to his people, with his signature mix of confession and didacticism, need hardly be emphasized.

The Buddha is the first historical person to appear in Indic antiquity: the first about whom we know enough biographical and chronological details so as not to doubt either his existence or the more or less exact duration of his life, as well as what happened in this life. But it is really only with Candragupta and Kauṭilya and their founding of a state that India emerges "out of the myth-smoke," as historian John Keay writes, and into "Gloria Maurya."[38] The history of India as told by Jawaharlal Nehru in his *Discovery,* and by imperialist historians before him as well as by nationalist historians after, is constructed as a series of subcontinent-sized polities, bookended by the Mauryan Empire in the beginning and the British Empire at the end, with other significant intervening moments being the Guptas in the first millennium and the Mughals in the second. None of these political formations strictly speaking resembles the postcolonial nation-state, but nevertheless, these become the nation's predecessors, mainly on account of their significant territorial scale, military power, economic wealth, and cultural achievements. If the Mauryans (post-Aśoka anyway) are Buddhist, the Guptas are Hindus, the Mughals are Muslim, and the British are Christians, so much the better as the diverse predecessors of secular India.

The Sarnath Lion Capital sits on a cylindrical disc, around which runs a carved band that is also included in India's state seal. On this band are four animals—a lion, a bull, a horse, and an elephant—interspersed with four small cakra discs. The appearance of the cakra both under the lions and immediately on top of them (in the original, now broken pillar) can be attributed to the immense importance of the dhammacakra to Buddhism's political theology. The cakra can be seen in Buddhist artifacts of all periods and in locations not just all over India, but indeed in all the catchment areas of ancient Buddhism, from Afghanistan in the west to Southeast Asia, and from Tibet in the north to Sri Lanka in the south. The Buddha, as already mentioned, set into motion the wheel of dharma after he attained Enlightenment. A righteous and powerful sovereign, in the Buddhist conception, is called a *cakra-vartin,* "wheel-turner," and a *dharma-rāja,* "dharma-king."

The life of Aśoka within the Buddhist canonical literature, the *Aśokāvadāna* (a text dated to roughly the second century CE), describes the transformation of Aśoka from a cruel despotic tyrant into an ethical Buddhist ruler to whom such epithets could be appropriately attached.[39] The *Cakkavatti-Sinhanāda-Sutta,* "Discourse Concerning the Lion's Roar of the Wheel-Turning King," a story in the foundational Buddhist text, the *Tipitaka* (Three Baskets of Stories) tells of how the dhammacakra literally shines in the sky like the sun: its setting and sinking indicates the decline of dharma, which brings a flourishing society to ruin; its rise indicates that the world is once again restored to a condition of normative order, necessary for human happiness.[40] Only a just and virtuous ruler, and pious monks of the Buddhist community, all engaged in their proper tasks in their respective spheres, can keep the dhammacakra buoyed in the firmament. In its absence, war and pestilence break out, social norms are violated, prosperity vanishes, and life spans are drastically shortened. Unless the wheel of law remains in place, there is sociobiological chaos.

The decisions to take the Lion Capital as India's seal and to place the dhammacakra at the center of the national flag suggest that Nehru wanted both to appropriate the antiquity of the Mauryan imperium to equip the new republic with a historical ancestor that had adequate political weight as well as desirable ethical standards, and to retain the idea of normative order (dharma) as central to the contemporary Indian conception of the political. In addition, he liked the idea of a history for the Indian state in which Indic political theory was being written well over 2,000 years ago—in fact, almost exactly at the same time as Aristotle's *Politics*—and Gandhi's current gospel of ahimsa was anticipated by the original turn to non-violence of Emperor Aśoka. It was a bonus that Candragupta was a state builder and Kauṭilya a strategic thinker, and that Aśoka sent Buddhist embassies all over Asia to propagate his message, expand his moral authority, and enter into peaceful relations with other rulers and their kingdoms, near and far. Recall Nehru's words to the Constituent Assembly:

> Now because I have mentioned the name of Asoka I should like you to think that the Asokan period in Indian history was essentially an international period of Indian history. It was not a narrowly national period. It was a period when India's ambassadors went abroad to far countries and went abroad not in the way of an Empire and imperialism but as ambassadors of peace and culture and goodwill.[41]

All of these significations latent in the Mauryan moment were seized upon by Nehru, as should be abundantly clear by now. And yet he had little or no stakes in the specifically Buddhist character of the Aśokan conception of the political—no interest in Aśokan dhamma qua Budhhist dhamma, no suggestion, at any stage, that India should adopt Buddhism, say, as its state religion. Nehru could see, as he wrote in *Discovery,* the Buddha giving his first sermon in the deer park at Sarnath; he could hear the voice of Aśoka speak to him from the edict carved on the Aśokan pillar there. But all of these visions and intimations were of a historical and not a religious nature: through them Nehru grasped some of the philosophical teachings of the Buddha and some of the moral strictures of Aśoka but more importantly the depth, complexity, and nobility of India's past, which had to now be recalled, marshaled, and adduced in the cause of nation building. Some aspects of the past were unsuitable for the purposes of nationalist pride, as Nehru acknowledges when he writes, "in some ways this Mauryan state reminds one of modern dictatorships."[42] Other aspects, like the Buddha's theory of the impermanence of identity and the transience of the self, Nehru can both understand and retain, without in the least taking them to be truths that warrant either faith or skepticism of a religious kind:

> Our bodies and our souls change from moment to moment; they cease to be and something else, like them and yet different, appears and then passes off. In a sense we are dying all the time and being reborn, and this succession gives the appearance of an unbroken identity. . . . It is remarkable how near this philosophy of the Buddha brings us to some of the concepts of modern physics and modern philosophical thought.[43]

If there is any system that can be described as religious or something close to religion toward which Nehru does express at the very least "an intellectual appreciation," it is Upaniṣadic monism: "I have been attracted toward the Advaita (nondualist) philosophy of the Vedānta, though I do not presume to understand it in all its depth and intricacy," he confesses in the very first chapter of *Discovery*.[44] The third and last national symbol that I discuss in this book is India's motto, *satyameva jayate,* which is taken from the *Muṇḍaka Upaniṣad,* usually counted as the fifth in a series of 108 Upaniṣads:

MU: 3.1.6:
satyameva jayate nānṛtamsatyena panthā vitato devayānaḥ|
yenākramantyṛṣayo hyāptakāmāyatra tat satyasya paramaṁ nidhānam||

Which translates, more or less:

Truth alone prevails, not untruth.
With the help of the truth
A divine path (a way of the gods) is laid out
On which the great sages
Whose desires are appropriate (/befitting)
Proceed to the ultimate abode of truth[45]

Yeats somewhat precariously translates this as follows: "Falsehood turns from the way; truth goes all the way; the end of the way is truth; the way is paved with truth. The sage travels there without desire."[46]

In his *Principal Upanishads* (1953), Radhakrishan translates this as:

> Truth alone conquers, not untruth.
> By truth is laid out the path leading to the gods
> By which the sages who have their desires fulfilled
> Travel to where is that supreme abode of truth.[47]

And notes immediately below it: *"satyam eva jayate:* truth alone conquers. This is the motto inscribed on the seal of the Indian nation." He also notes a different reading of one of the key words in this mantra that comes down to us in the textual traditions:

> *jayate v. jayati*

Based on this alternative reading that is noted by Radhakrishnan, the contemporary Sanskrit scholar Patrick Olivelle translates the mantra as:

> The real alone he wins, never the unreal.
> Along the real runs the path to the gods,
> On which the seers proceed, their desires fulfilled,
> To where that highest treasure of the real is found.[48]

Whether we translate "satya" as "the truth" or "the real" is not really the problem here; the question is, do we treat satya as the subject of the verb or as the object? In other words, does someone (X) conquer the truth and the truth alone (nothing other than truth); or does truth alone conquer (everything)? It is the latter sense that is favored in the national motto, and that Radhakrishnan chooses, following several premodern commentaries.[49]

In Olivelle's reconstruction, the implied subject is *ātman* (being/self/soul), indicated by the personal pronoun "he": "He wins [gains/gets/conquers] only the truth [the real], never untruth [the unreal]." We cannot know what exact role Nehru played in either selecting or approving *satyameva jayate* as the motto that would be printed below the state seal, but it seems safe to suggest that had he been presented with the difference between the implications of *jayati* versus *jayate,* given his determined personal atheism, he might have had a strong preference for "Truth Alone Triumphs" over "He [the implied Subject of All Advaita Vedānta] Conquers the Truth"—thereby reifying a non-personified, non-anthropomorphic, and fundamentally non-religious category like satya (truth/being/the real), rather than introducing into the national emblem any trace of a soul-like or godlike "Hindu" theological entity. As it stands, the credo is perfectly anodyne: drawn from a classical source, veridical, lofty, and non-sectarian. Nehru could not but have been rather pleased with it as the right motto for the Indian nation.

* * *

The Constituent Assembly debates, the rituals around Independence—such as the adoption of the national symbols, the speeches on the occasion of August 15, the formalities of the transfer of power from the British government to the Indian, and subsequently the promulgation of the Constitution of the Republic on January 26, 1950—marked a kind of crescendo in Jawaharlal Nehru's career as a nationalist leader. Once this threshold of decolonization had been crossed, and India had launched itself as an independent nation-state, the occasions for Nehru, as the prime minister, to write or speak in the particular exhortatory and grandiloquent vein noted in the preceding sections became fewer and fewer; he now had very pressing, very mundane tasks to take care of. These included dealing with the aftermath of Partition violence, rehabilitating millions of refugees, organizing—and fighting—the first elections to have a universal adult franchise, the integration of the former princely states, the linguistic reorganization of the states of the Indian Union, and putting into place the new executive, legislative, judicial, military, bureaucratic, and legal architecture of the nation-state.[50] No matter how great the level of "colonial continuity," the scale of the work at hand was enormous, as India emerged from colonial rule as the world's largest democracy and one of its poorest countries.

It was in this context of an almost unimaginable administrative burden and independent India's nominally federal yet highly centralized governance structure that Nehru instituted the practice of writing a fortnightly letter to the chief ministers of the different states, a practice he kept up over seventeen years more or less regularly for the remainder of his life and career.[51] The letters are now available to us in five thick volumes. Reading through them offers a way to reprise the eventful history of the period between 1947 and 1964, as Nehru pens his version of all kinds of significant domestic and international developments. Some letters are addressed to the chief ministers or administrative heads of particular states that might be undergoing a specific type of upheaval, such as Kashmir, especially in Volume 1 (covering the first years of Independence, when Kashmir was neither liberated nor fully absorbed into either India or Pakistan, occasioning the first war between the two neighbors in the winter of 1947–1948). While at no point does Nehru lose either his distinctive voice or his literary flair, and while the letters often have the reflective moments so typical of the man, the overall difference in tone between *The Discovery of India* and *Letters to Chief Ministers* is undeniable and marked. Nehru has clearly made an irreversible transition, from a popular nationalist leader to an elected statesman; from a principal dissenter to the head of the establishment; from a freedom fighter to the designated ruler. Concomitantly, "India" has gone from being his elusive dream to his concrete responsibility. Once the distant object of his quest, now it was the unremitting subject of his reality.

Nehru's letters have the characteristic features of what might be called periodic briefings or communiqués from the prime minister's office—today their equivalents would be sent out as e-mails. They discuss all manner of issues, from elections to foreign policy, from war to famine, from higher education to constitutional matters, from regional problems within India to India's relations with other countries. The wider public in any case would have followed everything that is here discussed by Nehru from his own perspective, in the national and international press. In other words, the letters do not have some sort of classified content where Nehru is sharing information to which he alone has privileged access, with a handful of other political leaders, at his own discretion. They are addressed to the heads of the different states, but they are all about the conduct of public business. In the ancient and mutually related sciences of politics, economics, political economy, and statecraft as these were theorized in Indic texts—principally in Kauṭilya's *Arthaśāstra,* in the *Mahābhārata,* and in the juridico-legal discourse of the *Dharmaśāstras*—the totality of all the ends that might elicit the kind of purposive, directed, measurable activity described by Nehru in his letters would be called artha.

Literally, artha means either "purpose" or "substance." When placed inside the traditional fourfold classification of the "ends of man" *(puruṣārtha)* widely available across the Sanskrit knowledge world, namely, dharma-artha-kāma-mokṣa, artha is usually taken to mean the sphere of economic activity, the pursuit of wealth, as distinct from the pursuit of metaphysical ends (dharma), the pursuit of corporeal pleasure (kāma), or the pursuit of transcendental liberation (mokṣa) from all pursuits as such. Naturally, Nehru's letters are not systematic or theoretical; they are rather descriptive and communicative; nonetheless, they show a side of Nehru that is very much about pragmatic problem solving, thoroughly engaged with the substantive aspects of running a nation. Of course these qualities must come to the fore if any politician is to qualify as a good administrator, as Nehru on balance undoubtedly was. Even Aśoka's edicts, in this sense, are equally divided between the expression of the sovereign's concern to preserve and propagate the values and virtues entailed by dhamma, and the cataloging of the actual steps he takes in order to make his realm as safe, just, peaceful, prosperous, and well managed as he possibly can. Without a willingness to deal with the nitty-gritty of artha—purposive, goal-directed action that will have immediate or long-term consequences—Aśoka would not have issued orders for the construction of rest houses and hospitals, the protection of flora and fauna, the planting of trees and the diversion of waters, the rehabilitation of prisoners and the ban on wanton hunting, and numerous other such aspects of what is in contemporary language called "good governance."

This book traces the search for the self in five of India's founding fathers, insofar as we are able to examine what classical texts these men read, to reconstruct how they negotiated their challenges in the present through the prism of traditions coming down from the past, and to find the categories of selfhood emergent from these intense engagements. What Gandhi took away from the *Bhagavad Gītā,* I have argued, was ahimsa; what Rabindranath took away from Kalidasa's poetry, particularly the *Meghadūta,* was viraha; what Nehru took from Aśoka and the Aśokan edicts was dharma and what he took from the Mauryan Empire (both before Aśoka and during his reign), and especially from Kauṭilya's *Arthaśāstra,* was artha. Aśoka's change of heart, his turn from tyranny to non-violence, from despotism to ethical sovereignty both attracts and moves Nehru; but he is also impressed by the capacities for empire building and realpolitik exhibited by Aśoka's grandfather Candragupta and his canny minister Kauṭilya. Perhaps one thing that Aśoka and Kauṭilya have in common—a certain intellectualism, the ability to elaborate, in language that will stand the test of time, their respective theories of the political—is also a key to what Nehru finds compelling about these otherwise historically remote, almost mythical or apocryphal figures.

Nehru's own personality, both as an intellectual and as a leader, shows the two tendencies, toward idealism in his nationalistic phase, and realism in his prime ministerial career; toward the signifying of the imperium of normativity through the dhammacakra on the one hand, and the shrewd harnessing of the indexical power/potent indexicality of the Lion Capital on the other. At one stage Nehru can produce the deeply affecting discourse of *The Discovery of India,* which will forever after be considered a classic of Indian nationalism; later he will churn out hundreds of the fortnightly or monthly *Letters to Chief Ministers,* which do nothing very much besides going over the ground incrementally covered by the nation as it slowly, almost ploddingly, proceeds into the future. He is capable of both the Aśokan flight of the aspiring self, straining to clarify its being and raise itself higher, closer to the final liberation, as well as the Kauṭilyan instrumentality that will help achieve some utterly realizable goal, serve some explicit and limited purpose, get done some job that needs doing without too much thought of past precedent or future implications.

The duality within Nehru in Indic terms we designate as Aśokan/Kauṭilyan and in modern terms as Gandhian/Nehruvian. The traditional categories of selfhood that they correspond with most closely are dharma/artha, or norm/purpose, or the self's aspiration/the self's instrumentality. These binaries can just as well be understood through MacIntyre's scheme, whereby the modern state as such—the modern state of which Nehru is an ideologue, a proponent, a theorist, an architect, a practitioner, and a product, indeed, an all-round exemplar—invariably has two faces, one turned toward the political imagination and the other toward bureaucratic rationality. If we want to follow the unfolding of each of these visages of the modern state in Nehru, we may do so by reading very carefully first *The Discovery of India,* followed by his statements regarding his choice of national symbols, followed by his *Letters to Chief Ministers.* In the text composed in jail just before Independence, Nehru must still write like a poet, capture the imagination of the

Indian people, appeal to them on the basis of their nationalist emotions; in choosing the regalia of the new republic, he must have an eye on both its symbolic power and its pragmatic efficacy; in sharing the burden of administration with his lieutenants and colleagues, he must keep his feet on the ground and his sights trained on the next difficult task to be tackled after the current one has been completed.

The tension within the self, between aspiration and instrumentality, between norm and purpose, mirrors or replicates a larger contradiction in the very nature of the modern state, which cannot but pull in these two opposite directions in order to present itself as ethically desirable and worthy of dying for, even as it delivers a set of rather banal goods and services to the citizenry, and becomes the ground on which they negotiate their respective self-interests. We want the poetry of revolution to nourish our souls, as MacIntyre drily observes, but we also expect the convenience of the telephone company to make our everyday life comfortable. Nehru was in the extraordinary and completely unique historical position of having to give India both its flag and its five-year plans, its credo and its credit, its perduring civilizational identity and its unprecedented democratic transformation. Rather than seeing him as flawed, fractured, and schizophrenic, I would rather we acknowledge his immense achievement in becoming the closest figure we may have seen in the modern world to a philosopher-statesman.

5

Bhimrao Ambedkar

Duḥkha, the Self's Burden

Of the five founders discussed in this book, B. R. Ambedkar (1891–1956) may have had the most agonized relationship to modern India's quest for an authentic self. Born a Mahar in Maharashtra, he grew up painfully conscious of the distance at which caste society kept the Untouchables. In the course of his remarkable life, he came to identify three men as his teachers—Siddhartha Gautama, the Buddha; Kabir, the medieval poet; and Jotiba Phule, the nineteenth-century Maharashtrian social reformer. For Ambedkar to arrive at a place from which he could embrace these three figures meant engaging with a vast spectrum of religious and political traditions that had appeared on the subcontinent from its earliest antiquity to its most recent colonial moment. It also meant working out what each of these traditions—Buddhism, bhakti radicalism, and non-Brahmin egalitarianism—had to offer to Untouchables by way of a bridge across the terrible chasm separating them from dominant Indian conceptions of self and sovereignty. For whatever Ambedkar might have claimed about his desire to break entirely with Hindu India, ultimately we cannot but regard the man as straining to build India anew, in such a way as to redefine the very basis of what it was to be Indian, away from the differential and hierarchical mechanism of caste, toward an inclusive and integrating idea of citizenship.

This new India—whose key text, the Constitution of 1950, Ambedkar shepherded into its inaugural form—had to be imagined on the basis of a kind of selfhood that would appeal as much to Hindus as to minorities, to upper castes as to Sudras and Untouchables, and to those in the mainstream as to those on the margins. Ambedkar tested every big and small, old and new religion available to Indians, trawled the texts and tenets of Hindus, Buddhists, Muslims, Sikhs, and Christians, and indeed made himself an entire career as a scholar of comparative religions alongside his enormously busy public life as a mass leader, a politician, and an intellectual. He was far more systematic than Gandhi as a self-taught student of different religions in India, far more thorough than Nehru as an amateur historian of India, far more imaginative and conflicted than the talented Tagores in his attempt to identify or construct an acceptable past for the emerging nation. Even as he stood every received theory about the origins and evolution of the caste system on its head, he declared his fervent intention to "annihilate" caste. It is no wonder that Ambedkar remains the least understood of the great moderns that India produced, and who produced India.

In this chapter, the focus is on Ambedkar's conversion to Buddhism in the last months of his life (October–December 1956) and on his final book, published posthumously, *The Buddha and His Dhamma* (1957).[1] Sangharakshita's riveting biographical account *Ambedkar and Buddhism* (1986) describes Ambedkar's journey toward Buddhism, from a book about the Buddha he received as a prize at age sixteen from his Brahmin high school teacher Arjun Keluskar, to the conflict with Gandhi over temple entry and separate electorates for Untouchables throughout the 1930s, to his increasing contact with Sri Lankan, Burmese, Japanese, and other Asian Buddhist groups from 1950, culminating in Ambedkar's formal conversion, together with that of some 400,000 of his Untouchable followers, in 1956.[2] Almost all major contemporary scholars of Ambedkar's life and works, including Zelliot, Rodrigues, Omvedt, Fiske, Fitzgerald, Tartakov, Jaffrelot, Nagaraj, Jondhale, and Gokhale have had something to contribute to our understanding of Ambedkar's conversion, and his founding of a sect of modern Indian Buddhism, Navayana, the "New Way."

Why, then, yet another attempt to examine Ambedkar's stance with regard to his neo-Buddhism? One of the hazards of entering into the history of Indian nationalism is that most accounts of Gandhi, say, will compare his traditionalism with Nehru's modernism; most accounts of Ambedkar's heterodoxy will insist on Gandhi's orthodoxy; Rabindranath's creativity and whimsy are easy contrasts to Ambedkar's prosaic and pragmatic approach. Thus it becomes difficult to keep several of these contemporaneous, equally important, and rather complex figures within a single frame of inquiry and judgment. It's as if we must take sides; condemn one in order to extol the other; separate out the secularists from the believers, the radicals from the reactionaries, the thinkers from the doers, and so on. I am not willing to take this approach. I do want to judge and analyze the five founders I have chosen, but not at each other's cost. To my mind, there is nothing to be gained in building up Ambedkar if most of one's effort is expended in tearing down Gandhi. Today, in the early part of the twenty-first century, we live as much in Gandhi's India as we do in the India of Nehru, Tagore, or Ambedkar, in certain ways; in other ways, India has pursued directions that none of these men could ever have predicted or endorsed.

Gandhi and Rabindranath, Gandhi and Nehru, Gandhi and Ambedkar, all had serious and long-running disagreements and conflicts with one another, which in my view only enhance the value of each of their legacies for independent India, rather than detracting from the stature of any of them individually. I turn to the question of why Ambedkar became a Buddhist, and of the nature of the new Buddhism that he authored, within a common framework of inquiry in which I have placed all the figures discussed in this book. This framework, as should be clear by now, encompasses the five founders in their engagements with particular texts of premodernity, examines the categories of thought that were central to these engagements, and traces how these categories underlie modern India's search for the self, the "swa" in swaraj. For Ambedkar, the relevant premodern texts were drawn from the Buddhist canon, especially the *Dhammapada,* in Pali. I argue that the key category that accounts for his close reading of these early texts of Indian Buddhism is duḥkha, or suffering.

However, Ambedkar does not simply appropriate the ancient religion of Buddhism for purposes of strengthening the political identity and self-respect of a modern community, the Untouchables. Nor is his turn to Buddhist tradition in search of the self the least bit easy for him, since he understands Untouchable subjectivity to be fundamentally at odds with "tradition" as such, given his perception of an upper-caste—in fact Brahmin—Hindu monopoly over the very idea of tradition throughout the recorded history of India. Moreover, Buddhism as he creates it anew, his Navayana, so deeply eviscerates Buddhism as it has been practiced in any number of its existing sectarian interpretations within and outside India that it almost becomes something else altogether, a religion all right, but hardly a type of Buddhism. He renders Buddhism unrecognizable as itself. Most significantly, for Ambedkar, duḥkha is not individual suffering rooted in *karma* but rather social suffering, and it springs from caste. In all these ways, Ambedkar's Buddhist moment is quite startlingly different from Gandhi's engagement with the *Bhagavad Gītā,* Tagore's with Kalidasa, Abanindranath's with Mughal and Rajput art, and Nehru's with Aśoka's edicts and pillars.

And yet my claim is that duḥkha, Ambedkar's category, shares with Gandhi's ahimsa, Rabindranath's viraha, Abanindranath's samvega, and Nehru's dharma the peculiar quality of being a hybrid between non-modern and modern meanings of the term; an apparently archaic concept deployed at an utterly unprecedented historical conjuncture for pressing political reasons; the distillate of centuries of thought about the self percolated through the filter of a sovereignty in crisis on account of colonialism. Ambedkar was undoubtedly at odds with his eminent contemporaries, both because he was an Untouchable and because he was so continuously and acutely conscious of being an Untouchable. But he was also of a piece with his peers: attending to history and refashioning history, immersed in tradition and in revolt against tradition, in mourning over a lost self and eagerly searching for a new self. The thread that keeps Ambedkar tied to India, even as he wants to smash India into smithereens and reconstruct it from the ground up, is his abiding commitment to solving the mystery of duḥkha, the suffering of the people—not just his people, the Untouchables, but all people, the people of India.

What exactly does Ambedkar do to Buddhism as he finds it, from his readings of the Buddhist canon, his travels in various countries of Asia, his dialogues with Indian and foreign Buddhists, and his parallel investigations into both Brahmin and popular Hindu traditions? Moreover, what does Ambedkar do to Buddhism that had not already been attempted in the course of several centuries of debate between Buddhists and Hindus (and

Jains and Greeks, for that matter) in Indic premodernity? To answer the latter question first, Ambedkar's discursive maneuvers and doctrinal innovations are uniquely a response to what he sees as the main problem before him in his capacity as the leader of India's Untouchables: the problem of abiding social inequality. Ambedkar has to put a particular pressure on Buddhism in order to make it an effective antidote to Hinduism's tenacious protection and preservation of the caste system. This is a tall order, because even after the coming of political modernity, together with democracy, liberalism, secularism, and rule of law, caste retained its customary hold over Hindu society.

Independence from the British Empire does not really liberate the Untouchables of India from their subservience to upper castes. The coming of equal citizenship does not make Hindus egalitarian. The promulgation of a constitution does not teach Indians the true meaning of fraternity between and across castes.[3] Maybe a reformist and revisionist Buddhism—after all, the advent of Buddhism 2,500 years ago was the very first "revolution" in India, according to Ambedkar—will achieve what Western values have failed to achieve in changing India's attachment to a caste-based social order. In other words, what Ambedkar does to Buddhism that has not been done before, in many centuries of argumentation, hermeneutics, and exegesis, is to redefine its purpose, from Nirvana to Equality; from the transcendence of the social to the amelioration of society; from "I must be free" to "Everyone must be equal." This is a laudable goal to seek, no doubt, in and of itself, but it is not the endpoint toward which Buddhist practice is oriented.

In Sangharakshita's telling, Ambedkar thought about Buddhism either actively or passively for at least five decades or so before he formally converted. His first major statement on Buddhism appeared in 1950, in an article in the *Journal of the Maha Bodhi Society,* published from Calcutta.[4] This article, "Gospel of Equality: The Buddha and the Future of His Religion," should be read in close conjunction with Ambedkar's unpublished work "Revolution and Counter-revolution in Ancient India," especially the piece therein titled "Krishna and His Gita."[5] His magnum opus, *The Buddha and His Dhamma,* had barely been completed as Ambedkar lay on his deathbed, and came out only after he had passed away on December 6, 1956. These works show Ambedkar to be struggling with what he regarded as Hinduism's decisive ideological defeat of Buddhism on Indian soil, mainly (though not solely) through the text of the *Bhagavad Gītā.*

Given that over a thousand years had passed since Buddhism had been driven (in Ambedkar's history) from the minds and hearts of Indians, and the Buddha's place firmly taken by Krishna, Buddhism itself needed to be reinterpreted in order for it to be made appealing, once more, to India's Untouchables, but also beyond, possibly to India's caste Hindus as well. Ambedkar's desire to present a refurbished Buddhism to its most likely modern converts, the Untouchables, led him to transform it in certain fundamental ways that, by the end, leave the agnostic wondering why the new creed needed to be called Buddhism at all, or whether it is indeed justifiable to call it that. In its travels from Gangetic India north to Tibet and south to Sri Lanka, Buddhism had long ago flowered into a complicated ecology of "systems" (-*vādas*) and "vehicles" (-*yānas*), but the Navayana of Ambedkar pushes against the outer limits of Buddhism to the point of nearly transgressing its boundaries altogether. It is only the persistence of the category of duḥkha, as I will show, that keeps Ambedkar's religion within the family of discursive traditions that we understand as being, broadly speaking, Buddhist.

* * *

Why did Ambedkar become a Buddhist? At least three main reasons may be adduced. The first is his own theory regarding the history of the Untouchables, presented in his book *The Untouchables: A Thesis on the Origin of Untouchability* (1948).[6] Without going into the details of this work, its main contention is that the Untouchables in the Hindu caste order are in fact none other than former Buddhists. Untouchability as an institution was the way in which Hindu society both destroyed Buddhism in India and incorporated its erstwhile enemies, the Buddhists, into its own social order, as servants and slaves. For modern-day Untouchables, then, to become Buddhists meant that they would be making a return to Buddhism and not a fresh entry into a religion with which they had had no prior historical contact. Ambedkar saw Buddhism as the natural home of India's Untouchables. They had every reason, he felt, to reclaim their rightful home, rather than continue to linger, despised and exploited, at the very margins of Hindu social life.

The objector points out that Ambedkar's brief and hastily written introduction to *The Buddha and His Dhamma* is just about long enough for him to make clear that he does not accept the Four Noble Truths, usually taken as the very foundation of Buddhism:[7]

1. *Duḥkha:* Suffering
   The truth of suffering
2. *Duḥkha Samudāya:* Origin/cause of suffering
   The truth of the origin of suffering
3. *Duḥkha Nirodha:* Cessation of suffering
   The truth of Nirvana
4. *Nirvāṇa:* Path that leads to the cessation of suffering
   The truth of the path to Nirvana

The Buddha did not intend for these four precepts to be taken as foundational, says Ambedkar, because if suffering is everything, then we cannot hope to build any kind of a social order that is oriented toward the end of suffering. The insistence on the Four Noble Truths, in Ambedkar's polemic, is an interpolation of later Buddhist commentators. In my view, by contrast, the second major reason for Ambedkar's turn to Buddhism is precisely his understanding of the primacy of duḥkha. As the leader of the Untouchables of Maharashtra, Ambedkar was never free of the consciousness of the suffering of his people. Indeed, for him, suffering is constitutive of the very identity of the Untouchables; it is the modality in which they experience their being in the world—especially since society, from their perspective, is created by and for those with caste.

The only thing that then explains Ambedkar's rejection of the Four Noble Truths is his interpretation of duḥkha—not as individual, karmic suffering, but as collective, social suffering. In other words, in undermining the Four Noble Truths, what Ambedkar challenged was the notion that all persons, of whatever caste, class, or gender, need to face and transcend their suffering; rather, according to him, suffering had to be seen as socially constituted and historically specific, and could be conquered only via a creed that placed suffering at the very center of its entire ethical architecture. Thus, even after moving the Four Noble Truths to one side, it was Buddhism that would best deliver the Untouchables as a group from their very specific duḥkha, which was discrimination and denigration at the hands of caste Hindus.

The third reason why Ambedkar chose Buddhism was not positive (an attraction toward Buddhism), but negative (a rejection of other religions).

Ambedkar announced in the mid-1930s that he wanted to leave Hinduism, and then proceeded to test the idea of converting to several other faiths, notably Sikhism, Christianity, and Islam. In the end, he rejected all these options in favor of Buddhism. Sikhism in his assessment was not sufficiently distinguished or distant from its parent Hinduism; Christianity and Islam, on the other hand, were too foreign relative to India as a whole.[8] To convert to either of these religions, he feared, would be to "denationalize" the Untouchables. In my reading, Ambedkar saw Christianity as somehow alien to Indians not so much because it is a Semitic religion, but because the recent record of Untouchable conversion to Christianity on the subcontinent was a direct outcome of colonial efforts to proselytize the victims of the Hindu caste order. In other words, Christianity, which might have had the right values in the abstract, had, within Indian history, been tainted by its association with colonialism. Ambedkar was simply not interested in helping British and European missionaries do their work in India, and most certainly not at the very moment when India was being decolonized at long last.

The reasons for Ambedkar's rejection of Islam, too, are more complicated than simply its putative foreignness. The fact was that regardless of its lands of origin, Islam had been thoroughly incorporated into the life of the subcontinent over a period of nearly 1,200 years. If, in addition to having a long history in India, Islam also offered strong tenets of equality and justice, then it could hardly be ruled out because of its non-Indian origins. Ambedkar's real reason for deciding against Islam, then, was that he learned a lesson, as it were, from Partition. India's Muslims had made, and partially won, an argument in favor of a separate homeland. Millions of Muslims had left for Pakistan during Partition. Millions had stayed behind, as well, but they remained as a numerically and politically diminished minority, present on sufferance, no longer—and possibly never again—properly integrated into the idea of India (for all that the Indian nation-state proclaimed its secularism).

I suspect Ambedkar feared that to convert to Islam would send the message that the Untouchables too were opting out of India. Even if they did not vote with their feet and actually go to Pakistan, by joining a religious collectivity that had only just tried to sever its historical and existential ties with India, and almost succeeded in doing so, the Untouchables would exchange their present position as a marginalized people for an even worse position, that of the enemies of the Hindus. Ambedkar wanted inclusion and parity for the Untouchables, not a complete and utter divorce between Untouchables and Hindu India. For him, opting for Islam presented the danger of further estranging caste Hindus and Untouchables from one another.

Does this decision against Islam not show Ambedkar up as a communalist? Both Dalit and secular pieties are outraged by even the hint of such an implication. But the fact is that Ambedkar had always been open to thinking about religion—and caste—as valid bases for the political identity of a community, any community. In this sense he was both a modernist and a pragmatist. In the 1930s, Ambedkar clashed with Gandhi because he contemplated demanding separate electorates for those at the bottom of caste hierarchy—Gandhi saw this as an attack on the unity of Hindu society. In the 1940s, in his *Thoughts on Pakistan* (1941) and *Pakistan or the Partition of India* (1945), Ambedkar argued that if the Muslims saw their interests as being safeguarded only by the creation of a separate state, then the Muslim League's "two-nation theory" should in fact be supported.[9] The elaborate legalistic arguments put forward by Ambedkar in these writings—listing the pros and cons of Islam and Hinduism, of Partition and a unified India, of various possible arrangements of power sharing between Hindus and Muslims—need not detain us here. Suffice it to say that it was not beyond the ken of his imagination that modern communities of caste or religion could constitute themselves, through acts of political self-determination, as nationalities. He also had a sufficiently long list of criticisms of Indian Muslims and their social practices, and of the unending social, political, and economic conflict between Hindus and Muslims, so as not to want to get the Untouchables in the middle of all that. In the end, he decided that not only would Untouchables be no better off as Muslims than they were as Hindus, but further, that by becoming Muslims, Untouchables would lose whatever weak footing they had in post-Partition India. He last remaining option, of any seriousness, was Buddhism.

Besides the centrality of duḥkha (read as social suffering), the history of the Untouchables that led from an original Buddhism back to a future Buddhism, and the fact that other religions, especially Islam, offered no real options, Ambedkar also had other reasons for his choice of Buddhism. These included Buddhism's challenge to the caste system, the very first of its kind in Indian history; its equal respect for both men and women, relative to other religions, especially Hinduism; its global character as a faith, such that it traveled beyond India to many other parts of Asia and the West; its political, intellectual, and theological dimensions, which make it a serious world religion, a Big Tradition, so to speak; and last but not least, a revival in Buddhism that went on in India and elsewhere throughout Ambedkar's lifetime.

The last is a theme I cannot pursue at any length, but it appears that Buddhism enjoyed a widespread renaissance in twentieth-century India, across castes and classes. This phenomenon spread in both Victorian Britain and its colonies on the subcontinent—India, Sri Lanka, and Burma. Ambedkar thus was not in the least bit isolated in his interest in Buddhism, whether as a scholar or as a practitioner; rather, he was but one figure in a climate of ideas where Buddhism was being reappraised and reinvented in the very lands where it had originated. The Orientalist Sir Edwin Arnold published his hugely and perhaps undeservedly influential poem about the Buddha, "The Light of Asia," in 1879; T. W. Rhys Davids founded the Pali Text Society in England in 1881; the Sinhala Anagarika Dharmapala set up the Maha Bodhi Society in 1891–1892, headquartered in Calcutta. For the next half-century or more, Buddhism was explored from every angle, by all sorts of different constituencies of South Asians and Westerners.

The Bengal School artists and art historians, working in Calcutta and Santiniketan—E. B. Havell, Ananda Coomaraswamy, Abanindranath Tagore, and Nandalal Bose—all wrote about or pictorially represented the past to give Buddhist art, architecture, and iconography an enormously important place in the very conceptualization of a history of Indian art. The Theosophists Colonel Olcott, Madame Blavatsky, and Annie Besant had their interpretation of the meaning and role of Buddhism in India. Indian philologists, historians, and literary critics like Harprasad Shastri, Gopinath Kaviraj, R. G. Bhandarkar, and his son D. R. Bhandarkar, as well as Hazariprasad Dwivedi, all made advances in Indological studies through their work on Buddhism in ancient India. Dharmanand Kosambi (1876–1947) and Rahul Sankrityayana (1893–1963), Brahmins and scholars both, converted to Buddhism and translated important Buddhist texts into Indian languages. Sankrityayana helped collect, catalog, preserve, and resuscitate key manuscripts of the vast Buddhist canon that had proliferated over the centuries.

Buddhist texts could be found not only in Pali, Chinese, Tibetan, Mongolian, and Buddhist Sanskrit, but also in a number of other classical and vernacular, dead and living Indian, Southeast Asian, and East Asian languages.

The growing sense of an active religious revival on the subcontinent was led by neo-Buddhists like Anagarika, Sangharakshita, and Bhadant Anand Kausalyayan. For reasons that at the moment are quite unclear, at least to me, several prominent socialist and neo-Gandhian thinkers and leaders in decolonizing and newly independent India, like Acharya Narendra Dev, Acharya Kripalani, Rammanohar Lohia, and Jayprakash Narayan, evinced an interest in Buddhism and engaged with it both as history and as doctrine.[10] Acharya Narendra Dev's monumental *Bauddha-dharma-darshan,* in Hindi, running over 600 pages and with an extraordinarily lucid preface by Gopinath Kaviraj, came out in 1956, the year that both Narendra Dev and Ambedkar died. In 1957 its author was posthumously was awarded a Sahitya Akademi prize, India's highest literary honor.

For many of Buddhism's critics and interlocutors in modern India, Buddhism's intrinsic value and interest were matched by the attractive prospect of solving one of the biggest historical puzzles of the country's complex past: Why did Buddhism "die" in India? What was it, in the long intellectual dialogue of Hinduism and Buddhism, and in the political and doctrinal struggles between Hindus, Buddhists, Greeks, Jains, and Muslims extending over most of India's premodernity, that drove Buddhism out of the subcontinent and into other parts of Asia? Was Buddhism in fact "dead" in its original home, or had it somehow been absorbed into its rival philosophies and theologies to such an extent as to become indistinguishable as a separate system or set of systems? (I don't think these questions have been answered satisfactorily, even today.)

Indologists and Buddhologists visited the relationship between the major texts of early (i.e., Indic) Buddhism and the major texts of Hinduism, such as the epics, the *Bhagavad Gītā,* Manu's *Dharmaśāstra,* Sankara's Vedānta commentaries, and many others. Which texts were older? Which texts presupposed other texts; how could the relative historicity of the Buddhist canon help stabilize and date the largely ahistorical textual traditions of the Hindus? Who came earlier, who came later? Strangely enough, mastering the intimate enemy of Buddhism, so to speak, turned out to be absolutely essential for modern scholars of Hinduism to get any overall sense of the actual history of a range of so-called Hindu sects and schools in pre-Islamic India.

Even within Ambedkar's lifetime, the sites and monuments associated with the story of the Buddha, with Aśoka the Maurya, and with other Buddhist rulers, teachers, monks, and intellectuals, were gradually brought out of their historical obscurity and reestablished as the loci of pilgrimage, worship, tourism, archaeology, and, inevitably, national pride. Where in 1850 these places might have been in ruins, by 1950 every educated Indian probably had some idea of what Sarnath, Nalanda, Bodh Gaya, Sanchi, Ajanta-Ellora, Kapilavastu, Kushinara, Uruvela, Rajagriha, Pataliputra, and countless other such points were supposed to signify on the map of the new nation. The Orientalism of the British Raj was as much responsible for this revival as was Indian nationalism, though the two forces came at the problem from opposite directions.

From Ladakh and Kashmir in the far north to Maharashtra and Karnataka in the Deccan, and from Bihar, Bengal, and Orissa in the east to the furthest western reaches of the Punjab bordering on Afghanistan, Indians realized that the imprint of Buddhism was all over their country (not to mention Pakistan, China, Sri Lanka, Burma, Nepal, and Tibet). The succession of grand imperial formations and knowledge ecumenes of a transregional character seems to have been more or less as follows: from Vedic to Buddhist to Hindu to Muslim to British. In the context of the nationalist movement, "older" usual meant "more prestigious," more likely to be claimed by the emerging postcolonial state as a part of its deep history. Even Nehru and Radhakrishnan's choice of the Aśokan dhammacakra and Sarnath Lion Capital for state emblems, although based on the ability of these symbols to signify ethical sovereignty rather than any particular religious identity, could be read as the mainstreaming of the idea of a Buddhist heritage for independent India. After a thousand-year eclipse, Buddhism made a small but significant comeback in its homeland.

Against this backdrop, admittedly very roughly sketched here, Ambedkar's turn to Buddhism was not as idiosyncratic as we might suppose. Dharmanand Kosambi's Marathi primer on Buddhism, *Buddha, Dharma ani Sangha* (1910, 1924) was well known in Ambedkar's native Maharashtra, and circulated more widely in other parts of North India via its Hindi translation. Kosambi had a rather complicated life and career, as a Saraswat Brahmin from Goa who converted to Buddhism; a husband, father, and family man who fervently wanted to—and sporadically did—lead the life of a *bhikkhu;* a Buddhist whose other brushes with ideological "conversion" included Marxism, socialism, and eventually the Gandhian way; a scholar, an ascetic, a social activist, an academic, an energetic participant in the national movement, and, not least, a feminist.[11] Both Dharmanand and Ambedkar were from very poor families, and struggled with poverty in their youth. In 1940–1941, Dharmanand published an important two-volume book, *Bhagavan Buddha*. His Marathi play, *Bodhisattva,* was published posthumously in 1949. In a speculative vein, it might be worthwhile to compare the complex, contradictory, and experimental nature of the Brahmin Dharmanand's life with that of the Untouchable Ambedkar, as these two extremely learned men, one generation apart in age but worlds apart in their caste backgrounds, brought Buddhism out of history and myth back into the lived experience of men and women in Maharashtra, the part of India that they both belonged to.

In fact, Sangharakshita points out that after an initial surge in conversion to Buddhism in Maharashtra, when nearly the entire Mahar community was converted either directly by Ambedkar himself in late 1956 or by others in the immediate aftermath of his death, in early 1957, the numbers ceased to grow (the count stabilized at about four million). He suggests that the reason for this stagnation was that the new converts had no one to tell them how to actually live a Buddhist life; what it meant to be a Buddhist, day in and day out; how to retain a sense of their difference from the Hindus who surrounded them and were hostile to their conversion in the first place; and what being Buddhist entailed, in practice, for a lay population of largely illiterate, very poor, and routinely persecuted former Untouchables. In many small towns and villages, Buddhism came to be realized as a sort of adoration, if not worship, of B. R. Ambedkar: Dalit Buddhists were more likely to build statues of Babasaheb than of the Buddha himself.[12] Had an erudite, charismatic, and passionate figure like Dharmanand lived longer, or had there been others like him after the last of the nationalist generations faded away, perhaps the chariot of Ambedkarite Buddhism, the Navayana, would not have come to such an abrupt halt in Nehru's India.

* * *

It could be asked, however, that if there was such a widespread revival, diffusion, and acceptance of the ideas and symbols of Buddhism in twentieth-century India, and such a noticeable incorporation of a Buddhist past into the nation's history after Independence, then what purchase, exactly, did the gesture of conversion have for Ambedkar and his followers? If every Indian was henceforth going to be a little bit Buddhist, in a manner of speaking, then was it really meaningful for Untouchables to actually become Buddhist? Why did Ambedkar, who was terribly ill in the last year or two of his life, go to such physical and psychological trouble to organize his own public conversion ceremony, and on that same occasion—October 14, 1956, in Nagpur—also convert nearly 400,000 Untouchables, en masse? In my reading, there are at least two very strong reasons why Ambedkar must have felt it necessary to formally convert to Buddhism.

One was his desire to publicly and incontrovertibly renounce Hinduism. When he took the vows of Buddhism—the Three Refuges, the Five Precepts—he also swore never to follow Hinduism in any way, shape, or form.[13] The conversion ceremony afforded two simultaneous gestures: the adoption of Buddhism and the rejection of Hinduism. For Ambedkar both were equally important. It also meant that all the new Buddhists, the 380,000 Mahars converted that day, were taken out of the fold of Hinduism, and thus removed from the awful curse of their erstwhile Untouchability. Many who thought of themselves primarily as Hindus regarded this move with skepticism—was Buddhism really that different from Hinduism, that those who converted to Buddhism would stop being Hindus? In some Hindu understandings, the Buddha had been incorporated as an avatar of Vishnu—next in line after Krishna. Many who considered themselves first and foremost to be Indians also found the decision somewhat mystifying, given that the Constitution, to such an important degree associated with Ambedkar himself, had already ruled out Untouchability several years earlier. For purposes of caste-based reservations, Indian Buddhists still retain access to Scheduled Caste/Scheduled Tribe status today; as far as religious identity is concerned, the Census of India does not count Buddhists as separate from Hindus.

But Ambedkar first regarded Hinduism and Buddhism as two entirely separate religions; then converted to Buddhism and left Hinduism both, at the same time, in no uncertain terms; and finally, in keeping with his understanding of the historically determined and socially defined character of communities, refused to grant that a sort of soft tolerance of Buddhism by privileged caste Hindus could ever mean the same thing as the active embrace of Buddhism by persecuted Untouchables. Conversion was what would set apart complacent, assimilationist upper castes from the Untouchables, who could never forget or renounce their difference, past, present, or future. It is also worth noting that on the one hand, Ambedkar often had quite a modern understanding of community identity—a community, for him, was defined by its numerical strength, its relationship to the state, its legal rights, its capacity for political representation, and its formal recognition by other communities with whom it competed for national resources. Yet in the final analysis he wanted the Untouchables to reconstitute themselves as a religious community in a more traditional sense of "religion." It was not enough that Untouchables had already been constitutionally recast as free and equal citizens of India and as eligible for Scheduled Caste/Scheduled Tribe status—they also needed their own religious identity. This way of thinking, too, drove him to the act of conversion.

If Ambedkar, of all people—himself an architect of the Constitution, and one of the creators of a reservation policy for the Indian state—found law, legislation, and politics to be insufficient as solutions to the problem of Untouchability, and saw no alternative but to convert the Untouchables to Buddhism, then we are justified in probing further. What properties or protections could a religion bestow upon Untouchables that the Constitution itself had failed to guarantee? What did a religion do for a community, especially a humiliated community, which citizenship and its attendant rights could not do? Here perhaps, paradoxically, Ambedkar came to a conclusion that was not so far after all from that of his old adversary Gandhi.

Gandhi always understood the issue of Untouchability to lie within the purview of religion. The problem of course was that in Gandhi's view, the relevant religion was Hinduism, and it was Hinduism that needed to reform and purify itself in order to get rid of this most debilitating practice, which he called a "sin." In his decades-long argument with Gandhi, Ambedkar averred that the solution to Untouchability lay not in the self-purification of Hindus but in the self-respect of the Untouchables themselves.[14] Untouchables would never be able to feel or assert such self-respect if they did not make a clean break with Hinduism; for Hinduism would not and could not make a clean break with the caste system if it were to remain recognizable as itself. Gandhi saw a space for criticism, reflection, and reform within the Hindu fold; Ambedkar had despaired of Hinduism by the early 1930s, after a series of debilitating tank and temple satyagraha campaigns that brought Hindu wrath upon the agitating Untouchables.

But Gandhi was killed in early 1948, long before Ambedkar converted to Buddhism. By the time of his conversion, he had also tried and failed to pass something called the Hindu Code Bill in the new Indian Parliament, a reformist piece of legislation that was opposed by both the Hindu Right and the centrist Congress, leading to Ambedkar's resignation from Nehru's Cabinet in 1951 (he had been the law minister). In 1936 Ambedkar had launched the Independent Labour Party, which went nowhere in its political fortunes; in 1956 he relaunched it under the new name of the Republican Party, which also went nowhere during and long after Ambedkar's lifetime. Clearly Ambedkar tried every possible route to the emancipation of the Untouchables, and hit a wall each time.

What a separate religious identity promised, eventually, was the prospect of a certain kind of horizon of authority; maybe not a separate God—for Buddhism, depending on the school, had both atheistic and theistic elements—but certainly a complete system of thought and practice that could govern and regulate the life of its adherents. Ambedkar was after the transcendentally authoritative character of a religion (any religion has this); the ability of religion as such to define and delineate everything about one's vision of reality, its characteristic property of creating the world in which its followers were to live. Gandhi's Untouchables were Harijans, literally, children of Hari, the God—or a god—of the Hindus. Ambedkar was not interested in this Hindu Almighty Father, but he did want for the Untouchables the all-encompassing, pervasive, authoritative universality of a proper religion, a religion of their own. No law, no legislative enactment, no rule, no political party, no constitution, even, could provide for them what a suitable religion could—the power to make an alternative world.

It was because Ambedkar sought a religious identity and not a secular ideology for Untouchables that he also could not have been content with the many other creeds that he came to engage with intimately, as a scholar, a politician, and a man given to deep and passionate convictions of various kinds. These include the Satyashodhak Samaj of his third guru, Mahatma Jotiba Phule (1827–1890), a social reformer who had revolutionized Sudra identity in nineteenth-century Maharashtra; the non-Brahmin and Dravida movements in South India in the early twentieth century, led by men like E. V. Ramasamy Naicker "Periyar" and Iyothee Thass; Marxism, which Ambedkar studied so seriously that he intended to write a book titled *Gautama Buddha or Karl Marx?*

(only an outline exists); and Communism, which took shape in Russia and China contemporaneously with Indian nationalism, and fascinated not just Ambedkar but several of his contemporaries, notably Jawaharlal Nehru and M. N. Roy.

From the 1970s onward, Maharashtra began to see new attempts to synthesize Ambedkar's Buddhism with the ideas of Phule and Marx, pooling as it were egalitarian, anticaste, emancipatory, and revolutionary tendencies from a variety of sources into a single progressive ideology; its coherence, effectiveness, and reach continue to be somewhat doubtful. (There was a parallel trend in the mid-twentieth century in North India, where socialists of various stripes tried to marry Marxism with Gandhian thought. The potentially fascinating question of the relationship of either Gandhian Marxian socialists or Phule-Ambedkarite Marxists with the organized Marxist Left in independent India has yet to be examined by historians.) But Ambedkar himself chose Buddhist religion over modern ideological formations—he wanted Untouchables to have access to a source of transcendent, world-making authority over and above the contingent and ultimately fleeting power of social movements, political parties, or state ideologies.

Ambedkar himself came from a family in which several strands of broadly "Hindu" faith were practiced: Ramanandi Vaiṣṇavism, Kabirpanthi bhakti, and a sort of default Puranic veneration of the *Rāmāyaṇa* and the *Mahābhārata,* as well as of the various Hindu gods and goddesses who appear therein. In an unpublished preface to *The Buddha and His Dhamma,* Ambedkar recounts how his father would encourage him to listen to recitations of the epics and would draw his attention to numerous lowly and outcaste characters in both texts: Karna and Vidura, Sabari and Surpanakha, Vali and Sugriva, and many others. Valmiki himself, the poet of the *Rāmāyaṇa,* was supposed to have been a hunter, that is, belonging to a caste that translated in terms of Maharashtra's *jati* structure into "Koli."

Ambedkar's father wanted his Untouchable son to feel his confidence boosted by looking at the talent, heroism, and loyalty of some of these figures, or by observing the affection with which they were treated by the great gods, kings, sages, and warriors of the narratives, or by following the way in which injustice meted out to such persons was always, in the moral order of the epics, duly punished. But Ambedkar, even as a young boy, felt only irritation and anger. He wanted no part of a real or imaginary world where Untouchables had only two choices: unkindness, or kindness. He did not want to be at the receiving end of either type of treatment from caste Hindus. He stopped attending the epic recitations organized by his father.

Another way of putting it is that unlike the previous generation of Mahars, including his own parents, Ambedkar did not see himself in these stories. Karna and Valmiki failed to answer his quest for an authentic self; they did not reflect his dilemmas, struggles, or desires back to him. Eventually that need was answered by the Buddhist literature. In Buddhist narratives, it seems, he found greater possibilities for identification and affiliation. Gautama Buddha had countless encounters—he engaged with men and women, high and low, educated and illiterate, hostile and worshipful, young and old. In that wealth of socially diverse characters who populate the *Dhammapada,* the *Tipitaka,* and Aśvaghoṣa's *Buddhacarita,* Ambedkar found the resonance, the presence, and the participation that he sought, on behalf of the inarticulate and excluded Untouchable self, in India's long habit of telling itself stories about itself.

The conversion, then, was Ambedkar's attempt to dissociate himself and his people from the humiliating roles assigned to them in the narratives so dear to the Hindus. He wanted to find a true persona—one that had in it elements of intellectual curiosity, ethical doubt, rich and diverse life experiences, questions about the larger meaning of mortal existence, and a range of human emotions—in the Buddhist literature instead. He was absolutely inflexible about the need for a proper conversion to Buddhism, with all of the attendant rituals, because he did not want his personal realizations to remain confined to him—he wanted his entire community to be able to benefit from the lessons he had so painstakingly worked out for himself over the course of his life. His refusal to like or learn from the epics had been a gesture of defiance by the young Babasaheb against his father, a small interaction that took place in the privacy of one Mahar home. He wanted to ensure that every Mahar in Maharashtra would have the courage to refuse, in turn, the lowly place given to the Untouchable in the caste Hindu imagination.

Ambedkar named Kabir as one of his three gurus, along with the Buddha and Jotiba Phule. His father was a follower of both Ramanand, who was Kabir's guru, and Kabir himself. Why did Ambedkar not think to convert all Mahars to the Kabirpanth, the religion of his own family? There could be several answers to this question. One is that many Mahars were already

Kabirpanthis. Another is that the Kabirpanth was a religion—or rather, a minor sect—associated mainly with Untouchables, Hindu as well as Muslim. Ambedkar, however, sought a creed that was not in any way confined to lower caste and outcaste groups—a major world religion, in other words, not a small sectarian identity that caste Hindus would denigrate just as much as they denigrated other Untouchable beliefs and practices.

The third reason is that through Guru Ramanand, a Brahmin who accepted the unlettered, Untouchable Muslim weaver Kabir as his student, according to some legends, Kabir had been folded into upper-caste Vaiṣṇavism, making Kabir's Ram much more of a Hindu deity than the formless God intended by Kabir in his invocation of that name. Hindus had absorbed the radical outsider, the greatest heterodox Kabir, as well, which meant that he no longer held any value as a true symbol of opposition to organized caste-based Hinduism, in Ambedkar's view. Ambedkar himself might have looked up to Kabir and followed the true import of his iconoclastic poetry, but he did not trust his followers to be able to keep Kabir apart from mainstream Hinduism.

It should be noted that Hazariprasad Dwivedi's monumental Hindi monograph, *Kabir: Kabir ke vyaktitva, sahitya aur darsanik vicaron ki alocana,* appeared in 1942, while Dwivedi was still at Santiniketan. This book was the first major critical and historical work in Hindi to completely reappraise the legend, the literary works, and the philosophy of Kabir for modern readers. It granted to Kabir pride of place in the history of Indian poetry, especially Hindi poetry. But it also raised Kabir up as a shining star in the firmament of India's poetic canon that stretched from Kalidasa to Rabindranath. Perhaps Ambedkar felt alienated from Dwivedi's Kabir, or perhaps he never had the opportunity to read this groundbreaking book. In any event, Ambedkar did not seem interested in converting anyone to the Kabirpanth. Kabir's primarily north and central Indian, Hindi-speaking provenance may also have been a deterrent for Ambedkar, who was looking mainly to uplift the Marathi-speaking Mahars of Maharashtra. Maybe the fact that it was Rabindranath who, as early as 1914–1915, had published an English selection and translation titled *One Hundred Poems of Kabir* also put Ambedkar off. (This is of course pure speculation on my part.)

It would seem that throughout the twentieth century, caste Hindus, especially Brahmin intellectuals, as well as secular Indians of the upper classes—

the nationalist elite—were as eager to claim the Buddha as they were to claim Kabir for India: the rising popularity of both these figures, who really ought to have been considered as symbols of social revolution and religious heterodoxy, must have alarmed Ambedkar. The mainstreaming of the Buddha and of Kabir undermined their oppositional energy, their ability to challenge caste society and orthodox Hinduism. But of the two, the Buddha was definitely the bigger figure: the founder of a major religion, known and venerated all across Asia for two and a half millennia. Kabir by contrast was never personally invested in any kind of institutionalized belief. He was a breaker, not a maker. Unlike the Buddha, he lived his life outside society and at war with it. Moreover, the Buddha's influence had spread over a continent; Kabir was recognized and his poetry sung only in one part of India. If indeed Ambedkar had to make a choice between these two, for purposes of conversion, he must have felt it a much more beneficial option to go for universal Buddhism rather than for the relatively provincial Kabirpanth.

* * *

The question that then arises is, if Buddhism was the best and only choice, and if a thorough conversion to Buddhism was to be undergone by the entire Mahar community, if not all Untouchables, then why did Ambedkar change Buddhism so much as to make it almost unrecognizable? Why did he create a neo-Buddhism, his Navayana? We noted already that he did not accept the Four Noble Truths as the foundation of Buddhism. This was a radical enough departure, tempered somewhat, in my reading, by the fact that he retained the category of duḥkha, reinterpreted as social suffering, even while dismantling the fourfold structure: duḥkha—duḥkha *samudāya*—duḥkha *nirodha*—Nirvana that defined an individual's quest for liberation from suffering in classical Buddhism. But Ambedkar's deviation from the *mārga* (the doctrinal highway, as it were) of Buddhism did not stop at his profound revision of the central category of suffering. He remained unimpressed by the widely disseminated account of the reasons behind the Śākya prince Gautama's *parivraja* or renunciation—the first step in his journey to attaining enlightenment and becoming the Buddha.

The story, known to most if not all Buddhists and many non-Buddhists as well, is that Siddhartha Gautama led the spoiled and sequestered life of a prince until the age of twenty-nine, when for the first time he encountered what are known, in the Buddhist vocabulary, as the Three Sights—the sight of a sick man, the sight of an aged man, and the sight of a dead man, or a corpse. He was so horrified at these shocking intimations of bodily suffering and unavoidable mortality that he decided to leave his wife Yashodhara and young son Rahula, his father Shuddhodana and his foster mother Gotami, his harem, his servants, his palaces, and the kingdom that was to be his, in search of a higher truth. The *parivraja* of Siddhartha—literally, his departure to go and dwell among strangers, his going away from the familiar world of material comforts and human attachments—is one of the most iconic moments in all of India's self-understanding. It is also unique among such moments in being quite precisely locatable within historical time, and in having occurred at a more or less determinable spot in the ancient geography of India.[15] The *parivraja* of Gautama, said Ambedkar, never happened in that way, or for those reasons.

To my mind, Ambedkar's inability to be persuaded that a young man, who was also a prince, could be driven to leave everything and embark on a quest for spiritual self-knowledge, or that the Three Sights could bring about such a monumental break in a human life, is symptomatic of Ambedkar's own distance from a category that for centuries has been absolutely central to all the Indic religions—renunciation. To not believe in God, soul, or eternity; to not believe in rebirth or karma; to not believe in the incarnation *(avatāra-vāda)* or the appearance *(darśana)* of the divine; to not believe in a teacher, a prophet, or an embodied divinity; none of these forms of skepticism is unknown in the history of Indic religions. But to not understand the act of renunciation (*sannyāsa* or *parivraja*), to be unable to imagine a situation in which a person might go down that road, and moreover, to not see the significance of this turn in the life of the Buddha, is for me really the furthest away that Ambedkar goes from the metaphysics of his fellow Indians, contemporaries as well as ancestors. At the risk of making an ethical judgment against Ambedkar, I would even go so far as to say that this is a failure of his imagination.

Without going into whether or not this is what the Śākya prince actually experienced (a traumatic and transformative encounter with sickness, age, and death), I do want to stress Ambedkar's skepticism and his inability to relate to the psychological state of a man on the verge of renunciation. He writes: "It is impossible to accept the traditional explanation that this was the first time he saw them. The explanation is not plausible and does not appeal to reason."[16] It seems to me that someone who finds the argument that disillusionment leads to renunciation to be completely incomprehensible and unpersuasive is very far indeed from a way of thinking about desire, detachment, and asceticism that is fundamental to all the Indic religions, whether Hindu, Buddhist, Jain, or Sikh.

What we can read in Ambedkar's point is not the logical fragility of the basic Buddhist narrative, but rather Ambedkar's own distance from a certain civilizational orientation with regard to the act of renunciation. If he did not relate to *parivraja,* it would seem that he would hardly be the most vocal advocate of Buddhism—one of the paramount *śrāmaṇika* (renunciatory) traditions of India, much like Jainism and certain kinds of Śaiva sects as well. But somehow Ambedkar moved ahead even with this fundamental doubt. His Gautama did leave, but for more mundane reasons, and with the full knowledge and consent of his family members, who all joined him eventually in his new life as the Buddha and themselves became the earliest converts to Buddhism.

Ambedkar described the Buddha as a *mārga-dātā* (giver of a path, guide) and not a *mokṣa-dātā* (giver of transcendental emancipation, deliverer).[17] He thought the Buddha to be more worthy of being followed than Jesus, who claimed to be the Son of God; Muhammad, who claimed to be the Prophet of God; and Krishna (a historical personage, according to Ambedkar), who claimed to be not just a god himself, but an avatar of the Supreme Godhead. Ambedkar found all these claims to be distastefully hyperbolic, megalomaniacal. The Buddha, he said, was a man and acted like one, knowing his limitations, recognizing that the knowledge he had attained might or might not be helpful for others, and never gesturing toward any kind of superhuman infallibility. He was a man and a man only: a mortal. His life showed the perfectibility of man, but he did not transcend the human condition. For Ambedkar, the Buddha was authoritative exactly because he did not demand that his authority be acknowledged by anyone. The Buddha asked that we trust our own experience, our reason, our faculties, and not the word of another. Ambedkar was really impressed by this humility in one of the greatest human beings who ever lived. He was also very attracted by the rationality, the verifiability, the humanism, and what he called the "scientific temper" of the teachings of the Buddha (thus reconstructed by him).[18]

In his fragmentary introduction—if only he had lived to complete it!—Ambedkar also expresses his discomfort with Buddhist doctrines of soul, rebirth, and karma, though it is not possible, in the purview of this meditation, to take his summary dismissal with any degree of seriousness, since he does not say which school of Buddhism he means, nor specify which of many doctrines on these subjects that are available from the vast canon of Buddhism. Further, Ambedkar means to rearrange the *saṃgha* or Buddhist community, to stipulate that the *bhikkhu* (monk) and the *bhikkhuni* (nun) be on an equal footing with the lay practitioner *(upāsak/upāsikā)*. He must do this, it seems, in order to attract ordinary people, especially poor, uneducated, and leaderless Untouchables, into the Buddhist fold. If Buddhism continues to be an intimidating and highly institutionalized order of renunciants, priests, and intellectuals, as it has become in Sri Lanka, Burma, Thailand, and elsewhere, then it is never going to draw India's Untouchables. Ambedkar also hints at conjoining the figure of the *bhikkhu* with an ethic of social service rather than a highly—in his view—antisocial discipline of self-knowledge and self-realization. We don't know how he might have elaborated these hints, nor can we say what response his challenging views might have elicited from the monkish orders of Buddhists in and outside India.

Suffice it to say that we may detect a certain internal consistency in all of Ambedkar's revisions, implicit or explicit, stated or explained, intended or accidental, to the core of Buddhist philosophy. His redefinition of duḥkha as a category denoting social suffering; his lack of interest in Nirvana, which is a category denoting transcendence; his rejection of rebirth, and his questioning of the structure and purpose of *saṃgha,* together begin to outline the alternative doctrine of his Navayana. This is to be a religion oriented toward collective deliverance and not individual liberation; the betterment of this life and not the care of the afterlife; the anchoring of the experientially knowable self within its material surround rather than in the abstract imaginings of a Universal Self or other selves conceived outside of humanly cognizable space-time. Nirvana, if there is such a thing, lies not in self-realization but in achieving an equal society; like suffering, enlightenment too can be only socially and not individually understood.

Ambedkar had to rethink Buddhism in all these ways, perhaps not because he was an incorrigible renegade, a contrarian, and an unbeliever, but because he had to craft a creed within reach of and acceptable to his followers, the Mahars. His biographers, Dhananjay Keer and Sangharakshita, both describe how in the last year or so of his life, Ambedkar had become estranged from many of his lieutenants, worked like a madman on his Buddhist opus, neglected his precarious health to spread the message of Buddhism as much as he physically could, and sometimes wept with despair at the thought of what would happen to the Untouchables after him. All the major schools of Buddhism that still existed flourished outside India and not on Indian soil. These meant nothing to the poorest sections of Indian society and were all equally far away from Maharashtra, in any case. Sangharakshita notes that hardly a decade after Ambedkar's death, even monks who had come to live in India from other countries went back, discouraged by linguistic and cultural divides that they could not surmount, by the difficulty of converting and educating a largely unlettered lay population, and by the poverty and backwardness of their flock, who could not support the monks in the fashion they were used to in their own societies. No wonder Ambedkar had to build a new Buddhism from scratch.

⋆ ⋆ ⋆

What do Ambedkar's insistence on a separate non-Hindu religious identity for Untouchables, his choice of Buddhism as the appropriate religion for his people, his creation of a new kind of Buddhism, the Navayana, and his obsession with the formality of conversion, together tell us about his relationship to tradition? If like Gandhi, Rabindranath Tagore, Abanindranath Tagore, and Nehru, Ambedkar too was on a quest for the self, then was his search part of or outside of India's traditions of thinking about the self? We might have the impression, going in, that of the many founders of the Indian republic, Ambedkar was likely to be the most hostile to tradition of any kind—that he would always regard all traditions with suspicion, because no tradition had ever really given a proper place to the Untouchables, whom he represented. But in fact it's not so simple to answer this question. Ambedkar's stated position on the subject of tradition might be one thing; but our analysis of his life and work may yield another outcome altogether.

The main difficulty is that Ambedkar in the end chose religion—there is something traditional, even conservative in that choice. However, he chose not just any religion, but Buddhism, which, at least in its original form, rejects the very notion of a unitary, stable, and identifiable self. So we could say that Ambedkar's search for the self led him to a doctrine of "selflessness" or "no-selfhood" *(anātmavāda, anattā)*. He picked a tradition, true, but that tradition has a non-traditional answer to the problem of self. Even within Buddhism, as he announced in his introduction to *The Buddha and His Dhamma,* he took issue with those sects which held certain beliefs about soul, rebirth, and karma that contradicted the idea of there being no self to persist over time and accrue merit or demerit. In other words, inside the Buddhist tradition, he wanted to stay close to what he understood to be the direct teachings of the Buddha, and not to accept the interpretations of later teachers and commentators. This, too, was a traditionalizing move, if you will.

As a student of religion, Ambedkar was fastidious in the extreme about reading primary works and secondary scholarship, and this was true no matter which religion he was investigating. He read Hindu and Buddhist texts with the most profound care; it seems highly likely, given what we know of his temperament and method, that he expended quite a lot of energy engaging with Islam, Christianity, and Sikhism as well, through books, articles, and discussions with scholars and experts. Several historians have traced Ambedkar's journey: from the first declarations of his intention to convert in the mid-1930s; through his exploration of Islam, Christianity, and Sikhism as possible religions for himself and other Untouchables and his subsequent rejection of these options; followed by his growing interactions with Buddhist leaders in the 1950s; to his actual conversion a couple of months before his death at the end of 1956.[19]

We also have some idea of the books that might have influenced Ambedkar directly and indirectly. These include Sir Edwin Arnold's *The Light of Asia* (1879), Krishna Arjun Keluskar's *The Life of Gautama Buddha* (in Marathi, 1898), the South Indian P. L. Narasu's *The Essence of Buddhism* (1907), and Dharmanand Kosambi's *Buddha, Dharma ani Sangha* (1910, 1924), as well as his later two-part oeuvre *Bhagavan Buddha* (1940, 1941). We can list the canonical and non-canonical Buddhist works that became Ambedkar's main sources for *The Buddha and His Dhamma:* the *Dhammapada* (Indian as well as Chinese versions); the Pali *Tipitaka* (especially the *Sutta Pitaka* and *Vinaya*

Pitaka sections); Aśvaghoṣa's *Buddhacarita;* and the *Milindapanha.* We know that Ambedkar read most of the Buddhist literature through English translations, possibly some through the Marathi translations and retellings that became available in his lifetime, and that he also tried to study Pali so as to be able to read original texts in it. He absorbed the most from the Theravada, Sarvastivada, and Mahayana schools of Buddhism.[20]

Although I cannot take this up in detail here, Ambedkar was as well, if not better, read in Brahmin literature as he was in the Buddhist. Even a cursory glance at his book *Who Were the Shudras? How They Came to Be the Fourth Varna in Indo-Aryan Society* (1946) shows his extensive knowledge of Hindu texts. Apart from this, a number of fragmentary, incomplete, and unpublished writings that were discovered at his death establish his deep curiosity about and serious engagement with the *Bhagavad Gītā,* the Tantric literature, the epics, the Vedas, the *purāṇas,* and whole slew of other Sanskrit sources. Of necessity he read these in English or Marathi, mostly the former, but it is quite amazing to calculate how much time he must have invested in this kind of research, and what a tremendous intellectual and physical effort it must have been for him to read and write so much, of such esoteric materials in classical languages, in the middle of a busy political career. From his strong criticisms of Brahmin texts, and his adoption and adaptation of Buddhism, my sense is that Ambedkar did not want to leave tradition—rather, he wanted to enter into it. And he wanted his entrance to be seen as a reentry, onto the historical stage of doctrinal disputation, of the long-defeated, long-banished Buddhist adversary of the Brahmin intellectual hegemon. In other words, Ambedkar sought, through the conversion to Buddhism (of himself and of the Untouchables), to reclaim a space, a role, and a voice for Hinduism's original adversarial conversation partner.

Brahmin traditions exclude the Sudra and the Untouchable in no uncertain terms. Islamic and Hindu theologies are so fundamentally incompatible that even a thousand or more years of close coexistence and interaction on the subcontinent failed to yield any actual understanding, synthesis, or syncretism of a doctrinally robust kind (though several popular practices mixed Hindu and Islamic elements now and again, to produce *encore un instant de bonheur*). Importantly, across Brahmin discourse, there was a common blindness to these others, whether low-caste, outcaste, or Muslim, a denial of the very existence of these groups and their belief systems that irked Ambedkar no end. Buddhism, on the other hand, had been a chosen, named, identified, and respected adversary for several centuries of Brahmin text making and intellectual argumentation. For about 1,500 years before the advent of Islam on the subcontinent, it seemed, Brahmins and Buddhists were engaged in an extended dialogue about self and no-self, God and no-God, language, mind, reality, soul, meaning, beauty, logic, ritual, divinity, poetry, existence, death, knowledge, realization, and all of the hundreds of categories that constituted the epistemic world of Indic premodernity. The two conversation partners may seldom have agreed, but they talked about their disagreements all the time, nevertheless. They talked in more than one language, in Sanskrit and Pali and the Prakrits. By the fourth or fifth century CE, a distinctive subtype of Sanskrit had developed in the Indic world specifically in order to carry on a discussion about topics in Buddhism.

According to Ambedkar's theory about "Broken Men," articulated in a number of his writings, sometime in the unspecified past, Buddhists had been relegated to the status of Untouchables, and Untouchables were now, in the twentieth century, going to become Buddhists again.[21] It seems plausible that Ambedkar must have projected their emergence out of the silence that went with Untouchability, into the vocal disagreement of Buddhism against its old enemy, Brahminism. He did not want to destroy tradition—he only wanted to be able to partake in it, in full. As an Untouchable, he could not speak (for the subaltern cannot speak, in a discursive context where Brahmins make the rules). As a Muslim, he could have spoken, maybe, but it was not clear that Hindus ever had or ever would have any interest in listening to what Islam had to offer. As a Buddhist, however, not only could he speak—he could speak against the Brahmin, and yet he would be heard. This, at any rate, was Ambedkar's fantasy. (It's interesting that the kind of speech situation he was fantasizing about could not unfold on the floor of the Parliament, in the modern courtroom, or in the Constituent Assembly debates.) In converting to Buddhism, he wanted to pull into an empty spot in the parking lot of tradition.

But whatever the historical validity or polemical force of the intertwined narratives of Brahmin, Buddhist, and Muslim knowledge systems and religious traditions as Ambedkar reconstructed them—and for the most part, his views were and remain unacceptable to secular, liberal, or left-leaning historians of India—the real test of Ambedkar's relationship with tradition lies in his treatment of the two central categories of Indic Buddhism: duḥkha and dharma/dhamma, righteousness. We noted already that even while adopting Buddhism, he rejected the Four Noble Truths *(catvārī-ārya-satyānī),* but retained duḥkha, yet reinterpreted it as social suffering. In the Brahmin worldview, he rejected the caste system *(varṇāśramadharma),* yet retained a stake in dharma, to the extent that Buddhism itself adapted dharma as dhamma. But here again, Ambedkar—ever the traditionalist, ever the iconoclast—insisted that Buddhist dhamma be read as "morality" and not "law," excising the injunctive core of Brahmin dharma and replacing it with an idea of dhamma that comes close to "responsibility."

Moral action is not the unreflexive, fastidious performance of rituals in obedience to an unbending and context-free Law; moral action is action premised on difficult moral judgments that we make all the time in response to the demands of our particular situation and within the limits of our fallible knowledge. It was as if, repeatedly, Ambedkar could not help hewing close to the tradition, but equally felt compelled to revise it in fundamental ways. For all we know, this is what he understood to be the essence of the Buddha's teaching—that our conduct as human beings must at all times be oriented to the cessation of our collective suffering (duḥkha), and that we must act responsibly toward all others (dhamma), as far as possible observing compassion, non-violence, friendship, and other virtues *(śīla).* Ambedkar may have called his type of Buddhism Navayana, but its quality of being new *(navya)* signaled a paradoxical return to what he understood to be the original import of the Buddha's words, not a radical departure from them.

In a larger theory of Indian history that Ambedkar was beginning to outline, but never managed to flesh out within his lifetime, the advent of Buddhism was the first "revolution" against Vedic social order and Brahmin dharma. The subsequent appearance of the *Bhagavad Gītā* was the counterrevolution of Brahminism against Buddhism. The figure of Krishna was in Ambedkar's reading the ultimate reactionary. Gradually Buddhism was defeated, by a combination of argument, assimilation, and outright coercion. Ideologically faltering Buddhists were rendered as social outcasts, the Untouchables. The Navayana, coming after the worsening injustice of centuries, was to be a long-needed corrective to the hegemony of the Hindus and their caste-ridden society. None but the Untouchables, reawakened to the moral power of the dhamma, and charged with a renewed sense of historical purpose, would be the converts, the proponents, and the beneficiaries of this—apparently—new religion. The Buddha's original challenge to the caste system would come back with exponential force, given that Ambedkar aimed to release the pent-up anger and political energies of a class of people who had been defeated, oppressed, and denied for millennia.

In Ambedkar's incompletely articulated but nonetheless profoundly ambitious theory of history, we begin to discern the convergence of traditional and modern, religious and secular, Indian and Western categories that I am arguing marks the thinking of all of the five founders under analysis in this book. When read as social suffering, duḥkha is after all nothing other than inequality. In the Hindu universe, caste pervades and subsumes reality itself, leaves no space for freedom (except transcendental freedom, which Ambedkar doesn't believe in). But because in the Hindu perspective, in this world there is no escaping difference, and outside of embodied existence, there is only non-difference, Hinduism offers no history of inequality. In Ambedkar's alternative history, by contrast, by grasping that duḥkha is precisely the social suffering that results from the caste system (and not the individual suffering that results from rebirth and karma), we can see the destruction that inequality has wreaked over hundreds if not thousands of years. Whether or not a person may find liberation in mokṣa and enlightenment in Nirvana, society can most certainly find emancipation in equality. It is beyond Hindus to be able to think in this way. Only the Buddhists—more precisely, Untouchables-turned-Buddhists—can play this revolutionary role in Indian history, as they did once long ago.

Now we can see that Ambedkar fought against inequality throughout his career: by his determination to get the best modern education the world had to offer, the tank-and-temple mobilizations of the 1920s, his work with non-Brahmin movements, entertaining the idea of separate electorates and minority status for Untouchables, resisting Gandhi in his efforts to reform Hinduism and uplift the Untouchables, supporting and critiquing Pakistan, crafting a reservation policy, drafting the Constitution, cooperating with Nehru, trying to pass the Hindu Code Bill, creating the International Labour Party in 1936 and the Republican Party in 1956. His struggle for justice, for a new social and political order founded on the principles of liberty, equality, and fraternity, was cosubstantial with his life itself. His final conversion to Buddhism was not a freakish deviation from this path: all that had happened was that he could at last see how duḥkha and inequality converged at a vanishing point, in the far distance where the social and the religious merge to yield the political. The independence of India, the conversion of Untouchables into Buddhists, and the transformation of Indian society such that the prison house of caste gave way to an emancipating principle of equal citizenship: these were all simultaneous and necessary conditions for the true achievement of an Indic modernity. Ambedkar came to this realization—his personal Nirvana, if you will—tragically close to the end of his very long journey.

As we look at the way in which Ambedkar finally reinstated a revisionist duḥkha and dhamma at the center of his philosophy of history (if we can call it that) after fighting against inequality and doggedly working with the categories of the law for five decades, are we to conclude that he somehow, in the end, managed to reconcile the traditional and the modern? It is tempting to wish for—nay, to find—a restful oasis of reconciliation in the incessant anguish and conflict of this man's thought. It's hard to imagine a destiny more difficult than that of B. R. Ambedkar, no matter how heroic we take him to have been. But when we look carefully at the language of his Buddhist opus, *The Buddha and His Dhamma,* we cannot help but notice that once again, he is torn about his stance vis-à-vis tradition. He writes (in his unpublished preface) that the life of the Buddha has to be retold in such a way as to marry narrative flow with the beauty of example, denotative simplicity with deontic power, character with teaching, norm with magic, directness with profundity.[22] He wanted to find a register in which to tell the truth of Buddhism, as it were, unmediated and unsullied by centuries of commentarial and exegetical accretions, detours, and errors of comprehension. He wanted to write like one of the Buddha's early companions, and not like the later Buddhists, who were indistinguishable from their adversaries, the Brahmins, in their turgid scholasticism. He wanted to write as though he had heard the Buddha speak. He wanted, he announced, to write the Buddhist Bible.

Rushing to finish his work while the winged chariot waited, as Sangharakshita says, staying up nights, feverish, crying, desperate, lonely, sick, and exhausted, what did Ambedkar produce?[23] A strangely unpoetic account of Siddhartha Gautama's life and teachings; a text so devoid of metaphor, so stripped down in its language, so bereft of the marvels and miracles associated for 2,500 years with the name and memory of the Buddha that, yet again, we have to wonder at just how distant Ambedkar was from the kind of imagination that had heretofore been at work in the Buddhist traditions. *The Buddha and His Dhamma* has none of the incantatory quality that he sets out as a desideratum—and perhaps this was at least partly because it was written in English. Its protagonist is deprived of the two most dramatic poles of his life, his renunciation *(parivraja)* and his enlightenment (Nirvana)—not that these don't occur, but Ambedkar takes away the causal factors and the psychological states that have been read into them by countless Buddhists. Thereby, to my mind anyway, he renders both these momentous events in desiccated versions, literally taking the aesthetic—and ethical—essence (rasa) out of them for future readers. Did Ambedkar forget that the Bible, too, is poetry?

Even if the Buddha was a man, a mortal, and no god, avatar, or prophet, even if he was completely and utterly this-worldly and real, so to speak, even if his message had to be communicated to the very simplest of folk, even if the end of suffering was more important than the narration and analysis of it, still, there is no good justification for making so semiotically potent a character banal. Somehow, that is what Ambedkar, ever prosaic, ever pragmatic, ever the realist, ends up doing. It's as though he was so eager to rewrite history that he never grasped the literary nature of his chosen task. The Buddha cannot be known either historically or in the sense of moral knowledge without the exercise of something like the literary imagination. Arguably up until Ambedkar, neither the Buddha nor his teachings exist for the people of the subcontinent (I can't speak for Buddhist cultures outside India) in any medium that is not poetic. Ambedkar allowed his own moral seriousness to get in the way of his moral imagination.

To me, this marks a grave sundering from tradition. Ambedkar is adrift in precisely the kind of modernity where Buddhism loses some of the character of a religion and approaches the state of politics. He might have deemed this necessary, even urgent, but is it, in the end, a good thing? It's difficult to say. The answer turns on what work it is that we expect religion, or religious experience, to do for us, whether as individuals or as a society. Did Ambedkar want the Untouchables to be able to walk the Eightfold Path to Nirvana? Did he wish to communicate the order of truth that the Buddha himself had tried to impart? Or were his actual agendas quite different—to reclaim a long-lost identity, to reengage with Hinduism, to annihilate caste, to find a solution to the suffering produced by inequality, to take the empty space left behind by an Islam that was apparently turning its back on India, to supplement the Constitution, to politicize his bereft community, and so on?

The *Bhagavad Gītā* spoke to Gandhi so vividly because it had achieved the supreme summit of poetry.[24] His visceral identification with the text came about precisely because it appealed to his moral imagination. He could feel Arjuna's bewilderment; he was soothed by Krishna's reasoning. Gandhi was able to think about the self and its freedom through the poem, in the vocabulary of the poem, in its metaphors, in its regime of truth. Ambedkar disliked and distrusted Krishna, as he made clear in his unfinished fragment, "Krishna and His Gita," a part, tellingly, of his projected book on revolution and counterrevolution.[25] He got nothing from the *Gītā* other than a defense and entrenchment of the caste system *(cāturvarṇya)*.[26] He said he took the Buddha as his guru, and yet, in some fundamental way remained tone-deaf to the Buddha as well.

Did Ambedkar hear the poetry of Kabir? I doubt it, though I don't know for sure. The fact is that one cannot really set aside the possibility of transcendence, one cannot take the problem of social suffering as the be-all and end-all of moral endeavor, and then get much worth out of any of these texts, whether the *Gītā,* or Kabir's poems, or the sermons and *sūtras* of the Buddha. Ambedkar, who had no interest (and worse, no faith) in the categories of transcendence, whether dharma, or *īśvara,* or *ātman,* or *jñāna,* or bhakti, or mokṣa, or Nirvana—categories that fluctuate back and forth between and across Hindu and Buddhist thought, and make it possible for the two traditions to converse with one another—had to struggle very hard indeed to make sense of such texts. If *The Buddha and His Dhamma* had been the only book Ambedkar left behind, we would have recognized him, with clarity, as being irremediably, irreconcilably estranged from the tradition.

* * *

As discussed at length in Chapter 4, the adoption of the Aśokan dhammacakra as the motif at the center of India's national flag, of the Sarnath Lion Capital as the state seal, and of the phrase *dharma-cakra-pravartanāya* as the motto of the Lok Sabha (the lower house of the Indian Parliament) were for the most part reflective of Jawaharlal Nehru's vision for the new republic.[27] His most vocal supporter in the Constituent Assembly, where these symbols were proposed and debated, was likely S. Radhakrishnan. I have not been able to see any clear indication in the historical record that Ambedkar either suggested these Buddhist icons himself in the first place, or that he worked particularly hard to persuade other members of the Assembly that these would be the most appropriate symbols for the Indian nation. Later on, however, Ambedkar did not seem entirely averse to retrospectively claiming these choices as his idea and as evidence of the importance of Buddhism to the history and future of India.

As nationalists, Nehru and Radhakrishnan were enthusiastic about the cakra and the Lion Capital for a variety of reasons—because of their historical age, dating back to the time of Aśoka; the prestige of the Mauryan Empire; their materiality as objects; their aesthetic properties: design, beauty, antiquity, and sculptural finesse; and, last but not least, their association with certain political ideas embedded within Buddhist discourse, such as non-violence and ethical sovereignty. By the mid-1950s, long after the Constituent Assembly debates were over, the state regalia had been adopted, and Ambedkar had quit Nehru's cabinet, he cited these symbols as proof of the high value given to Buddhism and Buddhist political power within the self-fashioning of the Indian republic. He was also relieved that the demands of the right wing—composed mostly of the upper castes—for more explicitly Hindu symbols had been sidelined, thanks to the mixture of secular and Gandhian compulsions that dominated the discussions of the lawmakers on this subject.

But the fact is that Ambedkar's imagination was so different from Nehru's that he had not thought to use such icons to signify his own version of India's history, in which Buddhism played a central role. Or perhaps Ambedkar had arrived at the conversion to Buddhism having traveled such a long and complex path that he could not think of the past as a resource for the present; could not use tradition in a straightforward way to authorize modernity; could not really believe that simply placing the ancient symbol of dhamma at the heart of the nation's self-representations would transform caste-ridden India into the equal society that Gautama Buddha had preached, or the moral polity that Aśoka the Maurya had envisioned. Certainly in Ambedkar's estimation, Jawaharlal Nehru, of all people, could not set the wheel of dhamma in motion—far from it.

Besides, Ambedkar understood that when most Indians, especially Hindus, looked at their new flag or their new currency, they were not thinking of ancient Buddhists or contemporary Untouchables, nor were they experiencing a newfound faith in egalitarianism and compassion for the downtrodden. They were most probably eliding the difference of Buddhism and assimilating it into Hinduism; taking undeserved pride in the imagined glories of ancient India and, if anything, denying the injustice and inequality that had sullied the long centuries stretching between the death of Indian Buddhism and the emergence of the Indian republic. No one, surely, was enamored of the national symbols because they evoked Buddhism in its capacity of being the first major historical critique of and challenge to Brahmin orthodoxy. Rather, Indians were fantasizing about the Mauryan Empire as the remote ancestor of modern India; Nehru was in all probability dreaming of Aśoka as a model and exemplar for himself as the ruler of India. Ambedkar could not have celebrated this iconography in any uncomplicated fashion.

A famous parable found in the *Digha Nikaya* of the Pali *Tipitaka,* titled "Discourse Concerning the Lion's Roar of the Wheel-Turning King," describes a state of human longevity and material prosperity that exists so long as the Wheel Jewel—the precious dhammacakra—risen up above the earth, dominates the sky and all those who walk below it.[28] The Wheel Jewel *(cakra-ratna)* retains its position high in the heavens only as long as the king and his subjects lead virtuous lives. As their virtue slips, so does the Wheel, and the quality of life sinks slowly into utter ruin. In this story, the cakra symbolizes a pervasive and powerful moral order: when dhamma, in its personal, religious, and political senses, is upheld, a society may flourish; in its absence, that same society will perish. The Buddha instructs his audience of monks in Magadha that without an overarching regime of morality, all social structures descend into a terrible condition of chaos and destitution. Even nature cannot sustain itself in this manmade anarchy. A true ruler—the Wheel-Turning King *(cakravartī rājā)*—is one who ensures that the Jewel remains shining at the highest point in the sky like the noonday sun, that is, that dhamma illuminates his kingdom at all times.

Gandhi and the Tagores were comfortable enough with tradition to be able to accept many aspects of it, as well as to criticize and if necessary discard, alter, or reframe other parts. Nehru had a far more instrumental attitude toward tradition: not one of intimacy, participation, and the critical reflection necessary for its renewal and perpetuation, but instead a canny assessment of how far it could be used to make certain arguments in the present more persuasive to a larger number of people. Gandhi, Rabindranath, and Abanindranath intervened in tradition; Nehru instrumentalized it; Ambedkar, however, was both attracted to and repelled by it, felt himself excluded from it, helpless to participate in or utilize it, but at the same time, deeply and painfully cognizant of its importance, were the Untouchables to find a proper place in the ongoing history of India. At least he realized this much: no individual, no caste community, no religious group could flourish in India without constructing some kind of relationship to tradition, some narrative of selfhood compatible with India's quest for its proper self, some foothold in the past to stabilize its presence in the future. In recasting the Untouchables as Buddhists, Ambedkar was conceding that tradition remained the firmament that would slowly flood with light as the sun of modernity climbed to its zenith, much like the dhammacakra that dominated the sky of the once and future righteous republic.

Conclusion

The Sovereign Self, Its Sources and Shapes

In the mid-eighteenth century, the master miniaturist Nainsukh, who belonged originally to Guler in the Kangra foothills of the Himalayas in northern India, painted a work showing an entire township aboard an ark, adrift on a river, while the far bank appears to be on fire.[1] The town was probably the Rajput fort-city of Jasrota, in Jammu, where Nainsukh lived for many years with his patron, the connoisseur Raja Balwant Singh, a royal who was exiled from his hill principality and spent a long time wandering in the plains, together with Nainsukh and other artists and retainers in his entourage. Two seated figures, Balwant Singh and in all likelihood his son, face one another at either end of the ark, while in between them is their entire city, with populace, animals, buildings, and even a mountain, crammed into the center of the boat. The protagonists of this painting, as well as their historical relationship with its painter, Nainsukh, have only recently been identified and deciphered by the scholars B. N. Goswamy and Eberhard Fischer.[2]

The contemporary Indian painter Gulammohammed Sheikh quotes Nainsukh's work, *A Boat Adrift on a River: Illustration to a Folk Legend* (c. 1765–1775) in his own monumental work, *Ark* (2008), a digital collage print made as the inner wall of a shrine called *Kaavad: Home.*[3] Sheikh's *Ark* is a complex image that refers not only to Nainsukh's painting, but also to several other medieval and modern Indian and European works, weaving a dense web of intertextual references.[4] Sheikh transforms Nainsukh's boat into an ark of Indian tradition. On one end of this ark sits Gandhi, quoted from a 1921 work by Abanindranath Tagore that shows Gandhi at Santiniketan in 1915, in conversation with Rabindranath Tagore and C. F. Andrews.[5]

On the other end of the boat sits Kabir, quoted from a work by Mangal Chatterra, made at almost exactly the same time as Nainsukh's painting, about 1760, either in Amber or elsewhere in Mughal India.[6] Stretching between Gandhi and Kabir inside the ark is what appears to be a water body, a bluish expanse, in which float tiny figures of sages, saints, skeptics, and Sufis, each one again a quotation, in Persian, Italianate, and Indic styles. This array of figures includes St. Francis of Assisi, Abdul Rahim Khan-i-Khana (Rahiman), and the twentieth-century artist and Sheikh's friend and colleague Bhupen Khakhar (1934–2003), as well as other known and unknown characters from history. Sheikh calls this a *sangat,* literally, an assembly of the virtuous.[7] The blue in which they are studded like small jewels is in fact a lake in the city of Baroda, Gujarat, where Sheikh lives and works (as did Khakhar). The palace of Jasrota, as well as the mountain shown in Nainsukh's painting, also make it onto Sheikh's ark.

The ark in Sheikh's painting floats in a turbulent expanse of dark, swirling waters, on the far extremity of which, poised like an island, is Surendranagar, where Sheikh grew up. The work has a visual richness that comes not only from the splicing of multiple other works into the body of the image, but also from the mixture of painting and photography on the one hand, and reproduction and interpretation on the other. I saw this painting on display in New Delhi, in October 2011. As I stood before it, looking at Gandhi and Kabir on either end of a huge ark, sheltering between their gigantic figures numerous small and often anonymous figures representing spiritual and skeptical, creative and analytic aspects of civilization, I understood in a single moment of apprehension—not unlike Coomaraswamy's samvega—that what Sheikh sought to depict was a composite image of India's traditions: religious, aesthetic, and learned. Sheikh does not invent his own Gandhi and Kabir ex nihilo; rather, he quotes Abanindranath's Gandhi and Chatterra's Kabir, both of whom are thoroughly historicized in the moments in which they are articulated—respectively, nationalist and Mughal.

The modern, political figure of Gandhi is in dialogue with and acts as a counterbalance for the medieval, mystical figure of Kabir. Both are necessary to keep the ark from foundering in the stormy waters of moral uncertainty and historical oblivion that surround the idea of India. India is neither the past nor the future, but a present that emerges out of the conversation between tradition and modernity, the concrete and the transcendental, the political and the poetic, the Hindu and the Muslim, Gandhi and Kabir. In a lovely postmodern gesture, the conversation between the painters Nainsukh and Sheikh, one a precolonial master, the other a postcolonial master, embodies and encapsulates the dialogue of tradition and modernity even as it takes that very dialogue as its subject. The recently deceased Bhupen Khakhar, set apart from the cluster of non-modern ascetics—Hindus, Muslims, and Christians—at the center of the boat, absorbed in his canvas at a distance from the others, perhaps stands in for Sheikh too, invoking the contemporary artist who at once is thoroughly individualistic, suffers from a very modernist alienation, and thinks deeply about the rich and sometimes mysterious past with which he may or may not be connected.

I take Gulammohammed Sheikh's *Ark* to be an almost perfect symbol of the argument I have tried to make in this book. Over the years that it took to write, political debates in India have naturally traversed a varied territory, from the rise and recession of the Hindu Right, to the electoral rout of the Communist Left, to the intensifying violence between the Indian state and its Maoist opponents, to the fluctuating fortunes of the Kashmiris, and, most recently, a public outcry over widespread corruption in the highest echelons of the government and the private sector. At different moments, developments and discussions in contemporary politics reminded me of the founders and their concerns, and of the promises of anticolonial nationalism that often seem to have been badly broken in our own time.

But I also began to see, as political life in India today changed and shifted, that many of my questions go to values and norms that are in a sense stable and abiding underneath the flux of news and current affairs. One wants to know how Hindutva as an ideology of majoritarian religious nationalism distorts and instrumentalizes history in order to persecute minorities, or how Anna Hazare, the aged farmer-activist leading a citizens' campaign against corruption in 2011, alludes to the memory of Mahatma Gandhi through the tactic of the hunger strike. But even if such queries were answered through a careful analysis of the present, one would still seek an account of how it was that by placing ourselves in a complicated yet determinate relationship to tradition, we actually became modern.

At the very beginning of my inquiry, I took as my talisman MacIntyre's insight that a crisis in the self is a crisis in the tradition that has formed the self. India's sense of self seems once again under stress, as the country enters its third decade of globalization and neoliberal economic policy, and they bring in their wake stronger manifestations of what Gandhi called "Western civilization" (or *kudharo:* literally, "the evil stream"), such as aggressive urbanization, rampant consumerism, and late capitalist hypermodernity. We may or may not be able to look objectively at the current crisis in sovereign selfhood, but by reflecting on the crisis that India went through less than a century ago—a crisis whose resolution provided the warrant for the new nation-state—we may discover what kinds of soul searching, acts of reading, and interpretive leaps are necessary at such junctures in history. It may be too much to ask for new minds of the order of Tagore, Nehru, and Ambedkar to apply themselves to the construction of India's future in the twenty-first century and beyond, but because we still have the work done by the founding generations as an example and a precedent before us, there is a plinth upon which we stand, and a vantage from which we may survey what is past, or passing, or to come.

On the banks of our river there are raging fires unleashed by economic liberalization. Urban settlements that are more slums than cities remain mired in polluted land, air, and water. Adrift in a time of turbulence, a delicate ark harbors the fragile resources for cultural renewal, civilizational memories that are also our only hope for salvation from the more virulently antihuman manifestations of modernity. Foregrounded in our consciousness are the ideas and words of giants like Kabir and Gandhi, boatmen who forded the confusions of their own times with insights, whether political or poetic, that restored balance and provided direction to societies—to our own society at earlier points in its history—that might otherwise have been plunged into extreme uncertainty and perhaps terminal decline. Traditions that do not renew and reorient themselves, that fail to make the epistemological breakthrough, that do not gather themselves and chart, with the help of the oars of criticism and creativity, a course through the onrush of the future, are doomed to founder and be forgotten.

About 250 years ago, Nainsukh saw his patron, Balwant Singh of Jasrota, plunged into a political crisis, howsoever local and personal its dimensions. Everything precious had to be sheltered and carried to safety, at least in the painter's imagination. Gulammohammed Sheikh, painting in Gujarat not long after the carnage of 2002, makes a similar plea for saving the traditions of self-examination and self-mastery, of peaceful coexistence and affective community, of rational inquiry and ecstatic transcendence, that have characterized India and kept it buoyed for at least a millennium. Sheikh's ark of tradition is both capaciously accommodating and precariously poised on stormy waters. His Gandhi is speaking to (an invisible) Tagore, the modern poet, but looks across to Kabir, the medieval poet, who weaves his subtle cloth as he always did, into the fabric of meaning. In this wordless, continuing, and resonant dialogue the ark is balanced and kept afloat, and perhaps by paying close attention to our ancestors, we too may be able to get across to safer shores.

Does this book offer an exhaustive narrative about the search for the self in modern India? About the role of the founders in marrying civilizational selfhood with national sovereignty? About the emergence of new political categories through a philological exploration of old texts? About the place of every community—major or minor, ancient or recent—in a collective effort to imagine India, to live India? The answer must certainly be in the negative, since my account is necessarily preliminary rather than definitive, and my aim has been more to open a door than to write a total history. I wanted to interrogate certain commonly held beliefs: for example, that the *Gītā* is a text about war and therefore it makes no sense that Gandhi lived by the *Gītā* and preached non-violence; that Nehru was such a fanatical modernist and determined secularist as to have no interest in or relationship to tradition; that Tagore's engagement with classical texts, especially Sanskrit poetry, was purely literary or romantic, but not political; that Ambedkar's hatred for caste led him to reject the past so vehemently as to secede from Indian history altogether; that the arts and aesthetics, as practiced by Abanindranath, Coomaraswamy, and the Bengal School circle, were tangential to mainstream nationalist struggles and to the political self-image of the emerging nation.

Most of all, I was keen to test the limits of some of the ideas that are now widely accepted as the strongest claims of the Subaltern Studies historians—the derivative, incomplete, and belated nature of Indian political modernity; the continuities, compromises, and collaborations between the colonial and the postcolonial state that undermine or even obviate the revolutionary character of the latter; the anomalous persistence of religion, caste, and other seemingly non-rational aspects of Indic premodernity into the present—all of which leave secular, liberal, and left-wing citizens uncomfortable and dissatisfied with their polity even six decades after independence from British rule and the establishment of the world's largest democracy in India. I wanted to be reminded of the intellectual breadth and ethical commitment of the founders of modern India; to return to a not-so-distant past when many ways of being, thinking, feeling, and communicating that now appear remote or indecipherable were still lived realities for Indians; to be surprised by the historically deep roots of Indian modernity as also by the relatively recent and invented character of Indian traditions. And perhaps I wanted to paint my own version of Nainsukh's boat, or of Gulammohammed Sheikh's ark, constructing an argument about the tension and exchange between past and future that can keep India safe even in the deluge of late capitalism.

In writing this book I found that a series of binaries that had hitherto been implicit in my understanding of the history of India in the nineteenth and twentieth centuries became complicated and sometimes broke down altogether. These included pairs like modernity/tradition, secular/religious, Hindu/Muslim, the social/the transcendental, egalitarianism/inequality, modern political society/premodern cultural communities, and so on. Part of the reason for this process—of complication, and even breakdown—was that the five figures I focused on all tested, straddled, or upset these divisions. Further, the categories of self that emerged from my reading of the founders were also complex and tended to be situated at the intersection of the past and the future in a way that never allows us to assimilate them on the one hand into any simple reconstruction of an Indian political tradition coming down from the very beginnings of history, or on the other hand into a narrative of derivation, influence, or belatedness with respect to Western political thought. In confronting and addressing the crisis of the self, the five thinkers I discuss, and in fact many more in the founding generations, had to begin their journey from a place of genuine uncertainty and painstakingly find their way to an unexpected clearing, a threshold, a ground upon which they could firmly plant their feet.

The founders had a certain proximity to a range of traditions that have now, about a century later, become remote, even inaccessible. Regardless, they did not take those traditions for granted. We know this because we can see how carefully they reopened and reread the texts of those traditions as though for the first time, without either assuming their own capacity to access the meaning of those texts or anticipating the precise meaning that they would find or fail to find in those texts. Gandhi's return to the *Gītā,* for forty years, week after week, demonstrates both a tenacity and a humility that today appears almost unimaginable for us. Similarly, Rabindranath, Abanindranath, Nehru, and Ambedkar—as I hope is made amply clear in the preceding chapters—display qualities of curiosity, skepticism, adventurousness, and intellectual independence that made it possible for them to creatively engage with a variety of traditions of a broadly moral and political character through texts that a lesser minds might have consigned to history, left to specialists, or unthinkingly venerated (and thereby condemned to a different kind of oblivion). Rabindranath went back to Kalidasa repeatedly over fifty years of writing poetry and prose; Abanindranath meditated on the Great Mughals also over a long period of time and through a body of his paintings; Nehru kept on discovering Indian history throughout the course of his adult life; Ambedkar delved into every aspect of the Hindu traditions that he was so thoroughly critical of, and the Buddhist traditions that he ultimately, in some fashion, embraced. For these founders, the meaning of the past was not predetermined and the question of tradition was an open one.

Kabir, who sits at one end of Gulammohammed Sheikh's ark, appears to me as a symbol of the self that India seeks—not because he appears in any direct or prominent way in the discourse of the founders (although all five knew of Kabir, obviously), but because Kabir exceeds the binaries in which Indian history remains imprisoned; because Kabir too ought to be read with the same seriousness, the same lack of presumption, the same willingness to encounter something completely unforeseen, and the same daring with which the founders read the texts that they felt called out to them from the welter of past traditions. Today Kabir's popular reception makes him well known, but his peculiar language leaves him poorly understood. We are too eager to make him into an icon of our concerns—secularism *avant la lettre,* early modernity, a poetic canon, linguistic innovation, syncretistic culture, social radicalism, premodern egalitarianism, subaltern consciousness, or any number of other desiderata and agendas that we love to foist on him.

But in fact these quick fixes and facile characterizations do not even begin to capture the imaginative worlds, the spiritual power, and the discursive fecundity of the poet Kabir. Even as we fill out the details of Kabir's life and times, even as we know more and more precisely his biography and historical surround, even as we sing and recite Kabir with alacrity, the full import of his metaphors eludes us. This ignorance on our part is a result of our inattention to what Kabir did, with and to language, in order to address the mutually constitutive crises of self and tradition that he faced in his own context, his own moment. Gulammohammed Sheikh's intuitions—that Kabir balances the boat, that he steadies the ark, that he fords the waters, that he weaves the fabric, that he converses with the modern even while remaining in and of the medieval—these for me image with an uncanny perfection the role that Kabir must play, and the quest that he represents, as we try to understand the relationship between crisis and self-fashioning at the very moment of India's emergence into presence within the horizon of capitalist modernity.

The motivation behind this book (i.e., my reason for deciding to write it) was my desire to pursue to its logical limit an intuition—the culmination of a few years spent studying some dimensions of India's history and reading, philologically, a handful of premodern Indian texts—that what is valuable in the idea of India and what makes India worth preserving is not just its modern political form as a plural, secular, egalitarian democracy, but its legacy of centuries of reflection on the avenues available to the human mind to transcend the suffering inherent in the human condition. Free India, India that had won its swaraj, the India hard fought and brightly envisioned by extraordinary figures like Gandhi and Ambedkar, Tagore and Nehru, was the dream of realizing both the norm of righteousness and the form of a republic. Accounts of its quest for sovereignty I found aplenty; I wanted to track its still elusive search for the self. Incomplete and insufficient as they may be, these are my findings.

Appendixes

Notes

Selected Bibliography

Acknowledgments

Index

Appendix A

The Indexical Complexity of Tagore's *Meghdūt*

(A map of the distribution of deictic markers in Tagore's poem, based on the translation of William Radice)

Proximal Deictic: "Here"

Here—in the easternmost part of India, in verdurous Bengal, I sit.

Here—the poet Jayadeva, too, watched the density of a sky in full cloud.

Time: the present

Today—is a dark day.

Distal Deictic: "There"

There—is the Amrakuta mountain; there—is the Reva river; there—along the banks of the Vetravati, are the villages of Dasarna; there—is that unknown stream along whose banks forest-girls wander; there—is Avanti and the Nirvindhya river; there—is Ujjayini, gazing at her own shadow in the Shipra river; there—is Kurukshetra; there—is the peak of Kanakhala.

There—is Alakā, heavenly, longed-for city

Who but you, O poet, could take me *there?*

There—is the bed of pining by the Manasa lake

It is something not of *this* world that takes us *there*

There—is the sunless, jewel-lit, evening land, beyond all the rivers and mountains of *this* world.

The India of the poet is "there"—but *where* is this "there"? It is not out *there* in the world; it is only in Kalidasa's poem.

Tagore is able to name all the rivers, mountains and cities of that India, he is able to point them out, "there," "there" and "there," but "where" are they, other than in the poem which he is reading, sitting "here," in the present, in Bengal, in the part of India where Jayadeva also lived?

"There" is no place, *u-topia,* Alakā, heavenly, longed-for city: "beyond all the rivers and mountains of *this* world"—i.e., beyond this, here world.

The "something not of this body" that "takes us there"—there, "beyond all the rivers and mountains of this world"—is poetry. Poetry takes us "there," "beyond" the lands of "this world."

You, O Poet, can take me *there.*
There—to the moonlit woods, to the golden-lotus-lake, to the sapphire rock, to the jewel-studded palace.

Rabindranath's heart travels "like a cloud, from land to land," lands that are "there," but only in the poem he is reading. Traveling "thus" his heart arrives in Alakā, *where* the beloved lives, *where* her house is, *where* she can be seen from the open window, weeping on her bed. "I too have entered *that* heaven of yearning"—yonder "heaven of yearning," "*where* that bereft and lonely being weeps her lament," "*where* alone and awake, that adored one spends her unending night." As soon as he reaches *there,* "the vision goes."

He watches the rain again, pouring steadily all *around* him, "here," where he sits, where he has been sitting all along, while his heart was out, traveling like a cloud from land to land.

Appendix B

Thirteenth Rock Edict of Aśoka

Beloved-of-the-Gods, King Piyadasi, conquered the Kalingas eight years after his coronation. One hundred and fifty thousand were deported, one hundred thousand were killed and many more died (from other causes). After the Kalingas had been conquered, Beloved-of-the-Gods came to feel a strong inclination towards the Dhamma, a love for the Dhamma and for instruction in Dhamma. Now Beloved-of-the-Gods feels deep remorse for having conquered the Kalingas.

Indeed, Beloved-of-the-Gods is deeply pained by the killing, dying and deportation that take place when an unconquered country is conquered. But Beloved-of-the-Gods is pained even more by this—that Brahmans, ascetics, and householders of different religions who live in those countries, and who are respectful to superiors, to mother and father, to elders, and who behave properly and have strong loyalty towards friends, acquaintances, companions, relatives, servants and employees—that they are injured, killed or separated from their loved ones. Even those who are not affected (by all this) suffer when they see friends, acquaintances, companions and relatives affected. These misfortunes befall all (as a result of war), and this pains Beloved-of-the-Gods.

There is no country, except among the Greeks, where these two groups, Brahmans and ascetics, are not found, and there is no country where people are not devoted to one or another religion. Therefore the killing, death or deportation of a hundredth, or even a thousandth part of those who died during the conquest of Kalinga now pains Beloved-of-the-Gods. Now

Beloved-of-the-Gods thinks that even those who do wrong should be forgiven where forgiveness is possible.

Even the forest people, who live in Beloved-of-the-Gods' domain, are entreated and reasoned with to act properly. They are told that despite his remorse Beloved-of-the-Gods has the power to punish them if necessary, so that they should be ashamed of their wrong and not be killed. Truly, Beloved-of-the-Gods desires non-injury, restraint and impartiality to all beings, even where wrong has been done.

Now it is conquest by Dhamma that Beloved-of-the-Gods considers to be the best conquest. And it (conquest by Dhamma) has been won here, on the borders, even six hundred yojanas away, where the Greek king Antiochos rules, beyond there where the four kings named Ptolemy, Antigonos, Magas and Alexander rule, likewise in the south among the Cholas, the Pandyas, and as far as Tamraparni. Here in the king's domain among the Greeks, the Kambojas, the Nabhakas, the Nabhapamkits, the Bhojas, the Pitinikas, the Andhras and the Palidas, everywhere people are following Beloved-of-the-Gods' instructions in Dhamma. Even where Beloved-of-the-Gods' envoys have not been, these people too, having heard of the practice of Dhamma and the ordinances and instructions in Dhamma given by Beloved-of-the-Gods, are following it and will continue to do so. This conquest has been won everywhere, and it gives great joy—the joy which only conquest by Dhamma can give. But even this joy is of little consequence. Beloved-of-the-Gods considers the great fruit to be experienced in the next world to be more important.

I have had this Dhamma edict written so that my sons and great-grandsons may not consider making new conquests, or that if military conquests are made, that they be done with forbearance and light punishment, or better still, that they consider making conquest by Dhamma only, for that bears fruit in this world and the next. May all their intense devotion be given to this which has a result in this world and the next.

Source: English rendering by Ven. S. Dhammika. The Wheel Publication No. 386/387 (Kandy, Sri Lanka: Buddhist Publication Society, 1993; DharmaNet edition 1994).

Appendix C

The State Emblem of India (Prohibition of Improper Use) Act, 2005

December 20, 2005

The Schedule: State Emblem of India: Description and Design

The State Emblem of India is an adaptation from the Sarnath Lion Capital of Aśoka which is preserved in the Sarnath Museum. The Lion Capital has four lions mounted back to back on a circular abacus. The frieze of the abacus is adorned with sculpture in high relief of an elephant, a galloping horse, a bull and a lion separated by intervening Dharma Chakras. The abacus rests on a bell-shaped lotus.

The profile of the Lion Capital showing three lions mounted on the abacus with a Dharma Chakra in the centre, a bull on the right and a galloping horse on the left, and outlines of Dharma Chakras on the extreme right and left has been adopted as the State Emblem of India. The bell-shaped lotus has been omitted.

The motto "Satyameva Jayate"—Truth alone triumphs—written in Devanagari script below the profile of the Lion Capital is part of the State Emblem of India.

Source: Government of India.

Appendix D

From Ambedkar's Published Introduction to *The Buddha and His Dhamma*

Anyone who is not a Buddhist finds it extremely difficult to present the life and teachings of the Buddha in a manner which would make it a consistent whole. Depending on the Nikayas, not only the presentation of a consistent story of the life of the Buddha becomes a difficult thing and the presentation of some parts of his teachings becomes much more so. Indeed it would not be an exaggeration to say that of all the founders of religions in the world, the presentation of the life and teachings of the founder of Buddhism presents a problem which is quite puzzling if not baffling. Is it not necessary that these problems should be solved, and the path for the understanding of Buddhism be made clear? Is it not time that those who are Buddhists should take up these problems, at least for general discussion, and throw what light they can on these problems?

With a view to raise a discussion on these problems, I propose to set them out here. The first problem relates to the main event in the life of the Buddha, namely, Parivraja. Why did the Buddha take Parivraja? The traditional answer is that he took Parivraja because he saw a dead person, a sick person and an old person. This answer is absurd on the face of it. The Buddha took Parivraja at the age of 29. If he took Parivraja as a result of these three sights, how is it he did not see these three sights earlier? These are common events occurring by hundreds, and the Buddha could not have failed to come across them earlier. It is impossible to accept the traditional explanation that this was the first time he saw them. The explanation is not plausible and does not appeal to reason. But if this is not the answer to the question, what is the real answer?

The second problem is created by the four Aryan Truths. Do they form part of the original teachings of the Buddha? This formula cuts at the root of Buddhism. If life is sorrow, death is sorrow, and rebirth is sorrow, then there is an end of everything. Neither religion nor philosophy can help a man to achieve happiness in the world. If there is no escape from sorrow, then what can religion do, what can Buddha do, to relieve man from such sorrow which is ever there in birth itself? The four Aryan Truths are a great stumbling block in the way of non-Buddhists accepting the gospel of Buddhism. For the four Aryan Truths deny hope to man. The four Aryan Truths make the gospel of the Buddha a gospel of pessimism. Do they form part of the original gospel, or are they a later accretion by the monks?

The third problem relates to the doctrines of soul, of karma and rebirth. The Buddha denied the existence of the soul. But he is also said to have affirmed the doctrine of karma and rebirth. At once a question arises. If there is no soul, how can there be karma? If there is no soul, how can there be rebirth? These are baffling questions. In what sense did the Buddha use the words karma and rebirth? Did he use them in a different sense than the sense in which they were used by the Brahmins of his day? If so, in what sense? Did he use them in the same sense in which the Brahmins used them? If so, is there not a terrible contradiction between the denial of the soul and the affirmation of karma and rebirth? This contradiction needs to be resolved.

The fourth problem relates to the Bhikkhu. What was the object of the Buddha in creating the Bhikkhu? Was the object to create a perfect man? Or was his object to create a social servant devoting his life to service of the people and being their friend, guide and philosopher? This is a very real question. On it depends the future of Buddhism. If the Bhikkhu is only a perfect man he is of no use to the propagation of Buddhism, because though a perfect man he is a selfish man. If, on the other hand, he is a social servant, he may prove to be the hope of Buddhism. This question must be decided not so much in the interest of doctrinal consistency but in the interest of the future of Buddhism.

Appendix E

From "Gospel of Equality: The Buddha and the Future of His Religion," 1950

How could this ideal of spreading Buddhism be realized? Three steps appear to be quite necessary.

First: To produce a Buddhist Bible.
Second: To make changes in the organisation, aims and objects of the Bhikkshu Sangha.
Third: To set up a world Buddhist Mission.

The production of a Bible of Buddhism is the first and foremost need. The Buddhist literature is a vast literature. It is impossible to expect a person who wants to know the essence of Buddhism to wade through the sea of literature.

The greatest advantage which the other religions have over Buddhism is that each has a gospel which every one can carry with him and read wherever he goes. It is a handy thing. Buddhism suffers for not having such a handy gospel. The Indian Dhammapada has failed to perform the function which a gospel is expected to. Every great religion has been built on faith. But faith cannot be assimilated if presented in the form of creeds and abstract dogmas. It needs something on which the imagination can fasten, some myth or epic or gospel—what is called in Journalism a "story." The Dhammapada is not fastened around a story. It seeks to build faith on abstract dogmas.

The proposed Gospel of Buddhism should contain:

1. A short life of Buddha.
2. The Chinese Dhammapada.
3. Some of the important Dialogues of Buddha.
4. Buddhist Ceremonies, birth, initiation, marriage and death.

In preparing such a gospel the linguistic side of it must not be neglected. It must make the language in which it is produced live. It must become an incantation instead of being read as narrative or ethical exposition. Its style must be lucid, moving and must produce an hypnotic effect.

Notes

Preface

1. Jawaharlal Nehru, *The Discovery of India* (New Delhi: Oxford University Press, 1989 [1981, 1946]), 37. A few pages earlier he has already written the rousing, reflective words:

> What is my inheritance? To what am I an heir? To all that humanity has achieved during tens of thousands of years, to all that it has thought and felt and suffered and taken pleasure in, to its cries of triumph and its bitter agony of defeat. . . . To all this and more, in common with all men. But there is a special heritage for those of us in India . . . more especially applicable to us, something that is our flesh and blood and bones, that has gone to make us what we are and what we are likely to be.
>
> It is the thought of this particular heritage and its application to the present that has long filled my mind, and it is about this that I should like to write, though the difficulty and the complexity of the subject appall me and I can only touch the surface of it. I cannot do justice to it, but in attempting it I might be able to do some justice to myself by clearing my own mind and preparing for the next stages of thought and action. (Ibid., 25)

Introduction

1. The book began as a genealogy of modern Indian political thought in classical texts from Indic antiquity that India's founding fathers read and engaged with during the nationalist period. In the years it has taken to write it, the book changed, partly because all of my principal terms—"genealogy," "modernity," "political thought," "classical texts," and "founding fathers," as well as the relationships that obtained between them—turned out to be far more complex in

the Indian case than I had at first anticipated. Partly also I began to realize that the subject of the political—a "self" to which the political projects of the founders had reference—was as much in need of discovery and definition as the politics that would create India as a nation.

2. Alasdair MacIntyre, "Epistemological Crises, Dramatic Narrative and the Philosophy of Science," in *The Tasks of Philosophy: Selected Essays,* vol. 1 (Cambridge: Cambridge University Press, 2006), 3–23.
3. The best insights into colonialism and its forms of knowledge still come from the eponymous volume of essays by Bernard Cohn; see Bernard S. Cohn, *Colonialism and Its Forms of Knowledge: The British in India* (Princeton, NJ: Princeton University Press, 1996).
4. Sheldon Pollock, "The Death of Sanskrit," *Comparative Studies in Society and History* 43 (2001): 392–426.
5. Sudhir Chandra, *The Oppressive Present: Literature and Social Consciousness in Colonial India* (New Delhi: Oxford University Press, 1992). For language-wise elaborations, see: for Hindi, Vasudha Dalmia, *The Nationalization of Hindu Traditions: Bharatendu Harischandra and Nineteenth-Century Benaras* (New Delhi: Oxford University Press, 1997); for Bengali, Sudipta Kaviraj, *The Unhappy Consciousness: Bankimchandra Chattopadhyay and the Formation of Discourse in India* (New Delhi: Oxford University Press, 1995); for Marathi, Prachi Deshpande, *Creative Pasts: Historical Memory and Identity in Western India, 1700–1960* (New York: Columbia University Press, 2007). The definitive literary histories of several Indian languages may be found in Sheldon Pollock, ed., *Literary Cultures in History: Reconstructions from South Asia* (Berkeley: University of California Press, 2003), but there is no special focus on modernity and its crises in this volume, which provides historical accounts of the trajectories of fifteen major Indian languages from premodern times to the present.
6. MacIntyre, "Epistemological Crises," 3–14.
7. Rabindranath Tagore, *The Home and the World,* trans. Surendranath Tagore (New York: Penguin, 2005 [1919, 1916]), and *Nationalism* (New Delhi: Rupa & Co., 1992 [1917]).
8. On the epiphanic preamble to Gandhi's writing of *Hind Swaraj,* see Chapter 1 of the book. On *claritas* (lucidity), *veritas* (truth), and other facets that qualify epiphanies, I am quoting here W. G. Sebald, "A Poem of an Invisible Subject" (interview with Michael Silverblatt), in Lynne Sharon Schwartz, ed., *The Emergence of Memory: Conversations with W. G. Sebald* (New York: Seven Stories Press, 2007), 77–86.
9. A. R. Venkatachalapathy, "Introduction: Tradition, Talent, Translation," in *Love Stands Alone: Selections from Tamil Sangam Poetry,* trans. M. L. Thangappa (New Delhi: Penguin, 2010), xiii–xlviii; A. R. Venkatachalapathy, "*Enna Prayocanam?*

Constructing the Canon in Colonial Tamil Nadu," *Indian Economic and Social History Review* 42.4 (2010): 533–551; and A. R. Venkatachalapathy, "Obituary: A. K. Ramanujan (1928–1993)," *Economic and Political Weekly* 35.31 (31 July 1993): 1571.

10. Ananya Vajpeyi, "Reading the 'Book of Books': The Critical Edition of the *Mahābhārata* in the 20th Century" (Unpublished MA thesis, South Asian Languages and Civilizations, University of Chicago, June 1998).

11. Arendt, in her "Tradition and the Modern Age," states: "Our tradition of political thought has its definite beginnings in the teachings of Plato and Aristotle. I believe it came to a no less definite end in the theories of Karl Marx." In *Between Past and Future: Eight Exercises in Political Thought,* intro. Jerome Kohn (New York: Penguin, 2006 [1954]), p. 17.

12. Partha Chatterjee also makes this point in *The Nation and Its Fragments: Colonial and Postcolonial Histories* (Princeton, NJ: Princeton University Press, 1993).

13. When asked about Western civilization, Gandhi reportedly quipped, "That would be a good idea." The same could be said for Indian intellectual history. The field does not have an unambiguous existence, nor a clearly demarcated scholarly literature associated with it. However, if one is willing to resort to construal, relevant materials may be cobbled together from a variety of disparate sources. See the Selected Bibliography at the end of this book. Besides these wide-ranging but utterly heterogeneous works, there are vast scholarly literatures—critical, historical, and biographical—dedicated to each of my five founders, especially Gandhi and Rabindranath Tagore, but also Ambedkar, Nehru, and to a slightly lesser extent Abanindranath Tagore. A self-conscious, self-identifying global intellectual history of India under the British Raj, whether tracking Indian political thought, Islam in modern South Asian history and politics, or a major modern discipline specific to South Asia, like Indology, thus far cannot be found.

14. For a reprisal, see Ananya Vajpeyi, "Political Traditions in the Making of India," *Economic and Political Weekly* 46.25 (18 June 2011): 39–42. See Ramachandra Guha, "Arguments with Sen, Arguments about India," *Economic and Political Weekly* 40.41 (8–14 October 2005): 4420–4428. Sen in turn crafted a careful but nonetheless spirited response to Guha; see Amartya Sen, "Our Past and Our Present," *Economic and Political Weekly* 41.47 (25 November–1 December 2006): 4877–4886.

15. *Pakistan* obviously continues to be used, but that is a special case, and one that need not detain us here.

16. Sunil Khilnani, "Democracy and Its Indian Pasts," in Kaushik Basu and Ravi Kanbur, eds., *Arrangements for a Better World: Essays in Honor of Amartya Sen* (New Delhi: Oxford University Press, 2008), 488–502.

17. Whatever the histories and sources of these words, today India is Bharat; Bharat is India. Sometimes politicians attempt to hijack "Bharat" for particular constituencies; thus "Bharat," they claim, stands for Hindu India, for rural India, for

the India that is not Anglophone, while "India" is supposed to mean the secular, urban, and English-speaking minority. I think this division is false and motivated by ill will. In popular parlance, across classes, in village India as in the cities, in English as in Indian languages, people in fact say "India," "Bharat," and also sometimes "Hindustan" interchangeably.

18. In Chatterjee, *Nation and Its Fragments.*
19. Shahid Amin, *Event, Metaphor, Memory: Chauri Chaura 1922–1992* (Berkeley: University of California Press, 1995).
20. Gandhi and Tagore used their own mother tongues, Gujarati and Bengali, respectively, while Nehru and Ambedkar used mostly English.
21. Alasdair MacIntyre, "Tradition and Translation," in *Whose Justice? Which Rationality?* (Notre Dame, IN: University of Notre Dame Press, 1981), 370–388.
22. Partha Chatterjee, *Nationalist Thought and the Colonial World: A Derivative Discourse* (Minneapolis: University of Minnesota Press, 1993 [1986]).
23. Ajay Skaria, "Relinquishing Republican Democracy: Gandhi's Ramarajya," *Postcolonial Studies* 14.2 (2011): 203–229; and Tridip Suhrud, "Reading Hind Swarajya/Swaraj in Two Languages," unpublished paper, Indian Institute of Advanced Studies, 2 July 2009.
24. Milind Wakankar, *Subalternity and Religion: The Prehistory of Dalit Empowerment in South Asia* (New York: Routledge, 2010).
25. Rabindranath Tagore, *Gitanjali* (London: Macmillan & Co., 1985 [1913]), 20.

1. Mohandas Gandhi

1. I spell *svarāj* as "swaraj" and *ahiṃsā* as "ahimsa" because the latter spellings, in both cases, have become acceptable in mainstream parlance. I do not italicize either word because they both occur too often in this book to merit that kind of typographic attention. The same goes for "swadeshi," which could have been spelled *svadeśī.*
2. Akeel Bilgrami, "Gandhi, the Philosopher," *Economic and Political Weekly* 38.26 (27 September 2003): 4159–4165.
3. This point has recently been made very well in Mithi Mukherjee, *India in the Shadows of Empire: A Legal and Political History (1774–1950)* (New Delhi: Oxford University Press, 2010).
4. See William Dalrymple, *Nine Lives: In Search of the Sacred in Modern India* (London: Bloomsbury, 2009), 78–111.
5. Anthony Parel, "Editor's Introduction," in M. K. Gandhi, *Hind Swaraj and Other Writings,* ed. Anthony Parel (Cambridge: Cambridge University Press, 2006 [1997]), xiii–lxii. On comparable epiphanies in spiritual and political literature, see ibid., xiii–xiv.

6. W. G. Sebald, "A Poem of an Invisible Subject" (interview with Michael Silverblatt), in Lynne Sharon Schwartz, ed., *The Emergence of Memory: Conversations with W. G. Sebald* (New York: Seven Stories Press, 2007), 77–86: "Well, I suppose if there is such a thing as a revelation, if there can be a moment in a text which is surrounded by something like *claritas, veritas,* and the other facets that clarify epiphanies, then it can be achieved only by actually going to certain places, by looking, by expending great amounts of time in actually exposing oneself to places that no one else goes to" (85).
7. Alasdair MacIntyre, "Epistemological Crises, Dramatic Narrative, and the Philosophy of Science," in *The Tasks of Philosophy: Selected Essays,* vol. 1 (Cambridge: Cambridge University Press, 2006), 3–23.
8. Ibid., 10: "For Shakespeare invites us to reflect on the crisis of the self as a crisis of the tradition which has formed the self."
9. Gandhi, *Hind Swaraj,* 26–29.
10. Partha Chatterjee, *Nationalist Thought and the Colonial World: A Derivative Discourse* (Minneapolis: University of Minnesota Press, 1993 [1986]), 85–130.
11. Mukherjee, *India in the Shadows of Empire,* chapter 4.
12. Nick Sutton, "Aśoka and Yudhiṣṭhira: A Historical Setting for the Ideological Tensions of the Mahābhārata?," *Religion* 27 (1997): 333–341.
13. On Raychandbhai Mehta, or Rajchandra, see Ajay Skaria, "'No Politics without Religion': Of Secularism and Gandhi," in Vinay Lal, ed., *Political Hinduism: The Religious Imagination in Public Spheres* (New Delhi: Oxford University Press, 2009), 145–148.
14. M. K. Gandhi, *Hindu Dharma* (New Delhi: Orient Paperbacks, 2005 [1950]), 155: "That the central teaching of the *Gita* is not *himsa* but *ahimsa* is amply demonstrated by the subject begun in the second chapter and summarized in the concluding eighteenth chapter." Further, "To one who reads the spirit of the *Gita,* it teaches the secret of non-violence, the secret of realizing the self through the physical body."
15. Ibid., 179: "In 19 verses at the close of the 2nd chapter of the *Gita,* Krishna explains how this state can be achieved. It can be achieved, he tells us, after killing all your passions. It is not possible to kill your brother after having killed all your passions."
16. M. K. Gandhi, *The Gospel of Selfless Action, or, The Gita according to Gandhi,* trans. Mahadev H. Desai (Ahmedabad: Navajivan Publishing House, 1933 [1929]), Introduction: "8. Even in 1888–89, when I first became acquainted with the *Gita,* I felt that it was not a historical work, but that, under the guise of physical warfare, it described the duel that perpetually went on in the hearts of mankind, and that physical warfare was brought in merely to make the description of the internal duel more alluring. This preliminary intuition became more confirmed

on a closer study of religion and the *Gita.*" All subsequent quotations are from the introduction. Full text available at http://wikilivres.info/wiki/The_Gita_According_to_Gandhi/Introduction. Another edition that is available online is M. K. Gandhi, *The Gospel of Selfless Action, or, The Gita according to Gandhi,* trans. John Strohmier (Berkeley, CA: North Atlantic Books, 2009 [1929]).

17. Ibid., "25. Thinking along these lines, I have felt that in trying to enforce in one's life the central teaching of the *Gita,* one is bound to follow Truth and *ahimsa.* When there is no desire for fruit, there is no temptation for untruth or *himsa.* Take any instance of untruth or violence, and it will be found that at its back was the desire to attain the cherished end. But it may be freely admitted that the *Gita* was not written to establish *ahimsa.* It was an accepted and primary duty even before the *Gita* age. The Gita had to deliver the message of renunciation of fruit. This is clearly brought out as early as the second chapter."

18. *Bhagavad Gītā,* chap. 13, vv. 7–10: "amānitvam, adambhitvam, ahiṃsā, kṣāntir, ārjavam, ācāry' opāsanaṃ, śaucaṃ, sthairyam, ātmavinigraḥ, indriy' artheṣu vairāgyam, anahaṅkāra eva ca . . . etaj jñānam iti proktam; ajñānaṃ yad ato 'nyathā." (Humility, sincerity, non-violence, patience, honesty, service to one's teacher, purity, steadfastness, self-control, indifference towards sense-objects, absence of ego . . . all this is called knowledge, and whatever is other than this is ignorance.) All *Bhagavad Gītā* quotations are taken from Alex Cherniak, trans., *Mahābhārata, Book Six: Bhishma,* vol. 1, *Including the "Bhagavad Gita" in Context,* Clay Sanskrit Library (New York: New York University Press, 2008). These verses and their translation appear on pp. 266–267 (they appear as 37.7–10 in the numbering system of this volume). Henceforth, Cherniak, *BG.*

19. *Bhagavad Gītā,* chap. 16, vv. 1–5; Cherniak, *BG,* 40.1–5: 280–281: "abhayaṃ, sattva-saṃśuddhir, jñānayogavyavasthitiḥ . . . daivī saṃpad vimokṣāya; nibandhāy' āsurī matā; mā śucaḥ! saṃpadaṃ daivīm abhijāto 'si, Pāṇḍava." (Fearlessness, essential purity, steadfastness in knowledge and yoga . . . non-violence [etc., are the virtues of a man who is born to the divine set of qualities, Bharata. Hypocrisy, conceit, etc. are the vices of the man who is born to the demonic set, Partha]. It is thought that the divine set of qualities leads to release, and the demonic set to bondage; but don't worry! You have been born to the divine set, Pandava.)

20. *Bhagavad Gītā,* chap. 17, vv. 14–16; Cherniak, *BG,* 41.14–16: 286–288: "devadvijaguruprājñapūjanaṃ, śaucam, ārjavam, brahmacaryam, ahiṃsā ca śārīraṃ tapa ucyate. . . . ity etat tapo mānasam ucyate." (Physical austerity is said to consist of respect for the gods, the twice-born, the teachers, and the wise, plus purity, honesty, non-violence, and chastity. Speech that is inoffensive, truthful, pleasant and beneficial is known as verbal austerity, as is regular textual recitation. Mental tranquillity, gentleness, economy of speech, self-control and mental purity are called the austerity of the mind.)

21. Gandhi, *Gospel of Selfless Action:* "27. In assessing the implications of renunciation of fruit, we are not required to probe the mind of the author of the *Gita* as to his limitations of *ahimsa* and the like. Because a poet puts a particular truth before the world, it does not necessarily follow that he has known or worked out all its great consequences or that having done so, he is able always to express them fully. In this perhaps lies the greatness of the poem and the poet. A poet's meaning is limitless." Further: "Thus the author of the *Gita*, by extending meanings of words, has taught us to imitate him. Let it be granted, that according to the letter of the *Gita* it is possible to say that warfare is consistent with renunciation of fruit. But after forty years' unremitting endeavor fully to enforce the teaching of the *Gita* in my own life, I have in all humility felt that perfect renunciation is impossible without perfect observance of *ahimsa* in every shape and form."
22. Gandhi, *Hindu Dharma,* 170: "[The] true Kurukshetra is our body. It is at once the Kurukshetra and the Dharmakshetra. If we regard it as, and make it, the abode of God, it is the Dharmakshetra. In this battlefield lies one battle or another always before us."
23. *Bhagavad Gītā,* chap. 6, v. 32; Cherniak, *BG,* 30.32: 220–221: "ātmāupamyena sarvatra samaṃ paśyati yo, 'rjuna, sukhaṃ vā yadi vā duḥkhaṃ, sa yogī paramo mataḥ." (He who by analogy with his own self sees the same thing everywhere, in joy or in sorrow, is reckoned to be the best yogi.)
24. *Bhagavad Gītā,* chap. 11, v. 55; Cherniak, *BG,* 35.55: 262–263: "matkarmakṛn, matparamo, madbhaktaḥ, saṅgavarjitaḥ, nirvairaḥ sarvabhūteṣu yaḥ, sa mām eti, Pāṇḍava." (Whoever acts for me, intent on me as the highest goal, devoted to me, without attachments and without animosity towards any creature, Pandava, comes to me.)
25. T. R. Krishnacharya and T. R. Vyasacharya, eds., *Srimanmahabharatam: Vanaparva III* [in Sanskrit] (Bombay: Nirnaya Sagar Press, 1908), 499: "tarko' pratiṣṭhaḥ śrutayo vibhinnā / naiko muniryasya mataṃ pramāṇam / dharmasya tattvaṃ, nihitaṃ guhāyāṃ / mahājano yena gataḥ sa panthāḥ" (*Mahābhārata: Vanaparva III: Āraṇeyaparva* 21: *Adhyāya* 314: v. 119).
26. Gandhi, *Hindu Dharma,* 177: "I have admitted in my introduction to the *Gita* known as *Anasaktiyoga* that it is not a treatise on non-violence nor was it written to condemn war. Hinduism as it is practiced today, or has even been known to have ever been practiced, has certainly not condemned war as I do. What, however, I have done is to put a new but natural and logical interpretation upon the whole teaching of the *Gita* and the spirit of Hinduism." Further: "I have endeavoured in the light of a prayerful study of the other faiths of the world and, what is more, in the light of my own experiences in trying to live the teaching of Hinduism as interpreted in the *Gita*, to give an extended but in no way strained

meaning to Hinduism, not as buried in its ample scriptures, but as a living faith, speaking like a mother to her aching child. What I have done is perfectly historical. I have followed in the footsteps of our forefathers."

27. Gandhi, *Gospel of Selfless Action:* "5. . . . At the back of my reading there is the claim of an endeavour to enforce the meaning in my own conduct for an unbroken period of forty years."
28. *Bhagavad Gītā,* chap. 3, v. 43; Cherniak, *BG,* 27.43: 200–201: "evaṃ buddeḥ paraṃ buddhvā / saṃstabhy' ātmānam ātmanā / jahi śatruṃ, mahābāho / kāmarupaṃ, durāsadam." (So know that which is higher than the understanding, steady yourself by means of the self, and slay the formidable foe, mighty-armed one, in the form of desire.)
29. Gandhi, *Hindu Dharma,* 180: "It is quite likely that the author did not write it to inculcate *ahimsa,* but as a commentator draws innumerable interpretations from a poetic text, even so I interpret the *Gita* to mean that if its central theme is *anasakti,* it also teaches *ahimsa.* Whilst we are in the flesh and tread the solid earth, we have to practice *ahimsa.* In the life beyond there is no *himsa* or *ahimsa.*"
30. Shruti Kapila and Faisal Devji, eds., "The *Bhagavad Gita* and Modern Thought," special issue, *Modern Intellectual History* 7.2 (August 2010).
31. The August 2010 *Modern Intellectual History* symposium on the *Gītā* is focused on its political uses over and above its social and religious import.
32. Tridip Suhrud, "Reading Hind Swarajya/Swaraj in Two Languages," unpublished manuscript. See also Tridip Suhrud, "Afterword," in Tridip Suhrud and Peter Ronald deSouza, eds., *Speaking of Gandhi's Death* (New Delhi: Orient Blackswan, 2010), 133–147.
33. Gandhi, *Gospel of Selfless Action:* "4. Again this rendering is designed for women, the commercial class, the so-called Shudras and the like who have little or no literary equipment, who have neither the time nor the desire to read the *Gita* in the original and yet who stand in need of its support. In spite of my Gujarati being unscholarly, I must own to having the desire to leave to the Gujaratis, through the mother tongue, whatever knowledge I may possess."
34. Gandhi, *Hindu Dharma,* 154: "And if it is difficult to reconcile certain verses with the teaching of non-violence, it is far more difficult to set the whole of the *Gita* in the framework of violence."
35. Ibid., 165: "I run to my Mother *Gita* whenever I find myself in difficulties, and up to now she has never failed to comfort me"; "Whenever under stress we hasten to the *Gita* for relief and obtain consolation, it is at once for us a Teacher—a Mother" (168). "To thousands it is the real mother, for it yields the rich milk of consolation in difficulties"; "I have called it my spiritual dictionary, for it has never failed me in distress" (181).

36. Ibid., 178: "Yes, we finish the entire *Gita* reading once every week."

37. Ibid., 169–170: "It is called *Arjuna-vishada-yoga. Vishada* means distress. We have to experience such distress as Arjuna experienced. Knowledge cannot be experienced without spiritual anguish and thirst for knowledge."

38. Gandhi, *Gospel of Selfless Action:* "26. But if the *Gita* believed in *ahimsa* or it was included in desirelessness, why did the author take a warlike illustration? When the *Gita* was written, although people believed in *ahimsa,* wars were not only not taboo, but nobody observed the contradiction between them and *ahimsa.*"

39. *Bhagavad Gītā,* chap. 1, v. 1; Cherniak, *BG,* 25.1: 172–173: "dhṛtarāṣṭra uvāca: 'dharmakṣetre kurukṣetre samavetā yuyutsavaḥ / māmakāḥ pāṇḍavāś c' aiva kim akurvata, sanjaya?'" (Dhrtarastra said: "When they assembled, eager to fight, on the field of righteousness, the field of Kuru, what did my sons and the sons of Pandu do, Sanjaya?")

40. Gandhi, *Gospel of Selfless Action:* "16. But desirelessness or renunciation does not come for the mere talking about it. It is not attained by intellectual feat. It is attainable only by a constant heart-churn. . . . This devotion is not mere lip worship, it is a wrestling with death."

41. Uday S. Mehta, "Gandhi on Democracy, Violence and the Politics of Everyday Life," *Modern Intellectual History* 7.2 (July 2010): 355–371. See also Uday S. Mehta, "Patience, Inwardness, and Self-Knowledge in Gandhi's *Hind Swaraj,*" *Public Culture* 23.2 (2011): 417–429.

42. See Gandhi, *Hind Swaraj,* 28: "EDITOR: You have well drawn the picture. In effect it means this: that we want English rule without the Englishman. You want the tiger's nature, but not the tiger; that is to say, you would make India English, and, when it becomes English, it will be called not Hindustan but Englistan. This is not the Swaraj that I want."

43. Mukund Lath, "The concept of *ānṛśaṃsya* in the *Mahābhārata,*" in R. N. Dandekar, ed., *The Mahābhārata Revisited* (New Delhi: Sahitya Akademi, 1990), 113–119; Sibaji Bandopadhyay, "A Critique of Non-violence," *Seminar* 608 "The Enduring Epic" (April 2010): 39–47.

44. John S. Strong, *The Legend of King Aśoka: A Study and Translation of the Aśokāvadāna* (Princeton, NJ: Princeton University Press, 1983). See especially chapter 2, "Dirt and Dharma: Kingship in the *Aśokavadāna,*" 38–70, and in the translation of the text of the *Aśokavadāna,* the section titled "Aśoka the Fierce," 210–213.

45. W. J. Johnson, trans., "Verses 3.311–315: About the Drilling Sticks," *Mahābhārata, Book Three: "The Forest,"* vol. 4 (New York: NYU Press, 2005), 277–333. "Yudhiṣṭhira uvāca: dharma eva hato hanti, dharmo rakṣati rakṣitaḥ. / tasmād dharma na tyajāmi, mā no dharmo hato 'vadhīt. / ānṛśaṃsyaṃ paro dharmaḥ paramārthāc ca

me matam. / ānṛśaṃsyaṃ cikīrṣāmi Nakulo yakṣa jivatu" (322). (Yudhiṣṭhira said: The Law hurt, the Law hurts: protected, it protects. Therefore, that the Law may not abandon us, I do not abandon the Law. Compassion I consider the highest Law, superior even to the highest goal. My wish is to practice compassion: *yaksha,* let Nakula live!" [323].) See also, V. S. Sukthankar, ed., *The Mahābhārata,* vol. 4: *The Āraṇyakaparvan (Part 2): Being the Third Book of the Mahābhārata, the Great Epic of India* (Poona: BORI, 1942), 1025–1033. The text here is not identical with the Clay Sanskrit Library edition above.

On the episode of the *Yakṣa Praṣṇa,* the best modern commentary remains David Dean Shulman, "The Yakṣa's Questions," in Galit Hasan-Rokem and David D. Shulman, eds., *Untying the Knot: On Riddles and Other Enigmatic Modes* (New York: Oxford University Press, 1996), 151–167. See also Ajay Skaria, "Gandhi's Politics: Liberalism and the Question of the Ashram," *South Atlantic Quarterly* 101.4 (Fall 2002): 955–986. On p. 982, note a brief discussion of Yudhiṣṭhira as the *dharmarāja,* or ethical sovereign. See also Skaria, " 'No Politics without Religion,' " 174.

46. See Johnson, *Mahābhārata,* 322–323: "Dharmaśīlaḥ sadā rājā iti māṃ mānavā viduḥ. / svadharmān na caliṣyāmi; Nakulo yakṣa jīvatu." (People know this of me: that the king is ever the Law personified. I shall not stray from my inherent duty: *yaksha,* let Nakula live!) And "Yathā Kuntī tathā Mādrī, viśeṣo n' āsti me tayoḥ / mātṛbhyāṃ samam icchāmi: Nakulo yakṣa jīvatu." (As is Kunti, so is Madri: for me there is no difference between them. I want the same for both my mothers: *yaksha,* let Nakula live!)
47. N. A. Nikam and Richard McKeon, eds. and trans., *The Edicts of Asoka* (Chicago: University of Chicago Press, 1959); P. H. L. Eggermont and J. Hoftijzer, eds., *The Moral Edicts of King Aśoka: Included: The Graeco-Aramaic Inscription of Kandahar and Further Inscriptions of the Maurian Period* (Leiden: E. J. Brill, 1962).
48. See Skaria, "Gandhi's Politics," 982.
49. On the dialogue, debate, and disagreement between Gandhi and Tagore, see Sabyasachi Bhattacharya, ed., *The Mahatma and the Poet: Letters and Debates between Gandhi and Tagore 1915–1941* (New Delhi: National Book Trust of India, 2008 [1997]). See also R. K. Prabhu and Ravindra Kelekar, eds., *Truth Called Them Differently (Tagore-Gandhi Controversy)* (Ahmedabad: Navajivan Publishing House, 1961). See as well, Homer A. Jack, *The Gandhi Reader: A Source Book of His Life and Writings* (Bloomington: Indiana University Press, 1956), 217–233.
50. See Suresh Sharma, "Swaraj and the Quest for Freedom: Rabindranath Tagore's Critique of Gandhi's Non-cooperation," *Thesis Eleven* 39 (1994): 93–104.
51. See Skaria, " 'No Politics without Religion,' " 161–162.
52. See J. B. Kripalani, *Politics of Charkha* (Bombay: Vora and Co., 1946); and J. C. Kumarappa, *Gandhian Economic Thought* (Bombay: Vora and Co., 1951).

53. M. K. Gandhi, *An Autobiography: Or the Story of My Experiments with Truth,* trans. Mahadev Desai, intro. Sunil Khilnani (New Delhi: Penguin Classics, 2001), 10.

2. Rabindranath Tagore

1. Amit Chaudhuri, "The Flute of Modernity: Tagore and the Middle Class," in *Clearing a Space: Reflections on India, Literature and Culture* (New Delhi: Black Kite, 2008), 69–84; Dipesh Chakrabarty, "Nation and Imagination," in *Provincializing Europe: Postcolonial Thought and Historical Difference* (Princeton, NJ: Princeton University Press, 2008 [2000]), 149–179; Ranajit Guha, "Epilogue: The Poverty of Historiography—A Poet's Reproach," and "Appendix: Historicality in Literature by Rabindranath Tagore," in *History at the Limit of World-History* (New York: Columbia University Press, 2002), 75–100; and Partha Chatterjee, "Whose Imagined Community?," in *The Nation and Its Fragments: Colonial and Postcolonial Histories* (Princeton, NJ: Princeton University Press, 1993), 3–13.
2. The Indian national anthem is titled "Jana Gana Mana"; the Bangladeshi national anthem is titled "Amar Sonar Bangla."
3. Perhaps Tagore compares better to Chaim Nachman Bialik (1982–1934), the Hebrew poet; Mahmoud Darwish (1941–2008), the Palestinian poet; and Agha Shahid Ali (1949–2001), the Kashmiri poet, all of whom died before their people attained nationhood, and who had a complex relationship to their countries as well as to the idea of nationality. All three, like Tagore, are regarded as the "national" poets respectively of Israel, Palestine, and Kashmir (of which the latter two, obviously, are not yet nations).
4. William Radice, "Introduction," in Rabindranath Tagore, *Selected Poems,* ed. and trans. William Radice (New Delhi: Penguin Classics, 2005 [1985]), 32.
5. Chronology of poems and essays (written over five decades):
   Meghdūt (collection *Mānasī*), written 1890/published 1888–1889
   Essay "The *Meghdūta,*" written 1907/published 1890
   Meghdūt (collection *Caitālī*), written 1896/published 1895
   "Dream"/"Svapna" (collection *Kalpanā*), written 1900/published 1897
   "Shah Jahan" (collection *Balākā*), written/published 1916
   "Yakṣa" (collection *Śanāī*), written/published 1940
   Essay "Sāhitye Aitihāsikatā," written/published 1941
6. See Chapter 3.
7. Discussed in Chapter 3.
8. Chaudhuri, "Flute of Modernity," 84.
9. Rabindranath Tagore, "The Ramayana," in *Selected Writings on Literature and Language,* ed. Sukanta Chaudhuri and Sankha Ghosh (New Delhi: Oxford University Press, 2001), 253.

10. Sudipta Kaviraj, *The Unhappy Consciousness: Bankimchandra Chattopadhyay and the Formation of Nationalist Discourse in India* (New Delhi: Oxford University Press, 1995); see especially chapter 3, "The Myth of Praxis: Construction of the Figure of Krsna in Krsnacaritra," 72–106. Sudipta Kaviraj, Partha Chatterjee, and Dipesh Chakrabarty all write extensively and significantly on Bankim, supported by a vast secondary literature of mixed provenance.
11. Rabindranath Tagore, *Nationalism* (New Delhi: Penguin Classics, 2009 [1991]), 131.
12. Sheldon Pollock, *The Language of the Gods in the World of Men: Sanskrit, Culture, and Power in Premodern India* (Berkeley: University of California Press, 2006), 223–258.
13. The relationship of kāvya (poetic language) to rājya (rule), *rāṣṭra* (polity), and *sattā* (power) in Indic premodernity is one of the principle problems to which Pollock devotes his magnum opus, *The Language of the Gods in the World of Men* (2006). I am suggesting that we raise the same question for modern India as well. In one of his essays on Tagore, Amit Chaudhuri explains that in speaking of the "aesthetic parameters" of Indian modernity, by "aesthetic" he means "the transposition of historical and political entities into forms of self-imaging and self-consciousness" (Chaudhuri, "Flute of Modernity," 76). Poetry is certainly a subset of the totality of aesthetic forms in India whose careers we would like to be able to trace from the premodern into the modern world. Further, we would want to correlate these aesthetic forms with their contemporary political forms, for, as Pollock has shown for Indic premodernity, sometimes such a correlation provides the strongest plinth on which to build a history of India.
14. The rainy season in the Hindu calendar traditionally stretches over the two months of Āśāḍha and Śrāvaṇa. Kalidasa's Sanskrit may say that the Yakṣa sees the cloud *praśama divase* or *prathama divase*—meaning "on the last day" or "on the first day" of the month of Āśāḍha: commentators are divided over the two readings. Tagore himself goes with "on the first day" in the longer of his two poems, both titled *Meghdūt,* discussed at length below.
15. Rabindranath Tagore, "The *Meghadūta,*" in *Selected Poems,* 50–52. This poem is cited as *Megh-T.* throughout the chapter. See also "Yakṣa," 116–117; "Shah Jahan," 78–81.
16. Chakrabarty, "Nation and Imagination," 149–179.
17. Martha C. Nussbaum problematizes patriotism and contrasts it to cosmopolitanism, through a discussion of Rabindranath; see her "Patriotism and Cosmopolitanism" in Joshua Cohen, ed., *For Love of Country?* (Boston: Beacon Press, 2002), 3–17.
18. Sanskrit: viccheda; Bengali: *bicched.* Tagore's Bengali is highly Sanskritic, which makes it difficult to settle on one diacritical convention, either that for Sanskrit or that for Bengali.

19. Chaudhuri, "Flute of Modernity," 72.

20. Here, rasa is emotional essence/affect/the experiential distillate of a work of art; *adbhuta* is wonder, amazement.

21. Kadambari Debi was married to Tagore's older brother, Jyotindranath, and committed suicide in 1884, at a young age, soon after Tagore's marriage to Mrinalini Debi in 1883. As a young and unmarried man, Tagore had been very attached to his older sister-in-law, and she to him; her tragic death caused him great grief. The nature of the love between the young Rabindranath and Kadambari is a complex subject. Tagore himself wrote about it years later, through his novella *Naṣṭanīḍ* (The Broken Nest), in 1901 (*Naṣṭanīḍ*, trans. Mary M. Lago and Supriya Sen [Minneapolis: University of Missouri Press, 1971]; and "Nashtaneer," in *Three Women*, trans. Arunava Sinha [New Delhi: Random House India, 2010]). His wife, Mrinalini, died in 1902, and Tagore never remarried. He and his wife had several children, not all of whom survived, but it seems that his marriage was not a particularly close or fulfilling one, at least for the poet. Satyajit Ray adapted Tagore's story for his 1964 cinematic masterpiece, *Charulata: The Lonely Wife.*

22. Giorgio Agamben, *The Man without Content,* trans. Georgia Albert (Palo Alto, CA: Stanford University Press, 1999 [1994]), 59–93; see especially chapter 7, "Privation Is Like a Face," and chapter 8, "Poiesis and Praxis."

23. Ibid., 72.

24. Buddhadev Bose, *Modern Poetry and Sanskrit Kavya,* trans. Sujit Mukherjee (Calcutta: Writers Workshop, 1997).

25. Well-crafted, which is what "Sanskrit" means.

26. Sawhney's exegesis is relatively more focused on Kalidasa's *Abhijñānaśākuntalam* rather than his *Meghadūtam,* though she does approach both the Sanskrit texts via Tagore and also Bose. Simona Sawhney, *The Modernity of Sanskrit* (Minneapolis: University of Minnesota Press, 2009), 20–50 and 158–164.

27. Here, *karuṇā:* both "pathos" and "the compassion aroused in us when we are moved by the suffering of another."

28. In a sense, Kalidasa's poem has given to us classical India: we cannot, now, at this point in time, see that India, the India of antiquity, at all, except through the window of Kalidasa's language, which opens out into an exquisite vista of the past.

29. Biographers and critics continually speculate as to which references in Tagore's work could be to Kadambari Debi, Jyotindranath's wife and Rabindranath's older sister-in-law, who committed suicide in 1884. (See note 21 above.)

30. "Yet recalling the past meant, in this Tagorean configuration, confronting the question: why, and at what point, had the Indian modern ceased to have recourse to it, as an entity clearly available to rational apprehension? . . . In his poem, Tagore brilliantly reworks Kalidasa's tale of separation from the loved

one into a narrative of the separation of the self from history. . . . While Tagore wrote charming, implicitly patriotic verses, often for children, about the heroes and heroines of pre-colonial India . . . he was also the first poet to articulate, to, in effect fashion an iconography for, the educated Indian's anxiety about the recovery of the past" (Chaudhuri, "Flute of Modernity," 72–73).

31. Rabindranath Tagore, "The *Meghadutam*," in Sukanta Chaudhuri and Sankha Ghosh, eds., Bhawani Prasad Chattopadhyay, trans., *Selected Writings on Literature and Language* (New Delhi: Oxford University Press, 2001), 222–225. Hereafter cited in the text as Tagore. Also in Tagore, *Selected Poems,* 180–182. This translation is slightly different.
32. Ujjayinī: Ujjain.
33. Guha, *History at the Limit,* 75–76.
34. Amit Chaudhuri has tried to place him, in interesting and complicated ways, relative to these two categories of thinkers who dominated the realms of history and literature in both Europe and India in the late nineteenth and early twentieth centuries. In Chaudhuri's reading, Rabindranath stood Orientalism on its head by claiming that it was because Europeans came into contact with the texts of ancient India—like the Upaniṣads, Kalidasa, and many others—that Enlightenment and Romanticism came about in Europe. Subsequently, thanks to the colonial encounter, India rediscovered its own past via European intermediaries. So if India owed its modernity to Europe, Europe already owed its modernity to India—a prior debt, as it were. Chaudhuri calls this Tagore's "revisionist" Orientalism, and places Kalidasa's work, especially his *Śakuntalā,* at the center of Rabindranath's argument. Chaudhuri, "Two Giant Brothers: Tagore's Revisionist 'Orient,'" in *Clearing a Space,* 122–139.
35. Isaiah Berlin, *The Sense of Reality: Studies in Ideas and Their History,* ed. Henry Hardy (London: Chatto and Windus, 1996), 260.
36. Pollock, *Language of the Gods,* 223–258.
37. The deixis in Rabindranath's *Meghdūt* poem—indicating and differentiating two locations, one proximal and one distal—is quite insistent and consistent. However, upon closer examination, the separation between them becomes more and more unclear; in fact, it turns out that they are pretty thoroughly entangled with one another, inseparable. I have listed all of the occurrences of spatial deictic markers in *Meghdūt*—"here" and "there"—in Appendix A.
38. Tagore, *Selected Poems,* 169. "Yakṣa," 116–117, from the same volume, is also quoted in this chapter.
39. Guha, *History at the Limit,* 96. "Historicality in Literature" *(Sāhitye Aitihāsikatā)* appears in the Appendix, 95–99.
40. Rabindranath Tagore, "Dream" (22 May 1897), from *Kalpanā* (1900), in *I Won't Let You Go: Selected Poems,* trans. Ketaki Kushari Dyson (New York: Bloodaxe Books,

1991). "History was like the subconscious; it had been buried, and now, in an act of translation, it was being recovered. It was as if Indians, in invoking history, were recalling a past they did not quite remember having forgotten" (Chaudhuri, "Flute of Modernity," 70). In the poem "Dream": "Tagore invokes his sense of his historical past not in the aestheticized language of the new nationalism . . . but in terms of a fantasy, loss, and incommunicability" (Chaudhuri, "Flute of Modernity," 73).

41. Ujjayinī (modern Ujjain) is an old city in central India, in a region known as Malwa, today falling within the state of Madhya Pradesh. The earliest references available (in the Buddhist literature and the *Mahābhārata*) describe it as the capital of the kingdom of Avanti. It seems to have been continuously inhabited as an urban center as well as a site for Hindu (Śaiva) pilgrimage, on the banks of the river Kṣiprā, for at least 2,400 years. It was the capital of the Gupta Empire during the reign of Candragupta II "Vikramāditya" (r. 375–415 CE), at whose court Kalidasa is said to have been the resident poet. Ujjain is India's Greenwich: the prime meridian, according to Indic timekeeping, passes through it. Like Kashi/Varanasi, Ujjain is one of India's oldest and holiest cities. See Amartya Sen's essay, "India through Its Calendars," in *The Argumentative Indian: Writings on Indian History, Culture and Identity* (New Delhi: Penguin, 2005) for a fascinating account of calendrical systems in precolonial India. One major calendar used across North India, the Vikram Saṃvat, with its zero point in 57 BCE, was supposed to have been instituted by Vikramāditya, and Ujjain, his capital, had strong traditions of mathematics, astronomy, and calendrical science in the middle of the first millennium.

42. Bose, *Modern Poetry*, 74.

43. Ibid.

44. Ibid., 75–76.

45. Sudipta Kaviraj, "The Theory of the Poem: Alienation Themes in *Meghaduta*," *Journal of the School of Languages* 4.1 (1976): 28–43.

46. Ibid., 39.

47. Ibid., 42.

48. Ibid.

49. Sawhney, *Modernity of Sanskrit*, chap. 1.

50. Ibid., 52–57. Abanindranath Tagore and J. P. Gangooly should be thought of in exactly the same fashion, albeit with respect to a different aesthetic form (painting, and not poetry). I turn to them both in Chapter 3.

51. Prathama Banerjee, "The Work of Imagination: Temporality and Nationhood in Colonial Bengal," in Shail Mayaram, M. S. S. Pandian, and Ajay Skaria, eds., *Muslims, Dalits, and the Fabrication of History* (New Delhi: Permanent Black, 2005), 280–322.

52. Pothik kāler morme jege ṭhāke bipul bicched . . . / Ei biśyo to tārī kābyo, mandākrānte tārī roce ṭīkā / Birāṭ dukkher pote ānander śudūr bhūmikā.
53. The original Bengali for "fire of creation" is *sṛṣṭīr agun.*
54. The phrase is from Kaviraj, *Unhappy Consciousness.*
55. Berlin, *Sense of Reality,* 266.
56. For imagery where time future and time past, as well as the nation and its history, are all figured as a beautiful but death-drenched tomb, see Chapter 3, where I discuss in great detail Abanindranath Tagore's paintings showing the Taj Mahal, together with Rabindranath's poem on the same theme, "Shah Jahan."

3. Abanindranath Tagore

1. A gold medal was not awarded to any work, so effectively Abanindranath won first prize. He won a gold medal at the Congress Industrial Exhibition in Calcutta for the same painting the following year (1903).
2. Amit Chaudhuri, "Two Giant Brothers: Tagore's Revisionist Orient," in *Clearing a Space: Reflections on India, Literature and Culture* (New York: Peter Lang, 2008), 125.
3. Ibid.
4. Abanindranath was also involved in various ways with other contemporary art bodies based in Calcutta, such the Indian Society for Oriental Art and the Bangiya Kala Samsad, a history richly and intricately recounted by Guha-Thakurta. Much of the actual work and discussion took place in the fabled "south verandah" *(dakshiner baranda)* of Abanindranath's section of the house on the Jorasanko property, which no longer exists. A few surviving sepia-tinted photographs of this space arouse an ineffable nostalgia: it's almost like looking into the famous salon of the Bloomsbury group that was later destroyed in the London Blitz.
5. It would not be wrong to count men as far apart as Sri Aurobindo (1872–1950) and P. C. Mahalanobis (1893–1972) in this select group—incidentally also Bengalis, both.
6. The most illuminating meditation on the idea of the classical in recent Indian thought is Sudipta Kaviraj, "The Myth of Praxis: Construction of the Figure of Kṛṣṇa in *Kṛṣṇacarita,*" in *The Unhappy Consciousness: Bankimchandra Chattopadhyay and the Formation of Nationalist Discourse in India* (New Delhi: Oxford University Press, 1995), 72–106. On post-Orientalist philology see Sheldon Pollock, "Future Philology? The Fate of a Soft Science in a Hard World," *Critical Inquiry* 35 (Summer 2009): 931–961. On the difficulties of referring to the varieties of religious experience in the academic discourse of the humanities: Gayatri Spivak spoke eloquently about the discomfort with what she described as "the intuition

of the transcendental," "the un-anticipatable emergence of the supernatural in the natural," and "the interruption of the epistemological by the ethical" in a lecture on the life of Sharada Devi (1853–1920), wife of the Bengali mystic Sri Ramakrishna (1836–1886) at the Harvard Divinity School, 10 April 2008; *Annual William James Lecture on Religious Experience 2008,* video stream at http://www.hds.harvard.edu/news/events_online/james_2008.html.

7. Rama P. Coomaraswamy, introduction to Ananda K. Coomaraswamy, *The Essential Ananda K. Coomaraswamy* (Bloomington: World Wisdom, 2004), 6.
8. In 1910 Abanindranath painted a portrait of Coomaraswamy, as did his brother Gaganendranath Tagore. According to R. Siva Kumar, Abanindranath's "image of the most penetrating scholar and connoisseur of Indian art who was active around 1910 . . . seems to reveal shadows of their 'imperfect encounter.'" R. Siva Kumar, *Paintings of Abanindranath Tagore* (Calcutta: Pratikshan, 2008), 190, 193.
9. Ananda Coomaraswamy, "*Samvega:* 'Aesthetic Shock,'" in *Essential Ananda K. Coomaraswamy,* 193–199.
10. Rabindranath Tagore, "Shah Jahan," in William Radice, ed. and trans., *Selected Poems* (New Delhi: Penguin Classics, 2005 [1985]), 78–81.
11. Kumar, *Paintings of Abanindranath Tagore,* 363.
12. Coomaraswamy, *Essential Ananda K. Coomaraswamy,* 193.
13. Ibid., 196–197.
14. Ibid., 197–199.
15. Ibid., 197.
16. Siva Kumar discusses these works at some length, as well as reproducing many of them; see his *Paintings of Abanindranath Tagore,* especially pp. 68, 70, 74, 85, 86, 107, 137, 196, 224, and 229. He is concerned with various aspects of these works: how they reveal Abanindranath's evolution from a copyist to a painter with a marked individual style; Abanindranath's interest in character over event; his use of landscape as a backdrop to convey mood; his recurrent study of persons engaged in reflection or communion with their own thoughts, turned away from the spectator, as it were—thus the evocation of a subjective interiority, even when showing highly public figures like the Mughal emperors (or even famous members of the Tagore family, as well as other prominent Indian nationalists who visited the Tagores, such as Gandhi); and the fine balance that the painter is able to strike, time and again, between "portraiture and narration, history and fiction" (224).
17. Partha Mitter, *The Triumph of Modernism: India's Artists and the Avant-Garde, 1947–1992* (London: Reaktion, 2007), 361. The reviewer was Suresh Samajpati, writing in the journal *Sāhitya* in 1910 and refuting Sister Nivedita's praises of Abanindranath. A hundred years later, Siva Kumar is rather more kind: "Thus, what looks

like an equestrian portrait of Shahjahan, is an image of the emperor lost in reverie as he rides out alone in the twilight. While the emperor is tangible and withdrawn, his horse is agile and slight to the point of immateriality. Together they suggest a movement slowed down to near stillness. . . . Abanindranath, one may say, wanted to paint a man caught in a dream as one might paint a man caught in a storm" (*Paintings of Abanindranath Tagore,* 85–86).

18. Chaudhuri, "Two Giant Brothers," 125.
19. Partha Mitter, *Art and Nationalism in Colonial India, 1850–1922: Occidental Orientations* (Cambridge: Cambridge University Press, 1995), 283–289.
20. Jadunath Sarkar, "The Passing of Shah Jahan," *Modern Review* 18.4 (October 1915): 361–368.
21. Ibid., 366.
22. Tagore, *Selected Poems,* 145.
23. Ibid., 146.
24. The line, in a highly Sanskritic compounded Bengali, literally reads: "The eternally-descended darkness of the past": the past is perpetual dark; night that has fallen once for all (*"atīter cira-asta-andhakār"* in Radice's rendering) (Tagore, *Selected Poems,* 100–101).
25. *Head of Dara* (1907).
26. *Shah Jahan in Old Age* (early 1920s).
27. *Jahangir* (1924); *Aurangazeb in Young Age, Aurangazeb in Old Age, Alamgir,* all early 1920s.
28. Tapati Guha-Thakurta, *The Making of a New "Indian" Art: Artists, Aesthetics and Nationalism in Bengal, c. 1850–1920* (Cambridge University Press, 1992); and Mitter, *Art and Nationalism.*
29. See Christopher Pinney, *Photos of the Gods: The Printed Image and Political Struggle in India* (London: Reaktion, 2004), to compare Abanindranath's *Mother India* with other images of the nation as goddess in the late nineteenth and early twentieth centuries, especially in popular and political art—posters, calendars, journals, magazines, newspapers, etc.
30. Martha C. Nussbaum, *The Clash Within: Democracy, Religious Violence, and India's Future* (Cambridge, MA: Harvard University Press, 2007), 80–121.
31. Rabindranath Tagore, *The Home and the World,* trans. Surendranath Tagore (New York: Penguin Books, 2005 [1919]).
32. Ibid. See also Pradip Kumar Dutta, *Rabindranath Tagore's "The Home and The World": A Critical Companion* (London: Anthem Press, 2004).
33. Partha Chatterjee, *The Nation and Its Fragments: Colonial and Postcolonial Histories* (Princeton, NJ: Princeton University Press, 1993).
34. Rabindranath Tagore, "Our Swadeshi Samaj," in *Greater India* (Madras: Triplicane, 1921), 1–33.

35. Santiniketan is about 140 kilometers (87 miles) from Kolkata, in Bolpur, built on land owned by the Tagore family since the mid-nineteenth century, from Rabindranath's father's generation.
36. Tagore, "Our Swadeshi Samaj," 5.
37. Ibid.
38. Not surprisingly, the word *melā* comes from the same root in Sanskrit that yields, in many North Indian languages including Hindi and Bengali, a family of terms meaning "meeting," "union," "conjoining," "mingling," and "mixture."
39. For a discussion and critique of the painting, see also Kumar, *Paintings of Abanindranath Tagore,* 82.
40. Ibid.
41. Rabindranath Tagore, *Nationalism* (New Delhi: Penguin Classics, 2009), 136.
42. Ibid., 138.
43. Ibid., 136.
44. Ibid., 117.
45. Ibid., 133.
46. Same year as *Hind Swaraj;* see Guha-Thakurta, *Making of a New "Indian" Art.*
47. Guha-Thakurta, in her *Making of a New "Indian" Art,* titles both paintings *The Banished Yaksha of Kalidasa's Meghaduta* (1992). Kumar in his *Paintings of Abanindranath Tagore* titles Abanindranath's painting *Cloud Messenger* (100).
48. The shorter poem is hereafter referred to as *Meghdūt (b).* In 2009, Sudipta Kaviraj alerted me to this poem in the Bengali; Rosinka Chaudhuri very kindly translated it for me at short notice. The original line reads: "Tomār birahabīnā sakaruṇa bāje." This *birahabīnā,* then, is the melancholy instrument whose strumming expresses the longing of the separated lover.
49. Sudipta Kaviraj, "Tagore and Transformations in the Ideals of Love," in Francesca Orsini, ed., *Love in South Asia: A Cultural History* (Cambridge: Cambridge University Press, 2006), 161–182.
50. Ibid., 170.
51. Mitter, *Art and Nationalism.*
52. Ibid.
53. Rabindranath Tagore, *Selected Writings on Literature and* Language, ed. Sukanta Chaudhuri and Sankha Ghosh (New Delhi: Oxford University Press, 2001), 225; emphasis added.
54. For a detailed reading of the national anthem, see Ananya Vajpeyi, "A Song unto Itself," *The Caravan* (January 2010), 60–65.
55. *Head of Dara* (1907).
56. In the later part of his career Abanindranath too withdrew from nationalism, and ceased to paint in a Swadeshi idiom; but that is a different story. See Kumar, *Paintings of Abanindranath Tagore,* chapters 4–8.

57. I read the absence of the nation in Rabindranath's paintings somewhat like the theorist of film and visual media, Geeta Kapur, reads the absence of the nation in Satyajit Ray's trilogy of films made in the 1950s, *Pather Panchali* (The Song of the Road). See Geeta Kapur, *When Was Modernism: Essays on Contemporary Cultural Practice in India* (New Delhi: Tulika Press, 2000). A new exhibition of Rabindranath's late artwork, *The Last Harvest,* traveled to different parts of India and the world in 2011. I had a chance to see it at the Asia Society in New York in late September 2011. See also R. Siva Kumar, ed., *The Last Harvest: Paintings of Rabindranath Tagore* (Ahmedabad: Mapin, 2011).

4. Jawaharlal Nehru

1. A style of painting-cum-storytelling known as "Pabu ji ki Phaḍ." See William Dalrymple, *Nine Lives: In Search of the Sacred in Modern India* (London: Bloomsbury, 2009), 78–111.
2. Jawaharlal Nehru, *The Discovery of India* (New Delhi: Oxford University Press, in conjunction with the Jawaharlal Nehru Memorial Fund, 1989 [1981, 1946]), and *Letters to Chief Ministers 1947–1964,* ed. G. Parthasarathi (New Delhi: Jawaharlal Nehru Memorial Fund, 1985–1989).
3. Ramachandra Guha, *Makers of Modern India* (New Delhi: Penguin Books, 2010), 484–485.
4. Alasdair MacIntyre, "Poetry as Political Philosophy: Notes on Burke and Yeats," in *Ethics and Politics,* vol. 2 (Cambridge: Cambridge University Press, 2006), 159–171.
5. Sunil Khilnani explores and elucidates Nehru's qualities as a statesman, an intellectual, a writer, and a stylist, in a series of deeply sympathetic essays of incomparable elegance—as though the historian seeks to match his own language with that of the man he takes as his subject. See Sunil Khilnani, "Nehru's Judgment," in Richard Bourke and Raymond Geuss, eds., *Political Judgment: Essays in Honour of John Dunn* (Cambridge: Cambridge University Press, 2009), 254–278; Sunil Khilnani, "The Discovery of Indians: Nehru and Political Possibility," *Kingsley Martin Memorial Lecture,* Cambridge, 21 November 2007 (draft manuscript from the author, personal communication); Sunil Khilnani, "Gandhi and Nehru: The Uses of English," in Arvind Krishna Mehrotra, ed., *An Illustrated History of Indian Literature in English* (New Delhi: Orient Blackswan, 2003), 135–156.
6. Nehru, *Discovery of India,* 40.
7. For purposes of this chapter, see especially Shyam Benegal, dir., *Bharat ek Khoj* (1988), Episode 14, "Asoka: Part 2," Aśoka's conversion and his propagation of dhamma (split into two segments, of thirty and five minutes).
8. Nehru, *Discovery of India,* 41.
9. Ibid., 44–45.

10. Ibid., 55.
11. MacIntyre, "Poetry as Political Philosophy," 161.
12. Ibid., 164.
13. Ibid., 168.
14. Nehru, *Discovery of India,* 49.
15. Partha Chatterjee, *Nationalist Thought and the Colonial World: A Derivative Discourse* (Minneapolis: University of Minnesota Press), 1993 [1986], 147.
16. Ibid.
17. Ibid.
18. Nehru, *Discovery of India,* 55–56.
19. Ibid., 38.
20. Ibid., 37.
21. Ibid., 56.
22. The official literature of the Government of India, for example on its Web site under "National Symbols" (http://india.gov.in/knowindia/national_symbols.php), simply states what the symbols are and what their historical or textual sources are, but does not point to how or why these were adopted by the founders at the time of the creation of the republic.
23. The motto of the Lok Sabha, the Lower House of Parliament in India's bicameral legislature, consisting of elected representatives, is precisely the Sanskrit *dharma-cakra pravartanāya,* "In order to set into motion the Wheel of Dharma," taken from the life of the Buddha and his first sermon after his Enlightenment, delivered in Sarnath.
24. See Nehru's speech to the Constituent Assembly of India, 22 July 1947, "Resolution on the Adoption of the National Flag," *Constituent Assembly of India,* vol. 4, http://parliamentofindia.nic.in/ls/debates/debates.vol4p7.htm; and Radhakrishnan's speech, Tuesday, 22 July 1947, "Resolution re National Flag," in B. Shiva Rao et al., eds., "The National Flag," in *The Framing of India's Constitution: Select Documents,* vol. 1 (New Delhi: Indian Institute of Public Administration, 2006 [1967]), Part 6.
25. Radhakrishnan, "Resolution re the National Flag."
26. Nehru, "Resolution on the Adoption of the National Flag"; emphasis added. This identification, incidentally, was not so subtly reinforced by Nehru's friend and colleague Radhakrishnan when addressing the very same forum about a month later:

> We are *lucky in having for our leader one who is a world citizen, who is essentially a humanist, who possesses a buoyant optimism and robust good sense* in spite of the perversity of things and the hostility of human affairs. We see the way in which his Department interfered in a timely manner in the Indonesian dispute. (Loud applause). It shows that *if India gains freedom, that freedom will be used not merely for the well-being of India but for Vishva Kalyan i.e., world peace,* the welfare of mankind.

See S. Radhakrishnan, speech to Constituent Assembly of India, Thursday, 14 August 1947, "Motion Regarding Pledge by Members," in B. Shiva Rao et al., eds., *The Framing of India's Constitution: Select Documents,* vol. 1 (New Delhi: Indian Institute of Public Administration, 2006 [1967]); emphasis added.

27. The member of the Constituent Assembly debates who brought this up was V. I. Muniswami Pillai.
28. Ramachandra Guha, *India after Gandhi: The History of the World's Largest Democracy* (New Delhi: Picador, 2007), 167–174. "The India-China/Sino-Indian joint agreement was signed in April 1954" (171).
29. Nehru, *Discovery of India,* 114; emphasis added.
30. Ibid., 124–125; emphasis added.
31. Ibid., 114–115.
32. Ibid., 124.
33. Jawaharlal Nehru, "Letter No. 24: Ashoka, the Beloved of the Gods, March 30, 1932," in *Glimpses of World History: Letters from a Father to His Daughter* (New Delhi: Penguin, 2004 [1934–1935]), 72.
34. Ibid.
35. Ibid.
36. Srinath Raghavan's recent diplomatic history shows Nehru to be a leader we can understand and relate to even as we follow his policy in the integration of the princely states after independence, and his multiple wars with Pakistan and China—difficult passages all, fraught with errors in political judgment, massive military effort, and tremendous human cost. See Srinath Raghavan, *War and Peace in Modern India: A Strategic History of the Nehru Years* (New Delhi: Permanent Black, 2010).
37. That Aśoka was religious and yet neither sectarian nor fundamentalist is repeatedly affirmed by Étienne Lamotte in *History of Indian Buddhism: From the Origins to the Saka Era,* trans. Sara Webb-Boin (Paris: Institut Orientaliste, 1988):

> Asoka was a pious and zealous ruler, and not a sectarian propagandist. It was never his intention to found a Buddhist State, but to chide his subjects and edify his neighbours. His envoys, inspectors, overseers were in no way Buddhist missionaries, but officials preoccupied with the present and future happiness of those under their administration. Nevertheless, by promulgating the edict of the Dharma all over India, they prepared people's minds to receive the Buddhist message and opened the way for religious propagandists. (234)
>
> The Asoka of the inscriptions shows himself to have been a zealous, conscientious ruler, preoccupied with the present and future happiness of his subjects and neighbours. Personally, he was a convinced Buddhist; however, even if his preferences led him to fa-

> vour the Samgha of bhiksus and to take special measures to ensure the duration [perdurance] and harmony of the order he retained enough insight to protect all the sects impartially. (238)

38. John Keay, *India: A History* (New York: Atlantic Monthly Press, 2000), chaps. 4 and 5.
39. John S. Strong, *The Legend of King Aśoka: A Study and Translation of the Aśokāvadāna* (Princeton, NJ: Princeton University Press, 1983). See especially the translation of the text of the *Aśokāvadāna,* the section titled "Aśoka the Fierce," 210–213.
40. The righteous king, *dhammiko dhammarāja;* wheel, cakra; jewel, *ratna;* when the celestial wheel-jewel slips down from its place in the sky, then the king must reiterate his commitment to dhamma in order for it to rise up again and for the kingdom to flourish. Otherwise people's life spans get shorter and shorter, and *adhamma* grows—moral anarchy and physical destruction beset society; see Steven Collins, *Nirvana and Other Buddhist Felicities: Utopias of the Pali Imaginaire* (Cambridge: Cambridge University Press, 1998), 602–615.
41. Radhakrishnan, "Resolution re the National Flag."
42. Nehru, *Discovery of India,* 116.
43. Ibid., 120.
44. Ibid., 16.
45. Translation mine.
46. Shree Purohit Swami and W. B. Yeats, *The Ten Principal Upanishads* (New York: Macmillan, 1937).
47. S. Radhakrishnan, *The Principal Upanishads* (New Delhi: HarperCollins, 1994 [1953]).
48. Patrick Olivelle, *Upaniṣads* (New York: Oxford University Press, 2008 [1996]).
49. I asked Olivelle why he preferred the former, and he provided a detailed philological explanation, which is reproduced verbatim below:

> Grammatically, both translations are possible, even though I do not think that Radhakrishnan's is correct. The discussion in the whole section is not about the victory of truth/real over untruth/unreal. See, for example, 3.1.10 where in a similar context we have jayate with an implied subject and the objects in the accusative. Also in 3.1.5 and in the second pada of the verse in question (3.1.6) we have satyena in the instrumental. The subject of these verbs probably is the person (as two birds) in verses 1 and 2.
>
> Hertel also proposes, justifiably I think, that a syllable has been dropped from this verse through metathesis. The first pada as you see is unmetrical with just 10 syllables, when it should have 11.

Hertel proposes that the verse should be: satyam eva jayate nānṛtaṃ sa. The metathesis is created because the next pada starts with satyena, thus there are two "sa"s coming after each other. If we take this emendation, then there is no doubt that satyam and anṛtam are the objects and not the subject in this sentence. (Olivelle's e-mail to me in response to my request for a clarification, 24 October 2010)

50. Two of the best accounts are Ramachandra Guha, *India after Gandhi,* and Sunil Khilnani, *The Idea of India* (London: Penguin, 1997).
51. The details are as follows: vol. 1, 1947–1949 (1985); vol. 2, 1950–1952 (1986); vol. 3, 1952–1954 (1987); vol. 4, 1954–1957 (1988); vol. 5, 1958–1964 (1989).

5. Bhimrao Ambedkar

1. B. R. Ambedkar, *The Buddha and His Dhamma* (Nagpur: Buddha Bhoomi Publications, 1957).
2. Sangharakshita, *Ambedkar and Buddhism* (New Delhi: Motilal Banarsidass, 2006 [1986]).
3. The most illuminating meditation on this subject remains Pratap Bhanu Mehta, *The Burden of Democracy* (New Delhi: Penguin, 2003).
4. B. R. Ambedkar, "Gospel of Equality: The Buddha and the Future of His Religion," *Journal of the Maha Bodhi Society* (April–May 1950).
5. B. R. Ambedkar, "Philosophic Defence of Counter-revolution (Krishna and His Gita)," in *Dr. Babasaheb Ambedkar: Writings and Speeches,* vol. 3, comp. Vasant Moon (Bombay: Education Department, 1987), 357–380.
6. B. R. Ambedkar, *The Untouchables: A Thesis on the Origin of Untouchability* (New Delhi: Amrit Book Co., 1948); also known by the title *The Untouchables: Who Were They? And Why They Became Untouchables.*
7. The full text of this introduction is reproduced in Appendix D. In Sanskrit, the Four Noble Truths are called the Catvari-Arya-Satyani (or Catvārī Āryasatyānī).
8. I am not sure why Ambedkar never considered Jainism, or, if he did, then why he ruled it out. I would hazard this might have been because Gandhi was deeply interested in and engaged with Jainism; Ambedkar might also have regarded Jainism, like Sikhism but unlike Buddhism, to be far closer to Hinduism than he would have liked. As major premodern Indic renunciatory *(śramaṇa)* systems of more or less the same antiquity, both associated with several polities and dynasties, in fact, Jainism and Buddhism are very close to one another. Unlike Buddhism, however, Jainism remained within India and never spread widely in other parts of Asia or the world. Candragupta (340–298 BC), the founding dynast of the Mauryan Empire, converted to Jainism near his death.

9. B. R. Ambedkar, *Thoughts on Pakistan* (Bombay: Thacker and Co., 1941), and *Pakistan or the Partition of India* (Bombay: Thacker and Co., 1945).

10. One might hazard all sorts of reasons for this, although it must be said that I have no wherewithal to test any of these suggestions myself: (1) The discourse of emancipation, both personal and social, embedded in Buddhism, was as attractive to Indian socialists as it was to Ambedkar himself; (2) Buddhism offered a historically grounded critique of caste, again, of common interest to Ambedkar and the socialists; (3) Buddhism was Indic even while being in many interpretations anti-Hindu, which made it an attractive option for those who wanted to attack Hinduism but not turn to Western, Semitic, or the new Marxist/Communist traditions as alternatives; (4) The figure of Gandhi, as a modern-day "mahatma," reminded many Indians of the Buddha himself; his charisma somehow stoked a deeply felt desire to explore, remember, and recount the Ur-narrative, as it were, of enlightenment available on the subcontinent. Obviously Gandhi did not remind Ambedkar of the Buddha, but it's entirely possible that Gandhians tended to read one "great soul" into the other.

11. Dharmanand was also the father of the mathematician-Marxist-archaeologist-historian D. D. Kosambi (1907–1966), one of several great polymaths that India produced in the first half of the twentieth century. See Dharmanand Kosambi, *Nivedan: The Autobiography of Dharmanand Kosambi,* ed. and trans. Meera Kosambi (New Delhi: Permanent Black, 2011); and Dharmanand Kosambi, *The Essential Writings,* ed. Meera Kosambi (New Delhi: Permanent Black, 2010). See Ananya Vajpeyi, "Monk, Mathematician, Marxist," *The Caravan* 4.2 (1 February 2012): 80–84.

12. G. M. Tartakov, "Art and Identity: The Rise of a New Buddhist Imagery," *Art Journal* 49.4 (Winter 1990): 409–416.

13. The Three Refuges are: the Buddha, the Dhamma, the Sangha. The Five Precepts *(pañcaśīla)* are: I will not take life; I will not steal or covet; I will not engage in sexual misconduct; I will not utter false speech; I will not imbibe intoxicants. Ahimsa is the first of the five śīlas or precepts.

14. An argument made best by D. R. Nagaraj in *The Flaming Feet and Other Essays: The Dalit Movement in India,* ed. Prithvi Datta Chandra Shobhi (New Delhi: Permanent Black, 2010 [1993]); see especially the chapter titled "Self-Purification versus Self-Respect." See also Ananya Vajpeyi, "Let Poetry Be a Sword!," *The Caravan* 3.12 (1 January 2011): 86–91.

15. Gautama Buddha: born in Lumbini; raised in Kapilavastu; enlightened in Gaya; first sermon in Sarnath; died in Kushinara. Dates: either 563–483 BCE (in which case 534 BCE is the date of the Three Sights) or 490–410 BCE.

16. Bhimrao Ambedkar, "Introduction," in *The Buddha and His Dhamma.*

17. Ibid.

18. Ibid.

19. Keer, Zelliot, Sangharakshita, Rodrigues, Jaffrelot, and Gokhale, at least, if not others as well.
20. The first critical edition of Ambedkar's *The Buddha and His Dhamma,* edited by Aakash Singh Rathore and Ajay Verma (New Delhi: Oxford University Press, 2011), became available after work on this book was completed. This edition tries to trace all of Ambedkar's sources and reinstates the critical apparatus that Ambedkar himself was unable to provide prior to his death.
21. Ambedkar, *Untouchables.*
22. See Appendix E in this volume. I am claiming that even though he says that the language of the new Buddhist Bible that he intends to write should have certain poetic qualities (like "incantation" and "hypnotic effect" rather than laying out abstract rules and regulations), in fact he de-poeticizes, de-metaphorizes, and de-metricalizes whatever Buddhist text he takes up.
23. Dhananjay Keer, *Dr. Ambedkar: His Life and Mission* (Mumbai: Popular Prakashan, 1990), 493–495.
24. M. K. Gandhi, *The Gospel of Selfless Action, or, The Gita According to Gandhi,* trans. Mahadev Desai (Ahmedabad: Navajivan Publishing House, 1956 [1933, 1929]), "Introduction," paras. 27 and 28.
25. Ambedkar, "Philosophic Defence of Counter-revolution."
26. Aishwary Kumar, "Ambedkar's Inheritances." *Modern Intellectual History* 7.2 (2010): 391–415.
27. The phrase *dharmacakra pravartanāya* literally means, in Sanskrit, "In order to set into motion the Wheel of Dharma." The Buddha's teaching to five monks in his first sermon after his enlightenment, delivered in the deer park at Sarnath, is called the *Dharmacakra Pravartana Sūtra.* The Buddha's first sermon is the first turning of the wheel of dhamma, as recognized by all extant schools of Buddhism.
28. Steven Collins, *Selfless Persons: Imagery and Thought in Theravāda Buddhism* (New York: Cambridge University Press, 1982).

Conclusion

1. See John Guy and Jorritt Britschgi, *Wonder of the Age: Master Painters of India, 1100–1900* (New York: Metropolitan Museum of Art, 2011); B. N. Goswamy, *Nainsukh of Guler: A Great Indian Painter from a Small Hill-State* (New Delhi: Niyogi Books, 2011 [1997]), 160–166.
2. Goswamy, "92. *A Boat Adrift on a River: Illustration to a Folk Legend,*" in *Nainsukh of Guler,* 234–235; and Eberhard Fischer, "An Evening with the 18th Century Pahari Painter Nainsukh," India International Centre, Webcast, 23 November 2011, http://www.iicdelhi.in/webcasts/view_webcast/an-evening-with-the-18th-century-pahari-painter-nainsukh.

3. Nainsukh's *Boat Adrift on a River: Illustration to a Folk Legend* (tinted brush drawing on paper, c. 1765–1775) is in the collection of Bharat Kala Bhavan, Varanasi. Gulammohammed Sheikh, *Kaavad: Travelling Shrine: Home* (New Delhi: Vadehra Art Gallery, 2008). In an e-mail, Gulammohammed Sheikh wrote: "It is entitled 'Ark,' a digital collage print in two parts (8'×4' each) made in 2008 made for the inner wall of shrine entitled 'Kaavad: Home.' 'Kaavad: Home' is now in the collection Kiran Nadar Museum in Saket, New Delhi. I have made a few smaller prints of 'Ark' on a single paper and a version of it (entitled 'Ark-II') shows figures in the lake in a spread out form." See also, Gulammohammed Sheikh, *City, Kaavad and Other Works* (New Delhi: Vadehra Art Gallery, 2011).
4. Sheikh, in *Kaavad,* writes at length on "quotation":

> The idea of quotation, the choice of quoting from everywhere, anywhere, incuding one's own past work, overturns the real and the imaginary, back and forth. What were "real" characters assume different form, become figures from fables, stories from an autobiography, enlarging the imaginary world. The mundane world of the autobiography turns into a larger biography that is then available to others. Much of the painting of Kaavad is based on quotes. . . . Besides looking at my own work in retrospect . . . I chose from Bizhad and the Lorenzettis, Giotto and Duccio, Govardhan, Sahibdin and Nainsukh and many others. . . . Perhaps it was a way to re-enter history and in a way also to re-write it. (10)

5. See *Tagore Gandhi and Andrews,* c. 1921, watercolor on paper (Kala Bhavana Collection), in R. Siva Kumar, *Paintings of Abanindranath Tagore* (Calcutta: Pratikshan, 2008), 212–213.
6. The Mangal Chatterra painting is titled *Kabir, the Mystical Weaver, with a Disciple and Young Visitor* (probably Amber or Mughal India, c. 1760), Christie's, http://www.christies.com/LotFinder/lot_details.aspx?intObjectID=5303195. In an e-mail (29 November 2011) Sheikh mentioned the source of the Kabir image that he quotes: "The Kabir painting I have been using is from the British library (or Museum). Dated mid-18th, there is no reference to who painted it, but is apparently within what is broadly known as 'Popular Mughal.' The tilak shows that he was already appropriated by the Vaiṣṇava establishment by this time."
7. In *Kaavad,* Sheikh writes:

> [The work *Home*] served to host a "*sangat*" (assembly) of all the characters from art and life to gather. A *sangat* is open and free, anyone can join. . . . In the *sangat* here, all who have gathered are listening . . . perhaps Gandhiji too is listening. . . . All the images are not of saints. They are of both saints and sceptics. . . . Most of them are anonymous or marginal figures. But for St. Francis, none of these

are principal icons. Even Gandhiji (from a painting of Abanindranath Tagore) belongs to a period much before he embarked upon his great mission, as a little man in his *topi* when he had returned from South Africa. . . . At one level they are emblems but at another level they are physical beings with presences. They are all, in a way, questioners. Maybe they are seekers or Sufis, *faqirs, sadhus,* who still people our life today in India. (9–11)

Selected Bibliography

Primary Materials

Modern Sources

MOHANDAS GANDHI

Gandhi, M. K. *The Gospel of Selfless Action, or, The Gita According to Gandhi*. Trans. John Strohmier. Berkeley, CA: North Atlantic Books, 2009 [1929].

———. *Hind Swaraj and Other Writings*. Ed. Anthony J. Parel. Cambridge: Cambridge University Press, 2009.

———. *An Autobiography or The Story of My Experiments with Truth*. Trans. Mahadev Desai, intro. Pankaj Mishra. New Delhi: Penguin, 2007 [1927].

———. *Hindu Dharma*. New Delhi: Orient Paperbacks, 2005 [1950].

———. *An Autobiography: Or the Story of My Experiments with Truth*. Trans. Mahadev Desai, intro. Sunil Khilnani. New Delhi: Penguin Classics, 2001.

———. "The Creed of Non-violence." In Rudrangshu Mukherjee, ed., *The Penguin Gandhi Reader*. New Delhi: Penguin, 1993, 93–122.

———. "Gandhi on Swaraj." In B. Shiva Rao, ed., *The Framing of India's Constitution: Select Documents*, vol. 1. New Delhi: Indian Institute of Public Administration, 1967, 33–34.

———. *Village Industries*. Comp. R. K. Prabhu. Ahmedabad: Navajivan Publishing House, 1960.

———. *The Gospel of Selfless Action, or, The Gita According to Gandhi*. Trans. Mahadev H. Desai. Ahmedabad: Navajivan Publishing House, 1956 [1933, 1929].

———. "The Poet's Anxiety." In Homer A. Jack, ed., *The Gandhi Reader: A Source Book of His Life and Writings*. Bloomington: Indiana University Press, 1956, 217–221.

———. *Sarvodaya (The Welfare of All)*. Ed. Bharatan Kumarappa. Ahmedabad: Navajivan Publishing House, 1954.

Ahluwalia, B. K., and Shashi Ahluwalia. *Tagore and Gandhi: The Tagore-Gandhi Controversy*. New Delhi: Pankaj Publications, 1981.

Bandopadhaya, Sailesh Kumar, ed. *Gandhi's My Non-violence*. Ahmedabad: Navajivan Publishing House, 1960.

Basham, A. L. "Traditional Influences on the Thought of Mahatma Gandhi." In R. Kumar, ed., *Essays on Gandhian Politics*. Oxford: Clarendon Press, 1971, 17–42.

Bhattacharya, Sabyasachi. *The Mahatma and the Poet: Letters and Debates between Gandhi and Tagore, 1915–1941*. New Delhi: National Book Trust, 2008 [1997].

Bilgrami, Akeel. "Value, Enchantment, and the Mentality of Democracy: Some Distant Perspectives from Gandhi." *Economic and Political Weekly* 44 (2009): 47–61.

———. "Gandhi, Newton, and the Enlightenment." *Social Scientist* 34 (2006): 17–35.

———. "Secular Liberalism and Relativism." *boundary 2* 31.2 (Summer 2004): 173–196.

———. "Gandhi, the Philosopher." *Economic and Political Weekly* 38.26 (27 September 2003): 4159–4165.

———. "Gandhi's Integrity: The Philosophy behind the Politics." *Postcolonial Studies* 5 (2002): 79–93.

Brown, Judith M. *Gandhi: Prisoner of Hope*. New Haven, CT: Yale University Press, 1991.

Brown, Judith M., and Anthony Parel. *The Cambridge Companion to Gandhi*. Cambridge: Cambridge University Press, 2011.

Buber, Martin. *Two Letters to Gandhi from Martin Buber and J. L. Magnes*. Jerusalem: Reuben Mass, 1939.

Dalton, Dennis. *Gandhi's Power: Nonviolence in Action*. New Delhi: Oxford University Press, 1998.

———, ed. *Mahatma Gandhi: Selected Political Writings*. Indianapolis: Hackett, 1996.

Devji, Faisal. "A Practice of Prejudice: Gandhi's Politics of Friendship." *Subaltern Studies* 12 (2005): 78–98.

Devji, Faisal, and Ritu Birla, eds. "Itineraries of Self-Rule: Essays on the Centenary of Gandhi's Hind Swaraj." *Public Culture* 23.2 (Spring 2011). http://publicculture.org/issues/view/23/2.

Diwakar, Ranganath Ramachandra. *Saga of Satyagraha*. New Delhi: Gandhi Peace Foundation, 1969.

Gandhi, Gopalkrishna, ed. *The Oxford India Gandhi: Essential Writings*. New Delhi: Oxford University Press, 2008.

———, ed. *Gandhi Is Gone: Who Will Guide Us Now?* New Delhi: Permanent Black, 2007.

Gandhi, Leela. *Affective Communities: Anticolonial Thought, Fin-de-Siècle Radicalism, and the Politics of Friendship*. Durham, NC: Duke University Press, 2006 [1966].

Gandhi, Rajmohan. *The Good Boatman: A Portrait of Gandhi*. New York: Viking, 1995.

Guha, Ramachandra. "A Prophet Announces Himself: Mahatma Gandhi's 'Hind-Swaraj' a Hundred Years On." *TLS* (September 2009): 14–15.

Heredia, Rudolf C. "Gandhi's Interrogation." *Economic and Political Weekly* 45.46 (12 November 2011): 30–32.

———. "Interpreting Gandhi's *Hind Swaraj*." *Economic and Political Weekly* 34.24 (18 June 1999): 1497–1502.

Herman, Arthur. *Gandhi and Churchill: The Epic Rivalry That Destroyed an Empire and Forged Our Age*. New York: Bantam Dell, 2008.

Jack, Homer A. *The Gandhi Reader: A Source Book of His Life and Writings*. Bloomington: Indiana University Press, 1956.

Jaju, Srikrishnadas, ed. *The Ideology of the Charkha: A Collection of Some of Gandhi ji's Speeches and Writings about Khadi*. Varanasi: ABSSS Prakashan, 1958.

Kabra, Kamal Nayan, and Laxmi Dass, eds. *Charkha and Chip: Rural Industrialisation and Technology*. New Delhi: Gyan Publishing House, 2006.

Kaviraj, Sudipta. "Gandhi and Tagore." Unpublished manuscript, Columbia University, April 2009.

———. "The Politics of Performance: Gandhi's Trial Read as Theatre." In Julia Trauss and Donald Cruise O'Brien, eds., *Staging Politics: Power and Performance in Asia and Africa*. London: I. B. Tauris, 2007, 71–89.

Khilnani, Sunil. "Gandhi and Nehru: The Uses of English." In Arvind Krisha Mehrotra, ed., *A History of Indian Literature in English*. New York: Columbia University Press, 2003, 135–136.

———. "Introduction: An Experimental Life." In M. K. Gandhi, *An Autobiography: Or the Story of My Experiments with Truth,* trans. Mahadev Desai. New Delhi: Penguin Classics, 2001.

———. "Gandhi and History." *Seminar* 461 (January 1998): 110–115.

Kripalani, J. B. *My Times: An Autobiography*. New Delhi: Rupa & Co., 2004.

———. *Freedom in Peril*. Madras: Gandhi Samaj, 1977.

———. *Politics of Charkha*. Bombay: Vora and Co., 1946.

Kumar, Aishwary. "The Ellipsis of Touch: Gandhi's Unequals." *Public Culture* 23.2 (Spring 2011): 449–469.

Kumarappa, J. C. *Gandhian Economic Thought*. Bombay: Vora and Co., 1951.

MacIntyre, Alasdair. "Epistemological Crises, Dramatic Narrative, and the Philosophy of Science." In *The Tasks of Philosophy: Selected Essays,* vol. 1. Cambridge: Cambridge University Press, 2006, 3–23.

Mehta, Pratap Bhanu. "Hinduism and Self-Rule." *Journal of Democracy* 15.3 (July 2004): 108–121.

Mehta, Uday Singh. "Patience, Inwardness, and Self-Knowledge in Gandhi's *Hind Swaraj*." *Public Culture* 23.2 (Spring 2011): 417–429.

———. "Gandhi on Democracy, Politics and the Ethics of Everyday Life." *Modern Intellectual History* 7 (2010): 355–371.

———. "Gandhi's Politics." Unpublished manuscript, Amherst College, 2009.

Merton, Thomas, ed. *Gandhi on Non-violence: Selected Texts from Mohandas K. Gandhi's "Non-violence in Peace and War."* Preface by Mark Kurlansky. New York: New Directions, 2007 [1964].

Mukherjee, Mithi. *India in the Shadows of Empire: A Legal and Political History, 1774–1950*. New Delhi: Oxford University Press, 2010.

Mukherjee, Rudrangshu. *The Penguin Gandhi Reader*. New Delhi: Penguin, 2007 [1993].

Murti, V. V. Ramana. "On Buber's Dialogue and Gandhi's Satyagraha." *Journal of the History of Ideas* 29.4 (October–December 1968): 605–613.

Nanda, B. R. *Mahatma Gandhi: A Biography*. New Delhi: Oxford University Press, 2008 [1958].

———. *In Search of Gandhi: Essays and Reflections*. New Delhi: Oxford University Press, 2002.

Pantham, Thomas. "Thinking with Mahatma Gandhi: Beyond Liberal Democracy." *Political Theory* 11.2 (May 1983): 165–188.

Parekh, Bhikhu. *Colonialism, Tradition and Reform: An Analysis of Gandhi's Political Discourse*. New Delhi: Sage Publications, 1999 [1989].

Parel, Anthony J. "Hundred Years of Hind Swaraj." Unpublished manuscript, 2009.

———. "Gandhi and the Emergence of the Modern Indian Political Canon." *Review of Politics* 70 (2008): 40–63.

———. *Gandhi's Philosophy and the Quest for Harmony*. New York: Cambridge University Press, 2006.

———. *Gandhi, Freedom, and Self-Rule*. Lanham, MD: Lexington Books, 2000.

———. "Mahatma Gandhi's Critique of Modernity." In Anthony Parel and Ronald C. Keith, eds., *Comparative Political Philosophy: Studies under the Upas Tree*. New Delhi: Sage Publiciations, 1992, 163–183.

Prabhu, Joseph, and Ravindra Kelekar, eds. *Truth Called Them Differently: The Tagore-Gandhi Controversy*. Ahmedabad: Navajivan Publishing House, 1961.

Prasad, Bimal. *Gandhi, Nehru and J. P.: Studies in Leadership*. Delhi: Chanakya Publications, 1985.

Radhakrishnan, Sarvepalli. *Mahatma Gandhi: Essays and Reflections on His Life and Work, Presented to Him on His Seventieth Birthday, October 2nd, 1939*. London: George Allen & Unwin, 1949 [1939].

Rolland, Romain. *Mahatma Gandhi: The Man Who Became One with the Universal Being*. New Delhi: Rupa and Co., 2002 [1924].

———. *Mahatma Gandhi: A Study in Indian Nationalism*. Trans. L. V. Ramaswami Aiyar. Madras: S. Ganesan, 1923.

Roy, Ramashray, ed. *Gandhi and the Present Global Crisis*. Shimla: Indian Institute of Advanced Studies, 1996.

Sebald, W. G. "A Poem of an Invisible Subject" (interview with Michael Silverblatt). In Lynne Sharon Schwartz, ed., *The Emergence of Memory: Conversations with W. G. Sebald*. New York: Seven Stories Press, 2007, 77–86.

Sharma, Suresh, and Tridip Suhrud, eds. *M. K. Gandhi's Hind Swaraj: A Critical Edition*. New Delhi: Orient Blackswan, 2010.

Skaria, Ajay. "Relinquishing Republican Democracy: Gandhi's Ramarajya." *Postcolonial Studies* 14.2 (2011): 203–229.

———. "The Strange Violence of Satyagraha: Gandhi, Itihaas, and History." In Manu Bhagavan, ed., *Heterotopias: Nationalism and the Possibility of History in South Asia*. New Delhi: Oxford University Press, 2010, 142–185.

———. "Living by Dying." In Anand Pandian and Daud Ali, eds., *Genealogies of Virtue: Ethical Practice in South Asia*. Bloomington: Indiana University Press, 2009, 211–231.

———. "'No Politics without Religion': Of Secularism and Gandhi." In Vinay Lal, ed., *Political Hinduism: The Religious Imagination in Public Spheres*. New Delhi: Oxford University Press, 2009, 141–178.

———. "Only One Word, Properly Altered: Gandhi and the Question of the Prostitute." *Economic and Political Weekly* 41.49 (9–15 December 2006): 5065–5072.

———. "Gandhi's Politics: Liberalism and the Question of the Ashram." *South Atlantic Quarterly* 101.4 (Fall 2002): 955–986.

Suhrud, Tridip, and Peter Ronald DeSouza, eds. *Speaking of Gandhi's Death*. New Delhi: Orient Blackswan, 2010.

———. "Reading Hind Swarajya/Swaraj in Two Languages." Unpublished manuscript, Indian Institute of Advanced Studies, 2 July 2009.

———. "Emptied of All but Love: Gandhi's First Public Fast." In Debjani Ganguly and John Docker, eds., *Rethinking Gandhi and Nonviolent Relationality: Global Perspectives*. London: Routledge, 2007, 66–79.

Tähtinen, Unto. *Ahimsa: Non-violence in Indian Tradition*. London: Rider, 1976.

RABINDRANATH TAGORE

Tagore, Rabindranath. *The Last Harvest: An International Exhibition of Paintings by Rabindranath Tagore*. New Delhi: National Gallery of Modern Art, Ministry of Culture, 2011.

———. "Nashtaneer (The Broken Nest)." In *Three Women*, trans. Arunava Sinha. New Delhi: Random House India, 2010, 1–72.

———. *Nationalism*. Intro. Ramachandra Guha. New Delhi: Penguin Classics, 2009.

———. *The English Writings of Rabindranath Tagore*. 3 vols. Ed. Sisir Kumar Das. New Delhi: Atlantic Publishers and Distributors, 2007.

———. *The Home and the World*. Trans. Surendranath Tagore. New York: Penguin, 2005 [1916].

———. *Selected Poems*. Trans. William Radice. London: Penguin, 2005.

———. *The Religion of Man, Being the Hibbert Lectures for 1930*. Rhinebeck, NY: Monkfish Book Publishing Company, 2004.

———. *Sancayita* [in Bangla]. Kolkata: United Publishers, 2002.

———. *Selected Writings on Literature and Language*. Ed. Sukanta Chaudhuri and Sankha Ghosh. New Delhi: Oxford University Press, 2001.

———. "Dialogue between Karna and Kunti." Trans. Ketaki Kushari Dyson. http://www.parabaas.com/translation/database/translations/poems/RT_Karna kunti.html, 2000.

———. "Asoka: The Great Emperor." In Hemendu Bikash Chowdhury, ed., *Asoka 2300. Jagajjyoti: Asoka Commemoration Volume 1997* A.D./2541 B.E. Calcutta: Bauddha Dharmankur Sabha, 1997.

———. *Selected Letters of Rabindranath Tagore*. Ed. Krishna Dutta and Andrew Robinson. New York: Cambridge University Press, 1997.

———. *I Won't Let You Go: Selected Poems*. Trans. Ketaki Kushari Dyson. Northumberland: Bloodaxe Books, 1991.

———. *Gitanjali*. London: Macmillan & Co., 1985 [1913].

———. *Selected Poems*. New York: Penguin, 1985.

———. *The Broken Nest (Nashtanir)*. Trans. Mary M. Lago and Supriya Sen. Columbia: University of Missouri Press, 1971.

———. *A Vision of India's History*. Calcutta: Visva-Bharati, 1951.

———. "Cult of the Charkha." *Modern Review* 38.3 (September 1925): 263–270.

———. "Striving for Swaraj." *Modern Review* 38.6 (December 1925): 681–685.

———. "The Call of Truth." *Modern Review* 30.4 (October 1921): 423–433.

———. *Greater India*. Madras: Triplicane, 1921.

Bardhan, Kalpana, ed. and trans. *Of Love, Nature, and Devotion: Selected Songs of Rabindranath Tagore*. New Delhi: Oxford University Press, 2008.

Berlin, Isaiah. "Rabindranath Tagore and the Consciousness of Nationality." In *The Sense of Reality*. New York: Farrar, Strauss and Giroux, 1996, 249–266.

Bose, Buddhadeva. *Selected Poems of Buddhadeva Bose*. Trans. Ketaki Kushari Dyson. New York: Oxford University Press, 2003.

Chatterji, Bankim Chandra. *Anandamath*. New Delhi: Orient Paperback, 2006 [1882].

Chaudhuri, Amit. "The Flute of Modernity: Tagore and the Middle Class." In *Clearing a Space: Reflections on India, Literature and Culture*. New York: Peter Lang, 2008, 69–84.

———. "Two Giant Brothers: Tagore's Revisionist Orient." In *Clearing a Space: Reflections on India, Literature and Culture*. New York: Peter Lang, 2008, 122–139.

Chaudhuri, Rosinka. "The Flute, Gerontion, and Subalternist Misreadings of Tagore." *Social Text* 78.22.1 (2004): 103–122.

Das Gupta, Uma. *Rabindranath Tagore: A Biography*. New Delhi: Oxford University Press, 2004.

Dutta, Krishna, and Andrew Robinson. *Rabindranath Tagore: The Myriad-Minded Man*. New York: St. Martin's Press, 1995.

Dutta, Pradip Kumar. *Rabindranath Tagore's "The Home and The World": A Critical Companion*. London: Anthem Press, 2004.

Kaviraj, Sudipta. "Tagore and Transformations in the Ideals of Love." In Francesca Orsini, ed., *Love in South Asia: A Cultural History*. Cambridge: Cambridge University Press, 2006, 161–182.

Kripalani, Krishna. *Tagore: A Life*. New Delhi: Malancha, 1961.

Nussbaum, Martha. *For Love of Country?* Ed. Joshua Cohen. Boston: Beacon Press, 2002 [1996].

———. *Poetic Justice: The Literary Imagination and Public Life*. Boston: Beacon Press, 1995.

Sen, Amartya. "Tagore and His India." *New York Review of Books* 44.12 (1997): 55–63.

Siva Kumar, R., ed. *The Last Harvest: Paintings of Rabindranath Tagore*. Ahmedabad: Mapin, 2011.

———, curator. *Santiniketan: The Making of a Contextual Modernism*. NGMA Exhibition, New Delhi, 1992.

Thompson, E. P. *"Alien Homage": Edward Thompson and Rabindranath Tagore*. New York: Oxford University Press, 1993.

———. Introduction to Rabindranath Tagore, *Nationalism*. Calcutta: Rupa & Co., 1992 [1917], 1–16.

ABANINDRANATH TAGORE

Tagore, Abanindranath. "Sadanga or the Six Limbs of Painting." *Modern Review* 18.4 (October 1915): 337–345.

Banerji, Debashish. *The Alternate Nation of Abanindranath Tagore*. New Delhi: Sage Publications, 2010.

Bose, Nandalal. *Vision and Creation*. Trans. K. G. Subramanyan. Calcutta: Visva-Bharati, 1999.

Chandra, Pramod. *On the Study of Indian Art*. Cambridge, MA: Harvard University Press, 1983.

Coomaraswamy, Ananda Kentish. *What Is Civilisation? And Other Essays*. Ipswich: Golgonooza Press, 1989.

———. *Indian Art*, vol. 1: *Themes and Concepts*. Jaipur: The Historical Research and Documentation Programme, 1985.

———. *Introduction to Indian Art*. Delhi: Munshiram Manoharlal, 1969 [1966, 1913].

Guha-Thakurta, Tapati. *Abanindranath, Known and Unknown: The Artist versus the Art of His Times*. Kolkata: CSSSC, 2009.

———. *Monuments, Objects, Histories: Institutions of Art in Colonial and Postcolonial India*. New York: Columbia University Press, 2004.

———. *The Making of a New "Indian" Art: Artists, Aesthetics and Nationalism in Bengal, c. 1850–1920*. Cambridge: Cambridge University Press, 1992.

Havell, E. B. *The Ideals of Indian Art*. New York: E. P. Dutton and Co., 1920 [1911].

Mitter, Partha. *The Triumph of Modernism: India's Artists and the Avant-Garde, 1947–1992*. London: Reaktion, 2007.

———. *Art and Nationalism in Colonial India, 1850–1922: Occidental Orientations*. Cambridge: Cambridge University Press, 1995.

Pinney, Christopher. *Photos of the Gods: The Printed Image and Political Struggle in India*. London: Reaktion, 2004.

Ramaswami, Sumathi. *The Goddess and the Nation: Mapping Mother India*. Durham, NC: Duke University Press, 2010.

Sarkar, Jadunath. "The Passing of Shah Jahan." *Modern Review* 18.4 (October 1915): 361–368.

Siva Kumar, R. *Paintings of Abanindranath Tagore*. Calcutta: Pratikshan, 2008.

JAWAHARLAL NEHRU

Nehru, Jawaharlal. *Glimpses of World History: Letters from a Father to His Daughter*. New Delhi: Penguin, 2004 [1934–1935].

———. "Speech On the Granting of Indian Independence, August 14, 1947." In Brian McArthur, ed., *Penguin Book of Twentieth Century Speeches*. London: Penguin Viking, 1992, 234–237.

———. *The Discovery of India*. New Delhi: Oxford University Press, in conjunction with the Jawaharlal Nehru Memorial Fund, 1989 [1981, 1946].

———. *Letters to Chief Ministers 1947–1964*. Ed. G. Parthasarathi. 5 vols. New Delhi: Jawaharlal Nehru Memorial Fund, 1985–1989.

Crocker, Walter. *Nehru: A Contemporary's Estimate*. New Delhi: Random House India, 2008 [1966].

Gopal, Sarvepalli. *Jawaharlal Nehru: A Biography*. New Delhi: Oxford University Press, 1989.

Iyengar, Uma, ed. *The Oxford India Nehru*. New Delhi: Oxford University Press, 2007.

Khilnani, Sunil. "Nehru's Judgment." In Richard Bourke and Raymond Geuss, eds., *Political Judgment: Essays for John Dunn*. Cambridge: Cambridge University Press, 2009, 254–278.

———. "Democracy and Its Indian Pasts." In Kaushik Basu and Ravi Kanbur, eds., *Arrangements for a Better World: Essays in Honor of Amartya Sen*. New Delhi: Oxford University Press, 2008, 488–502.

———. "The Discovery of Indians: Nehru and Political Possibility." Kingsley Martin Memorial Lecture, Cambridge, 21 November 2007.

Nanda, B. R. *The Nehrus*. New Delhi: Oxford University Press, 2008 [1962].

Raghavan, Srinath. *War and Peace in Modern India: A Strategic History of the Nehru Years*. New Delhi: Permanent Black, 2010.

Roy, Srirupa. *Beyond Belief: India and the Politics of Postcolonial Nationalism*. Durham, NC: Duke University Press, 2007.

Sahgal, Nayantara. *Jawaharlal Nehru: Civilizing a Savage World*. New Delhi: Penguin, 2010.

Tharoor, Shashi. *Nehru: The Invention of India*. New Delhi: Penguin, 2003.

BHIMRAO AMBEDKAR

Ambedkar, B. R. *The Buddha and His Dhamma: A Critical Edition*. Ed., intro., and annotated by Aakash Singh Rathore and Ajay Verma New Delhi: Oxford University Press, 2011.

———. *Speeches and Writings of B. R. Ambedkar*. New Delhi: Penguin, 2010.

———. "Buddha or Karl Marx." In *Dr. Babasaheb Ambedkar: Writings and Speeches*, vol. 3. Comp. Vasant Moon. Bombay: Education Department, 1987, 441–462.

———. "Philosophic Defence of Counter-Revolution (Krishna and His Gita)." In *Dr. Babasaheb Ambedkar: Writings and Speeches*, vol. 3. Comp. Vasant Moon. Bombay: Education Department, 1987, 357–380.

———. *Dr. Babasaheb Ambedkar: Writings and Speeches*. Bombay: Education Department, 1979.

———. *Annihilation of Caste with a Reply to Mahatma Gandhi*. Jullundur City: Bheem Patrika Publications, 1968.

———. *The Buddha and His Dhamma*. Nagpur: Buddha Bhoomi Publications, 1957.

———. "Gospel of Equality: The Buddha and the Future of His Religion." *Journal of the Maha Bodhi Society* (April–March 1950).

———. *The Untouchables: A Thesis on the Origin of Untouchability*. New Delhi: Amrit Book Co., 1948.

———. *Who Were the Shudras? How They Came to Be the Fourth Varna in the Indo-Aryan Society*. Bombay: Thacker & Co., 1946.

———. *Pakistan or the Partition of India*. Bombay: Thacker and Co., 1945.

———. *Thoughts on Pakistan*. Bombay: Thacker and Co., 1941.

Chatterjee, Partha. "B. R. Ambedkar and the Troubled Times of Citizenship." In V. R. Mehta and Thomas Pantham, eds., *Political Ideas in Modern India: Thematic Explorations*. New Delhi: Sage Publications, 2005, 73–90.

Das, Bhagwan, ed. *Thus Spoke Ambedkar*. New Delhi: Navayana Publishing, 2010.

Ganguly, Debjani. *Caste, Colonialism and Counter-modernity: Notes on a Postcolonial Hermeneutics of Caste*. New York: Routledge, 2005.

Guha, Ramachandra. "Have We Failed Ambedkar?" In "The Republic at 60," special issue, *Outlook* (1 February 2010): 22–30.

Jaffrelot, Christophe. *Dr. Ambedkar*. Paris: Presses de Sciences Po, 2000.

Jai Bhim Comrade. Directed by Anand Patwardhan. Mumbai, 2012.

Jondhale, S., and J. Beltz, eds. *Reconstructing the World: B. R. Ambedkar and Buddhism in India*. New Delhi: Oxford University Press, 2004.

Keer, Dhananjay. *Dr. Babasaheb Ambedkar: Life and Mission*. Bombay: Popular Prakashan, 1990 [1954].

Kumar, Aishwary. "Ambedkar's Inheritances." *Modern Intellectual History* 7.2 (2010): 391–415.

Moon, Vasant, ed. *Dr. Babasaheb Ambedkar: Writings and Speeches*, vol. 7. Bombay: Education Department, 1990.

Omvedt, Gail. *Dalit Visions*. New Delhi: Orient Blackswan, 2008 [1995].

———. *Ambedkar: Towards an Enlightened India*. New Delhi: Penguin, 2004.

Parekh, Bhikhu. "Ambedkar's Legacy." Lecture, Ambedkar University, New Delhi, 2009.

Rodrigues, Valerian, ed. *The Essential Writings of B. R. Ambedkar*. New Delhi: Oxford University Press, 2002.

Sangharakshita. *Ambedkar and Buddhism*. New Delhi: Motilal Banarsidass, 2006 [1986].

Skaria, Ajay. "Can the Dalit Articulate a Universal Position? The Exclusions of the Intellectual." Unpublished manuscript, n.d.

Thorat, Sukhdeo, and Narender Kumar. *B. R. Ambedkar: Perspectives on Social Exclusion and Inclusive Policies*. New Delhi: Oxford University Press, 2008.

Classical Sources

BHAGAVAD GĪTĀ

Aurobindo, Sri. *Essays on Gita*. Pondicherry: Aurobindo Ashram Trust, 2003 [1922].

Chakrabarti, Arindam. "Desire, Self-Control and Concealment: Bhagavadgita, Kant, and Nagel on Hypocrisy." Unpublished paper.

Chaudhuri, Amit. Introduction to *The Bhagavad Gita*. Trans. Juan Mascaró. London: Folio Society, 2011, v–xix.

Devji, Faisal, and Shruti Kapila. "The Bhagavad Gita and Modern Thought: Introduction." *Modern Intellectual History* 7 (2010): 269–273.

Malinar, Angelika. *The Bhagavadgita*. Cambridge: Cambridge University Press, 2007.

Radhakrishnan, Sarvepalli, ed. *The Bhagavadgītā*. Boston: Unwin Paperbacks, 1989 [1948].

Tilak, Bal Gangadhar. *Śrīmadbhagavadgītārahasya*. Trans. Bhalchandra Sitaram. Poona: Saka, 1936.

Vivekananda, Swami. *Thoughts on the Gita*. Calcutta: Advaita Ashrama, 1974 [1963].

KALIDASA

Bose, Buddhadev. *Modern Poetry and Sanskrit Kavya*. Trans. Sujit Mukherjee. Calcutta: Writers Workshop, 1997.

Kālidāsa. *Meghadūta of Kālidāsa*. Trans. R. D. Karmarkar. Delhi: Chaukhamba Sanskrit Pratishthan, 2001.

———. *Kālidāsa's Meghadūta*. Ed. E. Eultzsch. New Delhi: Munshiram Manoharlal Publishers, 1998.

———. *The Loom of Time: A Selection of His Plays and Poems*. Trans. Chandra Rajan. New York: Viking Penguin, 1990.

Kālidāsa, Dhoyī, and Rūpa Gosvāmin. *Messenger Poems*. Trans. Sir James Mallinson. Clay Sanskrit Library. New York: New York University Press, 2006.

Kaviraj, Sudipta. "The Theory of the Poem: Alienation Themes in *Meghaduta*." *Journal of the School of Languages* 4.1 (1976): 28–43.

AŚOKA

Aśoka. *The Moral Edicts of King Aśoka*. Ed. P. H. L. Eggermont and J. Hoftijzer. Leiden: E. J. Brill, 1962.

Basak, Radhagovinda, ed. *Asokan Inscriptions*. Calcutta: Progressive Publishers, 1959.

Chattopadhyaya, Sudhakar. *Achaemenids and India*, 2nd rev. ed. New Delhi: Munshiram Manoharlal Publishers, 1974.

McCrindle, J. W. *Ancient India as Described by Megasthenes and Arrian. Being a Translation of the Fragments of the Indika of Megasthenes Collected by Dr. Schwanbeck, and of the First Part of the Indika of Arrian*. London: Trübner & Co., 1877.

Nikam, N. A., and Richard McKeon, eds. and trans. *The Edicts of Asoka*. Chicago: University of Chicago Press, 1959.

Rich, Bruce. *To Uphold the World: The Message of Ashoka and Kautilya for the 21st Century*. New Delhi: Penguin, 2008.

Sen, Amulyachandra. *Asoka's Edicts*. Calcutta: Indian Publicity Society, 1956.

Strong, John S. *The Legend of King Aśoka: A Study and Translation of the Aśokāvadāna*. Princeton, NJ: Princeton University Press, 1983.

Thapar, Romila. *Asoka and the Decline of the Mauryas*. New Delhi: Oxford University Press, 1997.

———. *The Mauryas Revisted*. New Delhi: K. P. Bagchi & Company, 1987.

Woolner, Alfred C. *Asoka: Text and Glossary*. New York: Oxford University Press, 1924.

ARTHAŚĀSTRA

Kangle, R. P. *The Kautiliya Arthasastra, Part III: A Study*. Bombay: University of Bombay, 1965.

Law, Narendranath. *Studies in Ancient Hindu Polity*. London: Longmans, Green, and Co., 1914.

Rangarajan, L. N., ed. and trans. *Kautilya's The Arthashastra*. New Delhi: Penguin, 1992 [1987].

MUṆḌAKA UPANIṢAD

Olivelle, Patrick. *Upaniṣads*. New York: Oxford University Press, 1996.

Radhakrishnan, S. *The Principal Upanishads*. New Delhi: HarperCollins, 1994 [1953].

BUDDHISM

Almond, Philip C. *The British Discovery of Buddhism*. Cambridge: Cambridge University Press, 1988.

Archaeological Survey of India: Annual Report, 1904–05. Calcutta: Superintendent Government Printing, 1908.

Collins, Steven. *Nirvana and Other Buddhist Felicities: Utopias of the Pali Imaginaire*. Cambridge: Cambridge University Press, 1998.

———. *Selfless Persons: Imagery and Thought in Theravāda Buddhism*. New York: Cambridge University Press, 1982.

Ghosha, Ashva. *Life of the Buddha*. Trans. Patrick Olivelle. New York: New York University Press, 2008.

Kinnaird, Jacob N. *The Emergence of Buddhism*. Westport, CT: Greenwood Press, 2006.

Lamotte, Étienne. *History of Indian Buddhism: From the Origins to the Saka Era*. Trans. Sara Webb-Boin. Louvain, France: Institut Orientaliste, 1988.

Ling, Trevor. *Buddhist Revival in India: Aspects of the Sociology of Buddhism*. New York: St. Martin's Press, 1980.

Sahni, Daya Ram. *Guide to the Buddhist Ruins of Sarnath: With a Plan of Excavations and Five Photographic Plates*. Delhi: Antiquarian Book House, 1982–1983 [1922].

Queen, Christopher S., and Sallie B. King. *Engaged Buddhism: Buddhist Liberation Movements in Asia*. Albany: State University of New York Press, 1996.

MAHĀBHĀRATA

Bandyopadhyay, Sibaji. *The Book of the Night: A Moment from the Mahabharata*. Trans. Ipista Chanda. Calcutta: Seagull Books, 2008.

Bharati, Dharmvir. *Andha Yug*. Trans. Alok Bhalla. New York: Oxford University Press, 2005.

Bose, Buddhadev. *The Book of Yudhisthir: A Study of the Mahabharat of Vyas*. Trans. Sujit Mukherjee. Hyderabad: Sangam Books, 1986.

Chakrabarti, Arindam. "Non-cruelty of Speech and Hand: Hopes for Humanity Inspired by the Mahābhārata and the Buddha." Unpublished manuscript, n.d.

Cherniak, Alex, trans. *Mahābhārata, Book Six: Bhishma,* vol. 1, *Including the "Bhagavad Gita" in Context*. Clay Sanskrit Library. New York: New York University Press, 2008.

Dhand, Arti. *Woman as Fire, Woman as Sage: Sexual Ideology in the Mahābhārata*. Albany: State University of New York Press, 2008.

Dutt, Manmatha Nath, trans. *The Mahabharata*. 6 vols. Calcutta: H. C. Dass, Elysium Press, 1895.

Fitzgerald, James L., trans. and ed. *The Mahabharata,* vol. 7. Chicago: University of Chicago Press, 2004.

Ganguli, Kisari Mohan. *The Mahabharata of Krishna-Dwaipayana Vyasa,* vol. 3: *Vana Parva*. New Delhi: Munshiram Manoharlal Publishers, 2001.

Hiltebeitel, Alf. *Rethinking the Mahabharata: A Reader's Guide to the Education of the Dharma King*. Chicago: University of Chicago Press, 2001.

———. *Rethinking India's Oral and Classical Epics: Draupadi among Rajputs, Muslims and Dalits*. Chicago: University of Chicago Press, 1999.

———. *The Ritual of Battle: Krishna in the Mahabharata*. Albany: State University of New York Press, 1990.

Johnson, W. J., trans. *Mahābhārata, Book Three: "The Forest,"* vol. 4. New York: NYU Press, 2005.

Kaviraj, Sudipta. "The Second Mahabharata." In *Language, Culture, Power: New Directions in South Asian Studies* conference, Columbia University, 22–23 February 2008.

Krishnacharya, T. R., and T. R. Vyasacharya, eds. *Srimanmahabharatam: Vanaparva III* [in Sanskrit]. Bombay: Nirnaya Sagar Press, 1908.

Laine, James W. *Visions of God: Narratives of Theophany in the Mahābhārata*. Vienna: Gerold and Company, 1989.

Lath, Mukund. "The Concept of *Ānṛśaṃsya* in the *Mahābhārata*." In R. N. Dandekar, ed., *The Mahābhārata Revisited*. New Delhi: Sahitya Akademi, 1990, 113–119.

Mehta, J. L. "Dvaipayana, Poet of Being and Becoming." In R. N. Dandekar, ed., *The Mahabharata Revisited*. New Delhi: Sahitya Akademi, 1990, 104–111.

Roy, Pratap Chandra. *The Mahabharata of Krishna-Dwaipayana Vyasa,* vol. 3: *Vana Parva*. Calcutta: Oriental Publishing Co., 1972.

Sukthankar, V. S., ed. *The Mahābhārata,* vol. 4: *The Āraṇyakaparvan (Part 2): Being the Third Book of the Mahābhārata, the Great Epic of India*. Poona: BORI, 1942.

KABIR

Agrawal, Purushottam. *Akath Kahani Prem Ki: Kabir ki Kavita aur unka Samay* [in Hindi]. Delhi: Rajkamal Prakashan, 2009.

Devy, Ganesh. "Translation and Literary History: An Indian View." In Susan Bassnett and Harish Trivedi, eds., *Post-colonial Translation: Theory and Practice*. London. Routledge, 1999, 182–188.

Dharamveer. *Kabir: Baaj Bhi, Kapot Bhi, Papiha Bhi* [Kabir: Falcon, pigeon, and Papiha] [in Hindi]. Delhi: Vani, 2008.

———. *Kabir: Dr Hazari Prasad Dvivedi ka Prakshipta Chintan* [Kabir: The interpolated thoughts of Dr. Hazari Prasad Dvivedi] [in Hindi]. Delhi: Vani, 2006.

———. *Kabir aur Ramanand: Kimvadantian* [Kabir and Ramanand: Heresays] [in Hindi]. Delhi: Vani, 2004.

———. *Kabir ke Alochak* [Critics of Kabir] [in Hindi]. Delji: Vani, 1997.

Dharwadker, Vinay, trans. *Kabir: The Weaver's Songs*. New Delhi: Penguin India, 2003.

———. "A. K. Ramanujan's Theory and Practice of Translation." In Susan Bassnett and Harish Trivedi, eds., *Post-colonial Translation: Theory and Practice*. London: Routledge, 1999, 114–140.

Dwivedi, Hazariprasad. *Kabir: Kabir ke vaktavya, sahitya aur darsanik vicaron ki alocana* [in Hindi]. Delhi: Rajkamal Prakashan, 1973 [1940].

Eck, Diana. *Banaras: City of Light*. New Delhi: Penguin Books, 1999 [1982].

Hess, Linda. *Singing Emptiness: Kumar Gandharva Performs the Poetry of Kabir*. Calcutta: Seagull Books, 2009.

Hess, Linda, and Shukdev Singh, trans. *The Bijak of Kabir*. New York: Oxford University Press, 2002.

Kabir. *Songs of Kabir*. Trans. Arvind Krishna Mehrotra. New York: New York Review of Books, 2011.

———. *Songs of Kabir*. Trans. Rabindranath Tagore (with assistance of Evelyn Underhill, based upon the Hindi text with Bengali translation of Mr. Kshiti Mohan Sen). New York: Macmillan, 1915.

Mehta, Pratap Bhanu. "Your Kabir and Mine." *Indian Express*, 18 June 2010. http://www.indianexpress.com/news/your-kabir-and-mine/639844/.

Mishra, Rameshchander. *Kabir Akela* [in Hindi]. New Delhi: Sant Sahitya Sanasthan, 1999.

Sen, Kshitimohan. *Medieval Mysticism of India*. Trans. Manmohan Ghosh, foreword by Rabindranath Tagore. New Delhi: Oriental Books Reprint Corporation, 1974 [1936].

Shukla, Ramchandra. "Kavita Kya Hai?" *Cintamani* 1: 91–101 [in Hindi]. Jaipur: Shyam Prakashan, 2009 [1929] (first published in *Sarasvati*, April 1909).

Singh, Namvar. *Doosri Parampara ki Khoj* [in Hindi]. Delhi: Rajkamal Prakashan, 2008 [1982].

Wakankar, Milind. *Subalternity and Religion: The Prehistory of Dalit Empowerment in South Asia*. New York: Routledge, 2010.

Secondary Materials

Important Books

Agamben, Giorgio. *The Man without Content*. Trans. Georgia Albert. Palo Alto, CA: Stanford University Press, 1999 [1994].

Arendt, Hannah. *Between Past and Future: Eight Exercises in Political Thought*. Intro. Jerome Kohn. New York: Penguin, 2006 [1954].

Azad, Maulana Abul Kalam. *India Wins Freedom*. New Delhi: Orient Blackswan, 2009 [1959].

Balagangadhara, S. N. *"The Heathen in His Blindness": Asia, the West and the Dynamic of Religion*. Leiden: Brill, 1994.

Berlin, Isaiah. *The Sense of Reality: Studies in Ideas and Their History*. Ed. Henry Hardy. London: Chatto and Windus, 1996.

———. *The Crooked Timber of Humanity: Chapters in the History of Ideas*. Ed. Henry Hardy. London: John Murray, 1990.

Bose, Sugata, and Ayesha Jalal. *Modern South Asia: History, Culture, Political Economy*. New Delhi: Oxford University Press, 2004.

Calasso, Roberto. *Ka*. Trans. Tim Parks. London: Vintage Books, 1999 [1996].

Chakrabarty, Dipesh. *Provincializing Europe: Postcolonial Thought and Historical Difference*. Princeton, NJ: Princeton University Press, 2010 [2000].

Chandra, Sudhir. *The Oppressive Present: Literature and Social Consciousness in Colonial India*. New Delhi: Oxford University Press, 1992.

———. *Dependence and Disillusionment: Emergence of National Consciousness in Later 19th Century India*. New Delhi: Manas Publishers, 1975.

Chandra, Sudhir, and Alok Bhalla, eds. *Indian Responses to Colonialism in the Nineteenth Century*. New Delhi: Sterling Publishers, 1993.

Chatterjee, Partha. *Nationalist Thought and the Colonial World: A Derivative Discourse*. Minneapolis: University of Minnesota Press, 1993 [1986].

———. *The Nation and Its Fragments: Colonial and Postcolonial Histories*. Princeton, NJ: Princeton University Press, 1993.

Chaudhuri, Amit. *Clearing a Space: Reflections on India, Literature and Culture*. New York: Peter Lang, 2008.

Chesterton, G. K. *Saint Francis of Assisi*. London: Hodder and Stoughton, 1924.

Doniger, Wendy. *The Hindus: An Alternative History*. New York: Penguin, 2009.

Guha, Ramachandra. *Makers of Modern India*. New Delhi: Penguin Books, 2010.

———. *India after Gandhi: The History of the World's Largest Democracy*. New Delhi: Picador, 2007.

Guha, Ranajit. *History at the Limit of World-History*. New York: Columbia University Press, 2002.

———. *Elementary Aspects of Peasant Insurgency in Colonial India*. Durham, NC: Duke University Press, 1999 [1983].

———. *Dominance without Hegemony: History and Power in Colonial India*. Cambridge, MA: Harvard University Press, 1997 [1988, 1977].

Hadot, Pierre. *Plotinus, or the Simplicity of Vision*. Trans. Michael Chase. Chicago: University of Chicago Press, 1993.

Inden, Ronald. *Text and Practice: Essays on South Asian History*. New York: Oxford University Press, 2006.

———. *Imagining India*. Bloomington: Indiana University Press, 2000 [1990].

Jacobsohn, Gary Jeffrey. *Constitutional Identity*. Cambridge, MA: Harvard University Press, 2010.

———. *The Wheel of Law: India's Secularism in Comparative Constitutional Context*. Princeton, NJ: Princeton University Press, 2003.

Jalal, Ayesha. *Partisans of Allah: Jihad in South Asia*. Cambridge, MA: Harvard University Press, 2008.

Kaviraj, Sudipta. *The Unhappy Consciousness: Bankimchandra Chattopadhyay and the Formation of Nationalist Discourse in India*. New Delhi: Oxford University Press, 1995.

Keay, John. *India: A History*. New York: Atlantic Monthly Press, 2000.

Khilnani, Sunil. *The Idea of India*. London: Penguin, 1997.

MacIntyre, Alasdair. *After Virtue: A Study in Moral Theory*. Notre Dame, IN: University of Notre Dame Press, 2007 [1984].

———. *The Tasks of Philosophy: Selected Essays*, vol. 1. Cambridge: Cambridge University Press, 2006.

———. *Ethics and Politics: Selected Essays*, vol. 2. Cambridge: Cambridge University Press, 2006.

———. *Whose Justice? Which Rationality?* Notre Dame, IN: University of Notre Dame Press, 1988.

Mehta, Pratap Bhanu. *The Burden of Democracy*. New Delhi: Penguin, 2003.

Mehta, Uday Singh. *Liberalism and Empire: A Study in Nineteenth-Century British Liberal Thought*. Chicago: University of Chicago Press, 1999.

Menand, Louis. *The Metaphysical Club: A Story of Ideas in America*. New York: Farrar, Straus and Giroux, 2001.

Mishra, Pankaj. *Temptations of the West: How to Be Modern in India, Pakistan, Tibet and Beyond*. New York: Farrar, Straus and Giroux, 2006.

———. *An End to Suffering: The Buddha in the World*. London: Picador, 2004.

Nandy, Ashis. *The Illegitimacy of Nationalism: Rabindranath Tagore and the Politics of Self*. New Delhi: Oxford University Press, 1994.

———. *The Intimate Enemy: Loss and Recovery of Self under Colonialism*. New Delhi: Oxford University Press, 1988 [1983].

Nelson, Eric. *The Hebrew Republic: Jewish Sources and the Transformation of European Political Thought*. Cambridge, MA: Harvard University Press, 2010.

Nussbaum, Martha. *The Clash Within: Democracy, Religious Violence, and India's Future*. Cambridge, MA: Harvard University Press, 2007.

———. *The Fragility of Goodness: Luck and Ethics in Greek Tragedy and Philosophy*. Cambridge: Cambridge University Press, 2006 [1986].

Pollock, Sheldon. *The Language of the Gods in the World of Men*. Berkeley: University of California Press, 2006.

———, ed. *Literary Cultures in History: Reconstructions from South Asia*. Berkeley: University of California Press, 2003.

Rudolph, Lloyd I., and Susanne Hoeber Rudolph. *Postmodern Gandhi: Gandhi in the World and at Home*. New Delhi: Oxford University Press, 2006.

———. *The Modernity of Tradition: Political Development in India*. New Delhi: Orient Longman, 1999 [1967].

Sawhney, Simona. *The Modernity of Sanskrit*. Minneapolis: University of Minnesota Press, 2008.

Sen, Amartya. *The Argumentative Indian: Writings on Indian History, Culture and Identity*. New Delhi: Penguin, 2005.

Siva Sankara Sarma, Rani. *The Last Brahmin: Life and Reflections of a Modern-Day Sanskrit Pandit*. New Delhi: Permanent Black, 2007.

Slauter, Eric. *The State as a Work of Art: The Cultural Origins of the Constitution*. Chicago: University of Chicago Press, 2009.

Taylor, Charles. *Sources of the Self: The Making of Modern Identity*. Cambridge, MA: Harvard University Press, 1989.

Varshney, Ashutosh. *Ethnic Conflict and Civic Life: Hindus and Muslims in India*. New Haven, CT: Yale University Press, 2002.

Virmani, Arundhati. *A National Flag for India: Rituals, Nationalism, and the Politics of Sentiment*. New Delhi: Permanent Black, 2008.

Weber, Max. *The Religion of India: The Sociology of Hinduism and Buddhism*. New Delhi: Munshiram Manoharlal Publications, 2000 [1958].

Wilson, Edmund. *To the Finland Station*. New York: New York Review of Books, 2003 [1940].

Anthologies, Journal Issues, and Edited Volumes

Bassnett, Susan, and Harish Trivedi, eds. *Post-colonial Translation: Theory and Practice*. London: Routledge, 1999.

"The *Bhagavad Gita* and Modern Thought." *Modern Intellectual History* 7.2 (2010).

Bilimoria, Purushottama, Joseph Prabhu, and Renuka Sharma, eds. *Indian Ethics: Classical Traditions and Contemporary Challenges*. Aldershot: Ashgate, 2007.

Boussac, Marie-Françoise, and Jean-François Salles, eds. *Athens, Aden, Arikamedu: Essays on the Interrelations between India, Arabia and the Eastern Mediterranean*. New Delhi: Manohar, 1995.

Chaudhuri, Amit, ed. *The Vintage Book of Modern Indian Literature*. New York: Vintage Books, 2004.

Dallmayr, Fred, and G. N. Devy, eds. *Between Tradition and Modernity: India's Search for Identity: A Twentieth Century Anthology*. Walnut Creek, CA: AltaMira Press, 1998.

Dalmia, Vasudha, Angelika Malinar, and Martin Christof. *Charisma and Canon: Essays on the Religious History of the Indian Subcontinent*. New Delhi: Oxford University Press, 2001.

Dandekar, R. N., ed. *The Mahabharata Revisited*. New Delhi: Sahitya Akademi, 1990.

"D. D. Kosambi: The Man and His Works." *Economic and Political Weekly* 43.30 (26 July 2008).

Dehejia, Vidya. *Antal and Her Path of Love: Poems of a Woman Saint from South India*. Albany: State University of New York Press, 1990.

Docker, John, and Debjani Ganguly, eds. *Rethinking Gandhi and Nonviolent Relationality: Global Perspectives*. New York: Routledge, 2007 [2001].

Hasan-Rokem, Galit, and David Shulman, eds. *Untying the Knot: On Riddles and Other Enigmatic Modes*. New York: Oxford University Press, 1996.

Hawley, John Stratton, and Mark Jurgensmeyer, eds. and trans. *Songs of the Saints of India*. New York: Oxford University Press, 2004.

Houben, Jan E. M., and Karel R. Van Kooij, eds. *Violence Denied: Violence, Nonviolence and the Rationalization of Violence in South Asian Cultural History*. Leiden: Brill, 1999.

"An Intellectual History for India." *Modern Intellectual History* 4.1. (2007).

Jayal, Niraja Gopal, and Pratap Bhanu Mehta, eds. *The Oxford Companion to Politics in India*. New Delhi: Oxford University Press, 2010.

Jha, D. N., ed. *The Many Careers of D. D. Kosambi: Critical Essays*. New Delhi: Left Word, 2011.

Kartunnen, Klaus, ed. *India and the Hellenistic World*. Helsinki: Finnish Oriental Society, 1997.

Lubin, Timothy, et al., eds. *Hinduism and Law: An Introduction*. New York: Cambridge University Press, 2010.

Mayaram, Shail, et al., eds. *Muslims, Dalits and the Fabrications of History*. New Delhi: Permanent Black, 2005.

Mehrotra, Arvind Krishna, ed. *An Illustrated History of Indian Literature in English*. New Delhi: Permanent Black, 2003.

Mehta, V. R., and Thomas Pantham, eds. *Political Ideas in Modern India: Thematic Explorations*. New Delhi: Sage Publications, 2006.

Michael, S. M., ed. *Dalits in Modern India: Vision and Values*. New Delhi: Sage Publications, 1999.

Mukherjee, Rudrangshu, ed. *Great Speeches of Modern India*. New Delhi: Penguin, 2007 [1993].

Political Theory: An International Journal of Political Philosophy 18.4 (November 1990). Entire issue.

Public Culture 23.2, issue 64 (Spring 2011). Entire issue.

Rao, B. Shiva, ed. *The Framing of India's Constitution: Select Documents*, vol. 1. New Delhi: Indian Institute of Public Administration, 1967.

Thangappa, M. L., trans. *Love Stands Alone: Selections from Tamil Sangam Poetry*. New Delhi: Penguin Books, 2010.

Thesis Eleven: Critical Theory and Historical Sociology 39.1 (August 1994). Entire issue.

Vajpeyi, Ananya, ed. *Seminar*, vol. 623: "The Nation and Its Poet: 150 Years of Rabindranath Tagore, Life-Language-Legacy, 1861–2011" (July 2011).

———, ed. *Seminar*, vol. 615: "We the People: India's Constitution at 60, 1950–2010" (November 2010).

Art-Historical Materials

Agrawala, Vasudeva Sharana. *The Wheel-Flag of India*. Varanasi: Prithvi Prakashan, 1964.

Bose, Nandalal. *Vision and Creation*. Trans. Kalpati Ganapati Subramanyan. Calcutta: Visva-Bharati Publishing Department, 1999.

Brown, Rebecca M. *Art for a Modern India, 1947–1980*. Durham, NC: Duke University Press, 2009.

Chandra, Pramod. *On the Study of Indian Art*. Cambridge, MA: Harvard University Press, 1983.

Coomaraswamy, R. P., ed. *The Essential Ananda K. Coomaraswamy*. Bloomington, IN: World Wisdom, 2004.

Dadi, Iftikhar. *Modernism and the Art of Muslim South Asia*. Chapel Hill: University of North Carolina Press, 2010.

Dutta, Arindam. *The Bureaucracy of Beauty: Design in the Age of Its Global Reproducibility*. New York: Routledge, 2007.

Goswamy, B. N. *Nainsukh of Guler: A Great Indian Painter from a Small Hill-State*. New Delhi: Niyogi Books, 2011 [1997].

Guy, John, and Jorritt Britschgi. *Wonder of the Age: Master Painters of India, 1100–1900*. New York: Metropolitan Museum of Art, 2011.

Havell, E. B. *The Ideals of Indian Art*. New York: E. P. Dutton and Co., 1920 [1911].

Kapur, Geeta. *When Was Modernism: Essays on Contemporary Cultural Practice in India*. New Delhi: Tulika, 2000.

Mitter, Partha. *Art and Nationalism in Colonial India, 1850–1922: Occidental Orientations*. New York: Cambridge University Press, 1994.

Quintanilla, Sonya Rhie. *Rhythms of India: The Art of Nandalal Bose*. San Diego, CA: San Diego Museum of Art, 2008.

Sheikh, Gulammohammed. *City, Kaavad and Other Works*. New Delhi: Vadehra Art Galeery, 2011.

———. *Kaavad: Travelling Shrine: Home*. New Delhi: Vadehra Art Gallery, 2008.

General Books

Arendt, Hannah. *On Revolution*. New York: Penguin, 2004 [1963].

Austin, Granville. *The Indian Constitution: Cornerstone of a Nation*. New Delhi: Oxford University Press, 2005 [1966].

Bromwich, David. *A Choice of Inheritance: Self and Community from Edmund Burke to Robert Frost*. Cambridge, MA: Harvard University Press, 1989.

Cohn, Bernard S. *Colonialism and Its Forms of Knowledge: The British in India*. Princeton, NJ: Princeton University Press, 1996.

Dalmia, Vasudha. *The Nationalization of Hindu Traditions: Bharatendu Harishchandra and Nineteenth-Century Banaras*. New Delhi: Oxford University Press, 1997.

Dalrymple, William. *Nine Lives: In Search of the Sacred in Modern India*. London: Bloomsbury, 2009.

Deshpande, Prachi. *Creative Pasts: Historical Memory and Identity in Western India, 1700–1960*. New York: Columbia University Press, 2007.

Dirks, Nicholas. *Castes of Mind: Colonialism and the Making of Modern India*. Princeton, NJ: Princeton University Press, 2001.

Doniger, Wendy. *The Hindus: An Alternative History*. New York: Penguin, 2009.

Gandhi, Rajmohan. *Understanding the Muslim Mind*. New Delhi: Penguin Books, 2000 [1986].

Ghose, Aurobindo. *Nationalism, Religion, and Beyond: Writings on Politics, Society, and Culture*. Ed. Peter Hechs. Delhi: Permanent Black, 2005.

Goswami, Manu. *Producing India: From Colonial Economy to National Space*. Chicago: University of Chicago Press, 2004.

Habib, Irfan, and Vivekanand Jha. *A People's History of India: Mauryan India*. New Delhi: Aligarh Historians' Society in conjunction with Tulika Books, 2004.

Halbfass, Wilhelm. *India and Europe: An Essay in Understanding*. Albany: State University of New York Press, 1988.

Hasan, Mushirul. *A Moral Reckoning: Muslim Intellectuals in Nineteenth-Century Delhi*. Delhi: Oxford University Press, 2005.

Heesterman, J. C. *The Inner Conflict of Tradition: Essays in Indian Ritual, Kingship and Society*. New Delhi: Oxford University Press, 1985.

Jalal, Ayesha. *Self and Sovereignty: Individual and Community in South Asian Islam since 1850*. London: Routledge, 2000.

Kateb, George. *The Inner Ocean: Individualism and Democratic Culture*. Ithaca, NY: Cornell University Press, 1992.

Kosambi, D. D. *The Oxford India Kosambi: Combined Methods in Indology and Other Writings*. Ed. Brajadulal Chattopadhyaya. New Delhi: Oxford University Press, 2009.

Kosambi, Dharmanand. *Nivedan: The Autobiography of Dharmanand Kosambi*. Ed. and trans. Meera Kosambi. New Delhi: Permanent Black, 2011.

———. *The Essential Writings*. Ed. Meera Kosambi. New Delhi: Permanent Black, 2010.

Krishna, Daya, ed. *India's Intellectual Traditions: Attempts at Conceptual Reconstructions*. New Delhi: Indian Council of Philosophical Research, 2003 [1987].

———. *Prolegomena to Any Future Historiography of Cultures and Civilizations*. New Delhi: Project of History of Indian Science, Philosophy, and Culture, 1997.

———. *The Problematic and Conceptual Structure of Classical Indian Thought about Man, Society and Polity*. New Delhi: Oxford University Press, 1996.

Lohia, Ram Manohar. *Interval during Politics*. Hyderabad: Navahind, 1965.

———. *The Caste System*. Hyderabad: Widener, 1964.

Lutgendorf, Philip. *Hanuman's Tale: The Messages of a Divine Monkey*. New York: Oxford University Press, 2007.

———. *The Life of a Text: Performing the Rāmcaritmānas of Tulsidas*. Berkeley: University of California Press, 1991.

Mahathera, Dharmapal, et al., eds. *Mahapandita Rahula Sanskrityayana Birth Centenary Volume*. Calcutta: Bauddha Dharmankur Sabha, 1994.

Mehrotra, Rajiv. *Thakur Sri Ramakrishna: A Biography*. New Delhi: Hay House India, 2009.

Nagaraj, D. R. *The Flaming Feet and Other Essays: The Dalit Movement in India*. Ed. Prithvi Datta Chandra Shobhi. New Delhi: Permanent Black, 2010 [1993].

Naipaul, V. S. *India: A Wounded Civilization*. New York: Vintage Books, 2008 [1976].

Novetzke, Christopher Lee. *Religion and Public Memory: A Cultural History of Saint Namdev in India*. New York: Columbia University Press, 2008.

Olivelle, Patrick. *Between the Empires: Society in India 300 BCE to 400 CE*. New York: Oxford University Press, 2006.

Pollock, Sheldon, trans. *Ramayana, Book Three: The Forest*. Clay Sanskrit Library. New York: New York University Press, 2006.

Radhakrishnan, Sarvepalli. *Indian Philosophy*, vol. 1, 2nd ed. London: George Allen & Unwin, 1923.

Rao, Anupama. *The Caste Question: Dalits and the Politics of Modern India*. Berkeley: University of California Press, 2009.

Safdar Hashmi Memorial Trust. *Indian People in the Struggle for Freedom: Five Essays*. New Delhi: Sahmat, 1998.

Sarkar, Jadunath. *The History of Bengal*. Patna: Academica Asiatica, 1973 [1943].

Sartori, Andrew. *Bengal in Global Concept History: Culturalism in the Age of Capital*. Chicago: University of Chicago Press, 2008.

Schwab, Raymond. *The Oriental Renaissance: Europe's Rediscovery of India and the East, 1680–1880*. New York: Columbia University Press, 1984.

Sharma, Shashi. *Imagined Manuvad: The Dharmasastras and Their Interpreters*. New Delhi: Rupa & Co., 2005.

Shulman, David Dean. *The Wisdom of Poets: Studies in Tamil, Telugu, and Sanskrit*. New York: Oxford University Press, 2001.

———. *The King and the Clown in South Indian Myth and Poetry*. Princeton, NJ: Princeton University Press, 1985.

Von Tunzelmann, Alex. *Indian Summer: The Secret History of the End of an Empire*. London: Simon and Schuster, 2007.

Articles, Chapters, and Television Episodes

Ahmad, Aijaz. "Azad's Careers: Roads Taken and Not Taken." In *Lineages of the Present: Political Essays*. New Delhi: Tulika, 1996, 133–190.

Alam, Javeed. "Tradition in India under Interpretive Stress: Interrogating Its Claims." *Thesis Eleven* 39 (1994): 19–38.

Amin, Shahid. "Making the Nation Habitable." Unpublished manuscript, October 2006.

———. "Remembering Chauri Chaura: Notes from Historical Fieldwork." In Ranajit Guha, ed., *A Subaltern Studies Reader, 1986–1995*. Minneapolis: University of Minnesota Press, 1997, 179–239.

———. "Gandhi as Mahatma: Gorakhpur District, Eastern Uttar Pradesh, 1921–2." In Gayatri Chakravorty Spivak and Ranajit Guha, eds., *Selected Subaltern Studies*. New Delhi: Oxford University Press, 1988, 288–348.

Balagangadhara, S. N. "How to Speak for the Indian Traditions: An Agenda for the Future." *Journal of the American Academy of Religion* 73.4 (December 2005): 987–1013.

Bandopadhyay, Sibaji. "A Critique of Non-violence." *Seminar* 608, "The Enduring Epic" (April 2010).

Banerjee, Prathama. "The Work of Imagination: Temporality and Nationhood in Colonial Bengal." In Shail Mayaram, M. S. S. Pandian, and Ajay Skaria, eds., *Muslims, Dalits, and the Fabrication of History*. New Delhi: Permanent Black, 2005, 280–322.

Benegal, Shyam. "Asoka: Part 2," Episode 14, *Bharat ek Khoj* (television series). Produced by Doordarshan and Sahyadri Films, 1988.

Bose, Sugata. "The Spirit and Form of an Ethical Polity: A Meditation on Aurobindo's Thought." *Modern Intellectual History* 4.1 (2007): 129–144.

Bosworth, A. Brian. "Aristotle, India and the Alexander Historians." *Topoi: Orient Occident* 3.2 (1993): 407–424.

Brockington, John. 2004. "The Concept of *Dharma* in the Ramayana." *Journal of Indian Philosophy* 32.5–6 (December 2004): 655–670.

Bromwich, David. "Commentaries: Whitman and Memory, a Response to Kateb." *Political Theory* (November 1990): 572–576.

Chakrabarti, Arindam. "On What There Will Be: The Future in Quine." In *Empiricism and Two Dogmas*. Kolkata: Rabindrabharati University, Department of Philosophy, 2006.

———. "The Trouble with You." Paper presented at the International Workshop on Ego, Self-Knowledge and Freedom, Department of Philosophy and Sociology, Pedagogical University, Krakow, Poland, 23 November 2005.

Chandra, Sudhir. "The Oppressive Present." In Fred Dallmayr and G. N. Devy, eds., *Between Tradition and Modernity: India's Search for Identity: A Twentieth Century Anthology*. Walnut Creek, CA: AltaMira Press, 1998, 287–300.

———. "'The Languages of Modern Ideas': Reflections on an Ethnological Parable." *Thesis Eleven* 39 (August 1994): 39–51.

Chatterjee, Partha. "Culture and Power in the Thought of Bankimchandra." In *Nationalist Thought and the Colonial World: A Derivative Discourse?* London: Zed Books for the United Nations University, 1986, 67–91.

Chatterji, Suniti Kumar. "The National Flag." *Modern Review* 49 (1931): 683–687.

Chaudhuri, Rosinka. "History in Poetry: Nabinchandra Sen's Palashir Yuddha and the Question of Truth." *Journal of Asian Studies* 66.4 (2007): 897–918.

"Constituent Assembly of India, Volume IV. 22nd July, 1947." http://parliamentofindia.nic.in/ls/debates/vol4p7.htm.

"Constituent Assembly of India, Volume V. 14th August, 1947." http://parliamentofindia.nic.in/ls/debates/vol5p1.htm

Dallmayr, Fred. "Gandhi and Islam: A Heart-and-Mind Unity." In V. R. Mehta and Thomas Pantham, eds., *Political Ideas in Modern India: Thematic Explorations*. New Delhi: Sage Publications, 2006, 206–220.

Das, Sisir Kumar. Introduction to Sukanta Chauduri, ed., *Rabindranath Tagore: Selected Writings on Literature and Language*. Oxford: Oxford University Press, 2001, 1–21.

Dayal, Samir. "Repositioning India: Tagore's Passionate Politics of Love." *Positions* 15.1 (2007): 165–208.

Devji, Faisal. "Morality in the Shadow of Politics." *Modern Intellectual History* 7.2 (2010): 373–390.

———. "Apologetic Modernity." *Modern Intellectual History* 4.1 (April 2007): 61–76.

———. "A Shadow Nation: The Making of Muslim India." In Kevin Grant, Philippa Levine, and Frank Trentmann, eds., *Beyond Sovereignty: Britain, Empire and Transnationalism, 1860–1950*. Basingstoke: Palgrave Macmillan, 2007, 126–145.

———. "Hindu/Muslim/Indian." *Public Culture* 5.1 (Fall 1992): 1–18.

———. "Confounded though Immortal: Muhammad Ali Jinnah and the Modernity of Indian Politics: A Synopsis." Unpublished manuscript, n.d.

———. "The Prophet of Islam's Globalization." Unpublished manuscript, n.d.

Dhareshwar, Vivek. "Politics, Experience and Cognitive Enslavement: Gandhi's *Hind Swaraj*." Unpublished manuscript, 2009.

Eliot, T. S. "Tradition and the Individual Talent." In *The Sacred Wood: Essays on Poetry and Criticism*. London: Methuen & Co., 1928 [1921].

Fitzgerald, James L. "*Dharma* and Its Translation in the *Mahabharata*." *Journal of Indian Philosophy* 32.5–6 (December 2004): 671–685.

———. "The Many Voices of the *Mahabharata*." *Journal of the American Oriental Society* (2003): 803–818.

———. "Making Yudhisthira the King: The Dialectics and the Politics of Violence in the *Mahabharata*." *Rocznik Orientalistyczny* 54 (2002): 63–92.

Fitzgerald, Timothy. "Ambedkar Buddhism in Maharashtra." *Contributions to Indian Sociology* 31.2 (1997): 225–251.

Frank, Jason. "Aesthetic Democracy: Walt Whitman and the Poetry of the People." *Review of Politics* 69 (2007): 402–430.

Fuchs, Martin. "Introduction: India and Modernity: Towards Decentring Western Perspectives." *Thesis Eleven* 39 (August 1994): v–xiii.

Gandhi, Leela. "*Ahimsa* and Other Animals: The Genealogy of Immature Politics." In Debjani Ganguly and John Docker, eds., *Rethinking Gandhi and Nonviolent Relationality*. London: Routledge, 2007, 17–37.

Gandhi, Ramchandra. "The Swaraj of India." In Fred Dallmayr and G. N. Devy, eds., *Between Tradition and Modernity: India's Search for Identity: A Twentieth Century Anthology*. Walnut Creek, CA: AltaMira Press, 1998, 301–311.

Ganeri, Jonardon. "Contextualism in the Study of Indian Intellectual Cultures." *Journal of Indian Philosophy* 36.5–6 (2008): 551–562.

Grossman, Allen. "The Poetics of Union in Whitman and Lincoln: An Inquiry toward the Relationship of Art and Policy." *American Renaissance Reconsidered*, new series 9 (1985): 183–208.

Guha, Ramachandra. "The Loss of Recovery of Intellectual Bilingualism." *Economic and Political Weekly* 45.4 (23 January 2010): 70–72.

———. "The Rise and Fall of the Bilingual Intellectual." *Economic and Political Weekly* 44.33 (15 August 2009): 36–42.

———. "Arguments with Sen, Arguments about India." *Economic and Political Weekly* 40.41 (8–14 October 2005): 4420–4428.

Guha, Ranajit. "Discipline and Mobilize." In *Subaltern Studies: Writings on South Asian History and Society,* vol. 7. New Delhi: Oxford University Press, 1992, 69–120.

———. "The Prose of Counter-Insurgency." In *Subaltern Studies: Writings on South Asian History and Society,* vol. 2. New Delhi: Oxford University Press, 1983, 1–42.

Heredia, Rudolf C. "Gandhi's Hind Swaraj: Need for a New Hermeneutic." *Vidyajyoti Journal of Theological Reflection* 63.10 (October 1999): 733–748.

Hymans, Jacques E. C. "India's Soft Power and Vulnerability." *India Review* 8.3 (2009): 234–265.

Jalal, Ayesha. "Striking a Just Balance: Maulana Azad as a Theorist of Trans-National Jihad." *Modern Intellectual History* 4.1 (2007): 95–107.

Karttunen, Klaus. "Graeco-India." *Topoi: Orient-Occident* 3.2 (1993): 391–400.

Kateb, George. "Walt Whitman and the Culture of Democracy." *Political Theory* 18.4 (1990): 545–571.

Kaviraj, Sudipta. "Two Histories of Literary Cultures in Bengal." In Sheldon Pollock, ed., *Literary Cultures in History: Reconstructions from South Asia*. Berkeley: University of California Press, 2003, 503–566.

Krishna, Daya. "The Myth of the Ethics of *Purusartha* of Humanity's Life-Goals." In Purushottama Bilimoria, Joseph Prabhu, and Renuka Sharma, eds., *Indian Ethics: Classical Traditions and Contemporary Challenges*. Aldershot: Ashgate, 2007, 103–115.

Lal, Vinay. "The Gandhi Everyone Loves to Hate." *Economic and Political Weekly* 43.40 (4–10 October 2008): 55–64.

MacIntyre, Alasdair. "A Disquieting Suggestion." In *After Virtue: A Study in Moral Theory*. Notre Dame, IN: University of Notre Dame Press, 2007 [1984], 1–5.

———. "The Virtues, the Unity of a Human Life and the Concept of a Tradition." In *After Virtue: A Study in Moral Theory*. Notre Dame, IN: University of Notre Dame Press, 2007 [1984], 204–225.

———. "Poetry as Political Philosophy." In *Ethics and Politics: Selected Essays,* vol. 2. Cambridge: Cambridge University Press, 2006, 159–171.

———. "The Rationality of Traditions." In *Whose Justice? Which Rationality?* Notre Dame, IN: University of Notre Dame Press, 1988, 349–369.

———. "Tradition and Translation." In *Whose Justice? Which Rationality?* Notre Dame, IN: University of Notre Dame Press, 1988, 370–388.

Majeed, Javed. "Geographies of Subjectivity, Pan-Islam and Muslim Separatism: Muhammad Iqbal and Selfhood." *Modern Intellectual History* 4.1 (2007): 145–161.

Matilal, Bimal Krishna. "*Dharma* and Rationality." In Purushottama Bilimoria, Joseph Prabhu, and Renuka Sharma, eds., *Indian Ethics: Classical Traditions and Contemporary Challenges*. Aldershot: Ashgate, 2007, 79–102.

Mehta, Pratap Bhanu. "The Quest for Hinduism." In V. R. Mehta and Thomas Pantham, eds., *Political Ideas in Modern India: Thematic Explorations*. New Delhi: Sage Publications, 2006, 155–166.

———. "Empire and Moral Identity." *Ethics and International Affairs* 17.2 (September 2003): 49–62.

———. "The Ethical Irrationality of the World: Weber and Hindu Ethics." *Critical Horizons* 2.2 (2001): 203–225.

Mehta, Uday Singh. "Indian Constitutionalism: The Social and the Political Vision." Unpublished manuscript, Amherst College, 2009.

Mohanty, J. N. "*Dharma,* Imperatives and Tradition: Towards an Indian Theory of Moral Action." In Purushottama Bilimoria, Joseph Prabhu, and Renuka Sharma, eds., *Indian Ethics: Classical Traditions and Contemporary Challenges*. Aldershot: Ashgate, 2007, 57–78.

Moon, Vasant. "Pali and Other Sources of the Buddha and His Dhamma with an Index." In B. Ambedkar, *Dr. Babasaheb Ambedkar: Writings and Speeches,* vol. 11. Maharashtra: Education Department, 1995.

More, Paul E. "Rabindranath Tagore." *The Nation* 103.2683 (30 November 1916): 506–507.

Mufti, Aamir R. "Secularism and Minority: Elements of a Critique." *Social Text* 45 (Winter 1995): 75–96.

Mukherjee, Mithi. "Transcending Identity: Gandhi, Nonviolence, and the Pursuit of a 'Different' Freedom in Modern India." *American Historical Review* 115 (April 2010): 453–473.

"The National Convention of Congress Legislators: March 1937." In B. Shiva Rao, ed., *Select Documents, The Project Committee*. Delhi: Universal Law Publishing Company, 2006, 86–92.

Olivelle, Patrick. "The Semantic History of Dharma: The Middle and Late Vedic Periods." *Journal of Indian Philosophy* 32 (2004): 491–511.

Pantham, Thomas. "Religious Diversity and National Unity: The Gandhian and Hindutva Visions." In V. R. Mehta and Thomas Pantham, eds., *Political Ideas in Modern India: Thematic Explorations*. New Delhi: Sage Publications, 2006, 221–237.

———. "Thinking with Mahatma Gandhi: Beyond Liberal Democracy." *Political Theory* 11 (1983): 165–188.

Parekh, Bhikhu. "Hindu Theory of Tolerance." In Purushottama Bilimoria, Joseph Prabhu, and Renuka Sharma, eds., *Indian Ethics: Classical Traditions and Contemporary Challenges*. Aldershot: Ashgate, 2007, 337–349.

———. "Limits of the Indian Political Imagination." In V. R. Mehta and Thomas Pantham, eds., *Political Ideas in Modern India: Thematic Explorations*. New Delhi: Sage Publications, 2006, 437–458.

Pollock, Sheldon. "Is There an Indian Intellectual History?" *Journal of Indian Philosophy* 36.5–6 (2008): 533–542.

———. "The Death of Sanskrit." *Comparative Studies in Society and History* 43 (2001): 392–426.

Prabhu, Joseph. "Gandhi, Empire, and a Culture of Peace." In P. Bilimoria, J. Prabhu, and R. Sharma, eds., *Indian Ethics: Classical Traditions and Contemporary Challenges*. Aldershot: Ashgate, 2007, 395–410.

Qureshi, Mahmud Shah. "Literary Assessments of Tagore by Bengali Muslim Writers." *University of Toronto Quarterly* 77.4 (2008): 1133–1152.

Ramanujan, A. K. "Why an Allama Poem Is Not a Riddle: An Anthological Essay." In Galit Hasan-Rokem and David Shulman, eds., *Untying the Knot: On Riddles and Other Enigmatic Modes*. New York: Oxford University Press, 1996, 179–190.

———. "Is There an Indian Way of Thinking? An Informal Essay." *Contributions to Indian Sociology* 23.1 (January 1989): 41–58.

Ray, Rabindra. "Deciphering India." *Thesis Eleven* 39 (1994): 86–92.

Rodrigues, Valerian. "Reading Texts and Traditions: The Ambedkar-Gandhi Debate." *Economic and Political Weekly* 46.49 (8 January 2011): 56–66.

Roy, Srirupa. "A Symbol of Freedom: The Indian Flag and the Transformations of Nationalism, 1906–2002." *Journal of Asian Studies* 65.3 (2006): 495–527.

Rudolph, Lloyd. "The Occidental Tagore." *Boston Review* 19.5 (October/November 1994): 21–22.

Sahasrabudhey, Sunil. "On Alien Political Categories." *Gandhi Marg* 4.11 (February 1983): 896–901.

———. "Towards a New Theory." *Seminar* 273 (19–23 May 1982): 19–23.

Saran, A. K. "Gandhi's Theory of Society and Our Times." In Fred Dallmayr and G. N. Devy, eds., *Between Tradition and Modernity: India's Search for Identity: A Twentieth Century Anthology*. Walnut Creek, CA: AltaMira Press, 1998, 201–233.

———. "Gandhi and the Concept of Politics: Towards a Normal Civilization." *Gandhi Marg* 1.11 (February 1980): 675–726.

Sartori, Andrew. "The Transfiguration of Duty in Aurobindo's *Essays on the Gita*." *Modern Intellectual History* 7 (2010): 319–334.

Sawhney, Simona. "Gods, Heroes and Epic Translations." *Canadian Review of Comparative Literature* 26 (1999): 81–93.

Seely, Clinton B. "Keynote Address." Twelfth Annual Tagore Festival, University of Illinois, Champaign–Urbana, 21 October 2000.

Sen, Amartya. "Our Past and Our Present." *Economic and Political Weekly* 41.47 (November 2006): 4877–4886.

———. "The Right Not to Be Hungry." *Contemporary Philosophy: A New Survey* 2 (1982): 343–360.

Sharma, Suresh. "Swaraj and the Quest for Freedom—Rabindranath Tagore's Critique of Gandhi's Non-cooperation." *Thesis Eleven* 39 (1994): 93–104.

Shastri, Mahamahopadhyaya Haraprasad. "Causes of the Dismemberment of the Maurya Empire." *Journal of the Proceedings of the Asiatic Society of Bengal* 4.5 (May 1910): 259–262.

Shklar, Judith N. "Emerson and the Inhibitions of Democracy." *Political Theory* 18.4 (November 1990): 601–614.

Shulman, David Dean. "The Yaksa's Questions." In Galit Hasan-Rokem and David Shulman, eds., *Untying the Knot*. New York: Oxford University Press, 1996, 151–167.

Spivak, Gayatri Chakravorty. "Moving Devi." *Cultural Critique* 47 (Winter 2001): 120–163.

———. "Moving Devi." In Vidya Dehejia, ed., *Devi: The Great Goddess: Female Divinity in South Asian Art*. Washington, DC: Arthur M. Sackler Gallery, 1999, 181–200.

———. "Subaltern Studies: Deconstructing Historiography." In Donna Landry and Gerald MacLean, eds., *The Spivak Reader*. New York: Routledge, 1996 [1985], 203–235.

Srinivasan, Vasanthi. "Spirituality and Politics in Coomaraswamy, Radhakrishnan and Rajagopalachari." In V. R. Mehta and Thomas Pantham, eds., *Political Ideas in Modern India: Thematic Explorations*. New Delhi: Sage Publications, 2005, 238–260.

"The State Emblem of India (Prohibition of Improper Use) Act, 2005: No. 50 of 2005. 20th December, 2005."

Sutton, Nick. "Aśoka and Yudhiṣṭhira: A Historical Setting for the Ideological Tensions of the Mahābhārata?" *Religion* 27 (1997): 333–341.

Tagore, Saranindranath. "Tagore's Conception of Cosmopolitanism: A Reconstruction." *University of Toronto Quarterly* 77.4 (2008): 1070–1084.

Vajpeyi, Ananya. "The Guru Ambedkar." *Open Magazine* 4.18 (1–7 May 2012): 50–53.

———. "Monk, Mathematician, Marxist." *The Caravan* 4.2 (1 February 2012): 80–84.

———. "Let Poetry Be a Sword!" *The Caravan* 3.1 (1 January 2011): 86–91.

———. "Unfinished Symphony." *The Caravan* 3.5 (1 May 2011): 78–83.

———. "A Song unto Itself." *The Caravan* 2.1 (1 January 2010): 60–65.

Venkatachalapathy, A. R. "*Enna Prayocanam?* Constructing the Canon in Colonial Tamil Nadu." *Indian Economic and Social History Review* 42.4 (2010): 533–551.

———. "Introduction: Tradition, Talent, Translation." In *Love Stands Alone: Selections from Tamil Sangam Poetry*, trans. M. L. Thangappa. New Delhi: Penguin, 2010, xiii–xlviii.

Verma, Nirmal. "India and Europe—Some Reflections on Self and Other." In Fred Dallmayr and G. N. Devy, eds., *Between Tradition and Modernity: India's Search for Identity: A Twentieth Century Anthology*. Walnut Creek, CA: AltaMira Press, 1998, 326–352.

Virmani, Arundhati. "National Symbols under Colonial Domination: The Nationalization of the Indian Flag, March–August 1923." *Past and Present* 164 (1999): 169–197.

Wakankar, Milind. "The Moment of Criticism in Indian Nationalist Thought: Ramchandra Shukla and the Poetics of a Hindi Responsibility." *South Atlantic Quarterly* 101.4 (Fall 2002): 987–1014.

Wezler, Albrecht. "The Dharma in the Veda and the Dharmasastras." *Journal of Indian Philosophy* 32 (2004): 629–654.

Wolin, Sheldon S. "Political Theory as a Vocation." *American Political Science Review* 63.4 (1969): 1062–1082.

Acknowledgments

The writing of this book began in mid-October 2007 and ended in late November 2011 in conversation with Pratap Bhanu Mehta. The book was written over four years of continuous dialogue and argument with him. I could not have written it in any other way. No thanks would suffice.

For making it possible to write this book under contract and to work with an exacting, ambitious, and intelligent editor, I am grateful to Pankaj Mishra. For her being that editor, I am grateful to Sharmila Sen.

For crucial interventions with specific chapters, with interpretations of texts, with editorial conundrums, and with solving problems of meaning, archive, sources, or method, my deepest gratitude goes to Amit Chaudhuri, Ramachandra Guha, Lloyd and Susanne Rudolph, and Ajay Skaria. For extraordinary inspiration as well as practical help of all kinds in the last stages of writing and manuscript preparation, between October 2011 and May 2012, thanks to Rajeev Bhargava, John Keane, Ashis Nandy, Manas Ray, Gulammohammed and Nilima Sheikh, Dhirubhai Sheth, Malvika Thapar Singh, and Tridip Suhrud.

Profound and heartfelt thanks go to George Keller Hart for solving innumerable bibliographic problems at the speed of light.

For help with Bengali, thanks to Dipanwita Chakrabarti, Antara Datta, and Somnath Mukherji, as well as Rinka and Sharmila.

For inviting me to speak, write, and share work with colleagues, students, and readers, thanks to Sherman Teichman at the Institute for Global Leadership and Ayesha Jalal in the Department of History, both at Tufts University; Peter Ronald deSouza and Tridip Suhrud at the Indian Institute of Advanced Study, Shimla; Rosinka Chaudhuri and Tapati Guha-Thakurta at the Centre for the Study of the Social Sciences, Kolkata; Partho Datta, Kavita Sharma, Dilip Simeon, and Kapila Vatsyayana at the India International Center, New Delhi; Amit Basole and Sunil Sahasrabudhey at Vidya Ashram, Sarnath; Steven Kotkin and Daniel Rodgers at the Davis Center for Historical Studies, Princeton University; Eliza Kent at Colgate University, Hamilton, N.Y.; Bernadette Meyler at the Cornell Law School, Ithaca, N.Y.; Pratap Bhanu Mehta at the Centre for Policy Research, New Delhi; William Dalrymple and Namita Gokhale at the Jaipur Literary Festival; Harsh Sethi and Tejbir Singh at *Seminar;* Akeel Bilgrami at the Heyman Center for the Humanities, Columbia University; Faisal Devji (then) at the New School for Social Research; Jonathan Shainin (then) at the Abu Dhabi Review of *The National* newspaper; Arindam Chakrabarti and Peter Hershock at the University of Hawaii, East-West Center; Islam Dayeh and Georges Khalil at the Zukunftsphilologie Project of the Wissenchaftskolleg, Berlin; the South Asia Seminar at Harvard University; Vinod K. Jose, Anant Nath, and Jonathan Shainin at *The Caravan* magazine; Rudrangshu Mukherjee at *The Telegraph,* Calcutta; M. K. Venu (then) at *The Economic Times,* New Delhi; Heather Timmons at the "India Ink" blog of the *New York Times;* and Dr. C. Rammanohar Reddy at *Economic and Political Weekly,* Mumbai.

Thanks also to John Bowles, Nitasha Devasar, Sudipta Kaviraj, Amitava Kumar, Uday Singh Mehta, Anthony Parel, Gyan Prakash, Saranindranath Tagore, and Milind Wakankar.

For providing a superb work environment, thanks to my brilliant colleagues at the Centre for the Study of Developing Societies (CSDS): Hilal Ahmed, Sarada Balagopalan, Prathama Banerjee, Rajeev Bhargava, Abhay Dubey, Madhu Kishwar, Sanjay Kumar, Shail Mayaram, Ashis Nandy, Aditya Nigam, Rakesh Pandey, Awadhendra Sharan, Ravikant Sharma, D. L. Sheth, V. B. Singh, Ravi Sundaram, and Yogendra Yadav. Also at CSDS, thanks to Himanshu Bhattacharya, Ghanshyam Dutt, Jayasree Jayanthan, Avinash Jha, Preethi Nambiar, and Praveen Rai, along with all the other helpful staff. Thanks to my young friends and Centre Visiting Fellows, Sanjeer Alam, Devika Bordia, Ankur Datta, Yengkhom Jilangamba, Hemachandra Karah, Navpreet Kaur, Venugopal Madipatti, and Divya Vaid, for making the year 2011–2012 fly by.

Thanks to Ian Stevenson and Heather Hughes at Harvard University Press for their unflappable calm and reassuring manner in the face of my frequent bouts of panic and stress. All first-time writers should be so lucky. Thanks to Susan Wallace Boehmer, Susan Donnelly, Anne Zarrella, Lisa LaPoint, and Rebekah White at Harvard University Press, and to John Donohue and Manju Khanna for taking such good care of every aspect of the design, production, publicity, copyediting, and indexing of the book in the spring and summer of 2012. Thanks to William B. Sisler, director of Harvard University Press, for warm, wonderful meetings in Cambridge, Massachusetts, and New Delhi. Thanks to the two anonymous reviewers of my manuscript, whose comments were both highly encouraging and most helpful.

Let me also record my debt of gratitude to, as well as my deep sadness at the passing of, Dilip Chitre, in Pune, and Meenakshi Mukherjee, in Hyderabad, in 2009, as well as of N. Murari Ballal, in Udupi, in 2004. In memoriam, Rani Dubé, 1937–2010, who gave me my first introduction to Gandhi, around 1982.

For providing my two most consistent and conducive work spaces, I thank the staff at Widener Library, Harvard University, and the folks at Petsi Pies, on Putnam Avenue, Cambridge, Massachusetts, especially Paul and Elizabeth Clark. Thanks also to David Magier, of Columbia and Princeton, for access to Butler Library at Columbia University, where I spent some time writing.

Thanks to my wonderful students Omar Ocampo and Savvas Papadopoulos, and to my young friend Madhav Khosla, for help with the bibliography. Thanks to Ved Prakash Baruah for superb eleventh-hour assistance with manuscript preparation.

I thank my closest friends near and far who have made my life over the past five years of working on this book for the most part happy: Hartosh Singh Bal and Paminder Parbha, Rhitu Chatterjee, Chris Chekuri, William and Olivia Dalrymple, Christina Davis, Nonica Datta, Mahmood Farooqui and Anusha Rizvi, Gauri Gill, Rebecca Gowers, Laura Harrison, Rudi Heredia, Maya Jasanoff, Wim Klerkx, Lital Levy, Hardeep Mann and Balraj Gill, Isabelle Onians, Manue Ornon and my godson Adam, Chitra Padmanabhan and M. K. Venu, Davide Panagia, Annie Reinhardt and Arindam Dutta, Matthew

C. J. Rudolph, Rashmi Sadana and Vivek Narayanan, Dana Sajdi, Aadya Shukla, Osama Siddique and Paro Khan, Jaspal Singh, Vinay Sitapati, Matthew Smith and Bernie Meyler, Meera Subramanian and Stephen Prothero, and Michael Vazquez. Jalal Alamgir passed away on December 3, 2011, in a tragic accident at sea: the loss is irreparable.

My fondest thanks go to Teddy Weesner and Ravit Reichman, for helping me to settle into Cambridge when I first moved from New York, and for being my family far from home, ably assisted by Pep Vicente, Greta, Lucy, and now little Nadav Lee.

In New York, I thank Rupa Athreya and Taimur Hyat, Deborah Baker and Amitav Ghosh, Jessica Benko and Matthew Power, Siddhartha Deb, Suketu Mehta, Anjali Mody and Rathin Roy, Nauman Naqvi, Miriam Ticktin, Alex Travelli, and also Noga Arikha, though she left much too soon. Thanks to Patrick Dodd, whose paintings I live with and enjoy every day.

At the *New York Times* South Asia Bureau in Delhi, I thank Lydia Polgreen, Jim Yardley, and the feisty Candace Feit.

Thanks to the truly awesome Sarah Chalfant at the Wylie Agency in London and New York.

From the University of Chicago 1996–2004, where I learned how to be a scholar, I thank my teachers Muzaffar Alam, Arjun Appadurai, Dipesh Chakrabarty, Steven Collins, Wendy Doniger, Paul Griffiths, Ronald Inden, Matthew Kapstein, John Kelly, Bruce Lincoln, the late D. R. Nagaraj, Sheldon Pollock, and Michael Silverstein; Jim Nye at the Regenstein Library; and my extraordinary friends and peers who labored with me in what we used to call the trenches of academia, most especially Manan Ahmed, Dan Arnold, Frank Bechter, Tom Borchert, Whitney Cox, Spencer Austin Leonard, Rick Nance, Andrew Nicholson, Ajay Rao, Adheesh Sathaye, Prithvi Datta Chandra Shobhi, and Robert Yelle.

Thanks to my tiny family—Nanoo and Jiji in Delhi, the gang in NOIDA—and Bhai and his girls in Geneva. I wish my grandparents, Sardar Sher Singh and Manmohini Khurana, were still here. This book would have made them happy. Thanks to Mala and Jugnu, who make Delhi a city one is happy to return to and live in again.

Thanks to Kapil Kapoor, my professor in the English and Linguistics Centre at Jawaharlal Nehru University from 1992 to 1994, for first introducing me to Indian classical texts and intellectual traditions, which eventually became my principal area of study.

Thanks to Arindam Chakrabarti, who taught me portions of the *Bhagavad Gītā* in Delhi in 1995 and again in Hawaii in 2010, and who has a gift for always being on my mind regardless of where we are or how long it has been since we communicated.

Thanks to Jonathan Shainin, friend, editorial whizkid, and now Indophile par excellence, who knows how to turn text to gold. He helps me to make my writing more my own.

Thanks again to Pratap Mehta, without whom I could not have thought up or written down one word of this book. Provocative, learned, brilliant, patient, impatient, insightful, optimistic, ethical, balanced, biased, demanding, and unstintingly generous, one could not ask for a better interlocutor.

Thanks to Sheldon Pollock, who taught me everything I know and everything I don't know. From the day I first met him in Leiden, in November 1994, I have never stopped learning from him; his unparalleled scholarship makes the world a better place.

Thanks Basharat Peer, dearest love. I never knew what "happy" meant until you came along. It's conceivable that I didn't really know what "writing" or "editing" meant either, before you so surprisingly, so fortuitously came into my life.

Thanks to my beloved peerless parents, Roopa and Kailash Vajpeyi. My mother led me to Gandhi; my father to Kabir. Their shared love of poetry they passed on to their only child. Their faith made me get up and get on with it. Their integrity has shown me a way. Their sweetness makes it all worthwhile.

Index